REMOTE VIEWING

To my mother,
and the memory of my father.

REMOTE VIEWING

The history and science of psychic warfare and spying

TIM RIFAT

Century · London

First published by Century in 1999

Copyright © Tim Rifat 1999

Tim Rifat has asserted his right under the Copyright, Designs and
Patents Act, 1988, to be identified as the author of this work

First published in the United Kingdom in 1999 by Century
20 Vauxhall Bridge Road, London, SW1V 2SA

Random House Australia (Pty) Limited
20 Alfred Street, Milsons Point, Sydney,
New South Wales 2061, Australia

Random House New Zealand Limited
18 Poland Road, Glenfield
Auckland 10, New Zealand

Random House South Africa (Pty) Limited
Endulini, 5a Jubilee Road,
Parktown 2193, South Africa

Random House UK Limited Reg. No. 954009

A CIP catalogue record for this book
is available from the British Library

Papers used by Random House UK Limited
are natural, recyclable products made from wood grown in
sustainable forests. The manufacturing processes conform to
the environmental regulations of the country of origin.

ISBN 0 7126 7908 1

Typeset by SX Composing DTP, Rayleigh, Essex
Printed and bound in Great Britain by
Biddles Ltd, Guildford & Kings Lynn

Contents

Introduction

At the height of the Cold War, a new twist to weapons development occurred. The Soviet Union systematized its investigations into how to harness the paranormal and use it for military purposes. What in other times was seen as magic or witchcraft – laying a curse, predicting the future, having second sight – had already gained scientific respectability in the USSR with the recognition of clairvoyance and the acceptance of psychic phenomena.

Research had started in the Soviet Union in the twenties and thirties, but was stopped by Stalin, who thought it smacked of superstition. Now the Russians plunged into a large-scale research programme. Billions of roubles were poured into the investigation and development of psychic energy (psi) and electronic mind-control technology. To convince hard-nosed military men that psychic phenomena can win wars may, on the face of it, appear to be a forlorn task. But in the case of the Soviet Union it happened the other way around, as some of the leading minds in the military convinced their leaders to spend fortunes on this effort.

Science fiction writers have not come close to the reality of the actual research undertaken since then. The aim was no less than to produce psychic agents, capable of visualizing top-secret sites and installations located thousands of miles away, reading the minds of their country's enemies, intervening and altering thought processes, and even killing through psychic attack.

The first step was the development of remote viewing. People displaying psychic sensitivity were sought out all over the USSR and trained under the strictest secrecy as spies with a difference. They were required to focus on, say, a particular top-secret facility in the US or China, and conjure up a detailed picture of its location and personnel in their mind's eye, which they would then describe to their spy masters. Remote viewing, then, is a kind of psychic spying.

The Americans realized that something unusual was going on. 'Between 1969 and 1971, American intelligence sources began discovering and confirming that the Soviet Union was deeply engaged in so-called "psychic research". By 1970, it was discovered that the Soviets were spending approximately 60 million roubles per year on it, and over 300 million by 1975, according to Ingo Swann, the godfather of US remote viewing. In the early seventies he was commissioned by the CIA to develop a remote-viewing programme for the US military, to be operated from Fort Meade in Maryland.

Others in the United States also became aware of the possibilities – and dangers. In 1980, Colonel John Alexander wrote an article in Military Review, a respected Army journal, entitled 'The New Mental Battlefield'. The article described remote viewing and suggested that effective mind-influencing devices were already a 'lethal' reality. The US Army's partly classified 'Fire Support Mission Area Analysis' of 1981 talked about 'cryptomental technologies' and 'the relatively unexplored, unexploited human technologies in such areas as influence, communications, thinking, learning, and stress reduction. Discussions in this area represent an excursion into a largely unknown realm which appears to possess significant military application.'

Progress from that time has been rapid with the development of sophisticated techniques and technology. As this book will show, psychotronic (i.e. mind-control) weapons are the most top-secret class of weapons used not only by the Russians and Americans, but increasingly by the Chinese, Japanese, British, Czechs and Israelis.

It may be hard to believe that the Soviet Union and the United States could actually explore the paranormal in search of new military technology for decades in almost absolute secrecy, but the power and mastery to be attained by controlling the minds and wills of their perceived enemies was the spur. As long ago as 1975, when Leonid Brezhnev urged the US to agree to ban research into and development of new kinds of weapons 'more terrible' than anything the world has known (reported in the *New York Times*, June 1977), he was warning America that the USSR had the knowledge to end the Cold War by psychic means.

The first popular reports of this research appeared in 1970 in a book entitled *Psychic Discoveries Behind the Iron Curtain* by Sheila Ostrander and Lynn Schroeder. Martin Ebon's 1983 book *Psychic Warfare: Threat or Illusion?* took the subject of psi warfare much further; and David Morehouse's *Psychic Warrior: Inside the CIA's Stargate Program* (1996) tells an insider's story. Major Morehouse had been one of the US military's top remote viewers, and the US military are allegedly unhappy at his revelations.

Apart from the books, a few stories have filtered out into the public domain. For instance, the Associated Wire Press ran a story on 28 November 1995 under the headline 'US Used "Psychic" Spies':

For 20 years, the United States has secretly used psychics in attempts to hunt down Libyan leader Muammar Quaddafi, find plutonium in North Korea and help drug enforcement agencies, the CIA and others confirmed Tuesday.

The London *Daily Express* published an article on 25 September 1997 under the headline 'Reds Planned Psycho-wars':

> The KGB and the Red Army carried out experiments aimed at using hypnotic warfare against the West, it emerged yesterday. Revelations include a prototype satellite releasing electronic mind-bending signals to 'control and correct the behaviour of the population' over an area the size of England. Research into psycho-warfare was conducted in more than twenty institutes led by the Siberian scientific community of Novosibirsk, and only stopped in 1991. However fears were voiced yesterday that the technology could fall into the hands of the powerful Russian Mafia. The research was disclosed by the *Izvestia* newspaper under the headline 'They Could Produce Zombies in the USSR'. It is clear large-scale experiments were carried out on ordinary Russians and soldiers.

However, under the US Freedom of Information Act, previously unpublished files from the US Department of Defense Intelligence Agency (DIA) have now become available, which detail Soviet research in this area and add weight to the assertions made in the books, as well as giving credibility to the other stories. The documents given in Appendices I and II together provide the definitive work on Soviet psychical research up until 1975. They show the importance accorded the Soviet Union's advances in psychic spying and mind-control techniques by the United States authorities, and the countermeasures taken and parallel progress made.

I found all this hard to swallow when I first learnt of it, but my research into the scientific basis of the biophysical technology convinced me that the Russians *had* entered into new territories. They had begun the inner-space arms race, which they developed to undreamed of levels of power. After nuclear warfare, biophysical warfare is the second great crossroads for human civilization. Inner-space weapon systems had, and have, the potential to drive mad or even to kill entire populations by means of biophysical and electronic technology unknown to the West in the 1970s.

Whether or not you believe in remote viewing and the psychotronic weapons described in this book, by the end of the first part you will know that the US and Soviet military authorities believe in them.

During my research, I have become aware of how useful remote viewing can be in gaining information on topics that have proved impossible to analyse by any other method. Having developed basic do-it-yourself guides for beginners, I found that with these simple methods accuracy could be a problem. The new methodology, outlined in the second part of this book, will help people who want to practise controlled remote viewing as espoused by the Americans, as well as teaching a Russian-like version of extended remote viewing.

1

How it all started
– in Russia

Scientists in pre-Revolutionary [Russia] were studying the
area of parapsychology as did later such Soviet scientists
as V.M. Bekhterev, A.G. Ivanov-Smolensky and B.B.
Kazhinsky in the twenties and thirties. In 1922, a commission composed of psychologists, medical hypnotists,
physiologists and physicists worked on parapsychology
problems at the Institute for Brain Research in Petrograd
(Leningrad). Work flourished throughout the thirties with
research being reported in the literature in 1934, 1936,
and 1937. After 1937 further experiments in the field of
parapsychology were forbidden. During Stalin's time, any
attempt to study paranormal phenomena might have been
interpreted as a deliberate attempt to undermine the doctrines of materialism.

So stated the 1972 DIA report 'Controlled Offensive Behavior
– USSR' (Appendix I, document page 22). The Defense
Intelligence Agency is the military intelligence agency of the
US Department of Defense. Part of the military (mainly
army), they carry out intelligence work for the Pentagon.
According to an official CIA paper written by Gerald K.
Haines, the historian of the National Reconnaissance Office

6

(NRO): 'There is a DIA Psychic Center, and the NSA (National Security Agency) studies parapsychology, that branch of psychology that deals with the investigation of such psychic phenomena as clairvoyance, extrasensory perception, and telepathy.'

In 1960 the Stalinist taboo that had prohibited research into the paranormal was lifted, and the KGB and GRU (Soviet military intelligence) began a scientific exploration of the weapons potential of psychic energy.

Soviet interest in psi was reawakened in February 1960 by a story which appeared in the French magazine *Science et Vie* (*Science and Life*). The story was entitled 'The Secrets of the *Nautilus*', and it claimed that the US government had secretly used telepaths to communicate with the first nuclear submarine ever constructed, the *Nautilus*, while it was under the Arctic ice pack. This telepathy project involved, according to the article, President Eisenhower, the Navy, the Air Force, Westinghouse, General Electric, Bell Laboratories and the Rand Corporation. Communicating with submarines is difficult, as radio waves do not penetrate to the depths of the ocean. Extremely low frequency (ELF) waves are used, but only to signal the submarine to come to the surface to receive a message – these super-long waves penetrate almost anything including water but carry little information. So if telepathy could work it would be a perfect method of communicating with submarines while still deeply submerged. The story was almost certainly a hoax, but the Soviets were spurred into action, according to the DIA:

> Ship-to-shore telepathy, according to the French, blipped along nicely even when the *Nautilus* was far under water. 'Is telepathy a new secret weapon? Will ESP be the deciding factor in future warfare? Has the American military learned the secrets of mind power?' were some of the

headlines in the French press. In Leningrad the *Nautilus* reports went off like a depth charge in the mind of L.L. Vasilev. In April of 1960 Doctor Vasilev, while addressing a group of top Soviet scientists, stated: 'We carried out extensive and until now completely unreported investigations under the Stalin regime. Today the American Navy is testing telepathy on their atomic submarines. Soviet scientists conducted a great many successful telepathy tests over a quarter of a century ago. It's urgent that we throw off our prejudices. We must again plunge into the exploration of this vital field.' [Appendix I, document page 24]

From 1922 to 1959, this [negative] attitude [to parapsychology] gradually changed. Official recognition of parapsychology as a legitimate science was prompted to a considerable extent by the Party's recognition of other disciplines ... In 1959 Professor L.L. Vasilev published his 'Mysterious Phenomena of the Human Psyche', followed in 1962 by his 'Experiments in Mental Suggestion' ... the possible military implications were apparently overlooked in the West. [Appendix II, document page 15.]

Groups of scientists at many Soviet research institutes began to investigate and later harness psychic energy. The aim of this research was to produce deadly new weapons that could tip the balance of power during the Cold War. The DIA again:

Soviet parapsychology research gained impetus and sophistication, growing from a single laboratory into a co-ordinated USSR-wide effort; laboratories were also established in Czechoslovakia. Funds for research (reported at 20 million roubles in 1973) are believed to be primarily from military sources. This high level of support advanced Soviet research on human telepathy far beyond that of the West, and the USSR became the leader in sponsoring and participating in international parapsychology symposiums [Appendix II, document page 15] . . . by 1968 the Soviets already had: (1) established several research centers specializing in telepathic experiments on an academic and scientific level; (2) organized teams of scientists – physiologists, physicists, psychologists, mathematicians, cyberneticians, neurologists, and electronic engineers – to investigate telepathy, find out how it works, and devise means of practical application; and (3) conducted experiments involving long-range thought transference (Leningrad-Moscow [600km]; Moscow-Tomsk [4000km]). [Appendix II, document page 18] . . . Professor Vasilev was given state funds to establish at the University appropriately equipped laboratories for the study of telepathy . . . Following the example of Leningrad, other cities, including Moscow, Kiev, Novosibirsk and Kharkov, established similar laboratories and research centers, at which not only the phenomena described in world literature were examined, but a study was made of parapsychic features displayed by Soviet citizens. [Appendix I, document page 23]

Although the US Navy subsequently denied the reports of telepathic testing on atomic submarines, the Soviet hierarchy apparently heeded Doctor Vasilev's advice and gave support, both moral and financial, to his dynamic view that: 'The discovery of the energy underlying telepathic communication will be equivalent to the discovery of atomic energy.'

. . . In 1963, Doctor Vasilev claimed to have conducted successful long-distance telepathic experiments between Leningrad and Sevastopol, a distance of 1200 miles, with the aid of an ultra-short-wave (UHF) radio transmitter. As a result, Doctor Vasilev was convinced that his experiments, and those he conducted jointly with the Moscow-based Bekhterev Brain Institute, offered scientific proof of telepathic communications. His next goal was to identify the nature of brain energy that produces it . . .

The so-called Father of Soviet Rocketry, K.E. Tsiolkovsky, stated that: 'In the coming era of space flights, telepathic abilities are necessary. While the space rocket must bring men toward knowledge of the grand secrets in the universe, the study of psychic phenomena can lead us toward knowledge of the mysteries of the human mind. It is precisely the solution of this secret which promises the greatest achievements.'

There are reports that the Soviets are training their cosmonauts in telepathy to back up their electronic equipment while in outer space. One of these back-up schemes is known to involve coded telepathic messages. This method was previously demonstrated in March 1967, when a coded telepathic message was flashed from Moscow to Leningrad. The involvement of astronauts or cosmonauts in telepathy experiments is not necessarily unprecedented. In February 1971, during the Apollo 14 flight to the moon, astronaut Edgar Mitchell made 150 separate attempts to project his thoughts from inside the space capsule back to an individual on earth. [Appendix II, document pages 25–26]

In 1967, the Soviet *Maritime News* reported, 'Cosmonauts, when in orbit, seem to be able to communicate telepathically more easily with each other than on Earth. A psi (short for psychic faculty) training system has been incorporated in the cosmonaut training program'. Some informal reports indicate that the Soviets are working on psi systems for space use, involving not just telepathy, but precognition. [Appendix I, document page 33]

There are numerous reports on Soviet applications of clairvoyance, hypnotism, dowsing etc. in military operations. In the case of dowsing, this is also not unprecedented, since US forces have employed dowsing in Vietnam for locating enemy tunnels and caches. [Appendix I]

The Soviet Union is well aware of the benefits and applications of parapsychology research. In 1963, a Kremlin edict apparently gave top priority to biological research, which in Russia includes parapsychology. The major impetus behind the Soviet drive to harness the possible capabilities of telepathic communication, telekinetics and bionics is said to come from the Soviet military and the KGB. Today [1972] it is reported that the USSR has twenty or more centers for the study of parapsychological phenomena, with an annual budget estimated in 1967 at over 12 million roubles (13 million dollars) and reported to be as high as 21 million dollars. [Appendix I, document page xi]

In the early 1960s, Yuri Andropov, head of the KGB from 1967 to 1982 and President of the USSR from 1983 to 1984, issued the command to implement a psychotronic-warfare programme in order to develop a new form of strategic weapons system to augment nuclear weapons. According to Soviet journalist Emil Bachurin, writing in *Young Guard* magazine, in 1990, former KGB Major General Oleg Kalugin, head of foreign counter-intelligence for the Soviet Union in the seventies, told him that Yuri Andropov had been especially upset about several psi-weapons centres he maintained were located in Canada. 'Canadian research must be surpassed,' he ordered. Bachurin's sources also revealed that after the war the Soviets had scooped up masses of Nazi occult research, including some by the notorious Dr Mengele at the Dachau concentration camp. Building on these horrible experiments had sped Soviet success in developing psi weapons, they told him. V. Scheglov, a journalist for *Yaroslavl*, reported in 1993 that psi weapons had been developed and used on the civilian populations of not only the USSR but the West, and not once or twice, but again and again. The DIA thought they were capable of it:

> Doctor Y.A. Kholodov has investigated the effects of a constant magnetic field on rabbits. Whole-body exposures to fields between 30 and 2000 oersteds resulted in non-specific changes in the [animals'] electroencephalograms [EEGs] . . . natural and artificial fields in man's environment may have an influence on health and behavior via the nervous system and hypothalamus. [Appendix II]

In a 1992 ABC Television documentary shown in America, and in an earlier 1990 interview for *Young Guard* magazine, Major General Kalugin made more startling revelations about the Soviet Union's investigation into harnessing psychic energy in order to produce exotic weapons with which the West was unfamiliar. He said:

> They started to explore the mysterious powers of certain people and to simulate generators of this same nature in order to produce a similar effect. Russian scientists succeeded in developing generators of psychic force. Yuri Andropov issued personal orders to push full speed ahead with psychic warfare. Andropov's directive also urged scientists to forget being squeamish about injuring or killing research subjects in the race to achieve their goal.

Funding from the Military-Industrial Commission and the KGB was estimated at 500 million roubles.

The amount may be an underestimate. In Martin Ebon's 1983 book *Psychic Warfare: Threat or Illusion?* he claims that congressional sources stated the USSR psychotronic warfare research programme was funded to the tune of 500 million dollars per year.

2

ESP and beyond . . .

There has been massive interest in extra sensory perception (ESP) and spiritualism throughout the Western world since the nineteenth century. But Dr J.B. Rhine's work with card reading and manipulating dice at Duke University in the USA gave research into ESP a formal scientific base. He led the field in telepathy and ESP research in the West in the years before the Second World War. His work was controversial then, and even now is not generally understood.

Soviet scientists, however, took Dr Rhine's research many steps further. They had little interest in proving ESP existed; that was taken as proven by their research into telepathy and telepathic hypnosis from the thirties. What interested the Soviets was its military potential. They worked on the use of telepathy and ESP for psychic spying on US secret bases; but the main thrust of their initial endeavour was the use of ESP and telepathy to read an enemy's mind. The aim was the psychic interrogation of Nato commanders by using a technique known as scanning. The DIA again:

In summary, what is the strategic threat posed by the current 'explosion' in Soviet parapsychological research? Soviet efforts in the field of psi research, sooner or later, might enable them to do some of the following:

a) Know the contents of top secret US documents, the movements of our troops and ships, and the location and nature of our military installations.
b) Mold the thoughts of key US military and civilian leaders, at a distance.
c) Cause the instant death of any US official, at a distance.
d) Disable, at a distance, US military equipment of all types including space craft. [Appendix I, document page 40]

To this end, according to émigrés and intelligence reports, the KGB and GRU scoured the Soviet Union for psychics, searched the length of Siberia for mystics, and forcibly recruited them into the huge number of parapsychological research projects being undertaken. By the mid-seventies, the Soviets had apparently embarked upon a society-wide screening programme for talented psychics, covering senior schools, universities and Red Army soldiers. Children who displayed powerful psychic abilities were especially sought after.

Research was carried out at the Institute of Control Problems, attached to the USSR Academy of Sciences, and headed by a Dr Lev Lupichev. Special Department No. 8 in the 'science city' of Novosibirsk researched into military psi. The Institute for the Problems of Information Transmission, and the Pavlov Institute of Higher Nervous Activity, both well-guarded facilities in Moscow, also researched into psi warfare. The DIA documents in Appendices I and II listing the names of Soviet scientists involved, and the research institutes they worked at in the early seventies, show how extensive the commitment was. Much of this effort focused on developing the ability to control people's minds with an amalgam of psychic force and electronics. American research at the Stanford Research Institute was tiny in comparison.

As the research continued, it became ultra-clandestine. The laboratories at Odessa State University were hidden underground in the sub-sub-basement beneath the university's old botanical gardens. Only special couriers knew how to access any of these institutes, and KGB and GRU guards made sure there were no unwanted visitors. In utmost secrecy, bizarre new lines of research were followed. Remote viewing and remote influencing were seen as the targeting mechanisms for much more lethal paranormal-weapon systems. Psychotronics had become the catch-all title for a multitude of psi weapons, ranging from microwave mind-control devices to psychic remote killing.

Dr A.V. Kalinets-Bryukhanov, president of the All Union Scientific Research Association, was part of a top-secret KGB project at the Filatov Eye Institute in Odessa that looked into ways of artificially stimulating remote viewing. It was found that natural clairvoyants changed the magnetic field around themselves and that of the Earth in their immediate vicinity. If this frequency of magnetic field could be artificially generated in the brain, the Russians thought they might stimulate greater clairvoyance in their test subjects. They experimented on animals, bombarding their brains with these specific magnetic fields, with the result that the animals seemingly developed the ability to tell what was going on behind solid walls. Unfortunately, the high-power magnetic fields soon disintegrated the animals' brains and they died. Allegedly, condemned prisoners were used for human experiments with the same results. Something about natural clairvoyants, on the other hand, seemed to guard them against this disintegration.

The Odessa institute also carried on with research pioneered by parapsychologist Dr A.N. Leontyev in the fifties, by undertaking psychic-viewing experiments with blind patients. They thought it might be possible to train blind people to develop psychic ability. The experiments were centred on training the subjects to attain a deeply relaxed state, from which visualization of the body's energy fields led to what the scientists called eyeless sight, or bio-introscopy. Coloured paper was passed beneath the subjects' fingertips, and it was found that they could distinguish between black and white and red and green paper, even though they were completely blind. The colour of an object could be determined even after it had been removed; apparently the object left a 'colour trace' of itself in the air. This progressed to picture reading: the ability to run a hand over a photograph and describe what the photo showed. These techniques evolved into teaching blind subjects to travel in their mind's eye to distant rooms and places they had never been before. Once there, if they could describe the location's layout, psychic viewing had been achieved.

A. Ivanov's paper on 'Soviet Experiments in Eyeless Vision', published in the 1964 *International Journal of Parapsychology*, revealed this remarkable work to the Western world. Research into eyeless sight led the Soviets to study how energy fields were imprinted on matter and vice versa. Much research was carried out on how to attach harmful energy fields to objects. The idea was that these biophysically poisoned objects would be given to enemies to make them ill, or to 'infect' them with subliminal commands.

Eyeless-sight research also led scientists towards more sophisticated training methods for their sighted psychic spies. The same deeply relaxed state and visualization of biological energy fields (biophysical fields that surround the human body) were found to increase the efficiency of psychic spying.

Amplifying psi
Once they had confirmed that the potential for psi warfare actually existed, the Soviet scientists searched for further ways to boost the relatively weak, naturally occuring psi

faculty so it could be developed into weapons for causing harm. The deeply relaxed state used for eyeless-sight research was the theta state of consciousness found in dreaming sleep. The theta state is a level of consciousness at which the brain is deeply relaxed and the static and negative effects of other people's minds are blacked out, so that the subconscious and unconscious mind, with its heightened paranormal abilities, can come to the fore. Normal consciousness, the beta state, is measured at above 14 cycles per second of oscillations in electrical activity of the brain, by an electroencephalograph (EEG); alpha, the relaxed, daydreaming state, at above 7 cycles per second; and theta, the dreaming state, at above 3 cycles per second.

Hypnosis, drugs and meditation were tried to inculcate the theta state of consciousness. Autovisualization of the brain was very effective in inducing the states needed for remote viewing. Tesla coils (see pages 19–20) tuned to radiate extremely low frequency (ELF) waves at 7.8 cycles per second (Hertz), the Earth's natural frequency (known as the Schumann resonance), were found to amplify psychic ability tremendously by inducing a theta state in the remote viewer. The Schumann resonance is a naturally occurring standing wave, an ELF signal that circles the globe, resonating in the cavity between the ground and the edge of the atmosphere, a naturally occurring signal with which all life is in resonance. According to off-the-record interviews with US remote viewers and psi-warfare adepts, psychotronic-augmented spying enabled Soviet remote viewers to achieve almost perfect images. Brain implants designed to 'switch off' the brain stress system, the body's anxiety generator, were also found to be very effective, as were drug regimens and hypnotic suggestion. Magnetic fields at 7.8Hz were later found to be almost as good as the Tesla coils. Aided by this vast array of high-tech brain-state modifying systems, the Russians began to uncover the secrets of the energy field surrounding the body. They mapped out the neural currents in the brain, and found that in the normal waking state a negative-to-positive current runs from the front of the brain to the back, along the centre. By passing a low-voltage current from the front of the brain to the back, they could vary the subject's waking state. By artificially lowering the negative potential at the back of the brain, the remote viewer could be dropped into a theta state.

Dr Robert Becker of the Syracuse VA Hospital found that a person under anaesthesia or in a deep hypnotic trance has an altered brain potential. The normal brain potentials, which are negative potential at the front of the brain and positive at the rear , drop to zero in these people. (This is documented in Dr Becker's book, *Cross Currents*.)

The Soviets found that, by applying a low voltage to the front of the brain, they could knock people out. More importantly, they found they could also lower their remote viewers into the delta state found in deep, dreamless sleep. In the delta state apparently all manner of psi marvels such as telekinesis – moving things by the power of the mind – become possible. It is rumoured too that the delta state could lead to remote influencing.

Defence mechanisms – Tesla coils
The Russians were aware that the US was attempting to monitor their progress and had remote-viewing programmes of their own. They therefore devoted time and money to developing electronic devices to block out remote viewing of their own bases. In the course of this research, they found that Tesla coils interfered with psychic spying.

Nikola Tesla (1856–1943) was a genius who invented many new forms of electrical equipment towards the end of the nineteenth century, and developed a new branch of electrical technology using very high voltages running through special coils and transformers. Some of his inventions were so far ahead of their time that they were not fully understood until the Russians began to explore his work in the sixties. Tesla found that power could be beamed through the air at high voltages, as air's resistance breaks down. It was found that Tesla coils could in principle be used to transmit ELF oscillations that could cause a fault line to spasm and produce an earthquake, and that these ELF signals could also be tuned to influence people's minds.

Soviet scientists were taught Tesla technology at university, which may have encouraged a number of them to experiment with the effectiveness of Tesla coils in causing a 'whirlpool' effect that prevented remote viewing.

These anti-remote-viewing devices are now widely deployed in the top-secret bases of both Russian and US underground military and research facilities. In an off-the-record interview a retired US Special Forces, CIA-trained, psi-warfare expert involved in the remote-viewing programme has discussed this anti-remote-viewing technology, attesting to the fact that by the end of the century the US will have totally effective anti-remote-viewing devices in all their top-secret installations – so concerned are they about the effectiveness of remote viewing and remote influencing.

Telekinesis (Pychokinesis)
According to US intelligence:

> The apport technique is a form of astral projection in which the psychic subject transports his 'energy body' to a remote site, dematerializes an object, then transports it back and materializes it . . . Lack of information on Soviet interest in the technique represents a major intelligence gap. [Appendix II, document page 55]

It appears then that Soviet remote viewing was developing in a very different way to US remote viewing. Rather than picking up psychic images from the waking or deeply relaxed state, Soviet research involved actually projecting what had been known since theosophical research in the nineteenth century as the energy body to the location to be viewed. According to the DIA (Appendix II, document page 54) in 1970, 'Ostrander and Schroeder reported that the Soviets were studying out-of-the-body phenomena in Yogis'. Sheila Ostrander and Lynn Schroeder were the top American/Canadian psychic investigators.

The DIA paid great attention to Soviet research into psychokinesis (PK), the American term for telekinesis, and cited the work of G.A. Welk to explain the Soviet version of remote viewing and what was known as the apport technique:

Welk claims, based on many Soviet sources, that the so-called 'apport' technique is likely to meet valuable intelligence needs. When fully developed, this technique would make possible the abduction of actual objects (including documents) in enemy territory and their transfer to friendly territory. Objects so abducted are known as 'apports.' They could be returned to the point of origin without the enemy becoming aware of this temporary abduction . . . It is a known fact that the Soviet Union takes the appearance of luminous bodies very seriously as evidenced by the Kirlian photography of the human body's aura [see page 33–35 of document in Appendix I]. It appears that the Soviets may be considering that a hand which appears out of nowhere and can grasp, 'with the firm pressure of an old friend,' another person may have first-rate military possibilities. There has been some discussion recently about the prospects of being able to control the apport technique to a point of sophistication where individuals could control these 'luminous clouds.' The individuals who have studied these effects (real or otherwise) have suggested that since these bodies can travel unlimited distances and are able to pass through solid material (walls), they might well be used to produce instant death in military and civilian officials. It is further conjectured that these bodies could disable military equipment or communications. . .

Two things are certain: (1) that parapsychological phenomena are due to little-known faculties of the subconscious mind; and (2) that the powers of the subconscious mind are vastly superior to those of the normal consciousness. The fantastic memory of the subconscious mind (sometimes referred to as 'photographic memory') is a well-established fact. So is its extraordinary mathematical ability, which has baffled trained mathematicians no end. It seems probable that some of these little-understood faculties of the subconscious mind have something to do with its ability to put together again an object which it had previously disintegrated, and to manipulate the forces involved in this process. The only way one can learn more about these little-understood processes is through intensive study and experimentation. The stakes seem high enough. [Appendix I, document pages 27–29]

While the process by which matter is converted into 'force-matter' (and vice versa) may not be understood, nevertheless one is faced with the possibility that the human mind can disintegrate and reintegrate organic matter – a feat which seems far more complex than the disintegration and reintegration of, say, a stone, a piece of wood, paper, etc. Experiments show that a human body which has lost about half its weight can be reintegrated without loss of normal functions. Since this is possible, it does not seem safe to exclude – without further investigation – the possibility that inorganic matter might undergo a similar disintegration and reintegration. After all, apport phenomena in which physical objects have passed through solid walls have been observed and attested to by some of the world's most eminent scientists as well as by a host of other responsible witnesses. In view of what the human mind has demonstrated it can do with organic matter, and in view of the very real Soviet threat in this sector, the science of parapsychology should be investigated to its fullest potential, perhaps to benefit the national defense.

According to Pullman, Director of the Southeast Hypnosis Research Center in Dallas, Texas, before the end of the 1970s, Soviet diplomats will be able to sit in their foreign embassies and use ESP (in this case a form of apport technique) to steal the secrets of their enemies. Pullman states that a spy would be hypnotized, then his invisible 'spirit' would be ordered to leave his body, travel across barriers of space and time to a foreign government's security facility, and there read top-secret documents and relay back their information. Such 'astral projection' already has been accomplished in laboratory settings, Pullman said, adding that the Russians are probably now trying to perfect it. Pullman further states that the Soviets are at least 25 years ahead of the US in psychic research. According to Pullman, the Soviets have realized the immense military advantage of the psychic ability known as astral projection (out-of-the-body-travel). In this reference, details are given for some of Pullman's work in the US with astral projection. Other scientists . . . interested in this work are professor H.A. Cahn of Northern Arizona University, Doctor Charles Tart of the University of Southern California and Doctor V. Inyushin of Alma-ata. [Appendix I, document page 30]

[Doctor Genady] Sergeyev has conducted several years of intensive lab research on the outstanding PK psychic in Leningrad, Nina Kulagina . . . Sergeyev postulates that the 'bio-plasma' of the human body must interact with the environment to produce PK. Sergeyev emphasizes when target objects are placed in a vacuum, Kulagina is unable to move them . . . Reportedly, Kulagina has caused the movement of a wide range of non-magnetic objects: (under strict scientific control) large crystal bowls, clock pendulums, bread, matches, etc. In one test, a raw egg was placed in a salt solution inside a sealed aquarium six feet away from her. Researchers report she was able to use PK to separate the yolk from the white of the egg. Observations by Western scientists of Mrs Kulagina's PK ability has been reported with verification of her authentic ability. These same Western scientists have reported that as of February 1971, they have not been able to visit or observe Mrs Kulagina. A veil of secrecy has been placed on Sergeyev and Mrs Kulagina for some unknown reasons.

Rather than simply observing PK, the Soviets typically turned to instrumentation. Mrs Kulagina was subjected to a number of physiological electronic measuring devices and tested for important body functions during her PK demonstrations. The Soviets found that at the moment an object begins to move, all of Mrs Kulagina's body processes speed up drastically – heart, breathing, brain activity – and the electromagnetic fields around her body all begin to pulse in rhythm. Soviet researchers postulate that it was these rhythmic 'vibrations' that cause objects to be attracted to or repelled by her . . .

Scientists report that Kulagina has been able to stop the beating of a frog's heart in solution and to re-activate it! This is perhaps the most significant PK test done and its military implications in controlled offensive behavior, if true, are extremely important. [Appendix I, document pages 35–36]

Telepathic scanning

The aim of tuning into the thought processes of the West's military commanders spurred the Soviets on to develop telepathic scanning techniques, particularly with regard to tracking enemy agents in the field.

Soviet researchers went further, and found ways to tap into the telepathic conversations of other remote viewers. By introducing a third telepath who knew when information (in the form of a telepathic conversation) flowed between two other telepaths, the Russians found that the ESP data stream could not only be broken into but could be changed. The third telepath could substitute new ideas and words, in effect corrupting the telepathic message. The Russians thus learnt how to hack into telepathic conversations and substitute fallacious messages and images.

Doctor Milan Ryzl reports that secret psi research associated with state security and defense is going on in the USSR. Communist state authorities, the military and the KGB display an unusual, disproportionate interest in parapsychology. The Soviets are attempting to apply ESP to both police and military use ... According to Ryzl, some years ago a project was begun in the USSR to apply telepathy to indoctrinate and re-educate antisocial elements. It was hoped that suggestion at a distance could induce individuals, without their being aware of it, to adopt the officially desired political and social attitudes ... Reports of psi research in Soviet submarines help confirm military involvement in parapsychology. According to Stone, there is clandestine psi research going on at the

Pavlov Institute of Higher Nervous Activity in Moscow [and] the Durov Institute . . .

Kirlian fields

Energy fields that surround humans were first photographed by Semyon Davidovich Kirlian in 1939 in Krasnodar, capital city of the Kuban region in the south of Russia. Kirlian found that photography of biophysical fields around the body could be achieved with the use of high-frequency electrical fields and a spark generator oscillating at 75 to 200KHz. The generator causes a high-frequency field to emanate between two clamps, which hold the sample and photographic paper. The high-frequency electrostatic field causes the biophysical field to resonate and become excited. Once excited, the bio-physical field around the living object being photographed gives off photons. The 75 to 200KHz electric field causes photons of light to be radiated by the living tissue, which fall on the photographic paper and produce images of the bio-physical excitation. These are not actual pictures of the bio-physical field, but secondary effects, rather like the wake of a boat passing through water. Kirlian's photographs of leaves which had had sections cut out revealed entire biophysical fields that showed the entire leaf as if it was uncut. It was as if the biophysical field was the energetic blueprint for the leaf.

Later research has found that the human body has a bio-physical field around it composed of morphogenic fields, defined by cell biologists as the fields which switch genes on and off and control cell development. They determine whether a cell will become a skin cell or an eye cell, for instance. US military intelligence evaluated the Kirlian effect:

'. . .the Soviets seem preoccupied with the search for the energy that carries or facilitates telepathy transmission. Is it electromagnetic or not? The search for this unknown energy has led the Soviets to Kirlian photography; named after its inventors Semyon and Valentina Kirlian. The Kirlians developed a technique of photographing with a high-frequency electrical field involving a specially constructed high-frequency spark generator . . . Their first photographs showed turquoise and reddish-yellow patterns of flares coming out of specific channels within leaves. A magnified picture of a finger showed craters of light and flares. By the 1960s research on bioluminescence revealed by Kirlian photography was going on in many Soviet universities. Perfected techniques of photographing the play of high-frequency currents on humans, plants and animals, as well as on inanimate matter have set the Soviets on some striking discoveries about the energetical nature of man. 'Bio-plasma' is a term coined by the Soviets for bioluminescent phenomena or energy. Scientists at the Kazakh State University at Alma-ata have found illnesses tend to show up in advance as a disordered play of flares from the 'bio-plasma' long before they manifest in the physical body.

Doctor A. Podshibyakin, an electrophysiologist at the Institute of Clinical Physiology in Kiev, has found that by charting acupuncture points a correlation exists between the 'bio-plasma' and changes on the surface of the sun. At the exact moment solar flares (sun spots) occur, there are changes in the electrical potential of the skin's acupuncture points. These electrical charges are measured by a tobiscope (probably a simple wheatstone bridge device). In some way the 'bio-plasma' of the body is sensitive to these solar explosions the instant they occur even though it takes about two days for the cosmic particles to reach the earth.

The most significant use of Kirlian photography is in the area of psychokinesis or mind over matter (PK). Doctor Genady Sergeyev of the A.A. Uktomskii Military

Institute in Leningrad believes Kirlian photography may uncover the mechanism of PK. Sergeyev is a prominent mathematician for the Soviet military who works closely with an electrophysiologist from the University of Leningrad, Doctor L. Pavlova. Sergeyev has devised important mathematical and statistical methods for analyzing the EEG which allowed parapsychologists to follow the actions of telepathy in the brain. The type of work reported by Sergeyev in 1967 and 1968 is just now beginning to appear in the US efforts to understand the transmission of telepathy. Sergeyev has conducted several years of intensive lab research on the outstanding PK psychic in Leningrad, Nina Kulagina – Sergeyev registered heightened biological luminescence radiating from Kulagina's eyes during the apparent movement of objects by PK. [Appendix I, document pages 33–35]

The telepathic knockout

It seems scarcely credible that the Soviets trained their telepaths to be able to knock out a person simply by projecting a psychic punch at the victim. In fact, the Soviets poured a vast amount of time and money into exactly this.

The Soviets found that the biophysical field of the remote viewer flared out when he or she was lowered into the theta state. At the Schumann resonance point of 7.8Hz, the Earth's natural frequency, the human biophysical field seemed to merge with its surroundings and vanish for a split second. When it came back into being, it was many times larger than normal. While remote viewing, this biophysical field seemed to grow smaller, as if part of it was at the place being remotely viewed.

In Dr Vasilev's 'Experiments in Mental Suggestion', published in 1962 (English translation published in 1963), voluminous data is recorded by the Russian scientist on Soviet experiments in sleep-wake hypnosis. Discovered by the Russians in the thirties, this allowed a hypnotist to transfer commands telepathically to a subject, whether they were a few feet or a thousand miles away. Soviet scientists took this further and discovered that hypnosis could be examined by its affect on the biophysical energy body, which could be detected using Kirlian photography and other means, such as using the powers of the human biophysical field to enable people actually to see energy fields – auras.

Vladimir L. Raikov MD, a psychiatrist, monitored the mental state of a hypnotized person:

> Raikov has worked closely with V. Adamenko, a physicist who reportedly has invented the CCAP (conductivity of the channels of acupuncture points) device. This machine, it is claimed, registers energy flow in the body using as check points for its electrodes the acupuncture points of traditional Chinese medicine. Adamenko reportedly detects changes in body energy caused by alterations of consciousness and varying emotional states. With subjects attached to the CCAP, Raikov put them through various forms of hypnosis. At the end of many sessions the graphs from the CCAP were checked by Raikov and Adamenko. They claim to have found a pronounced difference between the different forms of hypnosis ... They report that these states are very hard to measure by any other method. [Appendix I, document page 46]

A US expert in remote viewing told me that their research showed that, when a paranormal-warfare expert remotely viewed another person, there was a change in the biophysical energy field of the remote viewer and the person being psychically spied upon. Pulsed ELF fields had been found to put people into a trance (see Appendix III for the far-reaching effects of ELF). Russian scientists found that if the remote viewer could mimic this ELF oscillation in his or her bio-physical body, then this field were placed over another person, the person would become unconscious. Following this discovery, the Russians trained their remote viewers to mimic pulsed ELF waves by use of Kirlian photography – the trainee watched the picture of his or her biophysical body while it was exposed to pulsed ELF waves – then tried to copy the effect.

Psychic batteries

Would it be possible to store psychic energy like electricity? was a question Soviet scientists asked themselves. With hard evidence from Kirlian photography and a wide variety of other electronic scanners designed to study the body's bio-physical field – which comprised biomagnetic, bioelectric and bioplasmic components – the Soviet physicists had access to experimental data needed for a new physics of the paranor-mal. Journalist Emil Bachurin's 1990 article in *Young Guard* magazine disclosed information on a number of top-secret psi-warfare projects that had been undertaken in the Soviet Union. Doctor A. Akimov, former director of the Soviets' Centre for Non-traditional Technologies, is quoted as claim-ing that Russian research had discovered a new class of phys-ical fields and particles and the effect they exerted on living and non-living organisms and inanimate objects. New terms such as 'spinor', 'torsionic' and 'microleptonnic' were being used to define these new classes of physical field. Scientists in the West, who have little appreciation of these remarkable advances made by the Soviets, called them 'scalar' fields. Russian psychotronic generators which stored 'torsionic radiation' were apparently found to cause destruction of the brain's neural network and the biophysical field around the brain – 'mind zappers'.

Moreover, if psychotronic generators could to store bio-physical energy, Russian psychic viewers might be able to link themselves to psychic amplifiers that boosted their paranormal powers. The DIA reports that psychotronic generators, devices that store psi energy, were developed by a Czech called Robert Pavlita. Czech researchers, like their Russian counterparts, had also come to the conclusion that biophysical energy is the field effect behind psychokinesis and remote viewing. Reference to the equivalent of the psychotronic generator had been uncovered in ancient alchemical texts, and Pavlita used modern technology to improve on this psychic battery effect. Psychotronic generators draw biophysical fields from a person and store them for later use.

The Czechs believed they had found two types of psychotronic generator – cosmic generators, of which the Egyptian pyramids are an example, and biological generators, the type to which Wilhelm Reich and his Orgone generator belong. Wilhelm Reich, a pupil of Sigmund Freud, found that boxes with alternate layers of wool and steel wool could store biophysical energy. His seminal work in the fifties led the Soviet researchers into bettering these early biological psychotronic generators. In their report 'Soviet and Czechoslovakian Parapsychology Research', the DIA gives a detailed appraisal of psychotronic-generator research:

> Psychotronic generators (also called Pavlita generators after the inventor) are small devices said to be capable of drawing biological energy from humans; the energy is accumulated and stored for future use. Once charged with human energy, the generators can do some of the things a psychic subject can do, but, according to the inventor Robert Pavlita, can be charged by individuals possessing no psychic ability.
>
> The concept of man as a source of unusual energy

dates back at least as far as ancient Chinese and Hindu teachings, in which it was called 'vital energy' or 'prana.' Between the eighteenth and twentieth centuries it was called various things (animal magnetism, odic force, motor force, n-rays, etheric force, etc.) by rediscoverers of its existence. In contemporary Soviet and Czechoslovakian parapsychology this energy is called bio-plasmic or psychotronic energy. The Czechoslovakian rediscovery of biological energy is credited to Robert Pavlita, who began work on his device over thirty years ago.

. . . It has been reported . . . that the devices are fabricated from various metals (steel, bronze, copper, iron, gold) and that their effects are as a result of their form.

Pavlita's generators can be charged by direct contact (e.g. rubbing or touching to the temporal region of the head) or by visually directing mental concentration upon them from a distance. The nature of the energy stored is still not understood, but over the years a number of observations about its effects have been reported. It can be reflected, refracted, polarized, and combined with other forms of energy. It creates effects similar to magnetism, heat, electricity and luminous radiation, but is itself none of these. The energy apparently can be conducted by paper, wood, wool, silk, and other substances normally considered to be good insulators. The devices have been tested by commissions of experts from the Czechoslovakian Academy of Sciences and the University of Hzadec Kralove in Prague. Static electricity, air currents, temperature changes, and magnetism were eliminated as possible explanations for the observed effects. In addition, the energy exerted its effect through glass, water, wood, cardboard, or any type of metal and was not diminished.

According to both Soviet and Czech researchers, one major advantage of studying psychotronic generators is the reproducibility of their effects; in addition they can be activated by nearly anyone, with or without any special psychic abilities. The devices may have other practical applications not related to parapsychology. The Czechs claim that irradiation of seeds with the energy enhances plant growth, and that industrial pollutants have been precipitated out of water by its action.

Pavlita has stated that some forms of his devices can exert both favorable and unfavorable effects on living organisms, including man. In experiments with snails exposed to the energy from a generator, a state similar to hibernation resulted. When flies were placed in the gap of a circular generator they died instantly. In another test, Pavlita aimed a generator at his daughter's head from a distance of several yards. Her electroencephalogram (EEG) changed, she became dizzy, and her equilibrium was disrupted. [Appendix II, document pages 33–34]

Researchers at the Metronomical Institute of the Academy of Sciences in Moscow studied Pavlita and his psychotronic generators. The DIA document continues:

In their present form and size, Pavlita's devices could probably exert an effect on humans at only relatively short range. It is possible that their size could be enlarged or their energy amplified, thereby extending their range. If the Czech claims for these devices are valid, biological energy might be an effective antipersonnel weapon. It would be difficult to defend against, since it apparently penetrates most common forms of insulation and its reported effects (changes in brain-wave characteristics, disturbance of equilibrium, dizziness) could result in personality changes or physical discomfort which might alter combat effectiveness.

Soviet or Czech perfection of psychotronic weapons would pose a severe threat to enemy military, embassy, or security functions. The emitted energy would be silent and difficult to detect electronically (although the Soviets claim to have developed effective biological energy sensors) and the only power source would be a human operator. [Appendix II, document page 34]

Were psychotronically boosted Russian remote viewers capable of enhanced remote influencing? A Ukrainian, Albert Ignatenko, publicly demonstrated that he could raise or lower the pulse rate of people who were remote from him. Vladimir Zironovsky, the Russian MP and ultra-nationalist, boasted on BBC television that Russia has psychics who could remotely kill anyone up to a thousand kilometres away. These boasts may indeed be based on fact!

Psychotronic mind control

Edward Naumov, a leading Russian parapsychologist, is on record as stating, 'A psychotronic generator can influence an individual, or a whole crowd of people. It can affect a person's psyche mentally or emotionally. It can affect memory and attention span. A psychotronic device can cause physical fatigue, disorientation, and alter a person's behaviour.' The Soviets built the world's largest transmitter, code-named Woodpecker by the US, to beam mind-control waves at the West (see Appendix III). It was powered by the Chernobyl nuclear power complex in the Ukraine.

A strange signal which disrupted short-wave transmissions around the world was detected in the early eighties. It was nicknamed Woodpecker due to its pulse modulation of 10Hz, which when listened to on radio equipment sounded like a woodpecker due to loud modulations in the signal. It emitted a peak estimated power of 14 million watts per pulse at frequencies of between 3.26 and 17.54MHz, making it the most powerful man-made, non-nuclear, non-ionizing (i.e. non-radioactive) radiation source on the planet. Seven awesome transmitters near Kiev, also powered by the Chernobyl nuclear power complex, beamed Woodpecker's emissions in the direction of western Europe, Australia, North America and the Middle East. As the document in Appendix III attests, these emissions permeated all obstacles. They were capable of penetrating underwater, and even into shielded bunkers.

So had the Soviets discovered a method of affecting the neurological functioning of entire populations? Woodpecker had been *designed* to alter the brain functions of Nato populations by using ELF modulated signals. It was found that these extremely low frequency waves could penetrate the skull and change brain patterns when broadcast at test victims – 6.66Hz makes the victim depressed, 11Hz can make a person manic and prone to riotous behaviour (see Appendix III). Of particular interest to the KGB scientists were the brain-wave maps of pathological criminals, hopelessly depressed mental patients and socio-psychopaths who had no regard for anyone but themselves; some Soviets hoped to remap the neural networks in the brains of the entire Western population in this way.

Prolonged exposure to ELF signals changes the brain's neural wiring permanently. Top neuro-scientist Dr Gerald Edelman has shown that neurones compete with each other, and that unused neural connections and brain cells die. If you can keep a person in one brain state, such as depression, by use of ELF transmitted by pulse-modulated microwaves, then the brain connections and cells for normal consciousness will be destroyed and the person will become a chronic depressive. Under a barrage of ELF signals from the Woodpecker transmitters the sane mental connections in the brain could gradually die out. Woodpecker's 10Hz ELF signal was broadcast from 1976 until the fall of the Soviet Union.

Doctor Robert Becker of the Syracuse VA Hospital, a Los Angeles physicist and former member of a top-secret US mind-control programme which looked into the effects of ELF, claimed, 'It's highly likely that the Woodpecker signal is causing neurological changes in thirty per cent of the population . . .'

Towards remote killing

Did the Soviets discover how to kill remotely decades ago? Dr Nikolai Khokhlov, a former KGB agent who defected to the West, was hired by the CIA in 1976 to uncover paranormal-warfare research in the USSR. He claimed to have found evidence of it at 20 top-secret, state-of-the-art, underground laboratories, staffed with hundreds of the Soviet Union's leading scientists. Khokhlov described a government laboratory in Moscow that mass-produced psychotronic generators, which were tested on prisoners. Telekinesis was also used on prisoners to paralyze sections of their spinal cord, by damaging the nerve cells with a telekinetic blast. (See Appendix II, document pages 41–47, for a detailed DIA evaluation of Soviet telekinesis.)

Research included the technique being used by Russian paranormal-warfare experts to stop the hearts of laboratory animals. Russian paranormal adepts trained in this remote-killing technique by raising or lowering the heart rate of a test subject in a separate room, simply by the use of remote influencing.

Khokhlov's evidence shows that the Russian research institutes were continuing to investigate telepathy in a rigorous way. In one experiment, new-born rabbits were separated from their mothers, who were hooked up to ECG and EEG monitors. When the new-born rabbits were killed, it was found that the stress levels of the mother were raised dramatically, even though the new-born rabbits were in another location. Telepathic biological links between mother and offspring were therefore shown to exist. To test whether water blocked out the telepathic signal, the mother rabbits were transferred to nuclear submarines. These rabbits were found to 'know' when their offspring were killed, even when they were deep underwater. This experiment showed that hundreds of feet of sea water could not block out the psi effect.

Psychotronic devices were designed to kill or disable humans, then tested out on enemies of the state. Telekinetic experiments were carried out to see how much damage a paranormal adept could cause to an untrained victim by use of mind over matter. Condemned prisoners had brain capillaries ruptured by telekinesis, causing massive embolisms in their brains. Telekinesis was also used to stop their hearts, bringing on a heart attack. 'Kulagina's highly publicized ability to affect living tissues might be applied against human targets,' said the DIA (Appendix II, document page 51).

The use of negative energy
One standard remote-viewing operation for a Russian paranormal-warfare expert was to hook oneself up to a psychotronic device called a theta-delta gun which, by reversing polarity in the brain, placed the psi-adept in the deep hypnotic-like state needed for psychotronic warfare. An ELF signal was then broadcast into the brain of the psi-adept that reproduced the perfect brain state for remote viewing. A room-sized psychotronic generator could then pump energy into the psi-adept, boosting his or her biophysical field so it could overpower any normal person's biophysical field.

The target to be remotely viewed was shown on a screen. Once the target had been located by psychic spying, the ELF-induced brain-wave entrainment was modified to the frequency that had been mapped as optimum for remote influencing. A list of hypnotic commands was then shown to the psi-adept, so that he or she could reprogramme the brain of the person being remotely viewed and influenced. If the person was to be remotely killed, the ELF signal for this was entrained in the psi-adept, enabling his or her power of telekinesis to be locked on to the body of the victim. With a psychotronic generator to power the psi-adept's biophysical body, remote influencing was made possible even over distances of thousands of miles. If the person was to be made ill, the specific frequencies that enabled the psi-adept to broadcast negative illness-inducing psionic energy was fed into his or her brain. Boosted by the psychotronic amplifier they were hooked up to, the Russian paranormal-warfare expert acted as a transmitter for negative energy; the process of remote viewing acted as the target locator, and remote influencing the way to focus this negative energy on the victim.

We all know that curses are supposed to bring us bad luck. Russian researchers expanded on this belief and used 'curses' for a new generation of psi weapons. KGB scientists, having proved that psi energy acted as the medium for remote viewing, began to experiment with remotely imprinting energy fields on matter. Doctor Abraham Shifrin worked at the psi-research institute in Kazakhstan, which was run by the Moscow Institute for Information Transmission, under the directorship of Dr Solomon Gellerstein. He managed to emigrate to Israel in the mid-eighties and disclosed that the Kazakhstan institute had been making psychotronic generators like Robert Pavlita's in Czechoslovakia. They had also found how to store psi energy in psychic accumulators. They studied how Siberian and Altai shamans, yogis, ascetics, psychics and witch doctors cursed or blessed talismans and amulets, and as a result learnt how to charge souvenirs, such as Russian dolls, which could then be given to unsuspecting victims. Depression and mental problems were easily passed on by these negatively charged objects, and in some cases health was adversely affected.

Doctor Boris Ivanov worked on charging water with psi energy at the Laboratory of Bioinformation at the Popov institute in the USSR. It was found that a paranormal-warfare expert hooked up to psychotronic amplification could charge water with negative psi energy that could shrivel plants or cause cancer. US subjects were allegedly given this negatively charged water in their drinks at state functions.*

In Leningrad, Dr Pavel Gulyaiev similarly found a way to scan another person's electromagnetic field at a distance, then to impose another field on to that person which would control their behaviour or make them ill. The neurology institute of Kharkov University experimented on rats, removing their brains and placing them in solutions that kept them partially alive. Remote viewers and sensors were then used to transmit emotions, thoughts, mental calculations and commands. The rats' brains responded to this telepathic link until they died, about three minutes later.

Doctor August Stern, who had worked in the multi-million-rouble psi labs in Novosibirsk, emigrated to France and revealed a wealth of secrets about other psi complexes such as the one at Kharkov.

KGB scientists were prompted to look into the transmission of negative psi energy by research at Novosibirsk:

A significant advance toward identification of the EMR [electromagnetic radiation] source of biological energy transfer was gained from recent research conducted at the University of Novosibirsk. Scientists there investigated the

---

*Psychic Warfare: Threat or Illusion? Martin Ebon (McGraw–Hill, 1983)

release of energy during cell division and during cellular damage and repair resulting from viral infection or toxic chemicals. In over 5000 experiments with cell cultures and animal organs, it was shown that damaged cells radiated some form of energy and that the energy released was capable of causing damage in adjacent control preparations of organs or cells. Further investigation revealed that a uniform pattern, code, or rhythm of radiation was emitted by normal cells. This pattern was disturbed when cellular damage occurred, becoming quite irregular. It was also found that the patterns were transmitted from experimental to control preparations only when the cells or organs were cultured in quartz containers. Since quartz transmits ultraviolet (UV) radiation and standard laboratory glassware does not, the Soviets concluded that UV radiation mediated cellular information transfer. The researchers subsequently correlated given irregularities of emission with specific diseases, and are now attempting to develop techniques for diagnosis and therapy by monitoring and altering cellular radiation codes. [Dr Jiri] Bradna feels that such stimuli influence the herd behavior of animals, and may also be a factor in altering human behavior under conditions of isolation or overcrowding. [Appendix II, document page 10]

As a result, remote viewers and psychotronics experts were apparently trained to transmit negative psi energy at the person they were remotely viewing, intended to make them ill. This barrage of negative psi energy also acted as a shock to the target's system, which made remote influencing much easier. If psychically induced trauma could be caused by projecting negative psi energy at the target, telepathic brainwashing could also be made more efficient.

After the Cold War

US remote viewing of the present-day Russian leadership shows that President Yeltsin, General Lebed and other leading lights in the Russian Federation are – or were – protected by psychic shields of an exotic and dangerous nature. Any remote viewer trying to influence them is attacked by the bio-physical logic bombs in these Russian psychic shields. A bio-physical logic bomb is a thought-form which acts as a mental virus, infecting the victim and causing death or madness. In 1992, former KGB Major General Oleg Kalugin said in an interview on ABC television in the US that, during the coup which brought down the USSR, he received a telephone call from a contact in a Ukrainian military lab. He was told that paranormal-warfare experts were using psychotronic generators and remote influencing against Boris Yeltsin to undermine his health, focusing on his heart in order to kill him. 'For the first time in my life,' Kalugin said, 'I took it [paranormal warfare] seriously.' After the coup, Yeltsin suffered a heart attack. Since then he has been treated by top Russian healers such as Djuna Davitashvili.

Pro-democracy psi-adepts were asked to create the psychic shield around Yeltsin. Remote influencers and psychic telepaths capable of scanning enemy paranormal-warfare experts, or indeed fellow Russians, keep Yeltsin and his chosen few protected from remote influencers and killers. They also use psychic scanning to protect the president's offices and home from psi attack and electronic bugs.

Many KGB paranormal-weapons experts have apparently gone into deep cover in foreign countries to act as special forces psi agents. Located in a hostile country, they could use their skills to spy on and attack the enemy. In the event of a Third World War, they were commanded to reprogramme the brains of the hostile country's leadership to follow the orders of the psi-adept. The Soviet Union could thus in theory ensure the Chinese and Nato leadership lost the war by making the wrong decisions on a consistent, planned basis, as psychically commanded by the psi-adept working under KGB directives!

Following the end of the Cold War, these psi agents and the paranormal-warfare experts in Russia have been redirected to the corporate theatre, focusing on economic espionage. They are also being used to view remotely government meetings in foreign countries and to influence remotely politicians and power brokers to manipulate the stock market and improve business opportunities for KGB-run organizations. By using advanced Russian methods, it is possible to fool the person being telepathically scanned into thinking they are asking themselves the questions being placed in their minds. In this way, the most secret information can be extracted from the target. This branch of psychic spying is referred to as remote sensing.

In post-communist Russia, paranormal research is one of the main priorities of the security service, as it is relatively cheap and very effective. It offers Russia a second strategic weapons system that does not rely on nuclear devices.

The deputy chief of President Yeltsin's security service has become a 'modern Rasputin', the 4 May edition of *Moscow News* reported. General Georgi G. Rogozin approves the horoscopes cast regularly for the country's top officials, communicates with the cosmos on budgetary and financial matters, rotates tables and saucers in his study, and creates a powerful field around the President. He also evaluates the decisions of the Supreme Personnel Commission by consulting the Kabala.

Anatoly Kashpirovsky, a psi-adept and ultra-nationalist, allegedly won a seat in the Russian parliament by use of remote influencing. When he lost his seat in the 1996 election, Kashpirovsky threatened to render impotent by psychic means any government employee who tried to evict him from the apartment that had come with the post.

The thrust of modern Russian psychotronic research is toward remote influence, telekinesis and biological-telekinesis. Doctor Edwin May, head of the US government psi-project Stargate (more about this in the next chapter on US remote viewing), and Soviet parapsychologist Dr Larissa Vilenskaya, in their overview 'Influence at a Distance, PK and Bio-PK', state that investigation into influencing the human brain telepathically with positive and negative psi energy and emotions, changing DNA in lab cultures by use of remote influencing, the growth of plants using telekinesis, and the healing effect of remote influencing on humans and animals, is part of present-day Russian research.

In the next chapter, we look at US paranormal mobilization, the other half of the inner-space arms race.

3

US psi-spies

News of Russian paranormal-warfare research eventually filtered out to the West. It was thought by CIA analysts that the
Soviets might be capable of telepathically controlling the
thoughts of leading US military and political leaders, as well
as being able to remotely kill US citizens. Could telekinesis be
used to disable US hardware such as computers, nuclear
weapon systems and space vehicles? The CIA report stated:
'The major impetus behind the Soviet drive to harness the
possible capabilities of telepathic communication, telekinetics, and bionics are said to come from the Soviet military and
the KGB.' No wonder they were worried!

The term 'eight-Martini effect' was coined by Norman
Jackson, a CIA spokesman and former technical adviser to
John McMahon, Deputy Director of the CIA. On the US TV
show *Night Line* (28 November 1995), which was about the
use of remote-viewing programmes in the mid-eighties, he said,
'"Eight-Martini results" is an in-house term for remote-
viewing data so good it cracks everyone's sense of reality.' After
one particularly spectacular demonstration apparently, the
CIA handlers had to have eight Martinis to calm their nerves.
The following is the story of how eight-Martini effects were
sometimes achieved by the US remote-viewing programme.

America gears up for psychic war

As early as 1972, it was feared that the Russians were developing a form of group-augmented telepathic telekinesis, whereby a large number of telepaths could create thought-forms out of the collective unconscious that would actually materialize. The Soviets could thus materialize their energy bodies in distant locations to steal top-secret documents or damage equipment (see Appendix I, document page 27, the apport technique). The US effort was stimulated by information that they received in 1973 about the top-secret psychical research base to the north east of Leningrad, code-named 'Black Box'. Doctor Igor Vladsky sent a letter to Harvard psychologist Gene Kearney, giving information about the Leningrad psychical research facility and its telekinesis experiments. The Russians' advances in ESP and telekinesis seemed to be leading them towards the ability to cause physical effects. This frightened the US missile command – if psychics could disable US ballistic missiles in their silos or in flight, American deterrent capability would be destroyed. In 1975, Thomas Bearden, a nuclear engineer, was asked by the US Army to investigate this area of Russian psychical research. By then, the DIA were discussing Soviet psychokinesis at length:

> All the Soviet and Czech research on PK is significant, especially that associated with the spectacular Soviet psychics Kulagina, Vinogradova and Ermolayev. Kulagina's highly publicized ability to affect living tissues might be applied against human targets; in like manner, Vinogradova's power to move objects, and Ermolayev's levitational ability could possibly be used to activate or deactivate power supplies or to steal military documents or hardware. Robert Pavlita's generators and Julius Krmessky's PK indicators could be (and possibly are now) used to train large numbers of lesser known Soviet and

Czech citizens to develop, enhance, and control their latent psychic abilities. Such a cadre of trained but anonymous individuals could be used for any number of covert activities. Less spectacular, but more significant, is the fact that Soviet and Czech scientists are pursuing an interrelated, unified approach to determining the energy sources and interactions underlying PK and appear to be far ahead of their Western counterparts in reaching this goal. It will be but a short step from understanding to application and there is little doubt that many applications can be directed toward man for whatever purpose, be it good or bad. [Appendix II, document page 51]

Both superpowers had soon become interested in telekinesis. Telekinetic effects may be small, but it does not take much force to ruin a circuit board in a missile-guidance system, or tear open a capillary in the brain.

In the early seventies, Soviet, Czech and Chinese paranormal-warfare projects forced the CIA reluctantly to start their own psi-spy programme. At first the number of scientists willing to help the CIA was very limited. However, two physicists, Russell Targ and Dr Hal Puthoff, agreed to help. They began remote-viewing research at the Stanford Research Institute in California. On 6 June 1972, the first psychic experiments were conducted on Ingo Swann, a leading clairvoyant. He had served in Korea, but by the seventies was an artist, who now began supplementing his income as a subject in parapsychology experiments. His remote-viewing abilities were eventually demonstrated to be of a high order and he was later to invent the six stages of protocols now used by all US remote viewers. On this first test, Swann succeeded in psychically influencing a magnetometer. There followed a series of remote-viewing experiments which proved hit and miss.

In the autumn of 1972, Yuri Geller visited the Stanford Research Institute and was tested by Targ and Puthoff. His talent was alleged to be quixotic, hard to pin down.*

Remote viewing was a term coined by Targ and Puthoff, a synergy created between telepathy and clairvoyance, initiated by Swann. The monitor in this psychic-spying game travels mentally to a specific location, and the guesser attempts to obtain a mental image of that location and then sketches what he sees.†

With this new form of remote viewing, Ingo Swann's efficiency increased to meaningful levels, and the CIA became interested enough to increase their initial funding of the project. When Puthoff gave Swann the co-ordinates of a place just east of California's Mount Shasta, the psychic's response was, 'Definitely see mountain to south-west, not far, also east.' The co-ordinates of a point 20 miles east of Mount Hekla volcano in southern Iceland produced: 'Volcano to south-west, I think I'm over ocean.' When Puthoff gave the co-ordinates of the middle of Lake Victoria in Africa, Swann described: 'Sense of speeding over water, landing on land. Lake to west, high elevation.' Puthoff thought Swann had described the target inaccurately, until he consulted the *Times Atlas of the World* and found his co-ordinates were those of the Tanzanian village of Ushashi, some 30 miles inland from Lake Victoria's south-eastern shore! Results such as this enabled Puthoff to win funding from the CIA Technical Services Division in the Directorate of Operations, which was transferred to the Directorate of Science and Technology, later to be called the Office of Technical Services. There was also funding from the CIA Office of Research and Development.

*_Mind Reach,_ Hal Puthoff and Russell Targ (Delacorte, New York, 1977)
†_Remote Viewers: The Secret History of America's Psychic Spies_, Jim Schnabel (Dell, New York, 1977)

Ingo Swann talks of an incident that occurred between 1975 and 1976 when he was asked to view remotely Soviet submarines:*

This was one of those 'big test' things that went on, with witnesses, and the room was filled with top brass. [I said,] 'Oh my God! Hal, I don't know what to do. I think that this submarine has shot down a UFO or the UFO fired on her. What shall I do?' And Puthoff was as pale as anything, you know, and he looked at me and whispered, 'Oh Christ! It's your show. You do what you think you should do.' So I sketched out this picture of this UFO and this brass (two- or three-star general) sitting on my right grabbed it and said, 'What's that, Mr Swann?' I said, 'Sir, I think it's rather obvious what that is.' And he took the paper and stood up, and when he stood up, everybody else stood up except me and Puthoff, and he walked out of the room, and so did the others. So Puthoff and I went back to the hotel and I said, 'Oh Christ, we've blown the program.' So we went out and got drunk on marguaritas and things like that. Three days later Puthoff got a call. The call said, 'OK, how much money do you want?'

While these early experiments with Swann were going on, Puthoff got a call from Pat Price, a retired police officer, who was offering his services. Price was tested by CIA liaison officer Richard Kennett, who gave him the approximate co-ordinates of his summer cabin in West Virginia. When Price responded with a detailed description of a secret US military underground base, Kennett thought he had failed; but when

*Ingo Swann interview on 'Dreamland' transcribed organization, University of Wisconsin, 12 December 1996. Quoted from 'Remote Viewing and the US Intelligence Community', Armen Victorian (*Lobster* magazine, June 1996, No. 31)

Kennett drove to his cabin sometime later he found the location that Price had described was situated nearby. The 'Sugar Grove' – a National Security Agency (NSA) underground spy satellite, communication and telephone interception centre – had been described perfectly. Price had even named three of the senior officers who worked there.

This generated a very serious DIA probe into Puthoff, Targ and Price. Suspected of being communist spies, the entire project was examined with a fine-tooth comb, as the Pentagon did not believe Price could have got such detailed information about the NSA base by psychic means. When no evidence could be found, the heat died down.

Price offered to view remotely the Russian counterpart to the NSA base, to soothe the CIA's discomfiture. He pinpointed the Russian base at Mount Narodnyna in a remote part of the northern Ural Mountains, and described the underground base, its high proportion of female personnel, radar dishes . . . The CIA were delighted.

Rivalry developed between Price and Swann, which was made worse by the fact that Price was acknowledged as the better psychic. Such was the power of Price's remote viewing that he could read numbers and words at the site he was studying. Price was asked by the CIA to view the Semipalatinsk military research facility. He successfully described the 60-foot-diameter steel spheres and the extremely large cranes that had been constructed with the use of sophisticated welding techniques to seal these nuclear-bomb containers together. Satellite photos showed that Price's remote viewing was correct. It was assumed that the Semipalatinsk complex was developing an exotic high-energy beam weapon, using nuclear explosions to power the proton or neutron beam.

Pat Price's death in 1975 under mysterious circumstances was highly controversial. It was alleged at the time that the Soviets had poisoned him, most likely with a mycotoxin. It would have been a top priority for the KGB to eliminate Price, as his phenomenal remote-viewing abilities would have posed a significant danger to the USSR's paranormal-warfare build-up. He may also have been the victim of an elite group of Russian psi-agents trained to kill remotely enemies of the Soviet Union. Whatever the true reason, Price, the leading US psi-spy, was probably the first casualty of the inner-space arms race.

Not to be outdone, Swann convinced Puthoff and Targ that he could train anyone in remote viewing. The aim was to train military personnel who had security clearance, rather than psychics who had none. Swann would persuade the military top brass who came to inspect the remote-viewing research to take part by pointing out that the training would enable them to view remotely top-secret files. Intelligence operatives from the CIA, the DIA, the NSA and other organizations also came calling. Such was the enthusiasm of the military and intelligence communities that they decided to fund a 20-year top-secret programme to train military remote viewers. This programme was called Star Gate.

Ingo Swann used his co-ordinate remote-viewing system to help train the new breed of military remote viewers. Today, Swann's agenda forms the basis for the commercially available courses sold in the USA, which cost $1000-7000 per week.

In 1976, the team started experimenting with precognitive remote viewing, which is a specialized version of clairvoyance, specifically designed to check on the future of the US embassy, which was being built in Moscow. But the remote viewers found it difficult to see that building in the future. When asked to describe the structure as it would be in the mid-eighties, they could not agree. What actually occurred was that the Russian construction teams planted so many bugs in the embassy (discovered by a giant X-ray machine brought in by the Americans), even using the steel supports as antennae, that eventually the building would have to be partly demolished at the request of the US government. This possibly explains why the US remote viewers could not home in on the building in the future – it had no future.

Project Grill Flame

In the late seventies, the US Army set up its own small remote-viewing programme. Taking orders from the army's assistant chief of intelligence in the Pentagon, only a few dozen officials in the intelligence community knew about this project, code-named Grill Flame. Documents obtained from US intelligence, published in part in *Lobster* magazine, show that Grill Flame was the operational wing of the overall Star Gate programme. In 1978, with the establishment of Detachment @G@ (later listed in the Intelligence and Security Command books as Grill Flame), the US Army was given a new mission – to utilize remote viewing as an intelligence-gathering tool. Eventually, the entire Defense Department's remote-viewing programme was moved under the administrative umbrella of Grill Flame.

Six people – Mel Riley, Joe McMoneagle, Ken Bell, Fern Gauvin, Hartleigh Trent and Nancy Stern – most of them army personnel, were tested by the Stanford Research Institute for the Grill Flame project and all were found to be suitable. Based at Fort Meade in Maryland, the home of the NSA, the largest US intelligence branch, this unit carried out remote viewing against a selection of Soviet and Chinese bases. In late 1978 its services were made available to anyone in the US intelligence community who had high enough access. General Ed Thompson, who was in overall command of the unit, increased funding so that Mel Riley, Joe McMoneagle and Ken Bell, nicknamed the Special Action Branch, could work full time on the project. In the summer of

1979, Mel Riley was assigned one of his first important remote-viewing targets – a Chinese nuclear-weapon test site near Lop Nor. He remotely viewed an airborne nuclear-weapon drop by the Chinese in which the weapon exploded but failed to go into a nuclear chain reaction. He also reported that it was much more sophisticated in its construction than anticipated, and made use of enrichment processes the intelligence people had not expected from China.*

Joe McMoneagle was asked by the NSA to view remotely a US consulate in the Mediterranean theatre from which the Russians were suspected of extracting information. McMoneagle correctly described a Russian listening post opposite the consulate, and the location of the electronic bug inside the consulate – he even psychically spied upon an NSA counterespionage team in a room beneath the Russians.†

McMoneagle sensed radioactivity when he was remotely viewing a Russian nuclear facility and 'saw' a greenish glow emanating from the nuclear reactor. In 1979, he remotely viewed a greenish glow around a nuclear weapon on the seabed off the coast of Spain. The weapon was rumoured to have fallen from an American nuclear bomber.

Like Joe McMoneagle at Fort Meade, Ingo Swann at the Stanford Research Institute was asked to detect any nuclear reaction. Using remote viewing, he was able to determine the moment a rocket motor was fired, and in another case, the event and time of a nuclear-weapon detonation in Nevada.

The Fort Meade group were set to predict the impact site of Sky Lab. When the space station finally fell to Earth, it struck Western Australia; McMoneagle had predicted this general area in his remote viewing. Ken Bell successfully

*'Operational project summary: an unofficial list of nineteen apparent RV successes, 1974–93' Dale Graff (CIA-sponsored report, 1995).
†*Remote Viewers: The Secret History of America's Psychic Spies*, Jim Schnabel (Dell, New York, 1977)

found a downed US helicopter in a remote part of Peru. He became distraught when he remotely viewed the burnt and broken corpses of the pilot and co-pilot.

One story claims that the Grill Flame group successfully psychically interrogated an agent in an Eastern European country. The CIA were suspicious of him but needed to know the right questions to ask to uncover his misdeeds. McMoneagle remotely viewed the agent, and discovered that he had received a large amount of money. During his next lie-detector test the agent, when questioned about the money, blurted out, 'How could you have known that!'*

The main aim of the CIA and DIA research teams at this time, however, was to develop a reliable psychic-spying method. To test out the powers of the US remote viewers, each subject was asked to spy psychically on US top-secret projects. McMoneagle remotely viewed a new, experimental XM-1 tank in a hangar, correctly describing its special armour, main gun and targeting system, and producing a detailed diagram of the tank – which was later to be the M1 main battle tank used by the US Army in the Gulf War. Riley psychically spied on the bat-like B1 stealth bomber, years before it was made public. Results like this proved to the military that remote viewing was a very powerful intelligence asset.

Unfortunately, the remote-viewing group's warnings that psi-poisoned gifts from the Russians to US diplomats should be removed, or at the very least be put in isolated rooms, fell on deaf ears and at worst generated ridicule. Mainstream US society was not ready to understand that the Soviet Union had developed paranormal weapons and thus instigated a whole new branch of warfare.

*Remote Viewers: The Secret History of America's Psychic Spies, Jim Schnabel (Dell, New York, 1997)

In their psychic spying, the US remote-viewing group (the team of six were by now nicknamed the Naturals) studied the new main Soviet battle tank, the T-72. They also remotely viewed how one of these T-72s was stolen by the CIA from Eastern Europe and brought to the USA by freighter.

McMoneagle's greatest display of remote viewing came in 1979, when he investigated a naval facility at Severodvinsk, on the White Sea near the Arctic Circle. Within a huge building in the facility, McMoneagle discovered a giant submarine, the size of a First World War battleship. With the aid of Hartleigh Trent, McMoneagle sketched the submarine, which had 20 canted tubes for ballistic missiles, a double hull and a new type of drive mechanism. During one remote-viewing session, McMoneagle saw the Russians dynamiting a channel from the building, which was 100 yards from the water's edge. Satellite photos confirmed the Typhoon-class submarine at the dockside some four months after McMoneagle's last remote viewing. His spectacular remote-viewing ability enabled him, in his own words, 'to gain access to the insides of filing cabinets, desk drawers, rooms, buildings in restricted areas of other countries for espionage purposes'.* The incident with the Typhoon submarine and his picture-perfect remote viewing of other sites demonstrated that Joe McMoneagle was now the finest remote viewer in the team. In fact, he was one of the US government's premier psi-spies. When this army intelligence officer left Star Gate in 1984, he was awarded a Legion of Merit for providing information on 150 targets that was unavailable from other sources.

US remote viewing expands in scope
While the Naturals were working on improving their technique, so other methods were constantly being developed, as

* *Mind Trek*, Joe McMoneagle (Hampton Roads Press, 1993)

CIA reports for their Research and Development Office (declassified in 1995) reveal. Targ and Puthoff at the Stanford Research Institute had refined many different training techniques. In 'outbound' remote viewing, for instance, an experimenter would mentally visit a target site while the remote viewer tried to visualize the experimenter's surroundings. Then the remote viewer was taken to the target site to get an actual look at what he had been seeing in his mind's eye. This training technique was extended to long-distance outbound remote viewing (without the final visit), which was used to look for kidnap victims, terrorist bombs etc., with much work being carried out on high-tech targets – including nuclear facilities and Mikoyan and Sukhoi, the Soviet aircraft design bureaux.

However, these all involved remote viewing from a normal state of consciousness, i.e. the beta state. The technique favoured by the Fort Meade military remote viewers was called extended remote viewing (ERV), whereby the remote viewer practised psychic spying from a deeper level of consciousness – the theta state, which as we have seen is normally achieved while asleep and dreaming. Biofeedback and EEG machines were used to train the remote viewer to put him- or herself into the theta state. A special room to cut out external stimuli was also used to facilitate ERV.

Ingo Swann continued to use the co-ordinate remote-viewing (CRV) method. In one notorious session, which he spoke about on the 27 August 1995 *Equinox* programme, The Real X-Files, on Channel 4, he psychically spied on a location in the Soviet Union which was being used for biological-weapons research on unwilling human victims. (This could have been the biological-warfare complex at Obolensk, in a forest to the south of Moscow.) Swann catalogued a number of such biological-weapons sites, including one at Stepnogorsk, an island in the Aral Sea called Vozrozhdeniye, Berdsk, and the city of Sverdlovsk, which in 1979 had suffered a deadly accident with anthrax spores that killed hundreds of Russians.

Gary Langford, another talented remote viewer from Stanford who was working with Swann, also tested CRV techniques on underwater Atlantic ridges, looking for Russian ballistic-missile submarines. In fact, the Stanford and Fort Meade military remote viewers worked together on many projects. According to the 'Operational project summary: an unofficial list of nineteen apparent RV successes, 1974-93', compiled by Dale Graff and selectively released by the CIA to sponsored investigators in 1995, the strategic use of remote viewing was made plain by the Stanford subjects being used by the air force to look for the new MX ballistic-missile sites. Soviet missiles were becoming so accurate that there was a possibility that they could destroy nearly all US land-based nuclear ballistic missiles in a single strike. In 1979, the air force had come up with the MX missile plan by which 200 mobile nuclear missiles were to be distributed on a special railroad 30 miles long, between 23 specially hardened silos. The Soviets would have to fire two missiles per silo, necessitating a total of 9,200 Russian warheads, which was thought to be too many nuclear weapons for the Soviets to be able to deploy.

The Stanford Research Institute was asked by the air force to see if remote viewing could be used to pinpoint the missiles in their specific silos. Two thousand students were tested for remote-viewing abilities. Groups of those who passed were set to find the silos, in a shell-game simulation. They achieved only ten per cent accuracy. But Mary Long, the remote-viewing prodigy of the group, reached 80 per cent accuracy! The air force were not pleased at this result, as it cast doubt on the efficacy of their plan. Since the Soviets were far more advanced than the USA in paranormal warfare, it was assumed that they had groups of remote viewers with Mary Long-like abilities. In the end only 50 MX missiles were built, and these were housed in old Minuteman silos at Warren Air Force Base in Wyoming and in Colorado.

CIA-sponsored research enabled Puthoff to make a study of the brains of remote viewers, to see if any neurophysiological changes could be found. Los Alamos National Laboratory gave the Stanford remote viewers brain scans, using super-conducting magnetoencephalographs. Puthoff and the CIA were keen to find the part of the brain involved with psi activity, and as a result of their experimentation they pinpointed the temporal lobes, which are situated to the front and side of the cortex, i.e. the uppermost grey matter of the brain (see Figure 1, document page 58).

In 1980, the CIA asked Ken Bell to help them with a suspected KGB agent who had been detained by BOSS (the South African intelligence organization) in South Africa. The KGB agent was proving difficult to break. Bell remotely viewed the KGB suspect and telepathically interrogated him. During this psychic interrogation, Bell asked the man questions which were telepathically transmitted so that they appeared in the man's thoughts as if he were asking them of himself. Bell discovered that the suspect was using a pocket calculator specially modified to decode messages from the KGB. One of the BOSS agents had taken the calculator home, and when it was recovered and examined, it enabled them to prove the man was a KGB agent.

The Fort Meade group was called upon to spy on the ultra-secret nuclear testing base at Semipalatinsk, as well as look for the crash site of a wrecked Soviet Tu-95 bomber – but their real test was to come with the task of finding the whereabouts of US hostages in Iran, who had been captured in 1979. In April 1980, Hartleigh Trent remotely viewed US special forces rappelling out of helicopters in Iran, and day after day the group used remote viewing to keep tabs on the hostages. However, on 25 April 1980 President Carter

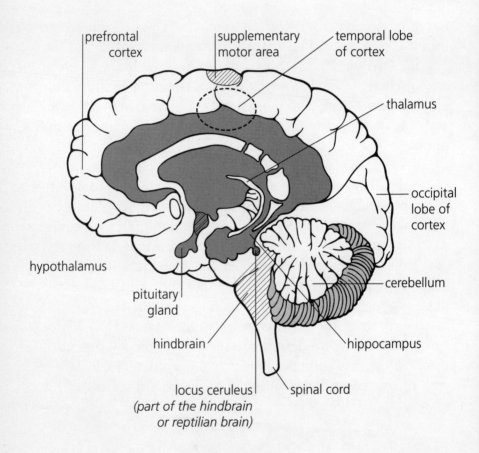

prefrontal
cortex

supplementary
motor area

temporal lobe
of cortex

thalamus

occipital
lobe of
cortex

hypothalamus

cerebellum

pituitary
gland

hindbrain

hippocampus

locus ceruleus
*(part of the hindbrain
or reptilian brain)*

spinal cord

Figure 1 The brain

announced that the rescue mission had been a debacle; Nancy Stern left the Grill Flame project, followed shortly by Fern Gauvin. By early 1981, most of the Grill Flame team had dispersed, Bell and Riley to the regular army and normal military work, while McMoneagle was nearing retirement. Hartleigh Trent died of cancer.

The need for new blood from the Stanford Research Institute to bolster the US remote-viewing programme was growing.

Amplifying remote viewing

By the early eighties, Ingo Swann was working for Jack Vorona of the DIA and for General Ed Thompson, who was still in overall charge of the Fort Meade project. Puthoff had found that two-thirds of the data gained by remote viewing was correct, but the aim, as always, was to improve accuracy.

Techniques used by US remote viewers in these early days included locking up their thoughts in a 'mental suitcase' – alpha- and theta-inducing mind machines, as now sold to the public.

Ingo Swann became interested in teaching pupils how to distinguish signal (or first impressions) from noise (or attempts to analyze). If the remote viewer's first impressions were recorded without any attempt to analyze them, the information tended to be of high accuracy. When the remote viewer tried to analyze what he or she was seeing, accuracy plummeted. This phenomenon was called analytical overlay. Within the first two seconds of studying an event, or part of the target, accuracy was high; once the remote viewer tried to analyze the image or information, the remote viewing became garbled or wrong.

Puthoff postulated that the left hemisphere of the brain was not involved in psi activity. Since the left part of our brains is involved in analytical, mathematical and alphanumeric data, he theorized that this part of the brain gets in the way of the deeper, non-language-based parts involved in remote viewing. It is rather like a person with a damaged left hemisphere who can see and draw pictures but cannot label them accurately. Swann developed remote-viewing methods of working that concentrated on raw data, and then, in later parts of each session, on bringing in analytical information when it was more likely to be right. In this way, Swann assumed that the brain could be trained to evaluate psi data. In effect, he was attempting to rewire the neural network of the brain, to build in a sixth sense. This was his method:

Stage One – doodle the first thing that comes into your mind after being given the co-ordinates of the remote-viewing target. The essence of the target could be seen in this ideogram. As the session develops, visual imagery could be brought in, and finally analytical information, which has been strictly avoided until this point.

Stage Two – allow visual and sensory data into your consciousness but discard any analytical mental processes. The raw data of remote-viewing perceptions should be to the fore, with no conscious thought about what it may or may not be.

Stage Three – put an overview of your remote-viewing perceptions into a bigger picture, possibly drawing numerous pictures.

Stage Four – make lists of the emotional and aesthetic impact of what you have seen in the remote-viewing session. List the tangibles and intangibles of which you were aware. Finally, make a sketch that incorporates all the information acquired in the remote-viewing session.

These four protocols, as Swann called them, were used in the early days. He later added a Stage Five, in which ways of improving remote-viewing resolution were implemented; and a Stage Six, in which a three-dimensional representation of the target was arrived at, by making a model. Later still, other teachers introduced a Stage Seven which involves reading documents at the remote-viewing location. These CRV protocols still form the basis for all remote viewing taught in the USA.

Puthoff theorized that remote viewing was a form of subliminal perception, rather like the image flashed on the screen too fast to be consciously seen but nevertheless perceived by the subconscious. It seemed as if the remote viewer was travelling to the target for the briefest of moments, picking up a subliminal perception of it, then alighting back in his body. As the remote-viewing process was repeated the remote viewer went back to the target, and slowly built up a picture of what he was seeing as a set of subliminal images and perceptions that slowly, tenuously, slipped into conscious awareness. In later chapters, we will discuss how this US research fits into an overall theory of how remote viewing works – the physics of the paranormal.

Remote viewing moves to wider circles

Psychic Noreen Renier, during a 1981 lecture at the FBI's training centre at Quantico in Virginia, predicted that President Reagan would be the subject of an assassination attempt that spring, which turned out to be correct. As is well-known, the White House at that time was very pro-paranormal; Ronald and Nancy Reagan regularly consulted astrologer Joan Quigley.

Freelance psi-spies such as Alex Tannous were kept busy by the CIA during the early eighties. When the CIA's station chief in Beirut, William Buckley, was kidnapped by Moslem terrorists, the agency's Directorate of Operations asked Tannous to view the captive. When Tannous reported the route of the kidnapping and stated that Buckley had been tortured to death by the terrorists, the CIA were not happy – especially when it turned out to be true.

Tannous's group of private psi-spies were also used by the secret service to find an assassin code-named the 'Cat', who was targeting Ronald Reagan.

A massive boost to official remote-viewing deployment in the US Army came with the appointment in 1981 of Major General Albert Stubblebine to head Intelligence Security Command (INSCOM). A true believer in remote viewing – 'I will tell you for the record that there are structures underneath the surface of Mars. I will also tell you that there are machines under the surface of Mars that you can look at. You can find out in detail, you can see what they are, who they are and a lot of detail about them . . . you can do that through remote viewing.'* – and the merits of paranormal warfare, Stubblebine had pushed through neuro-linguistic programming in the management training of staff officers and the teaching of out-of-body consciousness at the Monroe Institute. The military, under Major General Stubblebine, and with the help of Jack Vorona of the DIA and the technical expertise of Hal Puthoff, pushed forward the remote-viewing project at Fort Meade.

Colonel John Alexander oversaw many of these INSCOM projects for Stubblebine. Alexander, a true visionary who had published the seminal article in *Military Review* called 'The New Mental Battlefield', in which he described remote viewing and extolled its usefulness, suggested that effective mind-influencing devices were already a lethal reality.

Another innovation, according to Sally Squires of the

Nexus magazine, 'Remote Viewing', Vol 2 No 21, Aug-Sep 1994

Washington Post ('The Pentagon's Twilight Zone', 17 April 1988), was an army war college called Task Force Delta, which looked at the development of so-called paranormal warrior-monks. The project was to investigate strange philosophical practices for anything that might be of use to the military. Lieutenant Colonel Jim Chandler and like-minded officers from the task force came up with the name 'First Earth Battalion' – an ecologically minded, politically correct, warrior-monk vision for the future soldier. A 1982 report of a Task Force Delta meeting was reported by Colonel Mike Malone: 'I am one of the tribal elders . . . my name is "The Mullet Man." I am known as the one who casts nets. And I try to tell people that of all those who cast nets, most should focus more on the casting than the catching. I live with, fish for, and push the cause of the mullet, because he is a "low-class" fish. He is simple. He is honest. He moves around in great formations and columns. He does damn near all the work . . .'

According to documents in my possession, Jack Houck, a defence consultant and the US expert on psychokinesis, introduced Stubblebine and Alexander to spoon bending, which Stubblebine subsequently showed to INSCOM officers, as well as to General Thompson, directorate chief at the DIA, and John McMahon, deputy director of the CIA.

For some time, character clashes had been evident among the Stanford researchers and Fort Meade remote viewers, and now they became acrimonious. Russell Targ's finance was stopped by the DIA for alleged sloppiness, and in 1983 he and remote viewer Keith Harary left to go into business on their own. Initially they proved spectacularly successful in analyzing the silver-futures options for clients*, but again bitter acrimony was the end result.

*'The goose that laid the silver eggs: a criticism of psi and silver futures forecasting', *The Journal of the American Society for Psychical Research*, October 1992, volume 86.

In 1983, the military remote-viewing programme came under the auspices of INSCOM and the direct control of Stubblebine, and in the process received the new code-name of Center Lane. The unit was used to look for terrorists, among other things. When Brigadier General James Dozier was kidnapped by the Italian Red Brigade, the team at Fort Meade was asked to find him. Langford had predicted the blue van that was involved in the kidnapping; McMoneagle gave an exact description of the second-floor room in Padua in which Dozier was being held; another remote viewer, Ted Wheatley, identified the town. Dozier was eventually freed, thanks in part to signals intelligence by US special-operations teams. He was found in a second-floor room with a radiator on the wall, above a store with a distinctive facade on the ground floor, just as McMoneagle had described.

New blood was introduced by Stubblebine into the Fort Meade group at this time, including Lyn Buchanan and Ed Dames.

Ingo Swann's training enabled the new US military remote viewers not only to learn CRV and simple ERV, but to experience bilocation. This was seen as the first major step towards achieving Russian techniques of remote viewing. It enabled the remote viewer to perceive the target as if he or she were actually there. In the US, bilocation was seen as the pinnacle of remote viewing, a peak experience to be enjoyed when it occurred. Of all Swann's trainees, Tom Nance was the finest; he could make models of what he was remotely viewing – Stage Six of Swann's training.

Stubblebine's replacement by Major General Harry Soyster put the Fort Meade group into a strong decline; it was transferred to the DIA, and renamed Sun Streak. However, while the Army's remote-viewing group fell on hard times, the Stanford group blossomed, working for all branches of the US government. During 1984 and 1985, Jack Vorona of the CIA and Hal Puthoff lobbied congress, the military and intelligence agencies for funds. Remote-viewing demonstrations were held for the White House, the navy, the air force, the CIA, Joint Chiefs of Staff, the National Security Council, NSA, FBI, DEA, the Customs Service, the Coast Guard, and the Defense Advanced Research Projects Agency. As a result, the Stanford group won the support of a Pentagon-affiliated agency and a five-year, $10million research and development contract to work on the neurophysiology of remote viewing, and psi abilities such as psychokinesis. Sun Streak was given the job of remotely viewing high-tech Soviet weapons. In 1987, they psychically spied upon the Dushanbe satellite-tracking, communication and strategic laser complex in the USSR. Mel Riley and Paul Smith were among the unit's remote viewers. They located Chinese Silkworm missile emplacements in Iran, towards the end of the Iran-Iraq war. In 1988 and 1989, the unit helped the Drug Enforcement Agency (DEA) look for drug routes, vessels and barons. They also psychically searched for US POWs abandoned to their fate in Vietnam after the war.

With a new DIA operations officer, Fern Gauvin (a former Natural with Grill Flame), more exotic and occult techniques were practised at Fort Meade. Up until then, CRV and ERV had been the only techniques regularly used. Now channelling (allowing your body to be taken over by a spirit) was added to the portfolio of techniques. Written remote viewing, where the spirit 'dictated' the answer to questions, enabled Angela Dellafiora to find a rogue US Customs Service officer, Charles Jordan, in Lovell, Wyoming. She also predicted how Quaddafi would transport chemical weapons from the facility at Rabta by ship to another location, to avoid US surveillance and a presumed bombing raid. She even predicted a hijacking in Rome, or Athens, of US airline passengers by Moslem terrorists.

The channelling of information by discarnate spirits to enable remote viewing has a long history. Helen Duncan was a psychic who publicly stated at a seance during the height of the Second World War that a British battleship had been sunk. She was promptly jailed by the British authorities, who were keen to control the flow of bad news. It is known that Churchill was aware of psychic warfare during the Second World War; the lighting of candles and meditation on the powers of light was used to ward off the evil forces of Hitler*. Churchill was concerned that vital defence information may have been leaked by Helen Duncan if she was allowed to continue. A front-page article in *The Times* in January 1998, revealed that pressure was being put on the government to pardon Helen Duncan, Britain's first convicted psychic viewer. Until this very day, psychic viewing is looked on by the British establishment with horror. A country such as the UK, obsessed with secrecy, cannot allow remote viewing to become public knowledge – as I have found to my cost.

The twilight years of US military remote viewing

In 1988, the new US Secretary of Defense, Frank Carlucci, announced a $33 billion defence cut. A Pentagon inspector general's team arrived at Fort Meade to examine the work the US military remote viewers had been undertaking. Numerous files were shredded before the inspector general's team could examine them, and remote viewers were told to avoid the inspectors. Not surprisingly, the inspector general recommended that the remote-viewing unit be shut down. Many of the personnel left: Ingo Swann left Stanford in 1988; Ed Dames left the unit that summer, and Mel Riley retired in 1990.

The Spear of Destiny, Trevor Ravenscroft, Neville Spearman, 1973.

In fact, the unit survived, but only four remote viewers were left at Fort Meade when the Gulf War started in 1991. They were asked to find mobile Scud-missile launchers in the western desert of Iraq. Ken Bell and Joe McMoneagle, acting as private contractors, aided in this psychic hunt for the Scuds. Towards the end of the Gulf War, David Morehouse and two other independent remote viewers were asked by the DIA to examine the Iraqi army units which were torching the oil wells in Kuwait. Morehouse claims he saw the Iraqis releasing toxic agents into the conflagration. According to Morehouse's remote viewing, these nerve agents – myco-toxins and bacteriological substances – were spread at low concentrations to give US and UK troops chronic poisoning that would not show up at the time, but would disable or kill the soldiers years later; acute poisoning, which would have killed US and Allied troops on the battlefield, may have forced the USA to respond with nuclear weapons. If Saddam Hussein actually ordered this attack, as Morehouse states, he is responsible for over 10,000 US deaths from Gulf War Syndrome. To add to this horror, nearly 250,000 ex-service-men and women are now severely ill, many having children with birth defects.*

In 1994, the American Institute for Research (AIR) was asked by the CIA to evaluate the remote-viewing programme. Ray Hyman, a psychology professor at the University of Oregon in Eugene, and Jessica Utts, a professor of statistics at the University of California, helped prepare the study. Hyman was sceptical. 'My conclusion was that there's no evidence these people have done anything helpful for the government,' he said. Utts, however, thought some of the results were promising: 'I think they would be effective if they were used

*'Gulf War Syndrome: Biological Black Magic', David G. Guyatt, *Nexus* maga-zine, Aug–Sep 1997, Vol 4 No 5.

in conjunction with other intelligence,' she said. The statistical results were promising enough for her to recommend that research continue: 'I would like to see funding in the open science world – I think we're at the point that something needs to be explained.' However, David Goslin, who headed the AIR team, concluded that evidence for the 1993-94 period showed remote viewing to be not useful. This was a politically motivated decision, according to Dr Edwin C. May, Director of Research for Remote Viewing Programs for both the CIA and DIA: 'Dr May believes that the reasons for the cancellation of the RV programs were mainly due to the geopolitical shifts, and a review of priorities by the intelligence community.'*

Dr Marcello Truzzi a research scientist in this area adds:

The recent strange CIA/AIR report on the one hand indicates about fifteen per cent above chance guessing rate while somehow managing to conclude that RV is not operationally useful (bad enough but also dismissing the many hits in the operational, non-experimental efforts with RV). Given the low reliability of so many espionage methods and sources, one would have expected them to be delighted with fifteen per cent over chance. Obviously, the conclusions were dictated in advance of the evaluation study and were mostly politically motivated.

The decision to halt remote viewing was extraordinary. According to conventional science, remote viewing could not possibly work. Fifteen per cent accuracy (McMoneagle states it was 50 per cent and Morehouse gives 80 per cent) shows conventional science to be wrong. Russian science had

*Remote Viewing and the US Intelligence Community, Armen Victorian, Lobster magazine, Vol 31 June 1996.

expanded to encompass a theoretical basis for psi, while US remote viewing, lacking anything comparable, was easily dismissed by the sceptics as illusory.

In 1995, the CIA released information on the remote-viewing programme it had decided to discontinue. A 29 November Associated Press wire story stated:

> CIA confirms US used 'psychic' spies. Project 'Star Gate' employed psychics to hunt down Libyan leader Muammar Quaddafi, find plutonium in North Korea and help drug enforcement agencies. CIA spokesman Mark Mansfield confirmed the existence of the Star Gate study. 'The CIA is reviewing available programs regarding parapsychological phenomena, mostly remote viewing, to determine their usefulness to the intelligence community,' he said.
>
> But he noted that when the CIA first sponsored research on the program in the 1970s, the program was found to be 'unpromising' and was later turned over to the Defense Department.

Present-day psi research

The US remote-viewing programme was apparently run down by 1988, but in fact remote viewing is still being developed by the military, in absolute secrecy. DIA personnel and other secret groups in the US military are developing paranormal warfare along similar lines to the Russian research. The aim is to protect their democracy against Chinese paranormal-warfare projects, including remote influencing. A May 1992 DIA report, classified Secret/NOFORN (no foreigner), as well as open-source literature on the scope and thrust of the Chinese parapsychological effort, shows a five- to ten-year intelligence gap in this area.

The US military's official position on remote viewing was

stated by CIA spokesperson David Christian, who accepted that no further governmental US research into the project was warranted: 'We think the intelligence community shouldn't pursue research on this and that it is best left to the private sector.' However, a carefully planned campaign of disinformation to mask the continued and accelerated study of psi warfare became necessary, following a chance remark made by former president Jimmy Carter at a conference in South Africa in 1995. CNN reported on 20 September 1995:

> Carter: CIA used psychics to help find missing plane. Atlanta, Georgia – Former President Jimmy Carter said the CIA, without his knowledge, once consulted a psychic to help locate a missing government plane in Africa. Carter told students at Emory University that the 'special US plane crashed somewhere in Zaire' while he was president.
>
> According to Carter, US spy satellites could find no trace of the aircraft, so the CIA consulted a psychic from California. Carter said the woman 'went into a trance and gave some latitude and longitude figures. We focused our satellite cameras on that point and the plane was there.'

The Carter statement was circulated by Reuters in September 1995 ('Carter says psychic found lost plane for CIA').

Milton Friedman, a speech writer for President Ford with inside information, wrote in *Venture Inward* magazine, Jan-Feb 1996. In an article called 'Intuition is Alive in Washington' he said that:

> Remote-viewing accuracy was actually 60 per cent to 85 per cent (not 15 per cent as claimed). The programs have

not closed down but [have] been moved under a deeper cloak of secrecy. (Other agencies like the FBI are now training their agents to use intuition in investigations like the Oklahoma City bombing incident.) The budgets are enormous – much more than the alleged $20million over 20 years. The intelligence data picked up by psi-spies is called 'critical, crucial, vital and unavailable from any other source'. It was used by the highest echelons of the military and the government.

The highest ranks of the military are now involved in the new research.

Robert Gates, former Director of the CIA, estimated 'that the intelligence community had invested about $20million over the 16-year period during which the threat was under examination.' ('Night Line' TV show, 28 November 1995).

Ingo Swann responded on 1 December 1995:

A great deal was learned for those $20million, and our nation received a lot back for the bucks spent. And this knowledge, although somewhat on the shelf now, will soon come in handy again. Several quite respectable sources have informed me that two major nations are making advances in psychoenergetics applications, one of which is remote viewing. It is also alleged that a third, smaller nation with well-known and advertised hatred of the American way of life, is also making progress. I believe these sources, because I know that liberated Russia sold for big bucks the Soviet psychic secrets three times over in order to acquire needed foreign exchange monies.

The 15 per cent accuracy cited in recent public statements on behalf of the CIA is the baseline which ordinary non-gifted and untrained persons often do achieve. This figure was identified very early in the Stanford research phase. The minimum accuracy needed by the clients was 65 per cent. In the later stages of the development [training] part of the effort, this accuracy level was achieved and often consistently exceeded.

. . . remote viewers did help find Scud missiles, did help find biological and chemical warfare projects, did locate tunnels and extensive underground facilities and identify their purposes . . .

From the top of our system down, there are many who could stand up and be counted regarding the efficiency of developed remote viewing, and even regarding superior natural psychics. It has been circulated in the intelligence community that successful remote-viewing sessions probably saved the nation a billion-plus dollars in what otherwise would have been wasted, or misdirected, activities. Not a bad payback for the $20million.

The Japanese have brought psi warfare into the corporate arena. Any US firm that is not aware of it will be at risk. Russian researchers found they could remotely influence the decision-makers in foreign governments. *New Scientist* magazine (23 December 1995) revealed a major Japanese Corporation's attempts to use psychotronic technology in the business world to further Japanese interests. They are apparently developing mind-reading machines. US firms that are ignorant of psychotronics will be at a major disadvantage to foreign competitors who master this new field of study developed by the Soviet Union.

As we have seen there is also a danger that the Chinese are developing military remote influencers, who may be used against the USA and the West. Faced with these scenarios, there are secret psi-warfare projects spearheading US countermeasures.

At the end of the millennium, it seems that the USA has

indeed entered a new age, one in which American psi-spies stand between democracy and foreign powers. With the end of the Cold War, the inner-space arms race has not died down, but instead spread further afield.

4

Mind control and
the UK

As an offshoot of research into ways of enhancing psychic spying by electronic means, methods for remote influencing by purely electronic means – that is, without the psychic element – have also been devised.

Britain was the first discoverer of microwave technology, used for radar in the forties, and therefore it had a commanding lead over everyone else in the West in this field. Research into the use of microwave technology being specifically applied to mind control began in the fifties at a British research establishment, which looked for ways of controlling the British population by this means.

Project Pandora, launched in the sixties by the CIA, was a research programme looking into the effect of electromagnetic radiation on brain function*. One of the leading lights

*Ross W. Adey: 'Neurophysiologic Effects of Radiofrequency and Microwave Radiation', Bulletin of the New York Academy of Medicine, Vol 55 No 11, Dec 1979; 'The Influences of Impressed Electrical Fields at EEG Frequencies on Brain and Behaviour, in Behaviour and Brain Electrical Activity', Burch, N. and Altshuler, H.I., eds, Plenum press, 1975; 'Effects of Modulated Very High Frequency Fields on Specific Brain Rhythms in Cats', Brain Research, Vol 58, 1973; 'Spectral Analysis of Low Frequency Components in the Electrical Activity of the Hippocampus During Learning, Electroencephalography and Clinical Neurophysiology', Brain Research, Vol 23, 1967; 'Nexus, Military Use Of Mind Control Weapons', by Judy Wall, Vol 5 No 6, Nov 1998; *The Encyclopedia of Mind Control*, Adventures Unlimited Press, 1997; also *Secret and Suppressed* by Jim Keith, Feral Press, 1993.

in the Pandora project was a Dr Ross Adey. His work at the Brain Research Institute of the University of California has shown that there is a biological reaction in the brain to electromagnetic (EM) radiation. This reaction was found to be dependent on the frequency, amplitude and dose of the ultra-high-frequency (UHF) or microwave radiation used. The important factor in using microwaves for mind control was found to be extremely low frequency (ELF) signals. These ELF frequencies were picked up by the brain and, depending on their frequency, would modify behaviour and influence health. This meant that carefully modulated microwave beams could be used remotely to control brain function. Project Pandora was a programme established under the auspices of the Defense Advanced Research Projects Agency (DARPA) to investigate EM mind control utilising radio frequency, and direct 'neural manipulation by remote radar'. The Director of DARPA is on record as stating, 'The programme's initial goal was to discover whether a carefully controlled microwave signal could control the mind ... for potential weapons applications ... After testing a low-level modulated microwave signal on a chimpanzee, and within approximately a week causing stark performance decrements and behavioral disorganization, the potential of exerting a degree of control on human behavior by low-level microwaves seems to exist.'

The seventies brought an even darker side to the story, with the revelation to the American public that the Russians had been microwaving the US embassy in Moscow since 1965. One third of the staff developed abnormal white blood cell counts and suffered chromosomal damage. An unusually large number of illnesses were reported by the staff. US Ambassador Walter Stoessel developed a rare blood disease similar to leukaemia, suffering headaches and bleeding from the eyes. He was reported as telling his staff that microwaves could cause leukaemia, skin cancer, cataracts and various forms of emotional illness. Many other embassy staff developed lymphomas, and three ambassadors in a row suffered severe or terminal disease after taking up residence in Moscow*.

The use of ELF escalated when the Soviet Union built the first strategic mind control device. As we have seen, the world's largest radio frequency transmitter began to beam mind control waves at the West on 4 July 1976. This awesome mind-control transmitter was code named: 'Woodpecker'. The document quoted in Appendix III, describes the 'Woodpecker' mind-control ELF transmitter. Doctor Andrija Puharich, a top US expert on mind-control, states:

> Since July 4, 1976 the Soviet Union has been bombarding many parts of the world with ELF transmitters . . . a total of 14 giant transmitters are known to exist world-wide . . . When the Soviets went on the air in July 4, 1976 with their 100-megawatt transmissions of extremely low frequency waves (ELF) the intelligence community of the US was caught unaware of this new technology. The Soviets' ELF pulses covered the frequency range of the human brain. No one knew what the purpose of this new technology was. I had a hypothesis that this was a new mind-control weapon that could entrain a human being's EEG. Bob Beck and I designed an experiment that conclusively proved that the Soviet transmissions could indeed entrain the human brain, and thereby induce behavioural modification. I reported this finding to the intelligence community in the US, and my paper was promptly classified. A CIA commission of inquiry reported to President Carter

---

Secret and Suppressed by Jim Keith, Feral Press, 1993. *The Encyclopedia of Mind Control*, Adventures Unlimited Press, 1997.

that there was no substance to our findings. Today, five years later, all of our findings have been confirmed by various agencies of the US Government. However, they went one step beyond our findings, and proved that a certain ELF frequency (Classified) will cause cancer. I have repeated these experiments, and found this to be true.'

This gigantic mind-control weapon was – as we have also seen – powered by the Chernobyl nuclear power complex in the Ukraine. Edward K. Naumov, Director of the Institute of Technical Parapsychology, Moscow, is on record as stating:

A psychotronic generator can influence an individual, or a whole crowd of people. It can affect a person's psyche mentally or emotionally. It can affect memory and attention span. A psychotronic device can cause physical fatigue, disorientation, and alter a person's behaviour.

So with this development the Soviets had discovered a method of affecting the neurological functioning of entire populations. Appendix III, states:

1982, US Navy confirms that Soviet signals are indeed psychoactive and can cause mental depression at 6.66Hz and at 11Hz can lead to manic and riotous behaviour in humans.

As we have seen, top neuro-scientist Dr Gerald Edelman has shown that brain neurones compete with each other, and that unused neural connections within the brain cause those cells to die. This means that the brain connections are easily changed throughout life. Prolonged exposure to ELF may change the brain's neural wiring by stimulating behaviour and emotions that are not normal. Visualise a barrage of ELF from the 'Woodpecker' transmitters that forced normal brains into abnormal or unstable states of consciousness. The normal mental connections in the brain would gradually die out – if the ELF barrage was for long enough. 'Woodpecker's' 10Hz ELF signal continued transmission from 1976 until the fall of the Soviet Union – well over a decade. In time, the constant ELF stimulation of people's brains may have resulted in permanent adverse effects on the citizens of the West.

Doctor Robert Becker, a Los Angeles physicist, looked at the 'Woodpecker' broadcast and the effects of its ELF signals in the late seventies. He stated, 'It's highly likely that the Woodpecker signal is causing neurological changes in 30 per cent of the population.' Becker, now at the Syracuse VA Hospital, goes on to warn: 'The ultimate weapon is manipulation of our electromagnetic environment. We're dealing here with the most important scientific discovery ever – the nature of life . . . An informed public is the only defence.' The intended result of this strategic psychotronic weapon system was that it would make Western society more likely to implode, becoming more selfish and much less effective at fighting external enemies, turning instead against itself.

Margaret Thatcher, President Jimmy Carter and President Pierre Trudeau were sent a classified document by Puharich, on 13 March 1977, detailing the effects of ELF on human populations. Thatcher, who was at that time the leader of the opposition, as a chemistry graduate would have appreciated the true power of ELF mind control – if she did indeed read that document.

By the eighties Dr Ross Adey, working at the leading Pandora project, had performed many crucial experiments using radio frequency and microwave radiation for inducing mind control. As we have seen he used them as carrier waves for extremely low frequency (ELF) modulations, which enabled him to modify brain responses at a distance; Adey found he could change brain function and hence behaviour using these radio frequency and microwave beams. He found that radio frequency waves could mimic natural brain frequencies and override the normal brain rhythms with the ones broadcast by the microwave mind-control device.

It was now possible to broadcast mind-control commands directly into the brain by use of microwave beams. All that was needed was an ELF catalogue of every specific brain frequency for each mood, action and thought. Indeed it was found that each behavioural set in humans had a distinctive frequency: anger (11Hz), suicide (6.66Hz), aversion (4.5Hz), hysteria, trauma, serial killing, paranoia, lust . . . Microwave transmitters of this type can beam specific mood-inducing excitation potentials at the victims. In effect, Adey, had discovered that a mental state can be initiated by a coded ELF signal on a microwave carrier beam.

Similar wave forms were used by researcher C. S. Blackman in the 1970s*.

He noted a set of narrow field intensity parameters of microwave irradiation effects that was greatest at 0.75 mW/cm^2; this caused the neurones to release calcium ions to the greatest extent.

Adey repeated Blackman's experiments and confirmed that a specific microwave intensity between 0.1 and $1mW/cm^2$ had the most effect on brain cells.

The document in Appendix III shows that victims can also be made ill or even killed by use of microwave devices. It goes on to say:

One physiological effect which has been demonstrated is heart seizure . . . another possibility is alteration of the per-

*Electronics and Wireless World: 'The healing face of electromagnetic fields'; 1993.

meability of the blood brain barrier. This could allow neurotoxins in the blood to cross. As a result, an individual could develop severe neuropathological symptoms and either die or become seriously impaired neurologically.

Modern developments of psychotronic technology use special types of microwave beams called MASERs. These are the laser equivalent of microwave beams. Ludicrous though it sounds, these MASER (Microwave Amplification by Stimulation of Emitted Radiation) beams have been used to develop something called synthetic telepathy – the ability to read people's minds' from a distance. Effectively, this electronic scanning of victims' brains may be a possibility by using an array of MASERS to record sublocalised thought remotely by monitoring the electromagnetic (EM) emissions from peoples' brains.

Head of US Special Forces Major General Schacknow gave a lecture on synthetic telepathy in July 1992 at Fort Bragg, North Carolina.* 'Today the ability to remotely transmit microwave voices inside a target's head is known inside the pentagon as "synthetic telepathy",' he said. In synthetic telepathy, the weak electromagnetic signals in the brain, associated with subvocalised thought, are connected to a computer by use of electrodes, or in more advanced mechanisms by the aforementioned MASER beams. Sophisticated computer systems have apparently learnt to read the subvocalised thoughts in the brain, by associating a specific brain excitation potential with a particular word. Synthetic telepathy may detect the 15Hz, 5 milliwatt auditory cortex brain emissions that are linked with the excitation potentials in the brain associated with subvocalised thought.

*Source: Researcher on mind control, David D. Guyatt, in phone conversation with the author.

New technology, involving millimetre wave technology, has enabled devices to be built which can scan through walls and look inside bodies like X-rays. This enables security personnel to see a target in his own home and to track him throughout the house. Further to this, being able to see inside the victim's head would allow computer-controlled targeting of specific centres in the brain. The victim's brain emissions can be made to interact constructively or destructively with the pulsed-frequency MASER, so that remote monitoring of victims' thoughts might be possible.

Using ELF audiograms carried by a single pulse-modulated microwave device or MASER, subvocalised thoughts could be *placed* in the victim's brain. This gives synthetic telepathy operators the ability to enter into conversations with the person by the Frey effect, named after the US scientist who found that microwaves could be used to remotely transmit voices and sounds directly into the brains of humans. The DIA document states (*not included in this book*), 'Sounds and possibly even words which appear to be originating intracranially can be induced by signal modulations at very low power density.' In the future, visual cortex excitation potentials could also be broadcast into the person's brain so that illusory images are projected into the brain in order to build up a virtual reality.

Microwave phones and mind control in the UK

So that is what is possible. Imagine a British intelligence agent or agency willing to use this technology against its citizens.

The author has tested many microwave phones, and has found that they produce about 0.75 mW/cm^2 at the earpiece. This is the intensity that Dr Ross Adey found was optimal for mind control. ELF is also given off by cellular phones and their numerous transmitters, so that the brain of the user is affected by these signals. The phones are also pulse modulated, and carry ELF, like the signals Dr Ross Adey used. So in some respects mobile phones completely duplicate mind control devices. (It seems likely that regular use of the mobile phone may make you mentally tired, and interfere with memory, intelligence and the will to do things which require mental effort.)

Evidence that the GM900 (Hz) and GM1800 (Hz) microwave mobile phone network may be a major health hazard is now coming to public attention. The Defence Intelligence Agency (DIA) document entitled 'Biological Effects of Electromagnetic Radiation (Radiowaves and Microwaves) Eurasian Communist Countries' in Appendix IV, confirms that microwave frequencies similar to those of cellular phones may cause health problems. It states:

Histological examination of the cerebral cortex cells from rats exposed to UHF at 5 to 15 micro Watts per cm^2 revealed the onset of sclerosis and the formation of vacuoles in some of the cells – in plain language this is called brain damage.

Equipment to test the frequency and intensity of microwave phones shows that they produce signals similar to Soviet microwave weapons. Two cellular phones I examined were producing over 100 mW/cm^2 and 50 mW/cm^2 respectively. These levels of intensity are dangerous, as according to the DIA document in Appendix IV:

Examination of the brains of rabbits sacrificed after exposure to 10 cm microwaves at power densities of 20 to 30 mW/cm^2 revealed hyperemia of the meninges, distension of superficial vessels, and small extravasations of blood in deeper brain areas.

82

In an article in *New Scientist* entitled 'Cancer scare for cell-phone users' by Stewart Fist (10 May 1997), it was found that mice treated with microwave radiation from cellphone intensity sources for half an hour a day developed 2.4 times as many lymphomas after 18 months than unexposed mice. Consequently, 12 million mobile phone users in the UK may be at risk from developing cancer. Roger Coghill, a leading researcher in this area, found that mobile phones on standby mode lowered the activity of white blood cells to ten per cent of normal activity after exposure to cellphone microwaves. These cellphones may therefore cause significant health problems even if not used. A variety of cellphones have been tested to see how dangerous they are. Many of them fall into the range of intensities and frequencies used by Soviet microwave weapons as shown in the DIA document in Appendix IV. The DIA research dates from 1976, showing that the dangers were known about over twenty years ago.

It is a rule of the intelligence community that you hide things in plain view. Getting the public to accept microwave mind-control weapons which affect their behaviour under the guise of mobile phones would be a stroke of genius!

A UK land-line telephone can also be used for killing a targeted user, or mind-controlling the population. How is this possible? If one tests a UK phone with a frequency counter, it will be found that it gives off a signal of around 40 MHz. This carrier signal can then be amplitude modulated at ELF frequencies to induce these ELF mind-control signals into the brain via contact with the head. These ELF fields can alter the behaviour of human cells or the body in general.

Eldon Bryd, a scientist for the Naval Surface Weapon Center of the US Navy, in one of his 1986 lectures on the effects of microwaves, stated: 'We can alter the behaviour of cells, tissues, organs and whole organisms; you can cause up to six times higher foetus mortality and birth defects in laboratory animals, and these fields are so weak you can hardly detect them. You can also do genetic engineering with ELF weak magnetic fields without micro-surgical techniques that are currently employed to do genetic engineering. It is known how to induce malignant tumours in human cells – and how to remove them. You can entrain human beings' brain waves across a room with very weak magnetic fields.'

So one can see how ELF transmitted down the phone line can be used to induce paranoia in people (4.5Hz), depression (6.66Hz), mania (11Hz), or to give them cancer – a silent and covert way of eliminating UK dissidents.

One can also use gun diodes as methods of disabling 'problem' individuals by placing them behind their vehicles' dashboards so that they are irradiated by a 10 GHz-frequency microwave beam which can be focused by a small horn antenna. This will cause the driver of the car to have headaches, sickness, eventual brain damage and may lead to tumour development.

Non-lethal weapons

So what if British intelligence agencies were to use this technology to its full potential? For a start, microwave weapons are impossible to detect unless you have a detector. They are classed as non-lethal weapons, because they are devices that disable or slowly kill the victim, rather than conventional weapons which are designed to kill quickly. Lasers designed to blind the enemy, ultrasonic devices to stun, glue to stick victims to the ground, microwave weapons, pepper sprays to blind temporarily and incapacitate: the list of non-lethal weapons is extensive, but very little is published concerning them beyond manufacturing specifications. So if British intelligence agencies were to use them, they could be sure they would be difficult to trace. For example, it is not beyond the bounds of possibility that British intelligence agents or agencies could run a fleet of psychotronic weapon-carrying vans, as well as portable microwave weapons that could be deployed near a dissident's home, in which case the weapons could be disguised as communications equipment. The microwave weapon could have ELF frequencies superimposed upon it that would influence the behaviour and health of targets within the van's range.

These devices, as we have seen, can in principle be used to cause nerve damage, cancers, mental collapse leading to suicides, or tissue failure leading to heart attacks.

The massive number of microwave masts and antennae that dot the country, some of which are used for the microwave phone network, all use pulse-modulated microwaves and carry ELF signals which affect the brain, giving them a potential as strategic mind-control devices. It would be practical for British intelligence to use them against the civilian population in times of trouble. In modern democracies it is no longer acceptable to shoot rioters, or torture dissidents by normal means – but microwave weapons leave no marks or gaping wounds.*

My own research has shown how it is possible to build a variety of these devices, from tactical microwave mind-control weapons to the strategic devices used by the Soviet Union.

The latest in surveillance techniques
The technology exists in the form of sophisticated millimetre wave scanners to look through walls, so that people can be seen in their homes. Ten GHz, which is used for police speed traps on every major road in Britain, is an ideal frequency for this type of weapon, as it propagates as a beam one can target

*The Encyclopedia Of Mind Control by Jim Keith, Adventures Unlimited Press, 1997.
Defense Intelligence Agency, 'Psychotronic Warfare: Spiritual Access', 1982.

85

at specific individuals. When firing such microwave beams through walls at one specific target, bricks and concrete are relatively transparent to this radiation, although some materials such as steel block the beam. If a victim is to be driven mad or disabled without anyone else being aware that he or she is being targeted, the technology for this is easy to build; a simple 10 GHz device would suffice, fired at them through their own windows. To harm a whole household with microwaves is even simpler: the 2.4 GHz signal is ideal as it spreads out to encompass a wider area, and is at a frequency one can legally broadcast in the UK – as it is used by microwave ovens.

It would now be possible for British intelligence agents were they so motivated to discredit well-known people by driving them mad. Victims could be exposed to pulse-modulated microwaves which carry different types of madness and behavioural aberrations, encoded as ELF excitation potentials.

A simple technology exists in the form of 2.4 GHz transmitters which could easily be used for targeting the homes of victims, and a 10 GHz weapon for specific individuals. This is all that is needed to carry out microwave mind control and torture. MASERS, microwave lasers that fire a beam of microwave at the target rather like a ray gun, could also be used. These microwave weapons could even be used to burn out the gall bladder of the victims, or cause severe brain damage and brain tumours. Irradiating the optic nerve of the victim with the same ELF signal that is sent to the brain by this nerve (in this case 25 Hz) could cause the nerve tissue to overload, so that the victim would be blinded. As mentioned previously in the DIA document, if a microwave beam containing the ELF signals given off by the heart were to be fired at the chest, it would put the heart into a chaotic state, often explained as a heart attack.

As can be viewed in Appendix IV, document pages 25-6:

One physiological effect which has been demonstrated is heart seizure. This has been accomplished experimentally in frogs by synchronizing a pulsed ultrahigh frequency microwave signal of low average-power density with the depolarization of the myocardium and beaming the signal at the thoracic area. A frequency probably could be found which would provide sufficient peneration of the chest wall of humans to accomplish the same effect. Another possibility is alteration of the permeability of the blood-brain barrier. This could allow neurotoxins in the blood to cross. As a result, an individual could develop severe neuropathological symptoms and either die or become seriously impaired neurologically.

A study published in 1972 by the US Army Mobility Equipment Research and Development Center, titled 'Analysis of Microwaves for Barrier Warfare' examines the plausibility of using radio frequency energy in barrier-counterbarrier warfare. It discusses both anti-personnel and anti-material effects of lethal and nonlethal applications for meeting the barrier requirements of delay, immobilization, and increased target exposure. The report concludes that:

a. It is possible to field a truck-portable microwave barrier system that will completely immobilize personnel in the open with present-day technology and equipment.
b. There is a strong potential for a microwave system that would be capable of delaying or immobilizing personnel in vehicles.

Paralysis could be induced in the target by use of this method of broadcasting preparatory sets encoded on microwave beams: a pulse-modulated microwave beam, carrying an ELF signal identical to the one in the motor neurone centre of the brain (around 10 Hz), may be used to jam the victim's motor co-ordination. This is analogous to radar jamming, using a more powerful signal at the same frequency to swamp out the enemy's radar. Pulse-modulated microwave weapons which broadcast the ELF preparatory sets of the motor cortex at the victim, will paralyze the victim without killing them. Breathing and heartbeat are involuntary actions controlled by another set of frequencies in another part of the brain. By disrupting the connections between brain cells, memory may be clouded or even erased. Research by the US Navy and a leading British Company looked at a way of heating specific parts of the brain using microwave weapons to cause brain damage. A silent way of inducing brain damage in dissidents?* We have the technology.

Orwellian Britain
It seems that low-level microwave radiation excites the hydrogen bonds in the cell and can interfere with meiosis (cell division). This causes cell division to go wrong, which leads to cancerous cells and hence tumours. It seems strange that a few milliCuries of ionising radiation will get the National Radiological Protection Board excited, while high-intensity cancer-inducing non-ionising microwave radiation goes unchecked. So high are levels near the microwave transmitters that litter the countryside, that frequency counters show dangerous levels of radiation similar to the levels used by the Soviets for their microwave weapons (as documented in the DIA document of Appendix IV. This constant radiation with ELF signals superimposed by the mobile phone network could at these power levels cause a constant leakage of

Secret and Suppressed, Jim Keith, Feral Press.

calcium ions from the nerve and brain cells. The effect of this might be mental befuddlement, or a lack of energy for aggressive action or active, difficult thought. Since calcium flow out of brain cells affects memory and other thought processes, a decrease in intelligence can be attributed to these transmitters. Placing them near schools and hospitals would seem to be a grave mistake.

Microwave transmitters that can induce stress and confusion, and damage health, cover the rooftops in Britain's inner cities. These transmitters may broadcast extremely low frequency (ELF) signals which mimic natural brain waves and thus interfere with them. This, together with the massive increase in mobile phones, has given the UK security forces the ability – if they so desired – to mind control the UK population.

Greenham Common protesters displayed symptoms of vertigo, retinal bleeding, face burns (received even at night), nausea, sleep disturbances, palpitations, loss of concentration, loss of memory, disorientation, severe headaches, temporary paralysis, faulty speech co-ordination, irritability, and a sense of panic in non-panic situations A malignantly motivated security service could in theory have caused these symptoms. Some of the women peace protestors subsequently died of cancer.

5

Notes toward a scientific understanding of remote viewing

Unravelling the nature of reality

Physics used to be an experimentally based science; that is to say theories were developed to explain new experimental data. In recent times, more and more complex theories have been developed, but little experimental work has been carried out, partly because the high energies involved require particle accelerators that Western governments do not fund because of the enormous cost. The next 20 years will therefore be full of increasingly complicated mathematical physical theories, which to all intents and purposes are unprovable by experiment. Physicists have, in effect, become highly educated science-fiction writers. My research into remote viewing has forced me to reappraise the nature of reality, in order to begin to come to terms with how it could possibly work. Mainstream science has therefore overlooked the implications that remote viewing has for the nature of physical reality. According to mainstream physics and biology, remote viewing is not theoretically possible and therefore the evidence which we have been reviewing is deliberately overlooked. On the other hand the maverick work of some brilliant individuals within the scientific community – particularly Rupert Sheldrake and Gerald Edelmann – has pointed to directions where an overall theory of scientific viewing may be found.

Biophysics

Advances in developmental cell biology during the last ten years have enabled the science of biophysics to include psi. Remote viewing uses biophysical fields to enable perception to occur outside of the physical body. This can be explained as biophysical awareness, or a sixth sense, and is the basis for out-of-body experiences, clairvoyance or remote viewing, ESP and telepathy.

The physical body is surrounded by a mantle of electromagnetic energy. In fact, our eyes pick up this low-level light emission, but 90 per cent of it is filtered out in the thalamus area of the brain, the part that deals with attention. The thalamus is controlled by the brain's limbic system, which looks after our emotions, decision-making and memory. The information that gets through this mental filter is fitted into a visual mental model which we see as reality. The advanced mental training involved in remote viewing enables the remote viewer to clear the neural and mental blockages that make ordinary people perceive but a pale shadow of the real world. Children are taught to see the world as their parents and teachers do, and in the process they condition themselves to block out imagery that does not conform to the norm, such as auras around people, imaginary friends and empathic awareness.

Once visual perception is unfiltered using remote-viewing training programmes, auras, the emission of visible light around people, can, for example, be seen. Stimulation of the brain by the use of autovisualization can affect brain function so that deeper, more relaxed states of mind, which are the gateway to remote viewing, can be achieved. The Russians discovered that visualizing a set of physical actions in the mind's eye, such as gymnastics or shot-putting enabled Soviet athletes to train their bodies better to accomplish the athletic event. They also discovered that autovisualization of the immune system could boost its efficiency. Doctor Carl Simonton developed this methodology in the United States. He taught cancer patients to visualize their immune system's white blood cells eating cancer cells. Autovisualization was found to increase the life expectancy of these terminal cancer patients. I have found that autovisualization of the brain itself can alter consciousness and enhance development of remote-viewing abilities without recourse to expensive biofeedback and EEG machines, as used by the Russian and US military for remote viewing.

Electromagnetic Fields

The electromagnetic field around the body consists of infrared and visual-range radiation, together with electric and magnetic fields. My research interest has been in the biological and biophysical basis of paranormal phenomena. Since the body has an intrinsic electromagnetic mantle, could this electromagnetic field be projected outside the body? Could information gleaned by roving biophysical electromagnetic field effects be the basis for remote viewing? These electromagnetic fields could be picking up information, then transferring it to the brain. Could remote viewing be a case of 'mental radio', one mind picking up what another mind is seeing by mechanisms similar to a wireless tuning into a radio station? Russian research pointed to ELF waves being the carrier for remote-viewing information. ELF waves below 20 cycles per second can pass through the cranium and be picked up by the brain. Remote viewing could well work on an analogous mechanism; it seems a valid basis. Unfortunately it is not the whole picture.

The *Sunday Times* reported that Ingo Swann, in a remote-viewing session, was asked to look at Jupiter. He reported that the planet had a ring around it. At the time this was thought to be incorrect. Swann assumed his 'discovery' was a mistaken view of Saturn. In a 1977 account of their findings, Hal Puthoff counted it as an error. Two years later, Voyager 1 sent back pictures of Jupiter showing the planet did indeed have a ring around it. No time delay in Ingo Swann's remote viewing of Jupiter had been noted. This indicates that electromagnetic radiation is not the carrier for remote viewing. Experiments have been conducted in which remote viewers try to look at distant locations from shielded rooms which block out all electromagnetic radiation. The shielded rooms offer no impediment. The conclusion to be drawn is that something other than electromagnetic radiation must be involved in remote viewing.

As an experiment, I built a Faraday cage room from which to carry out remote-viewing experiments. A Faraday cage room is a metal-lined enclosure that is earthed so that it blocks out electromagnetic radiation. I experienced no negative effect; in fact it seemed to boost remote viewing by blocking out extraneous signals. Russian remote viewers regularly psychically visited US facilities supposedly protected by electromagnetic 'flytrap' field generators, such as those deployed at Dulce (a miles-deep super-secret US base) and Cheyenne Mountain, home of Strategic Air Command. All of this adds weight to the idea that something beyond the simple mental radio concept, where electromagnetism is used as the radio wave, is acting as the carrier for remote viewing.

Biophysical consciousness – the spirit in the machine
Dr Gerald Edelman, a leading neurophysiologist, has formulated the theory of neural Darwinism. This postulates that neurones, which are the connections between brain cells, compete with each other by natural selection. It is as if each brain cell and each connection fights each other for survival.

Only the fittest survive, and in the case of the brain that means only those connections which are frequently used. In the process, neural networks form which have the capability of primary consciousness; or in plain language, the connections make a pattern of brain cells so that the subject can be aware of what is going on around it through the senses.

This work, taken in conjunction with Russian research and my own, lead to the intriguing possiblity that there is a mechanism by which the biophysical body may begin to develop the ability to think separately from the physical body. If we practised remote viewing, perhaps the biophysical body would develop from its latent state to one in which it had a mind of its own.

The mechanism for remote viewing and ESP

To become a powerful remote viewer or controlled telepath, the biophysical fields that comprise our mind would have to evolve through primary consciousness – the state of being aware of surroundings – to high-order consciousness, where the biophysical field is self-aware: a process which as we have seen is analogous to the development of consciousness by neuronal selection in our own brains.

To achieve this evolution of the psyche, we would have to train our biophysical fields to become fully aware. Raising the consciousness of biophysical fields is very difficult, because we are programmed from birth to believe they do not exist. When children mention their awareness of this biophysical world, they are told to stop daydreaming and grow up. Biophysical awareness is suppressed and our psyche remains stunted. What we think is our mind is in fact the brain, while the psyche lies in the biophysical arena – and we normally only touch upon it in dreams and day-dreaming states.

Remote viewers have to develop their biophysical fields to

become aware of their surroundings, which enables them to view information in distant locations. This takes time and practice.

Brain Rhythms

Normally, people function in the beta state of consciousness, so that in day-to-day life their thoughts have no conscious effect on what goes on in their own brains. Remote viewing can be seen as a form of brain programming. We need to be able to input directly to our own brains in order to alter the programming.

Alpha training, encouraging work in the 7-14Hz range, seems to open up psi abilities. Ed Dames has confirmed that military remote viewers operate in the theta state, a brain-wave frequency of 4-7Hz. It may be that the lower frequencies are more powerful for psi activity. Since the energy of the electromagnetic wave is related to frequency, if we lower the frequency of the brain waves, we can think with less energy, and more energy is available for remote viewing, which is therefore more efficient. Theta consciousness is the doorway to remote viewing and psi.

Quantum reality

In the early part of this century, Dr Erwin Schrodinger and Werner Heisenberg formulated the basic laws of quantum mechanics. This theory describes the physics of the subatomic world. They maintained that in the world of quantum mechanics, subatomic entities such as the electron could behave not only as a particle, but also as a wave. This ability is supposed to disappear as the entities get bigger, so that in the normal world it is non-existent.

What if the biophysical fields used for remote viewing are a new form of quantum fields? If this were so, then such 'large-scale quantum-mechanical events' could explain how the biophysical field can be in two places at once – over the target site and over the remote viewer.

Doctor John Bell developed the theorem of quantum mechanics named after him, which shows that a subatomic particle (or photon) which splits in two is forever linked; each separate particle, which was at one time a unit, shares the same characteristics. If the biophysical body is a quantum field, then when it splits into two for remote viewing, each component part would know what the other paired bio-physical field was perceiving. Quantum transmission could explain how information is passed from remote-viewing site to remote viewer. In quantum mechanics, the notion that an entity can be in two different states at the same time is called superimposition of states.

In Schrodinger's wave equation, instead of a particle being localized, it is smeared across space and it can only be given a probability of its location. This equation states that quantum events are non-localized, potential possibilities. The observer collapses the quantum wave function to produce an event. It is as if the act of observation deflates the many potential quantum wave functions and forces it to manifest in only one specific fashion. So while remote viewing, the biophysical field of the remote viewer travelling to the target site may in fact be a quantum wave function smeared into many possible states.

A dualistic reality
Could remote viewing be the result of a biophysical field moving in a parallel reality, which is contiguous with our own but makes itself known to us only in the quantum realm? Perhaps this parallel reality is seen in lucid dreaming and out-of-body-experiences and is glimpsed in daydreaming states? Australian aborigines have a range of beliefs about this dreamtime reality. Perhaps remote viewers are relearning abilities that our ancestors knew of millennia ago.

Memes – mental software

Memes are acquired mental software which mould our neural networks in unique ways. Speaking a language, driving a car, are examples of acquired memes. Memes are highly contagious, and resist being eradicated once they are in your consciousness. A considerable number of the memes we acquire throughout our lives degrade health and mental and physical capacity and capability. An example is smoking – once it has become a habit it is hard work to stop. These negative memes will resurface unless they are replaced by positive ones.

Ideas have the power to spread through a population almost as if they have a life of their own. It was Dr Richard Dawkins, the eminent biologist, who first called these 'contagious' ideas memes; they have also been called mental viruses. In remote-viewing parlance, positive memes used to inculcate the remote-viewing state of mind are referred to as new mental software or success software. These switch off the negative mind-sets that keep individuals in a state of anxiety, inhibiting remote viewing. If you imagine a world full of infectious mental viruses and their mutants – which use humans as their breeding grounds and carriers and which are passed on to other humans by word of mouth, culture, the media, or by biophysical means – you can see the sense in which our world is shaped by memes.

Table manners, throwing frisbees, wearing fashion shoes – all are memes. Our culture is built up from a complex composite of memes that define who we are, what we think and what we do. People can only think and do what they know. In my view, memes are biophysical fields that mould the brain's neural network, i.e. the ideas that are carried in the biophysical field of the meme are transferred into a patterning of the neural network of our brains. The memes that comprise our culture are hardwired into our brains. As we will now see, language is itself a set of memes found in the biophysical field.

The destructive feedback cycle

This basic introduction to memes and memetics leads us on to the negative meme structure that we all find in life. Meme structures are a series of interlocking memes, which together build up a model of reality. In the case of the destructive feedback cycle, this negative meme structure locks us into the consensus reality upheld by the PDF – the 'psi-damping field', a common consensus of consciousness which tries to exorcise the paranormal from the generally accepted state of reality. If you can escape the effects of this destructive feedback cycle, you are half-way to saving all the energy that is needed for advanced ERV. Think of the biophysical field as a battery that is run down by the destructive feedback cycle. If this draining effect can be eliminated, the biophysical field will not run down after a normal day, and you can use this surplus adaptive energy for remote viewing.

To understand the destructive feedback cycle and how it affects remote viewing, let us first address the principles that apply: all remote-viewing training material has to be processed through the brain; new remote-viewing data is not dealt with in isolation, but is incorporated with old material of a similar nature. Emotional content (the way you felt at the time of remote viewing) is incorporated into the memory of the data gleaned by remote viewing, and is then linked to similar feelings that you have had in the past. Learning how to use remote viewing is linked with memories of other times when you tried to change your habitual ways of acting. In most cases this caused stress, so new material will bring with it not only the stress it causes while it is being taught to you, but a whole gamut of previous similar situations imprinted on your memory. This means that when you try to implement this new material you will get considerable negative feedback, most of which comes from past stressful experiences which are related to this new material. This goes back to the indoctrination you were subjected to at school, which has implanted negative memes that interfere with remote viewing, i.e. remote-viewing training must go against the common-sense view of the world you have been trained to uphold.

You will try to alleviate this stress by slowing down implementation of the new material, or finding excuses not to carry on. Therefore it is important, as we shall see later on, that stress-reduction systems be incorporated into remote-viewing training at an early stage, so as to connect a feeling of relaxation and well-being with remote-viewing practice.

Morphogenetic fields – life-shaping energy fields

Many cell developmental biologists believe that the human genome does not contain enough information to turn a clump of fertilized egg cells, called a blastocyst, into an embryo. Morphogenetic fields are needed to 'switch on' specific gene groupings dependent on their position in the blastocyst in the womb. These biophysical morphogenetic fields switch on specific genes and turn off others, all based upon their location in the clump of cells. If they are near the top axis, they become eye and gullet cells, at the bottom axis, an anal opening, in the centre of the blastocyst the gut tube, on the surface, skin cells, etc.

It was a profound revelation to me when I realized that the biophysical field contains large amounts of information not held in the genome, and that it can control gene expression. Like the neurones affected by neural Darwinism, I realized that perhaps morphogenetic fields could evolve through primary consciousness to high-order consciousness. In effect, by exercising the biophysical body using remote-viewing techniques, the morphogenetic fields of which it is composed might evolve (with long practice) to become self-aware. Could consciousness itself be in the biophysical field?

I believe that that the brain and the biophysical field can

both be conscious, independently of one another. Biophysical fields that have the potential to be conscious explain out-of-body-experiences, dreaming, doppelgangers and a host of other paranormal phenomena. Doctor Rupert Sheldrake has suggested that if we are influenced by morphogenetic fields from particular individuals to whom we are linked, then it is possible that we might pick up thoughts, images and feelings from them, while we are waking or dreaming, even though they may be thousands of miles away. In controlled ESP, the operator sends his biophysical field to interact with the person being scanned. In spontaneous telepathy, other people's biophysical fields might impinge on our own, causing their ideas to enter our heads. This for example may be as prosaic as knowing someone is going to ring or visit us just before the event occurs, or it may be the remote viewer looking inside the monitor's brain to see the target to be remotely viewed. The world of soul and spirit is, in these scientific terms, filled with morphogenetic fields and is a place of luminous bio-physical quantum reality.

Group consciousness
The theta state is important partly because it allows the person imprisoned in consensus reality to escape the shackles of the real world. The summation of everyone's belief is in my view amplified by their group 'psi-fields', and the six billion people on the planet produce a very powerful 'psi-field' that effectively hides paranormal phenomena.

In order to escape consensus reality and practise 'impossible' paranormal phenomena such as remote viewing, the psi-operator must attune his biophysical body with the Earth's biophysical field. By this means, the much larger biophysical field of the Earth can erase the effects of the psi-damping field generated by humanity. The theta state allows the remote viewer to resonate with the biophysical field of the planet.

This boosts the biophysical field of the psi-operator to the extent that paranormal phenomena can become possible. The Earth resonates at about 7.8Hz, the natural frequency of the planet. Theta begins at this frequency. It is as if the bio-physical body of the remote viewer in the theta state resonates with the planet's biophysical field – at the magic 7.8Hz.

In order to enter the theta state, it is better if there is a group involved. The group's biophysical fields join together when remote viewing is carried out in unison. This merged group consciousness boosts the remote-viewing capacity of all the remote viewers in the group. By working in teams, there is a synergistic amplification of remote-viewing poten-tial in all the individual members of the group.

Probable futures

When we factor in the paranormal forces of each individual human on the planet, each of us can have a massive effect on the future outcome of events. If we think of the future as a quantum-mechanical event, along the lines discussed on page 96, it can be in all possible states until it is collapsed by the act of observation. Since there are six billion human observers, the particular future that is manifested by the group is dependent on the psi-damping field (PDF). As the PDF defines what is possible and what is not possible, only a small subset of possible futures is ever revealed. Of these, only one becomes the future we all will live in.

An example of this is the National Lottery. A large per-centage of the population are willing their numbers to come up with all their might. This situation generates a lot of emo-tion, which as we have seen is conducive to generating para-normal phenomena. These people are using all their latent paranormal powers to influence the balls telekinetically, as well as subconsciously to remotely view the future numbers. US researchers, such as Robert Jahn, have found that people can influence the falling pattern of ball bearings, or the random counting of a computer, using telekinesis. By generating such emotional desperation, the lottery amplifies this telekinetic effect. A remote viewer trying to foresee the outcome of events has to look through a paranormal blizzard of conflicting telekinetic intents, where tens of millions of people are subconsciously trying to influence the fall of the numbered balls in the lottery machine.

On 'The Paranormal World of Paul McKenna' shown on British television, the audience was asked to concentrate on six specific numbers. When the lottery was run, two of these numbers came up and a third came up as the bonus number. The National Lottery immediately changed its rules, so that if too many people got three numbers, it would not be obliged to pay them.

The hundredth monkey effect

As we have seen, groups of people concentrating on the same site at the same time amplify their remote-viewing capabilities. There is a merging of the biophysical quantum-state functions of the field effects involved that boosts remote-viewing efficiency. This is the so-called hundredth monkey effect. A Japanese monkey once learned to get rid of the sand in its wild rice by washing handfuls of it in the sea. Other members of its troop copied this behaviour. Once a hundred or so of its peers had learnt this action, the behaviour miraculously appeared in other monkey troops on other islands, far removed from its original progenitor, even though the monkeys never came in contact with each other. My research into biophysical field effects and how they can interact with other members of the species seems to indicate that, when a threshold number of biophysical fields belonging to a group have learnt a new meme, the intent for that meme is spread by spontaneous telepathy. The first US remote viewers spent 12 hours a day, seven days a week, for 18 months, learning remote viewing. This training time has now been cut to six months. I am informed the more recent subjects are also more accurate than the original trainees. Remote viewing, is becoming easier to learn because of the hundredth monkey effect. In the future, many more people will be able to practise remote viewing and with greater accuracy.

The brain and remote viewing
The areas of the brain that are involved in remote viewing were studied at the Stanford Research Institute by Hal Puthoff, funded by the CIA. His team found that the temporal cortex is active while a person is remote viewing. The cortex is used for visualization, and the occipital cortex is used to process visual information. The older limbic system, which lies beneath the spongy grey matter we call the cortex, is used for decision-making. All our decisions are taken on an emotional level; we intellectualize them afterwards. The limbic system mediates information processing, while the hypothalamus is used for memory and the thalamus for attention. The reticulate gyrus is also concerned with information processing. Since emotional content plays such a large part in remote viewing, the amygdala, a small structure in the limbic system which is concerned with emotions and is the pleasure centre, is also involved.

I believe that remote-viewing information is transferred to the brain by quantum mechanical interactions between the biophysical body and the brain. At a higher level, memories from the biophysical body and from the brain are transferred by use of biophysical fields which affect the neurones; this is tied up with control of calcium concentrations in the brain.

Cell developmental biologists have found that the morphogenetic fields which control cell activity can change the calcium levels in the cells. Thus morphogenetic fields control cellular chemistry. We have so many avenues of communication between biophysical body and brain that the interaction must be seen as hierarchical – in a similar manner to how competitive cell death establishes primary and high-order consciousness in the brain by means of Darwinian selection. At the top of the hierarchy in the brain is the temporal cortex, which combines the remote-viewing data into the complex mental image.

How the brain sees the future

The areas of the brain which enable precognition are little understood. American experiments in showing people pornographic photographs, which are placed in a larger pack of non-emotive pictures such as those of the countryside, have shown an elevation in physical responses five seconds before the pornographic photo was observed. The responses were measured by sophisticated devices like lie-detectors. This was taken to indicate that, at a deep subconscious level, precognition of emotive events occurs.

Airline records show that planes that suffer fatal crashes have an abnormally large number of cancellations prior to take off. In combat, this sixth sense of danger is also heightened. Vietnam veterans tell of numerous paranormal experiences such as remote viewing of mines, bullets being seen in flight, Vietcong traps being sensed. Fighter pilots have to develop a sixth sense which is called situational awareness – a brain state where both hemispheres of the brain are working equally and in synchrony. This is an almost Zen-like state, where there is no chaos inherent in one's thinking and everything seems more real. Situational awareness means the pilot instinctively takes in a wealth of information, evaluating it and reacting correctly, with a panoramic view of everything in his or her mind's eye. American fighter pilots call it 'having the clue'.

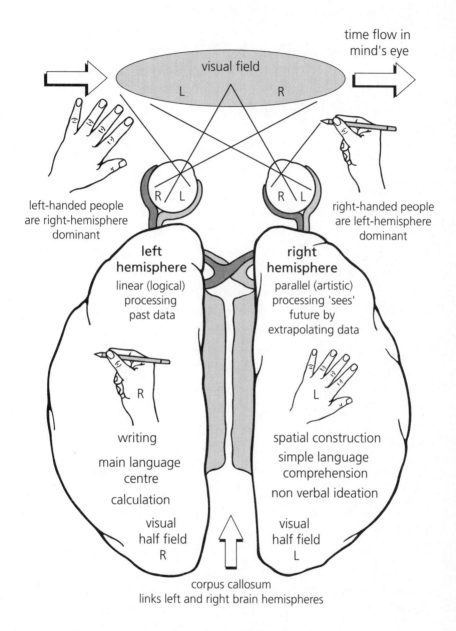

Figure 2 Functional division of the brain hemispheres

Is brain-centre balancing a key aspect of looking into the future? Significantly, when the remote viewer enters the theta state, this balancing of brain hemispheres takes place naturally.

Theta brain rhythms also enable more of the information received from the biophysical body to be left unmolested. Ninety per cent of the information we receive is filtered out by the thalamus, which is in the limbic system of the brain. Neurophysiologist Karl Pribram of Stanford University describes perceptive filtering as the Bowery Effect. The Bowery was an elevated railroad in New York. When it was demolished – and after the late-night service ended – the police were inundated with phone calls reporting something strange happening at exactly the time the train would normally pass through that neighbourhood; this went on for months after the railway had gone. People were subconsciously picking up on the lack of noise at the time they were expecting the train, and panicking because they did not hear its passing. Consciously they thought something was wrong, so they phoned the police.

Theta enables us to unblock these mental filters that blinker us to remote viewing and other paranormal phenomena. For precognitive remote viewing, we have to look at how the brain hemispheres process information.

The left hemisphere of the brain deals with data and thoughts in a step-by-step manner. It runs through data in a linear fashion, moving from a to b to c. The right hemisphere deals with thought processes in the form of a mental map, where the relationship between data is as important as the data itself (Figure 2). Finding patterns in data is one of the right hemisphere's abilities. It carries out parallel processing, whereby ideas are connected to make a bigger picture, like linking notes to compose a symphony. Perception for remote viewing the future appears to be processed by the right hemisphere. Since this side of the brain is visually connected to the left eye and field of vision, future events which are remotely viewed can appear to glide into one's mental field of vision from the left-hand side of one's awareness. In contrast, the left hemisphere seems to process past events. It is connected to the right eye and the right field of vision. In one's mind's eye, events the left hemisphere processes can appear to come into the left field of vision, but when remote viewing the past, the mental image appears from the right-hand field of our mind's eye.

Mechanism of remote Influencing
How can remote influencing plant suggestions that are sub-consciously acted upon by the victim? A brain structure which seems a likely candidate for the remote-influencing effect of biophysical fields is the supplementary motor area (SMA). Researchers in this field have postulated that the interface between mind and body occurs in the SMA, an area which lies in the top centre of the brain, underneath where the soft spot is located in infancy (see Figure 1, page 58). When you decide to carry out any conscious action, the SMA is the first part of the brain to register an excitation potential. Every time you decided to do something, this is the first area which generates electrical activity.

The SMA was first identified in the twenties by the late Canadian neurophysiologist Wilder Penfield. It was a chance discovery in his search for the epileptic initiator in the brain. Neurophysiologists Robert Porter and Cobie Brinkman surgically placed micro electrodes in the SMA of a monkey, and found that one tenth of a second before the monkey pulled a lever to obtain food, the brain cells in the monkey's SMA fired off electrical signals. This SMA activity was well ahead of any in the cells in the motor cortex, the area of the brain concerned with muscular control.

In the sixties, the neurophysiologists Luder Deeke and Hans Kornhuber discovered a method for measuring tiny electrical signals that ran through their patients' scalps. They discovered a readiness potential – i.e. nearly one second before carrying out a simple conscious action, the brain generated a gentle increase in negative electrical impulses. This negative electrical potential was the brain's means of preparing to make a conscious action, and was greatest in the SMA.

In the eighties, a research group headed by neurophysiologists Per Roland and Nils Lassen of the University of Lund in Sweden used radioisotopic scanning to look at blood flow through the brain. They found that the blood flow in a specific area of the brain which is in use is proportional to the brain's activity. They also discovered SMA and motor area excitation during conscious action. It was when they carried out a variation of the motor sequence test that they discovered their momentous and controversial results. In a slight modification of the experiment called the 'internal programming test', a patient was asked to perform the same difficult motor sequence test in his mind but with no physical action. When patients carried out this test, there was no increase in the blood flow through the motor area; in comparison, the SMA had as much increase in blood flow as if the actions had been carried out. When the action became habitual and could be carried out with no conscious thought, the increase in blood flow in the SMA vanished. This meant that the SMA had been pinpointed as the part of the brain that determined conscious action. If you told someone you were going to do something and your SMA did not fire, that would mean you had no intention of carrying out that action. Similarly, if the SMA fired, you would carry out the action as stated. The SMA is the conscious intent beacon in the brain, which lights up every time you consciously will yourself to carry out an action.

Sir John Eccles, a famous neurophysiologist, was particularly excited by this discovery. He stated: 'It is important to recognize that this burst of discharge of the observed SMA cell was not triggered by some other nerve cell of the SMA or elsewhere in the brain. . . So we have here an irrefutable demonstration that a mental act of intention initiates the burst of discharges of a nerve cell.' Eccles drew the following conclusions: that each conscious activity produced different excitation potentials in the SMA; that a neurological code is being played through the SMA; and that the non-physical mind is actually using the 50 million or so neurones in the SMA region as if they were controls of some sort, rather like a pianist playing the keys of a piano. These learned sets of sequential neurological code, Eccles believed, are the process of a lifetime of learning physical action and language.

It seems then that the SMA mediates the flow of information between the biophysical body and the brain. This occurs because every time you make the conscious decision to do something and you carry it out, the SMA fires. By using directed attention on your own SMA, you can programme your brain to carry out actions you wish to do but always make excuses not to do, e.g. giving up smoking. Self-activation of the SMA is the best means of self-motivation, and if executed correctly is invariably successful. Visualizing an action in your mind's eye has almost the same effect on your body as carrying out that action.

I come to the example of athletes who go through their performance in their mind's eye to get into 'the zone' of ultimate performance. Alpha and theta states are normally necessary for getting into 'the zone', but by programming your SMA while visualizing performance, the brain is programmed to carry out the action no matter what negative stimuli try to block it.

Similarly, in order to influence someone else's brain in its activating capacity, it is necessary to use concentrated attention on its SMA. However, before such an advanced aim may be properly contemplated, we should look at the elementary techniques.

6

How remote viewing
is taught

We have seen the amount of time and money the Soviets and Americans have invested regarding the techniques of remote viewing and remote influencing. How are these techniques actually taught to these operatives?

US training methods
This section of the book provides a complete guide to learning remote viewing. It gives a much fuller account than any previously published work of the actual methods used by the superpowers, covering more ground than any other available courses. US courses, which cost between $3000 and $7000, tend to concentrate on the simpler and less efficient co-ordinate remote viewing (CRV). This book teaches simple, scientific CRV, but goes further – including for the first time my versions of Russian super-advanced extended remote-viewing (ERV) techniques. To my knowledge, these are the most advanced remote-viewing instructions on the market.

CRV was developed by the Stanford Research Institute and taught to the US military remote viewers. It is carried out from normal consciousness, the beta state. Now it is recognized that certain steps must be followed to fixate the conscious mind on the biophysical body, which is actually carrying out remote viewing. Since the US researchers disregarded notions of a biophysical body, theirs was a rather hit-and-miss method. The psi-damping field (PDF) is in full operation outside of the theta state (see Chapter 5), so CRV is hampered by negative feedback. Systematic steps are therefore necessary to keep the psychic window to the biophysical field open against these adverse conditions.

CRV – US peliminary praining steps
Ingo Swann's methods are still used in the US:

> Stage One – get a blank piece of paper and pencil. In your mind's eye, visualize yourself opening a psychic window to the target, which is defined by map co-ordinates. Numbered photographs in sealed envelopes are easy alternatives to map co-ordinates. When you have visualized this psychic window in your mind's eye, start sketching lines on the paper. Draw lines or curves depending on how you feel. Don't think about the process, just sketch the first thing that comes into your mind. Do not rationalize.

> Stage Two – allow visual and sensory data into your consciousness through the psychic window to the target, but discard any analytical mental processes, giving no conscious thought to what it may or may not be. Imagine yourself peeking through this psychic window, getting glimpses of shapes and shadows, and odd sounds. Do not try to analyze these, but list the first impressions – smells, tastes, tactile data etc. Then let the far stronger auditory cues enter your perception. Finally, let the strongest of the data, the visual cues, come into your mind's eye. (They would swamp out the other information if allowed in first.)

> Stage Three – include dimensionals, putting your per-

REMOTE VIEWING

ceptions into a bigger picture. Imagine you are an artist sketching the target. Make a series of simple drawings of what comes into your psychic window. As you draw, try to link them with the perceptual cues you gained in Stage Two.

Stage Four – list the emotional and aesthetic impact of things that have come from the remote-viewing session. List the tangibles and intangibles of the target, 'wooden' and 'pastoral' for example. Look at your Stage Two list of perceptual cues and your Stage Three drawings; write down the feelings you get from these cues next to them. Try to expand your list of what the target is like.

Analytical information can be brought in for the final sketch, which is a coming together of all the information acquired in the session. Write what you think you are seeing next to the perceptual cues and the drawings.

Stage Five – meditate on the psychic window and visualize yourself opening it up to produce a clearer channel to the target. Imagine that fresh insights about what you are remotely viewing come flooding through the psychic window, which allow you to develop Stage One through to Stage Four data with a fresh mind.

Stage Six – make a three-dimensional representation of the target. Use plasticine, a sand pit, wire – whatever feels most applicable – and build a model of the actual target.

Stage Seven – can be added later, when you are more experienced, for a more detailed analyis. Try to pick up the name of the target. Do this by seeing which letters of the alphabet spring to mind, and building on them. You can also visualize written signs and text, so a catalogue of what is written down at the site can be developed over time. The monitor can help you to zoom in on specific areas of interest.

Monitored CRV – more preliminary steps

This technique requires two people and a photograph. One person acting as a guide, or monitor, directs the other to the target shown in the photograph (which the remote viewer is, of course, not allowed to see), and asks a series of questions based on the photograph. The monitor should not lead the remote viewer, but should record exactly what he or she says. As more information is forthcoming, the monitor should concentrate on a specific area of the photograph and ask a series of questions to tease out information from the remote viewer, such as:

Question (Q): Is the target light or dark?
Answer (A1): This could be a night target.
A2: A barren desert landscape.
Q: Is the target surrounded by objects?
A1: This could be a valley surrounded by hills.
A2: A room surrounded by walls.
Q: Is the target in a room or chamber?
A1: No.
A2: An underground bunker.
Q: Are there any objects in the target?
A1: These could be cows in a field.
A2: There are computers in an underground bunker.
Q: Are their any graphic representations in the scene?
A1: No.
A2: These could be military computer screens, signs flashing on them.
Q: Is any part of the target moving?
A1: No.

A2: This could be a train moving into an underground tunnel, or machinery in a nuclear-bomb factory (such as ultracentrifuges in Iraq).

Q: What colours do you sense in the scene?

A1: This could be green grass in a pastoral scene.

A2: Stainless steel coloured, grey metal containers.

Q: What sounds do you hear?

A1: Wind blowing through the trees in a forest.

A2: This could be screams of infected animals in a biological warfare lab in an underground complex.

Q: What creatures do you see at the target scene?

A1: This could be cows and sheep in the fields.

A2: Scientists in a laboratory.

Q: Is the target man-made?

A1: No, it is a pastoral scene.

A2: Yes, it looks like a series of man-made caves.

Q: Is the scene flat or are their tall objects dominating the scene?

A1: The scene seems to be in a valley.

A2: The underground complex is hidden under a mountain.

Q: Are there many objects of the same sort in the scene?

A1: There are many trees and a lot of cows and sheep.

A2: This could be a series of nuclear or biological missile silos, or electric pylons running into the mountainside.

Q: Are there any mechanical devices in the target scene?

A1: No.

A2: This could be Sukhoi 27 fighters at a nearby Chinese air base. Or the nuclear or biological processing facility underground.

Q: Are there straight lines, paths, roads or other landmarks in the target scene?

A1: No, just a river running into a small lake at the centre of the pastoral scene.

A2: There could be an airfield, road, long underground access tunnel, air vent tunnels.

Q: Does land dominate the scene?

A1: The scene is dominated by the central lake.

A2: This could be the mountains.

Q: Is the target underground?

A1: No.

A2: This could be the underground complex, or missile silos.

Q: Does flora or fauna dominate the scene?

A1: Grassland and woodland surround the lake.

A2: This could be desert-like conditions around the mountains, beneath which is the underground complex.

Q: If the scene is man-made, describe if it contains buildings.

A1: It is not man-made.

A2: This could be the massive underground complex for nuclear and biological warheads for Chinese intercontinental ballistic missiles aimed at the USA.

Q: If the scene is man-made, enter the target and walk around within it, reporting all you see.

A1: Negative.

A2: It is a Chinese underground nuclear and biological weapon facility.

The remote viewer draws what he has reported on a blank piece of paper. In the above example, A1 was a pastoral scene, with a central lake surrounded by fields of cows and sheep, with a small wood between the fields; A2 was a Chinese underground military complex in mountainous territory.

This training exercise can be repeated many times, with

different photographs and the monitor and remote viewer changing roles each time.

Stress and its effects

Stress levels have to be lowered for paranormal abilities to show themselves. Stress interferes with the mechanism of remote viewing; it also interferes with our immune response and a host of other biological processes. Research published in *New Scientist* in 1996 shows that stressed people are at least a thousand times more susceptible to poisons than non-stressed individuals. The process of activating remote-viewing abilities reduces the high levels of neurohormones and the blizzard of electrical over-stimulation of the nervous system, which blinds us to remote viewing.

I believe there are two main factors which elevate human stress levels: over-stimulation of the brain stress system (see page 129), and the acquisition of negative memes that degrade human performance (see Chapter 5). Improving remote viewing and finding effective stress-management systems go hand in hand; basal stress levels should be naturally reduced to alpha or theta. A corollary to this is that with a reduction in stress there is also a marked improvement in physiological and mental functioning. Augmented powers of mind over matter only occur when the brain is in the quiescent state of theta, which is also optimal for boosting the immune system and suppressing psychosomatic diseases. By switching off the body's habituated electrical storm of anxiety, with its concomitant sea of stress-inducing neurochemicals, the brain state which comes about from remote viewing also boosts life-span and makes the practitioner of biophysically augmented healing much more resistant to disease.

Our mental processes are locked into negative feedback cycles that severely degrade our ability to function appropriately. These negative mental programmes and memes that afflict humanity are reinforced by the organizations we work within; managers and staff endlessly externalize negative memes in the work place. Organizations therefore suffer from the human stress disease and all its associated memes, but on a grander scale. Individuals within these organizations are afflicted by stress and pass it on to the company culture. The average working person is probably constantly conditioned to be in exactly the stressed-out state which will inhibit remote viewing.

Relaxation techniques
When you begin to practise remote viewing in earnest, you will find that stress blocks it out. The following is a set of simple progressive steps for lowering brain rhythms, i.e. relaxing. It is a good idea to tape the relaxation programme, and the other sets of instructions in this book, and listen to them with eyes closed.

1. Lie down on the bed and close your eyes.
2. Visualize your feet.
3. Imagine that all the muscles in your feet are becoming limp.
4. Visualize your ankles.
5. Imagine that all the muscles in your ankles are becoming limp.
6. Visualize your calves.
7. Imagine that all the muscles in your calves are becoming limp.
8. Visualize your knees and thighs.
9. Imagine that all the muscles in your knees and thighs are becoming limp.
10. Visualize your lower body.
11. Imagine that all the muscles in your lower abdomen are becoming limp.

12. Visualize your chest and back.

13. Imagine that all the muscles in your chest and back are becoming limp.

14. Visualize your arms.

15. Imagine that all the muscles in your arms are becoming limp.

16. Visualize your neck.

17. Imagine that all the muscles in your neck are becoming limp.

18. Visualize your head.

19. Imagine that all the muscles in your head are becoming limp.

20. Now imagine yourself floating off to a grassy meadow.

21. Visualize the grass; hear the birds sing; feel the sun on your skin and the ground beneath your body; smell the grass.

22. Visualize all your worries drifting from your body and evaporating in the sunlight.

23. Feel the sunlight filling your body with energy that washes away the anxieties you have accumulated.

24. Tell yourself that you feel better than you have ever felt in your life.

25. Imagine your past experiences that caused you anxiety.

26. See the black vapour of these old anxieties being expelled from your body, to be replaced with positive feelings.

27. Replace these old worries with new, positive feelings such as love.

28. Choose one positive feeling and mental state each day you practise, and visualize each new, positive emotion easing out the old anxiety-inducing emotions. These positive emotions will become linked with your

practice of remote viewing, which will set up a positive feedback cycle – the more you practise remote viewing, the better you feel.

Once you are comfortable with this ritual and feel deeply relaxed, you can begin the set-up procedure for simple ERV. In your mind's eye, visualize yourself repeating the following axiomatic remote-viewing memes:

1. The goal is to manifest the true potential within myself.
2. A remote viewer sees only the total reality of him/herself.
3. A remote viewer lives in total reality.
4. A remote viewer must step outside of group perception, and hence group reality.

The reasoning behind each one is this:

1. Your perception of yourself is incomplete, due to filtering by the brain and imprinting of negative memes by the environment – which compete with and warp proper perception.
2. We carry a number of memes that specifically cut off all paranormal functioning. Our perception affects reality and vice versa.
3. Total reality is a state of perfect perception, where reality is not compromised by negative memes and preconceptions about how you think you are. These negative memes reconfigure the neural networks in your brain to block out all paranormal phenomena.
4. Group consciousness defines group reality. Memes not only warp the neural networks, but reprogramme the latent biophysical fields so that they are crippled. The magic key to success is knowledge of biophysics. Once

you can perceive unfiltered reality, with no preconceptions about what you can and cannot do, you are
able to leave the common consensus. Having stepped
outside the flow of group consciousness, you can begin
to appreciate hidden potentials. Remote viewing is
then available to the individual. Enabling you to know
your true self and to use all your psi abilities is the goal
of remote-viewing technology.

Continue thus:

1. In your mind's eye, fixate your awareness on your
   brain.
2. Visualize the three different areas of the brain – cortex,
   limbic system and reptilian brain-stem areas – as three
   concentric circles, with the reptilian brain in the middle,
   joined to your spinal cord (see Figure 1, page 58).
3. Visualize your biophysical field becoming stronger and
   'soaking' into the brain, linking with the brain cells.
   This process primes your biophysical fields to interact
   with your brain on a higher level than morphogenic
   fields. Imagine a ghost-like biophysical field being
   sucked into your brain and the three concentric circles
   of your idealized brain becoming suffused with the
   energy of your biophysical field. You are putting the
   ghost in the machine.
4. Visualize an energy field which overlays your body –
   the biophysical field that is contiguous with your
   physical being – becoming imprinted with the four
   repeated axiomatic memes. In effect, you are now programming the ghost in the machine.
5. Imagine the biophysical field commanding your brain
   centres to become compliant with the axiomatic
   memes, thus preparing your brain for remote-viewing

activity. You are programming the 'machine' for remote viewing.

This technique of programming the biophysical field is very important because it primes the specific brain centres for remote viewing. Biophysical fields carry information, and they can be fed information just like a computer. Your biophysical field is, in effect, a quantum computer that has to be programmed before you command it to begin remote viewing.

Once you have mastered the above exercises, it is time to send your biophysical awareness to a place you find of interest.

Further steps to remote viewing

1. Visualize yourself, from the above relaxed state, sending your biophysical body to the target. For the moment this should be somewhere you know well, as you are simply training the biophysical body to follow your commands and getting used to remote viewing.
2. The first step in processing the information the biophysical field sends back to your brain is to list the perceptual cues you receive, e.g.

Sense	Perception
tactile	wet
	sandy
aural	roaring noise
	sound of wind
visual	sunny
	blue sea

Remember to list the non-visual data first, as visual

information dominates the attention once you fix your awareness upon it. Build a picture in your mind's eye of what it is. In the above case, the target was a sandy beach at Bournemouth in the summertime, with a south-easterly wind blowing. It is helpful to use the monitored remote-viewing technique to help build up your perceptual cues, if there are two of you.

3. Imagine another place you know well. Keep repeating this visualization of actual places in order to train your biophysical body to become aware of distant locations. Practising helps to raise the biophysical awareness from its latent morphogenetic state to self-awareness; you are training your biophysical fields to become aware of the outside world. Visualize yourself walking around the places you 'visit', studying the details.

4. Keep a log of your remote viewing and check on its accuracy. Ask a friend to put anomalous objects at a target site you know well, such as the office or their home, and seek them out. This is a gentle but effective introduction to psychic spying.

5. The next step is to look for people in their own homes. Relax, send your biophysical awareness to the person's house, and hunt through the rooms until you feel or see his or her presence. Afterwards, telephone to see whether you were correct. You can also look for the person as an energy field. Look for a glowing shape rather than the physical image of the person. Decide which is the most efficient way of locating someone.

This is a preliminary exercise which develops the bifunctional viewing capacity of your remote-viewing biophysical fields. Your remote-viewing perception can look at things as physical objects, or at their energy field. In the realm of remote viewing perception is a duality, analogous to the particle-wave duality found in quantum mechanics. A person has a physical body and an energy field; which one you look at depends on your psychic intent.

6. You will have found in these preliminary exercises that accuracy can be a problem. In untrained people, an accuracy rate of 15 per cent is normal. If yours is better than that to start with, it shows you have a greater than normal complement of psi genes.

   Body and mind are linked; chaos and separation in this interface cause disease and block all remote viewing. You must optimize your self-image and change your reaction to environmental stimuli, to cut out chaos (entropic decay). Relax and visualize yourself as accurately as possible. In your mind's eye, list your characteristics and emotional reactions to various situations. For example:

Positive characteristics	Negative characteristics
hard-working	stressed
reliable	easily angered
modest	over-ambitious – bite off more than I can chew

This exercise is important because it makes you aware of yourself and helps to cleanse your being of the numerous negative characteristics (memes) that limit your capabilities.

7. Now you can begin to reprogramme yourself with new memes and software by intending what you wish to be and what you do not wish to be (see Chapter 5 on memes for more detail).

What I wish to be	What I do not wish to be
a remote viewer	psychically blind
empathic	unaware of what people are really feeling
intuitive	not being able to read people

8. Know that you have the ability to be aware using your biophysical fields. Visualize your ghost-like remote-viewing biophysical field leaving your body and travelling to locations of your choosing. First visualize it examining the room you are in from its point of view. Then visualize it travelling further afield and psychically viewing what is going on at a distant location you have chosen.

9. Buy or borrow some slow, repetitive music, such as Purcell's *Pavanne* and *Chaconne*, or the adagio from Marcello's Oboe Concerto in C Minor. If you concentrate on it, it will automatically put you into the alpha state, as the Eastern bloc parapsychological researchers discovered (Figure 3). In the alpha state, the brain functions much more efficiently than in beta. Languages can be learnt by people who can achieve the alpha state in six weeks.

   Play the music while you repeat the above exercises. Note how the efficiency of your remote viewing improves and how it is easier to contact the biophysical fields. The use of baroque music helps to develop neural networks which are alpha-functioning, and by a process of positive feedback leads to the 'hard-wiring' of the brain in a way conducive to psychic viewing. It is as if the music moulds the brain to function in alpha, enabling remote viewing to take place.

10. With the baroque music playing in the background,

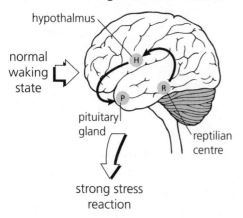

strong brain stress reaction

hypothalmus

normal
waking
state

pituitary
gland

reptilian
centre

strong stress
reaction

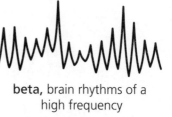

beta, brain rhythms of a
high frequency

*signals of brain stress
system reduced*

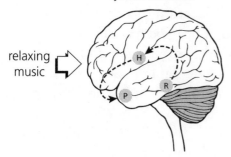

relaxing
music

alpha, brain rhythms of a
reduced frequency

*signals of brain stress
system supressed*

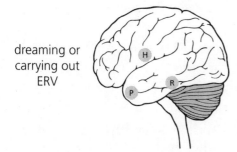

dreaming or
carrying out
ERV

theta, brain rhythms of
low frequency

Figure 3 The brain and its rhythms

pick a place for remote viewing that interests you, and look for anything that catches your attention. By choosing places that interest you, your attention is kept at a high level which boosts your remote-viewing efficiency. Keep a log of your remote viewing and see how it progresses as you learn more and more techniques to boost your accuracy.

Improving the signal-to-noise ratio in remote viewing

The remote viewing of underground sites or military facilities was the original intent of the US remote-viewing programme. American military personnel were trained to receive operational-anomalous cognition, which was used to describe the remote-viewing phenomenon. In plain language, this meant the ability to see distant locations clairvoyantly.

In the intelligence scenario, a near-perfect description of a foreign site may be of little value, because the information is well known through use of satellite data or such like, while a poor anomalous cognition that would not score well in a laboratory trial may provide vital information unavailable by any other method. This means that the skills of multiple remote viewers, using anomalous cognition simultaneously, may be of especial use when remotely viewing sites of interest which are so secret that no information is available on their real nature and function. For this, there are special instructions:

A – Managing the target pool. Make sure that you look for clearly defined targets; broaden the scope later. In the case of foreign sites, the first thing to look for is the presence of life forms. From there, look at the tunnel complexes, then the equipment that fills these chambers; targeting remote viewing makes recognition much easier than looking at everything, getting swamped by data or losing your way in the mental labyrinth.

B – Bandwidth. Keeping a focused train of attention is vital. It is easy to lose your remote viewing capability by letting the mind wander. Using directed attention on areas of the site you find of especial interest is necessary to keep your remote viewing fixated on the target; efficiency declines rapidly when you remotely view areas you find of little interest. Describing endless trivial target sites to sceptical researchers is a sure way to lose bandwidth by boring yourself stupid. When you get bored, the brain stress system becomes activated and you enter the beta state, which blocks remote-viewing activity. If you wish to show off your remote-viewing ability to other people, remotely view things you find of intense interest to keep accuracy levels high. This works by using goal direction to switch off the brain stress system. The relaxed state is linked with remote viewing, causing a positive feedback effect which amplifies remote viewing in future.

C – Switch off the internal chatter. To increase the signal-to-noise ratio, it is vital to reduce stress levels so you can enter the theta state. Switch off the internal chatter in the mind by using directed attention and the cinema method (see Chapter 8).

D – Use group-augmentation. This entails remotely viewing the same target in groups and then sharing your data. Feedback on the actual site will enable you to build up your accuracy level and improve your signal-to-noise ratio. Group augmentation of remote viewing works by training the biophysical field to high-order consciousness, a state where it is self-aware. The group's biophysical fields meld together when remotely viewing the same site, and boost their potential an effect which lasts after the session and rapidly advances the individual biophysical field's remote-viewing ability. From there it can be developed to the state where remote sensing and influencing become more useful. This was why military remote viewers worked in groups.

E – Noise reduction. This occurs when the brain rhythms are lowered by use of advanced stress-management techniques and memetic biophysical-enhancement systems, which have already been given in this book. Further to this, group-augmented remote viewing can be used to filter out noise so that the 15 per cent accuracy rate of untrained individuals may be of use for gleaning information from foreign sites. Each member of the group that remotely views the same site will see glimpses of the same thing. When they compare notes, the similarities in their remote viewings will be easy to pick out. Only the actual target information will be similar. This similarity in the signal can be used to suppress the noise, as methods can be developed to ignore any data which does not agree with the group.

Russian ERV
(extended remote viewing)

To carry out ERV as practised by Russian military remote viewers, it is necessary to be in the theta state. Both US and Russian extended remote viewers use biofeedback and EEG monitoring to achieve this, but I have developed a specialized technique to enable the remote viewer to enter the theta state without electronic biofeedback.

The brain stress system

Let us first look again at the stress-related processes that make the alpha and theta relaxed states so difficult to achieve. Within the brain's ancient neurological systems, the brain stem underpins our higher brain structure. These 'reptilian' brain-stem structures have evolved in such a way that they are now enclosed by the limbic system, and surrounding this, the cortex (Figure 4). These major brain structures are connected intimately to each other. Their interaction controls our state of stress.

The hippocampus, which controls memory and is intimately connected with data retrieval and storage, is also centred in the limbic system, as is the thalamus, which is the organ of attention. Stress destroys our ability to remember and concentrate on complex subjects – as all exam-takers

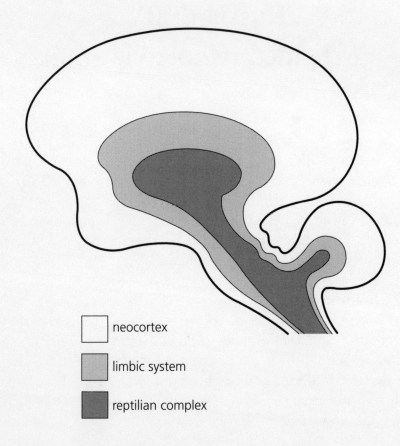

neocortex

limbic system

reptilian complex

Figure 4 Schematic division of the brain

can testify. Anxiety and the level of activity of the brain stress system therefore have an immense effect on the mechanism of remote viewing. Anything which ameliorates the high levels of chemical and electrical over-stimulation found in anxious people will have profound effects on their remote viewing and related data acquisition and retrieval.

Any disputes about dominance will constantly affect the brain stress system. Any change from the status quo will constantly stimulate the brain stress system. And an environment in which people don't know exactly what they are doing will have a similar effect. This is because the reptilian brain likes ordered, ritualistic behaviour.

To become master of your own mind and body and to develop remote viewing, it is necessary to reprogramme the reptilian brain so that it becomes fixated on the goal of remote viewing; in this state, you can ignore stressors that would normally put you into a state of high anxiety.

Steps for stress management
(Figure 5)
1. Relax using the relaxation techniques on pages 117–9.
2. Visualize your attention focused on the thalamus part of the brain (see Figure 6), which is in the limbic system, controlling attention.
3. Concentrate your attention in the thalamus; visualize yourself in this brain centre – the person that is you standing in your mind's eye in your thalamus.
4. Visualize yourself in the thalamus picking up a laser-beam gun, which is the mental representation of your will activating the thalamus; visualize yourself unleashing this mental laser from your thalamus.
5. Visualize the mental laser being so powerful it ignites your thalamus, which bursts into a flashing ball of light and gives off a mental laser that illuminates your entire

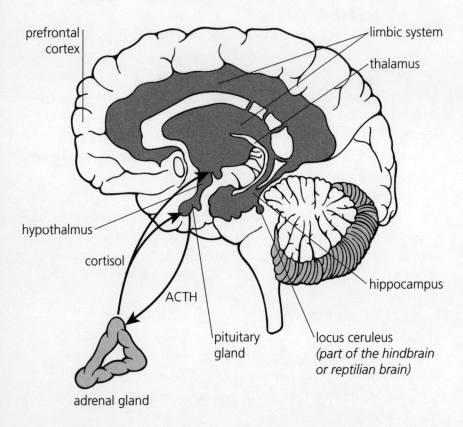

prefrontal cortex

limbic system

thalamus

hypothalmus

cortisol

ACTH

hippocampus

pituitary gland

locus ceruleus
(part of the hindbrain or reptilian brain)

adrenal gland

Brain stress system extends from the hindbrain and hypothalamus to cerebral destinations inside and outside the limbic system. When activated the system affects mood, thought and indirectly the 'stress' hormone cortisol, secreted from the adrenal gland and activated by pituitary ACTH.

Figure 5 Brain stress system

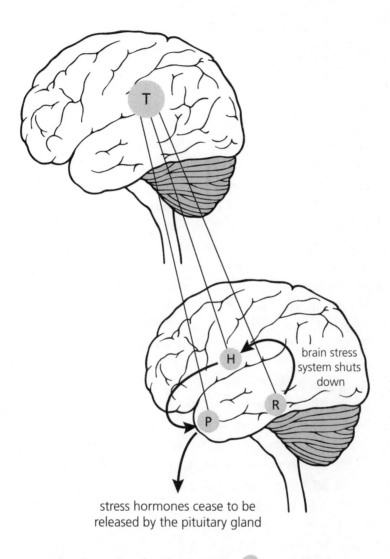

brain stress system shuts down

stress hormones cease to be released by the pituitary gland

Visualize yourself in the thalamus T in your brain. Vizualise the mental laser of your directed attention switching off the reptilian brain R ; then the hypothalamus H ; then the pituitary gland P . Lower your conscious mind into the theta state

Figure 6 Relaxing the brain stress system

brain in an explosion of light. This mental laser light is called directed attention and is epicentred in this brain area.

6. Control your directed attention and focus this beam of mental laser light on the locus ceruleus in your reptilian brain. Command the locus ceruleus to shut down, preventing it from detonating the brain stress system. So powerful is your mental laser that its light can reprogramme your brain centres.

7. Reprogramme the locus ceruleus to be totally fixated on remote viewing and to ignore all stressors unless they are actually life-threatening, by willing these thoughts down the mental laser beam at your reptilian brain.

8. Next, focus the mental laser on your limbic system. Zoom in on the hypothalamus, to lower the neurochemical and electrical stimulation of your brain stress system, so that you reach the theta state of consciousness.

9. Reprogramme the hypothalamus to ignore all stressors unless they are actually life-threatening. An example of how to programme these non-language areas of the brain is to visualize your state of stress as a big balloon of air which slowly deflates as you relax.

10. Next, let your mental laser beam travel to your pituitary gland and command this gland to shut down the stress hormones that keep your brain and body in a heightened state of anxiety all through the day. Visualize yourself turning a tap to close the flow of stress-inducing chemicals.

11. Return to the pituitary gland and follow the hormonal pathways to the adrenal glands on top of the kidneys. Fire your mental laser at these glands and command your adrenal glands to shut down the fight-or-flight hormonal response system, and to boost the feedback to

shut down the brain stress system. Command the whole hormonal system to shut down the brain stress system response, so your limbic system is flooded with positive responses by use of remote viewing. By this means, a very powerful feedback system is set up that lowers your body's stress levels every time you use remote viewing.

The above techniques are the most advanced form of stress management on the planet, used by the Russians.

Energy used by the brain and the biophysical fields is proportional to frequency. In the beta state, the frequency can be around 28Hz when anxious. In the theta state, the frequency can be around 7Hz. This means that by operating in theta, you can think using one quarter of the energy that is used in the beta state. By having such an energy-efficient mode of thinking, the person in theta has enough energy to think four times better, which can be four times faster, or four times more in content. Using only one quarter of the energy you would use in the beta state of consciousness enables you to extend the time you can think and work by a factor of four.

This augmented intelligence and stamina can be put to use for remote viewing. Psi activity requires energy for visualizing the information coming from the biophysical fields. What is more, a lot of energy is required to open a link to the biophysical fields. Rather like lighting a match to ignite a fire, the biophysical field needs energy to be released from the physical body, to resist the PDF and to merge with the Earth's field for bilocation.

The last step in ERV, after inculcating the theta state, is to visualize the perceptual cues you get when you try remotely to view a site of interest, for example:

Sense	Perception
tactile	hard
	metallic
aural	rattle of cables
	wind
visual	iron tower
	columns of iron

As before, remember to zoom in with your remote viewing on the non-visual data first, as visual information dominates the attention once you fix your awareness upon it. Build a mental image of the attributes of your remotely perceived site, followed by a complete picture of what it is. In the above case, the target was the Eiffel Tower. Use the monitored remote-viewing method to build up your perceptual cues if there is someone available to guide you through advanced ERV.

Once you are in the theta state, repeat the simple ERV exercises from this heightened state of consciousness. You will find that your remote viewing dramatically improves. It will take at least a month of practice before you can shorten the relaxation steps needed to enter theta, but as the months go by, the theta state will become more and more habitual with the concomitant increase in psi ability, mental functioning and physical health.

Checklist for ERV
1. The theta state of mind is the first step in setting up extended remote viewing.
2. Knowledge of the brain stress system mechanisms involved in lowering the frequency of brain rhythms is the vital second step.
3. Next, develop focused thought processes, directed attention.
4. This directed attention is used to reprogramme the brain

stress system to drop brain frequency from the beta state into the theta state. It can also be used to focus on the immune system to cure or ameliorate disease.

5. Awareness can be projected out of the body, the basis of remote viewing. The theta state is the doorway to the biophysical realm. When in theta, the biophysical field resonates with the Earth's natural frequency. In this state, the negative effect of the PDF is suppressed by the Earth's larger biophysical field. This enables the biophysical body to leave the physical body and begin extended remote viewing. When your consciousness awakes in the biophysical body, bilocation – the feeling of really being at the target – begins. This is an analogous state to lucid dreaming.

6. Checklisting the sensory input you get from remote viewing map co-ordinates can give useful information upon which to begin remote viewing.

7. Directed attention fixated on the biophysical field, which is sent to places you know, gives rise to remote-viewing awareness. Repeated use of this awareness develops remote-viewing accuracy.

8. Sending your biophysical awareness to view places of interest is the next step. The more this technique is practised, the stronger your remote-viewing attention becomes.

9. A useful next step is to view remotely people you know or find of interest. This leads to remote sensing.

10. In advanced remote viewing, as practised by the Russians, directed attention can grow to the point where you can remotely view documents of interest and even access computer data by remote viewing.

8

The cinema method and directed attention

As we have seen, for psi activities it is essential to stop the internal chatter, the incessant conversation we all have going on inside our heads. Imagine a remote viewer projecting his/her awareness at a target site; the biophysical field transmits information back to the brain. Someone who is constantly thinking about other things will not be a clear receiver for the remote-viewing information. A clear mind has a better chance of accurate remote viewing. When watching the cinema screen, we concentrate on what's going on, switching off the internal dialogue. Mental silence is the second major initiator of remote viewing (the first is achieving the theta state).

Clearing the mind of internal chatter is achieved by focusing your attention on remote-viewing imagery, like watching a cinema or TV screen. To link in with a common television fixation would provide a most powerful way of developing remote viewing, a guided use of perception. Once you have mastered the technique, you can use it to focus on the information the biophysical body uploads while remotely viewing.

Try to stop thinking to yourself for ten seconds. You will find that internal mental silence is extremely difficult to achieve. The reason is that the memes we are infected with from birth condition us to talk to ourselves, constantly review our life and experiences by use of non-stop mental dialogue. Our parents and elders infect us with this meme. Our brains force us to talk to ourselves in our mental world, blocking out the subtle paranormal signals we may be picking up. This neural network conditioned by memes interferes with remote viewing and all other psi activity.

The cinema method is a powerful technique because it uses the potent meme of watching television to eradicate the internal-chatter meme. Since both memes are very powerful, they cancel each other out, paving the way for the mental silence needed to establish a clear link between the biophysical field and the physical body's brain.

Directed attention may be defined as a state of awareness in which the focus of attention is coherent and concentrated on one spot, rather like a laser beam. Use it as a tool to increase efficiency of mind, brain and body to optimize remote viewing. Modern living and TV have caused a diminution in our attention to the level where in some cases the mind can digest only 20-second sound bites. To progress in remote viewing, you must be able to fix your attention on the target, and improve concentration until it reaches this coherent laser-like level, as described above.

Exercises to help facilitate directed attention
   – Diaphragm breathing. Breathe in through your nose – your diaphragm drops while your stomach rises. Breathe out through your nose – your diaphragm rises while your stomach drops. This increases lung capacity and induces your heart rate to drop while stimulating nerve endings in your nose which are connected to the brain. This exercise links your directed attention with your body, something we have learnt to ignore as we grow older. This bodily awareness is vital for remote sensing.

– Concentrate on your pulse/heartbeat. You can learn to lower your pulse or heartbeat at will, thus linking directed attention with a relaxed state of being. This may inculcate deep alpha states. (This exercise is vital for remote sensing and remote influencing when directed attention is used to influence heart function in others by telepathic means. Slow pulse or heartbeats [originally heard in your mother's womb] have a profound effect on internal bodily states, automatically lowering brain-wave rhythms. Conversely, loud, chaotic sounds have a negative, destabilizing effect on the mind.)

Practising directed attention
Repeat steps 1–5 on page 131, using the visualization diagram (Figure 7) as a rough map.
6. Once you have focused directed attention inside your hindbrain, command the locus ceruleus to ignore everything which is not life-threatening and has no bearing on your goals.
7. Visualize all your goals as if you had completed them. Do this in chronological order starting with your life's goal(s) and finishing with immediate goals. Add the caveat that every time you are in this state, you can upgrade your goals as your knowledge and experience increase.
8. Feel the positive neurochemical state achieved by bringing the reptilian brain into synchrony with the rest of the brain stress system.
9. Command yourself to feel this positive state every time you do something to achieve your goals, and practise remote viewing. This positive feedback helps you to do both, so you will find them invigorating rather than difficult.

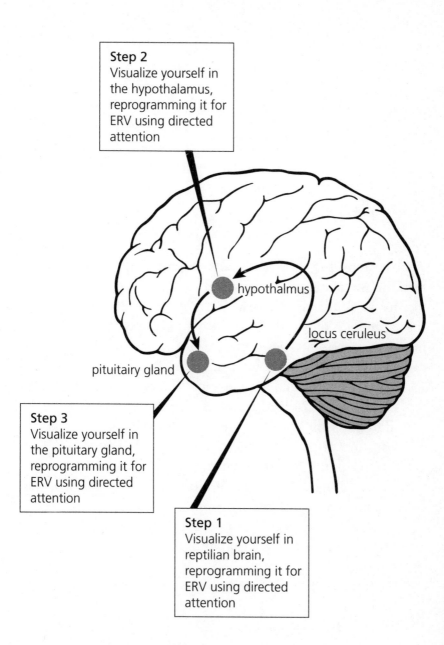

Step 2
Visualize yourself in the hypothalamus, reprogramming it for ERV using directed attention

hypothalmus

locus ceruleus

pituitairy gland

Step 3
Visualize yourself in the pituitary gland, reprogramming it for ERV using directed attention

Step 1
Visualize yourself in reptilian brain, reprogramming it for ERV using directed attention

Figure 7 Visualization diagram for using directed attention

Using directed attention and the cinema screen for remote viewing

Using directed attention enables you to raise your biophysical field from morphogenetic latency to become aware of its surroundings (primary consciousness), after which you can direct it to leave your body and remotely view distant sites. To achieve this, your concentration must be absolute. By visualizing your thalamus, you can reprogramme your brain to elevate your attention, analogous to changing a torch beam into a laser beam.

Steps

Repeat steps 1–5 of stress management on page 131. Relax into the theta state. The more relaxed you are, the better the picture you will get. Once you are in full theta, an image of the target site will appear. Once you are visualizing yourself inside the thalamus, get a mental broom out and metaphorically clean out all blockages and data filters.

4. Command the thalamus to let all sensory data through. Go systematically through all six senses (remote viewing/ESP is the sixth) and clean all the data channels. See your attention as a bright star epicentred in your thalamus. Command the epicentre of attention to shine a bright white light of perception into the thalamus, that becomes coherent and focuses down into the mental laser light of directed attention. Command this mental laser to illuminate your entire thalamus and focus on the goal of remote viewing.

5. Command your thalamus to give you an unlimited attention span; to eliminate all negative programmes; to engage all unused neurones and neuronal networks, so as to boost your attention to directed attention; and then to elevate this directed attention to fixate on remote-viewing data being received by your biophysical vehicle.

142

6. Now use this directed attention laser to inscribe a cinema screen in lines of blue fire, drawn in a clockwise direction, in your mind's eye. This is the cinema screen upon which you will see the remote-viewing picture relayed to you by your biophysical field, located at the remotely-viewed target site. Once you have drawn the cinema screen, fill it with blue fire; see a blue screen of lambent energy which now faces your mental gaze.

7. Then visualize your directed attention travelling from your thalamus, through the cinema screen – which is the doorway into the biophysical realm. As this occurs, visualize the screen becoming transparent, a perfect medium for the information you will pick up from your biophysical field. This practice initiates your biophysical consciousness to become aware of the outside world. The mental cinema screen can be thought of as the entrance to the world of psi; simply by stepping through it, your attention can be transported to anywhere you wish to go. It is a magic doorway to the great beyond.

8. Next, practise your remote viewing from this state of consciousness. Use this 'magic doorway' approach to remote viewing, and project your awareness to the places you wish to view psychically. With practice, every time you engage directed attention on the cinema screen, your brain and biophysical fields will automatically engage the cinema method programme. By positive feedback, the practice of directed attention will make you more and more efficient at ERV (Figure 8).

9. Use directed attention to inscribe the cinema screen, and will your biophysical field to travel to the target to be remotely viewed. Use the mental laser light of directed attention as the cursor in the biophysical cyberspace of your paranormal world, to direct your biophysical field to the target. Once at the target site, command your

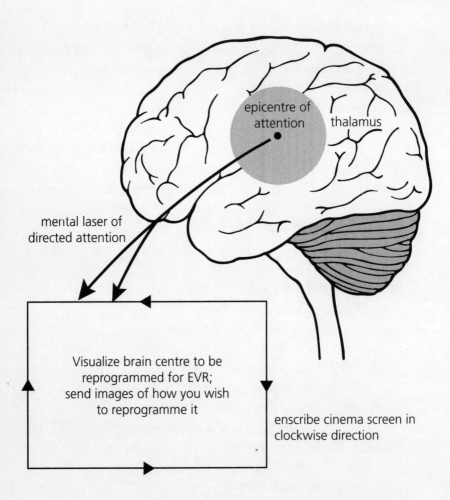

Figure 8 Using directed attention to reprogramme brain function

biophysical field to transmit information, via its quantum computer link to your brain, to your cinema screen.

10. This technique can be used to enter into remote-viewing bilocation, where you feel you are actually at the target site, as if you were in a lucid dream.

What is actually happening in bilocation

David Morehouse, interviewed by Uri Dowbenko for the article 'The True Adventures of a Psychic Spy', in *Nexus* Vol 4 No 5, Sep 1997, describes bilocation as:

> It's folding space, folding time and space. It's like bringing the event to you without ever going to the event, if you tap into it. It's omnipresent while traversing back and forth on the time-space continuum. What does it mean? It means you're everywhere at the same time. So the only way you can be everywhere at the same time is because everywhere is where you are. So folding space is the best analogy I can think of – like an accordion that folds in on itself, where you don't move. I was taught to believe that it was like the pages of a book, of an encyclopaedia. There are planes that are separated, yet they're connected by the spine of the book. The spine of the book corresponds to the unconscious.

The biophysical body can travel in its own quantum reality, in effect tunnelling through space-time. The physical body can be at one end of this quantum-reality wormhole, while the biophysical field is at the target site at the other end. When bilocation occurs, this quantum-reality wormhole is created.

But these wormholes need energy, so where does it come from? It comes from the quantum vacuum, an endless sea of energy underlying reality, which is accessed by using the Earth's biophysical field when the ERV adept is in theta. This source of energy is not available in beta (stressed consciousness, brain rhythm greater than 14 cycles per second) because paranormal reality is blocked off by the PDF; or in alpha (unstressed consciousness, the most efficient waking state, 7-14 cycles per second) in which a window can be opened to the biophysical body but it lacks real energy. The quantum vacuum can be accessed only in theta (4-7 cycles per second) or in delta (4 cycles per second or less). In this state, you are dead to the world in deep, dreamless sleep – if you are untrained.

This is the gateway to psychotronic realms. In delta, you can access the quantum vacuum for telekinesis, remote influencing.

Checklist for the cinema method

1. Relax by using the stress management techniques on pages 131–135.
2. Imagine the mental laser light of your directed attention forming in your thalamus, and firing out of this brain centre into your mind's eye to create the cinema screen. Remember to inscribe the cinema screen in your mind's eye in a clockwise direction with blue laser light from your mental laser, then fill in the screen with blue fire.
4. Once the cinema screen is constructed, see your biophysical field staring at you through it.
5. Visualize the epicentre of attention, the I part of your mind, flowing from your thalamus, via the link of directed attention, into the centre of the biophysical field.
6. Direct the biophysical field to the target site; command the biophysical field to broadcast the images and sensory data it is picking up on your cinema screen.
7. Watch your mental cinema screen and focus on the pictures being sent to you from the target site you are remotely viewing.

The sixth sense

Doctor Rupert Sheldrake has found that over 50 per cent of people know when they are being stared at, and register subliminal signals showing that their subconscious is aware of them being in someone else's field of gaze.

Directed attention and the cinema method can be expanded to encompass the sixth sense, or situational awareness – a state of heightened awareness where visual spatial stimuli are directly integrated with intellect, instinct and memory.

Steps
1. Use directed attention to create the mental cinema screen in your mind's eye.
2. On this cinema screen broadcast the sensory impressions your biophysical field is getting while it remains over your body, i.e. practise remote-viewing techniques while your biophysical body is over your physical form. This develops your sixth sense and allows you to have 'eyes in the back of your head'.

Putting directed attention to work

Wasted time on and waiting for trains, buses and planes, and any slack periods, can be used for practising directed attention with the eyes open. Use it during the day to recharge your batteries by breaking negative memes (see page 96) that have slipped into your mind. Do this by using your mental blue laser light to destroy the contagious memes you have contracted as a form of mental infection, which drain your energy. Eliminate them, and in the process release adaptive energy.

Super advanced ERV techniques

The goal of these advanced techniques is to be able to inculcate a theta state in your waking state, so that you are always in sympathy with the Earth's biophysical field. By constantly operating in the theta state, you become more and more detached from humanity's psi-damping field, and latent psi abilities come to the fore. Remote viewing may be the first of these, followed by remote sensing and remote influencing.

The limbic system is thought to control volition in humans. We make decisions on the basis of emotional processing in the limbic system, then we rationalize how we came to make that decision using the cortex. The limbic brain centre controls human behaviour, and reprogramming this area is vital for all aspects of psi performance.

Steps
1. Focus your mental laser light of directed attention, which is fired from your thalamus, on to the rest of the limbic system which you command to ignore all stressors that are not life-threatening. Visualize your will flowing down the mental laser beam, reprogramming every brain centre it touches.
2. Reprogramme the hypothalamus to depress your basal brain stress level to theta by focusing your mental laser on this brain centre and willing it to shut down your anxious state.
3. Reprogramme the amygdala, your brain's pleasure centre, to activate your pleasure receptors every time you carry out remote viewing, so that your limbic system is flooded with positive emotions every time you practise it. By this means a positive feedback system is set up, by which your limbic system gets an emotional high every time you practise remote viewing. Since the limbic system controls choice, this means that you will motivate yourself to carry out more and more remote viewing the more you practise it. In time you will so stimulate the limbic system that

every time you use your senses, remote viewing will be incorporated. You will have developed a permanent sixth sense.

4. Finally, see the limbic system as a totality, and see all its connections with the cortex and hindbrain. Concentrate on the temporal lobes, which are associated with remote viewing. Programme them to enable remote viewing. Through these connections, flood the rest of the brain with positive emotional stimuli via neurochemical transmitters and neuroelectrical signals, to the point that the whole of your brain experiences an orgasm-like trance condition every time you practise remote viewing.

By this means the brain can be driven into the lower levels of delta that enable you to link into deeper and deeper shells of the Earth's biophysical fields. From there, you can reach the elevated trance-like state of the Russian remote influencers who have psi power at their fingertips, or the yogic masters who have augmented control over their bodies and the world around them.

Afterword

It seems from the standpoint of conventional science that the concept of remote viewing cannot possibly exist. Unfortunately, there are numerous declassified CIA and DIA documents – amounting to tens of thousands of pages, some key examples of which are reproduced in this book – cataloguing the US government's top-secret remote-viewing programme. First-hand corroboration of the US military's secret remote-viewing projects comes from actual military remote viewers such as Joe McMoneagle and Lyn Buchanan, who now teach the subject to the general public. More extraordinary are the declassified documents released by the US government which document the Soviet paranormal-warfare programme – which includes psychotronics, giving Russian psi-operators the ability to influence remotely, affect electronics by telekinesis, and even remotely kill. These documents are freely available under the American Freedom of Information Act, and I recommend the serious researcher to look at these papers. The idea of the superpowers being engaged in an inner-space arms race using psi-agents seems far-fetched, but sometimes truth is stranger than fiction. It is alleged that both US and Russian psychics engaged in a secret paranormal war, remotely influencing and remotely killing each other.

The ramifications of the knowledge that remote viewing

and psi warfare not only exist, but have a long history of development by the superpowers, leads to a rather disturbing new vision of recent history and the prospect of the new millennium which will be dominated by psi. If humanity and its nation states develop more and more powerful weapon systems, the ability to view remotely top-secret installations will be secondary to the ability to influence remotely the politicians and generals who control them. It does not matter how powerful the weapon, if the brain that controls it can be remotely influenced. The strategic implications of being able to influence all the decision-makers in the West have not been lost on the Chinese, whose thinking is long term. Japan too has bought a large amount of psychotronic research from the Russians. A major research centre in Japan has been developing it for use in the business field; remote viewing and influencing in the commercial field have obvious uses.

The ethical and moral implications of this new psi technology are a minefield. What about the right of privacy? When people can remotely sense, are thoughts private any longer? With remote influencing, are your thoughts your own? The spectre of remote killing brings a new meaning to the old saying 'it's all in your mind'.

'What you don't believe in can't hurt you,' they say. Don't believe it.

Appendix I

Defense Intelligence Agency document: Controlled Offensive Behavior – USSR, July 1972

A complete table of contents and selected sections are reproduced here. The numbers in brackets refer to sources, which are listed at the end of the document.

ST-CS-01-169-72

DEFENSE INTELLIGENCE AGENCY

CONTROLLED
OFFENSIVE BEHAVIOR — USSR (U)

PREPARED BY U.S. ARMY
OFFICE OF THE SURGEON GENERAL
MEDICAL INTELLIGENCE OFFICE

CONTROLLED OFFENSIVE BEHAVIOR - USSR (U)

AUTHOR

JOHN D. LaMOTHE
CAPTAIN, MEDICAL SERVICE CORPS

SHORT TITLE

ST-CS-01-169-72

DIA TASK NUMBER
T72-01-14

DATE OF PUBLICATION
July 1972
Information Cut-off Date
31 January 1972

This is a Department of Defense Intelligence Document prepared by the
Medical Intelligence Office, Office of The Surgeon General, Department
of the Army, and approved by the Directorate for Scientific and Technical
Intelligence of the Defense Intelligence Agency.

(ii)

ST-CS-01-169-72
July 1972

PREFACE

(U)   This report summarizes the information available on Soviet
research on human vulnerability as it relates to incapacitating
individuals or small groups. The information contained in this
study is a review and evaluation of Soviet research in the field of
revolutionary methods of influencing human behavior and is intended
as an aid in the development of countermeasures for the protection
of US or allied personnel. Due to the nature of the Soviet research
in the area of reorientation or incapacitation of human behavior,
this report emphasizes the individual as opposed to groups.

(U) It is not within the realm of this report to make an in-depth
study of research and utilization of the multitudinous aspects of
psychology and psychiatry. It is strongly suggested that these
subjects, and the military use thereof, should be established as
separate studies. The importance of basic and applied research in
these areas should not be overlooked.

(U) The information reported covers the period from 1874-1972 and
has been drawn from scientific, medical and military journals, intelligence reports, magazines, news items, books, conferences, and other
reports as referenced. The information cut-off date for this report
was 31 January 1972.

(U) The author of this study is Captain John D. LaMothe, Medical
Intelligence Office, Office of The Surgeon General, Department of
the Army, Washington, DC 20314. Constructive criticism, comment
and suggested changes are invited from readers. These should be sent
to the author through the Defense Intelligence Agency, ATTN: DT-1A,
Washington, DC 20301.

iii
(Reverse Blank)

ST-CS-01-169-72
July 1972

TABLE OF CONTENTS

v

ST-CS-01-169-72
July 1972

ST-CS-01-169-72
July 1972

ST-CS-01-169-72
July 1972

LIST OF ILLUSTRATIONS

ST-CS-01-169-72
July 1972

LIST OF TABLES

ix
(Reverse Blank)

ST-CS-01-169-72
July 1972

SUMMARY

(U)   Controlled offensive behavior as defined within the scope
of this report includes Soviet research on human vulnerability as
it applies to methods of influencing or altering human behavior.
There is an ever increasing amount of information emanating from
the USSR (samizdat or underground press) that suggests that certain
authoritarian institutions in the USSR are engaged in the practice
of "mental reorientation" of numerous individuals who are classed
as political dissenters. The "mental reorientation" is being accomplished through various means including confinement, isolation and
psychopharmaceutical administration. This treatment of so-called
insane individuals is causing alarm among an international cross section of psychiatrists. The literature contains sufficient data on
human mental manipulation and, therefore, warrants surveillance by
interested parties. It appears that the USSR stresses physical and
medical "treatment" of its political detainees under the guise of
psychiatric-care rehabilitation.

(U)   The Soviet Union is well aware of the benefits and applications
of parapsychology research. The term parapsychology denotes a multi-
disciplinary field consisting of the sciences of bionics, biophysics,
psychophysics, psychology, physiology and neuropsychiatry. Many
scientists, US and Soviet, feel that parapsychology can be harnessed
to create conditions where one can alter or manipulate the minds of
others. The major impetus behind the Soviet drive to harness the
possible capabilities of telepathic communication, telekinetics, and
bionics are said to come from the Soviet military and the KGB. Today,
it is reported that the USSR has twenty or more centers for the study
of parapsychological phenomena, with an annual budget estimated at
21 million dollars. Parapsychological research in the USSR began
in the 1920s and has continued to the present. Based on their "head
start" and financial support, it could be concluded that Soviet
knowledge in this field is superior to that of the US.

(U) Methods for controlling behavior of the human being are
numerous. Not all of the possibilities were included in this report,
but an attempt was made to elaborate on those areas where there is
intensive research by the USSR. The use of sound, light and color,
or odors have been determined to be possible means for Soviet exploitation in order to alter human behavior. In the area of color and
lights, usually in a flickering mode, there have been reports of
actual "trials" by the Soviets (Air Force and Navy) on US or allied
personnel. The Soviets have shown an in-depth knowledge in the effects
of sound and light on biological systems. It appears that with their

xi

ST-CS-01-169-72
July 1972

knowledge, it would be a rather simple procedure to make the transformation (from scientific research to the applications phase). The area of pheromone research has interested the Soviets; however, their data is sketchy and it is conceivable that they are not yet aware of the tremendous potentials that these substances provide for causing human behavioral changes. It is also a possibility that the USSR has realized the military benefits and are not publishing or conversing about their research and development efforts concerning pheromone synthesis and uses.

xii

164

ST-CS-01-169-72
July 1972

PART 1

INTRODUCTION TO HUMAN BEHAVIOR MANIPULATION

SECTION I - BACKGROUND

1. (U)   Methods for manipulating or influencing the human mind
exist and are being thoroughly researched by members of the Soviet
scientific community. For background and introductory information
it would be best if some of these methods were briefly mentioned.
Techniques studied by the Soviets include biochemicals, sound, light,
color, odors, sensory deprivation, sleep, electronic and magnetic
fields, hypnosis, autosuggestion, and paranormal phenomena (psychokinesis, extrasensory perception, astral projection, dream state,
clairvoyance, and precognition). Paranormal phenomena have caused great
excitement in recent years in the Soviet Union; so much so, that it
has been reported (1) that the Soviets had 20 or more centers in
1967 for the study of this area. It was also reported that the
annual budget for 1967 for paranormal research was approximately
$20 million.

2. (U)   The purpose of mind altering techniques is to create
one or more of several different possible states in the conscious
or unconscious area of the brain. The ultimate goal of controlled
offensive behavior might well be the total submission of one's
will to some outside force. It is more realistic to assume that
lesser degrees of mental aberration would be the purpose of Soviet
research in this field. Some areas of human mind manipulation
that apply to this report are morale lowering, confusion, anxiety,
loss of confidence, loss of self reliance, fatigue, persuasion,
disruption of social cohesion, or complete incapacitation. Since
the desired end product of this type of research is some change
in the human mind, only the non-lethal aspects are discussed
in this report. It should be remembered, however, that some
techniques have lethal thresholds.

3. (U)   The purpose of this study is to portray the Soviet
research in mind manipulation and its possible use on US or allied
individuals (e.g. PW's) or troops. Controlled offensive behavior,
however, has other connotations. Certain methods of altering
mental or physical states of man may have application on one's
own individuals. The apport technique and astral projection are
examples which will be discussed in this report. These two methods
allow the enemy to impart certain behavioral characteristics on
its own people to the detriment of US or allied personnel or missions.

1

ST-CS-01-169-72
July 1972

SECTION II - CURRENT EVENTS

PART A - Events in Northern Ireland

1. (U) The following discussion is based on 1971 and 1972 literature
dealing with the manipulation of human behavior. The events that
have been reported to have occurred are not Soviet originated but
provide an excellent example of the type of efforts that this
report is expressing.

2. (U) Recently there has appeared in the press some discussion
elaborating on the techniques and procedures for detaining, treating,
and interrogating prisoners in Northern Ireland (2,3). According
to the report, once the detainees are in prison, they come under
three types of regime which create in men a state of great confusion,
suggestibility, and distress. The first regime contained various
methods to produce sensory isolation. The men were made to stand
still against a wall with their hands in the air for four to six
hours at a time. The total length was 43 1/2 hours. Hoods were
placed over the men's heads to further abolish visual input.
Sensory input was further decreased by having loud noise generators
turned on in order to mask meaningful sounds. The detainees were,
therefore, isolated from their sensory world.

3. (U) The second sensory regime has the effect of increasing
confusion and disorientation. Some men were rushed out, hooded
and doubled up, past barking dogs, loaded into a helicopter, doors
closed, engine revved up, then unloaded, then reloaded, with the
procedure repeated three times. In another incident, detainees
without shoes were made to move quickly over rough ground by
military police.

4. (U) The third type of treatment has the effect of increasing
stress and anxiety and reducing resistance to the disorienting
effect on the two types described above. It appears that dietary
intake was restricted to bread and water at six hour intervals.
Maximum weight loss was achieved it appears. One detainee lost
eight pounds in seven days. To accompany the diet restrictions,
no sleep was allowed the first two or three days. Forty-eight
hours sleep deprivation, in certain individuals, has been known
to precipitate psychotic-like states.

5. (U) Psychological torture and physical abuse has been used
on Catholic detainees in Northern Ireland. High-frequency sound
waves (range not given in report) and sensory deprivation - research
methods that have been outlawed for use on humans by the American

2

166

ST-CS-01-169-72
July 1972

Psychological Association - were being used to undermine the
dignity and destroy the effectiveness of the Catholic minority
of Northern Ireland. The case of one 40-year old released
prisoner has been reported. Upon release, the man's mental and
physical condition suggested senility - a condition inconsistent
with his health at the time of his internment. The man walks
like he is 65, whimpers in the dark and has an attention span so
short he cannot carry on a conversation.

6. (U) The Northern Ireland procedure can be expected to greatly
increase the pliability of detainees under interrogation since
sensory deprivation increases suggestability and lowers intellectual
competence. Stress-isolation techniques can reach the extent of
eliciting false confessions where both prisoner and interrogator
are convinced the statements rendered are true. It is hoped
that the above examples impart to the reader a feeling for the
type of mind manipulating procedures that will be discussed later
in this report.

7. (U) Since it appears that the research behind sensory deprivation
has been put to current use on humans, the interested reader might
peruse Biderman and Zimmer's 1961 publication entitled "The Manipulation
of Human Behavior" (4). The book represents a critical examination
of some of the conjectures about the application of scientific
knowledge to manipulation of human behavior. The problem is explored
within a particular frame of reference: the interrogation of an
unwilling subject. Attention has been focused on interrogation
because of the central position this topic has had in public
discussions of prisoner of war (PW) behavior.

PART B - Events in the Soviet Union

1. (U) The use of psychiatric detention to silence political
dissenters appears to be a method being utilized by the Soviet
Union. There is extensive documention from "samizdat" (self-
published) sources in the Soviet Union, notably "A Question of
Madness" by Soviet geneticist Zhores Medvedev, excerpts from
which were published in the Sunday New York Times Magazine of
November 7, 1971 (5). British Sovietologist Peter Reddaway asserts
that the number of such political detainees in the USSR has grown
sharply in the last two years, perhaps to several hundred (6).
Peter Reddaway has published several articles that give brief
accounts of several political detainees as well as publishing
letters received from the Soviet underground (7,8,9).

3

167

ST-CS-01-169-72
July 1972

2. (U)   On the surface, the fact that the Soviet Union has
been subjecting political dissenters to psychiatric institutions
may not appear relevant to this report. However, as one probes
into this area, he discovers that the medical and physical treatment
of these prisoners borders on the subject of controlled offensive
behavior. Since the techniques are reportedly being applied to
Soviet citizens, it is simple enough, as the researchers gain
knowledge and expertise in this area, to assume that alien personnel
could someday be subjected to it as well.

3. (U) From the many reports, some coming from the Soviet Union
underground press, the article that best relates some of the
medical and physical treatment to political detainees is discussed
below (10). The article was written about Vladimir Bukovsky who
is frequently quoted in the feature story. Bukovsky has spent
six of his 27 years in Soviet prisons, asylums and labor camps.
(On January 5, 1972, Bukovsky was sentenced to a 12-year confinement
to include prison, hard labor camp, and internal exile.) In 1962,
Bukovsky organized an illegal exhibition of paintings by abstract
artists not approved by state censors. In May 1963, Bukovsky was
arrested by the KGB. He was declared insane by the Serbsky Psychiatric
Institute. That December, he was transferred to a prison asylum
in Leningrad (name not mentioned) where he spent, in his own words,
"15 months of hell." "There were about 1,000 men in the asylum,
political prisoners and insane murderers," says Bukovsky. "The sick
raved, the healthy suffered." Doctors were technically in charge
of the inmates, but the real masters were brutal turnkeys and
prisoner trustees. "Only the crafty survived, you had to be nice
to the guards.... you had to bribe them. Otherwise, they can
beat you until you are nearly dead and tell the doctors you mis-
behaved. Or they could recommend medical punishment."

4. (U) The worst, according to Bukovsky, was medical punishment.
The three methods of medical punishment known to Bukovsky are
described as follows:

    a. On the recommendation of a trustee or turnkey, doctors
would inject a drug (not mentioned) that produced severe stomach
cramps, fever, intense pain, and a temperature of 104. The sickness
lasted two or three days and left the inmate very weak.

    b. Another drug reserved for serious misbehavior induced
sleep and dulled the brain. Inmates were punished with ten days
of daily injections. They woke up as human vegetables. Some
regained their senses after two months, others did not.

4

ST-CS-01-169-72
July 1972

c. The third punishment was the canvas bandage. An inmate
would be tightly swathed in wet canvas from neck to toes while
others in his ward were forced to watch. "The canvas shrinks
as it dries. It is not a pretty sight. They usually only do it
for two or three hours. A nurse is always in attendance, and the
bandages are loosened when the pulse grows weak."

5. (U) A thousand-word telegram by Andrei D. Sakhaiov to Colonel
Nikolai A. Shchelokov, Minister of the Interior, relates further
information on the use of drugs to alter mental behavior (11).
Sakhaiov, a physicist and civil-rights champion, charged that a
violation of human rights and medical ethics is occurring in the
Soviet Union. The contention is that drugs are being administered
forcibly to inmates in an effort to have them change their political
beliefs. In addition, some prisoners are threatened with the possible
use of electrical-shock "therapy." According to Sakhaiov, medicine,
one of the most humane of the professions, is thus being turned
into a servile handmaiden of the regimes correction agencies.
It is further reported that with the help of medicine, an attempt
is being made to make people literally lose their minds by chemical
and physical means if they refuse to adapt their mind to the
standards of the regime.

6. (U) One of the few references that mention a drug by name
is a London Times feature by Richard Preston (12). In several
cases, Soviet authorities forced political prisoners to submit
to the use of mind-bending drugs, specifically aminazine and
haloperidol. Aminazine is the Soviet brand of a phenothiazine
derivative known as chlorpromazine. Haloperidol is a butyrophenone.
Both drugs are in the tranquilizer class of therapeutic agents.
An excellent discussion on both of these drugs has been prepared
by Goodman and Gilman (13).

7. (U) Information on the plight of political prisoners in mental
wards and other examples of internal Soviet repression is contained
in Issue 18 of "A Chronicle of Current Events." The chronicle
has just passed its third anniversary despite the increasing
efforts of the KGB to shut down this underground publication.
The last issue discusses the case of Vasily I. Chernyshov who
was arrested in March of 1970. The chronicle quotes Chernyshov....
"I am terribly afraid of torture. But there is an even worse
torture - meddling with my brain with chemical substances. I
have now been informed of the decision that I shall be given
treatment. Farewell!" Chernyshov's compulsory "treatment" was
prescribed after only a five minute interview with the authorities.
The concluding statement from the panel of doctors was, "The main
thing for us is that you shouldn't think at all."

5

ST-CS-01-169-72
July 1972

8. (U) A document that contains several case histories of political detainees has been prepared by Abraham Brumberg (14). The article summarizes the procedure that is used in the Soviet Union from arrest to confession. According to the report, the KGB performs the search, arrest, and initial investigation. The medical "experts" cooperate in furnishing bogus diagnoses and the court confirms the findings of the doctors. The victim is then sent off to a prison asylum to languish until "cured" (which in most cases consists of the patient's confession that he is indeed guilty of some form of mental aberration).

9. (U) The legal procedures involved in detaining an "undesirable" have been drastically reduced by the "1961 Directives" (15). V.N. Chalidze (16) in an underground document, explains how the "1961 Directives" allow for the immediate detention of a sane individual who is not a criminal in the legal sense. Chalidze sums up his argument by noting that the viciousness of the present-day practice, not based on the law, of psychiatric preventive measures is due to the absence of any public means of defense for the patient. The "1961 Directives" are included in this report in Appendix IV.

10. (U) The office that prepared this study has copies of various reports from the Soviet Union that deal with some of the more celebrated political detainees. There are three reports available that illustrate the forensic-psychiatric examinations of I. A. Yakhimovich. Two of these documents list the names of the psychiatric teams that carried out the examination (17-19). By reading these reports, one can trace the fate of Yakhimovich up to early 1970. No further reports were available so the ultimate fate of the individual is unknown.

11. (U) A report is available on A. Volpin (20) that was apparently prepared by the individual while in detention. There have been several cases where these documents have been "smuggled" out of the asylum. An outpatient report on V.E. Borosov is available (21). This report condemns Borosov to compulsory psychiatric treatment. Reports are available on the plight of N.E. Gorbanevskaya (22,23) as well as several letters that she wrote while interned (24). An appeal for human rights written by V. Fainberg while he was incarcerated is on file (25) as well as documents relating to the sanity proceedings for General P.G. Grigorenko (26-28).

12. (U) The possible use of drugs by Soviet psychiatrists in order to manipulate behavior can be emphasized by an account from Vladimir Gershuni, a Soviet idealist. The event that follows occurred at the Oryol Hospital which is some 170 miles

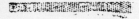

ST-CS-01-169-72
July 1972

southwest of Moscow. Mr. Gershuni gives a description of the
conditions in which mental patients (both genuine and political)
are held. "Eight people to a 16 or 17 meter cell. . . . (Comment:
This seems large enough for eight people if figure is correct.) There
is no room to move. One is allowed to go along the corridor, but
only if it's absolutely necessary – to the toilet, or to get some
food from the nurse. . . . The toilet is a cesspit: four holes
in the ground and two taps for 54 people. . . . From 7 to 8:30
in the evening we're allowed to use the dining room for writing
letters, or to play dominoes and chess. The bedlam is indescrib-
able." Mr. Gershuni talks about the use of drugs, one of which
is aminazine, a powerful substance administered orally or by
intramuscular injections, which causes depressive shock reactions
and frequently malignant tumors. Sometimes drugs are given as
a form of punishment. "Any phrase spoken incautiously to a doctor
or nurse can serve as a pretext for a series of aminazine injections.
Sometimes these injections are prescribed without any pretext,
simply because of some doctor's whim . . . without any medical
examination. . . . This medicine makes me feel more horrible
than anything I've ever experienced before; you no sooner lie
down than you want to get up, you no sooner take a step than
you're longing to sit down, and if you sit down, you want to walk
again – and there's nowhere to walk." Mr. Gershuni finishes
his account by describing the fate of a young man, once brilliantly
"alive and alert," who as a result of repeated doses of aminazine,
"and God only knows what else," had been reduced to a vegetable:
"his head on one side, his speech languid and indistinct, his eyes
glazed." "He was thus," concludes Mr. Gershuni, "cancelled out for
five whole months. Hail to Soviet 'special psychiatry'! I kiss
you all."

13. (U) To belabor this subject of political detention is not
the intention of this section. However, it is believed to be
of sufficient importance that this much material had to be presented.
It is difficult to judge the overall validity of much of the referenced material because of its source (primarily samizdat and
letters), but if true, it bears watching and possible investigation
for future developments. Portions of this material contain
sufficient data on human mental manipulation and therefore warrants
surveilance by interested agencies. From the information available
at this time, it appears that the Soviet Union stresses physical
and medical "treatment" of its political detainees under the
guise of psychiatric-care rehabilitation. No data is available
on the use of sound, lights, or hypnosis as methods of obtaining
confessions or reorientating the beliefs of these prisoners.
For a listing of personnel and institutes involved in political-
psychiatric care, see Appendix I. Many personalities involved

7

ST-CS-01-169-72
July 1972

in the maltreatment of detainees are not listed but can be found
in the references listed. An attempt was made to list only the
top professional personnel.

PART C - Soviet Response to Events in the USSR

1. (U) The Soviet government, quite naturally, has denied the
charges made in the USSR and abroad that mentally stable persons
were being detained in psychiatric hospitals because of dissident
activities. The Soviet authorities had said little about the
accusations until an article written by S.P. Pisarev was
obtained by Western sources from the Soviet underground (30).
Pisarev, 69, member of the Soviet Communist party since 1918
and minor party official, in 1970 directed a letter to the Soviet
Academy of Medical Sciences protesting the Soviet police practice
of sending political prisoners to "psychiatric institutions" such
as the infamous Serbsky Institute in Moscow.

2. (U) Disputing the type of charge mentioned by Pisarev, Soviet
authorities contended persons remanded by a legal psychiatric
commission to special mental institutions were those "who committed
socially dangerous acts while not responsible for their actions or
became ill during a pretrial investigation, during actual court
proceedings or after the passing of sentence." According to
the Soviet government, such cases are reviewed every six months
and committed persons are released if sufficient improvement is
found in their mental health (31).

3. (U) A.V. Snezhnevskiy (32), USSR Academy of Medical Sciences
academician and director of the USSR Academy of Medical Sciences
Psychiatric Institute says:

> "Yes, I, too, have read these absurd reports that in
> the USSR healthy people are put into psychiatric
> hospitals. Like all my colleagues, I cannot express
> my feelings of profound indignation at this wild fan-
> tasy. Soviet psychiatrists - a detachment of Soviet
> medical workers consisting of many thousands - do not,
> of course, need to be defended from insulting attacks
> of this sort. In our country and abroad fame and
> deserved authority are enjoyed by such psychiatrists
> as A.D. Zurabasvili, V.M. Morozov . . . ." etc.
> (Snezhnevskiy mentions eight other psychiatrists).

Snezhnevskiy continues his argument by listing the members of a
US mission that toured Soviet psychiatric facilities. The mission
says in its conclusion . . . . "It appears that the Soviets are leading."

8

ST-CS-01-169-72
July 1972

The US guests stressed the high degree of effectiveness of the
Soviet psychiatric first aid centers, and the better quality of
their staffs compared with US centers. The US delegation did
visit the Serbsky Institute. As for compulsory treatment, the
mission stated . . . . "It is possible that people who need
treatment should be compulsorily hospitalized for their own good."

4. (U) Snezhnevskiy, in another document (33), said that when
mentioning "brainwashing" many absurd allegations have been made,
such as the talk of injecting a substance which paralyzes a person's
will. Snezhnevskiy contends that "brainwashing," from a scientific
point of view, is absurd. He further believes that the people
dedicated to this sort of propaganda have very few scruples and
direct the propaganda to laymen who know nothing about medicine.
Interviews with Snezhnevskiy and Lebeden, chief of psychiatry at
the Pavlov hospital in Leningrad, were obtained just prior to
the Fifth World Psychiatric Congress in Mexico City which was
held in early December 1971 (34).

5. (U) The literature from Soviet authorities denying the maltreatment of detainees or other charges does not mention any of
the more celebrated prisoners with the exception of Zhores Medvedev
who was released after a very short stay. One can draw some obvious
conjectures based on the avoidance of such personalities as Gershuni,
Grigorenko, Bukovsky, Fainberg, and Borisov in the Soviet statements.
The issue of inhumane treatment is usually responded to with the
use of platitudes and counter-propaganda. If the Soviets have
nothing to conceal, then it would seem that one could expect more
scientific and concrete responses as to the actual situation in
political detention and behavior manipulation with drugs.

SECTION III - SOVIET PSYCHOLOGY AND PSYCHIATRY

PART A - A General Review

1. (U)   The past fifteen years have witnessed a definite
acceleration of growth in Soviet psychology (35). It has been observed
by some American psychologists that an upward trend in the quality and
quantity of Soviet published research began around the middle of the
1950's. Research designs improved, greater experimental controls
were employed, and the level of sophistication in laboratory techniques
started to rise perceptibly. Many new people are entering into the
area of psychology and the increase has been (1966) as much as a
factor of 2,3, or 4 (36). According to this source (36), Soviet

9

ST-CS-01-169-72
July 1972

psychology is in a growth stage which appears to have sprung up
coincident to the man-in-space program. Contrary to the reference
above (36), this source (36) believes that despite the growth and
acceptance by the Soviet scientific community, the Soviets are merely
duplicating or extending to some degree the research that is already
known. In the opinion of this source, there is definitely a tie-in
between the Soviet engineers, psychiatrists and psychologists. It must
be remembered that the Soviets are presently in a growth stage and,
therefore, are merely making their investments at this time. According
to this source, once they have reached the level off period then this
coordination of the disciplines will pay off handsomely in returns to
the Soviet psychological society. The source believes that in the area
of human engineering the Soviets are moving very rapidly and at least in
many respects are close to US levels. In behavior studies, the Soviets
are stagnant. They lean too heavily on the conditional response approach
of Pavlov. In the neurosensory areas, source believes that the Soviets
are considerably behind the US and accept the US as the leader in this
field.

2. (U)   According to one report, there is apparently
classified psychological research work going on in the area of cybernetics. One area that surveillance would appear fruitful is Soviet
research in the area of artificial intelligence. This report contains
a substantial number of institutes and personalities which is reflected
in Appendix I (37).

3. (U) It is concluded that, in spite of their ideological
resistance to theoretical psychology, Soviet behavior scientists
share a distinguished experimental tradition and possess the ability
to incorporate and combine the principles of biocybernetics, physiology,
learning, memory, and transfer under a common group of laws (38).

4. (U) The following brief discussion of Soviet psychiatry is
based primarily upon a report by Persic (39). The report contains
a brief history of psychiatry in the Soviet Union followed by a
section that relates to the scientific and investigative work in
psychiatry. Also included is a section on the organization of
psychiatric care including statistics on the number of patients,
beds, and medical personnel in the Soviet Union.

5. (U) According to Persic there are 94 medical institutes and
a greater number of medical research institutes. The following
research institutes in psychiatry exist in Moscow: the Psychiatric
Institute at the Academy of Science; the Psychiatric Institute at
the Ministry of Health for the Russian Federation, and the Institute
for Forensic Psychiatry at the Institute of the Ministry of Health

10

UNCLASSIFIED

ST-CS-01-169-72
July 1972

of the USSR (Serbsky Institute). The research institutes are either
of a general type or of a specialized type which study certain
mental diseases e.g. schizophrenia, epilepsy, or alcoholism. The
psychiatric research institutes have similar organizational schemes:
clinical departments, laboratories, and methodics departments.
The Psychiatric Institute of the Academy of Sciences in Moscow
is the post-graduate school for psychiatrists. At the Institute
for Forensic Psychiatry in Moscow (Serbsky) are clinics for schizophrenia, psychoorganic disorders, and alcoholism. (Naturally
there is no discussion in this report of some of the more infamous
areas of the Serbsky Institute.)

6. (U) The task of psychiatric institutes is to deal with the
educational matters of students, and physicians specializing in
psychiatry. This work is conducted in the form of seminars and
in the form of continuous education. The psychiatric research
institutes are connected with psychiatric hospitals, departments
and dispensaries in advancing psychiatric work and the organizing
of psychiatric service. Great attention is devoted to health
education in the USSR. A great network of institutions devoted
to health instruction exist. They are affiliated with many groups
which dispense health advice. Included in the general health
education is also education concerning mental health. There are
360 health institutes in the USSR which are devoted to teaching
health. The Central Institute for Health Education in Moscow
is engaged in research in the field of health education, education
of experts, training in the methodology of health education and
organizing health training. This Institute employs a method of
providing health education for schools, students of medicine, for
workers in industry and hospitals. There is also cooperation
with physicians concerning public health and seminars are held
where practical matters are discussed. There is also a functional
connection with health agencies so that officials of these agencies
cooperate with the Institute and attend seminars. These health
agencies also receive support from the Institute in the form of
trained help and literature which the Institute publishes through
its own printing outlets. Table I depicts the instructional
requirements for psychiatric specialization. These figures were
prepared by Persic. Table II illustrates statistics on the number
of neurologists and psychiatrists in the USSR in 1962 (Persic) and 1967.
The 1967 data was compiled by Fry (40). Fry, in his report, combined
neurologists and psychiatrists into one figure.

11

UNCLASSIFIED

ST-CS-01-169-72
July 1972

TABLE I

Plan of Instruction and Stages in Psychiatric Specialization—USSR

Subject	Hours of theoretical training	Hours of practical training
Psychopathology	16	60
Clinical psychiatry		
Schizophrenia	16	
Manic depressive psychosis	6	
Infectional psychosis	16	
Toxic psychosis	6	
Epilepsy	6	
Noninfectional symptomatic psychosis	8	
Brain trauma	4	400
Arteriosclerotic psychosis	6	
Brain tumors	2	
Presenile psychosis	4	
Senile psychosis	4	
Oligophrenia	2	
Psychopathy	4	
Psychogenic reaction	4	
Organization of Psychiatric Service	4	
Total	108	460

12

176

ST-CS-0i-169-72
July 1972

TABLE II

Comparison of the Number of Psychiatric Specialists in USSR-1962 and 1967

	1962	1967
Population	220,000,000	230,000,000
Physicians	400,000	480,000
Psychiatrists	6,140	Combined Psychiatrists and Neurologists total: 24,000
Neurologists	9,850	
One physician per	520 people	480 people
One psychiatrist per	35,835 people	Combined Psychiatrists and Neurologists total: 20,000 people
One neurologist per	22,335 people	

7. (U) The figures in Table II, if valid, represent a substantial growth in the number of specialists in mental health care. The number and quality of both psychology and psychiatry research reports is increasing, especially in the behavioral fields. There appears to be an ever increasing link between the psychology and psychiatry fields with the pharmacology, human engineering, bioelectronics, physics, and parapsychology disciplines. Some of the multidiscipline aspects of Soviet research will become evident later in this study as it relates to the subject of this report. The above information on psychology and psychiatry was intended to be a review because it is believed that there is a definite relationship between the two disciplines and mental manipulation. It is not within the scope of this report to delve into basic psychological research and discuss its military implications.

PART B - Soviet Military Psychology

1. (U) The purpose of this report is to make determinations and report findings on methods of controlling human behavior. One aspect of this subject is the possible use of certain novel techniques to disrupt or confuse combat troops. Based on Soviet literature dealing with military psychology, it appears that the Soviet military authorities might well suspect their potential enemies as already being able to do this. The available Soviet literature on military psychology emphasizes the protection of their troops against such possible attempts e.g. demoralization and confusion.

13

ST-CS-01-169-72
July 1972

2. (U) In 1967, a book entitled "Military Psychology" was published
in the Soviet Union. The authors, Colonel Dyachenko and Major Fedenko,
are Candidates of Pedagogical Sciences (41). This book is primarily
intended for commanders and military doctors. The book deals with the
various aspects of the personality of the soldier including his cognitive, emotional, and volitional processes, his fighting skill, and his
psychological readiness for battle. All of the psychic phenomena are
based on the service, training, and fighting activity of enlisted and
commissioned personnel. One of the more interesting areas is found in
Chapter 8 which is entitled "Will Power." The chapter contains information on will power as a psychic process. The chapter continues by
discussing the qualities of will power necessary to a soldier as well
as methods of training will power. The discussion on will power appears
to be a very important topic because if one's will power is sufficiently
developed, the use of techniques to demoralize or confuse could well be
nullified. Part one of the book describes the general problems of
military psychology, followed by a discussion on psychic processes of
the soldier and concluding with the psychological analysis of the
activity of Soviet soldiers.

3. (U) The group of people most susceptible to offensive behavior
manipulation appear to be rear-zone troops and small patrol groups.
The Soviets again seem to recognize the fallibility of such groups.
Lieutenant General Tyurnev (42) reports that the moral-psychological
training of administrative support troops in operations under
conditions of modern war is a quite urgent and complicated problem.
The report suggests training and propaganda methods to increase
the morale-psychological condition of rear-zone troops. The
training, to include evening seminars, propaganda sessions, political
indoctrination and field exercises is suggested in Tyurnev's report.
The word moral and morale seem to be interchanged frequently in the
report. It seems to be a problem in translation, because the author's
thoughts are still meaningful.

4. (U) Two further reports from the Soviets have appeared recently.
One report (43) discusses the role of medicine and military medical
personnel in the psychoprophylaxis in morale-psychological preparation.
A 1970 report by Stolyarenko (44) reinforces the thoughts of Tyurnev.
From the above discussion and a thorough perusal of the documents
referenced in this section, it could be stated: if the Soviets practice
what they preach, the psychological training of Soviet troops is as
good as or better than US soldiers. This does not include the special
training afforded to US pilots on anti-interrogation methods.

14

ST-CS-01-169-72
July 1972

SECTION IV - PSYCHOLOGICAL PHENOMENA/PSYCHOLOGICAL WEAPONS

(U)   One of the purposes of this report is to evaluate
research in the field of influencing human behavior in order that
the US may be in a position to develop certain countermeasures.
Therefore, before beginning specific sections in this report on
Soviet research, it is desirable to review some of the more feasible
areas of exploitation in the development of a technique that might
alter human behavior. Some of these characteristics will be studied
in depth in later sections of this study.

15

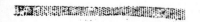

ST-CS-01-169-72
July 1972

PART A - Temperature

1. (U) An increase in body temperature decreases the body water
level and creates a salt-water imbalance. With a large intake
of water, but little replacement of sodium chloride, painful spasms
of the skeletal and abdominal muscles may develop as may also
faintness, weakness, nausea, and vomiting. With an internal
temperature above 41 degrees C or below 31 degrees C, brain
function is usually impaired. Irreversible damage to the skin
occurs at about 44-45 degrees C (46,47).

2. (U) The sensitivity and tolerance for temperature changes
is different for certain races. Negroes have a greater tolerance
for humid heat than Caucasians, and conversely, Negroes are
more susceptible to injury from cold stress than Caucasians.

3. (U)   It is believed that the use of temperature manipulation
as a technique to influence human behavior is practical. In order to
be effective it would seem necessary to apply this technique to
individuals or small groups that are already under one's influence
such as prisoners of war. The application of unnatural temperature
in field situations appear to be most difficult. Further, there
appears to be very little applicable research in the USSR in
this area other than some isolated work in the areospace field.
It may be concluded that temperature fluctuations could be used for
altering human behavior, but would probably not be as useful as other
available methods.

PART B - Atmospheric Conditions

1. (U)   There has been some work reported on the physiological
or psychological effects of atmospheric or geophysical parameters
(48-51). The works referenced here are free world but there is
little doubt that the Soviet Union has investigated similar effects
especially in relation to their space program. The utilization of
any of the techniques to alter human behavior by changing atmospheric
conditions seems remote for field application. These techniques,
like temperature effects, are more suitable for controlled groups or
individuals.

2. (U) An increase of 0.2 percent carbon dioxide doubles the
volume of air breathed. Breathing becomes deeper, more rapid,
and eventually violent. Depletion of oxygen or the increase
of carbon dioxide decreases auditory sensitivity as well as visual
sensitivity. Ten percent of oxygen for 15 to 30 minutes sometimes

16

180

ST-CS-01-169-72
July 1972

results in a hearing deficit for several hours. With severe or
prolonged anoxia there may be nausea, vomiting, extreme weakness,
and eventually convulsions and cardiac failure (52). Perhaps
the applicable symptoms of anoxia to this report are the homeo-
static inbalances in the brain: loss of ability to carry on complex
activities, restlessness, loquacity, delirium, confusion, and
unconsciousness.

3. (U) Intermittent exposures to negatively ionized air produces
a sedating effect on humans. There are some researchers who believe
that positively ionized air causes irritation and anxiety which is
applicable to altering behavior.

PART C - Olfactory Phenomena

1. (U) Seven primary odors have been identified; they are campho-
raceous, musky, floral, minty, pungent, putrid, and ethereal (53).
From the seven primary odors, every known odor can be made by
mixing them in certain proportions.

2. (U) Man expresses pleasure or displeasure to various odors.
If the smell is foul or irritating enough, man will attempt to
avoid it. If escape is hindered or if odors are used with surprise
they may elicit certain behavioral changes in the individual.
Odors are suitable for use in controlled situations and in the
field. For these reasons odors will be discussed more fully
later in this report.

PART D - Light

1. (U) Although it is customary to specify the wavelength range of
visible light as lying between 400 and 750 millimicrons (mµ), nevertheless, with sufficient energy, the eye can be stimulated up to
1050 mµ. Also, the fovea (phototopic vision) can be stimulated down
to about 320 mµ. It is thought that 1150-1200 mu marks the limit
at which radiant energy would cease to be seen and would be
readily felt as heat (54).

2. (U) Yellow light has maximum effect on the retina and is
most effective in eliciting photophobia. Non-rhythmic bright
lights can interrupt or prevent sleep. It has been claimed that
if sensory stimulation is sufficient, sleep can be prevented even
if fatigue is carried to the point of death (52). The physiological

17

ST-CS-01-169-72
July 1972

and psychological effects of flashing lights (stable) and photic-
flicker appear to have raised interests in the Soviet Union.
Since lights can be utilized in the field or in controlled situations
and do cause certain behavioral changes in man, this subject will
be discussed in detail later in this report.

PART E - Sound

1. (U) Sound, from one source or another, has been used to elicit
behavioral changes in man in every war ever recorded. It may be
a simple bugle call or battle cry or a mechanical siren device;
but whatever is used there is normally a psychological response
by the receiver. Regardless of the absolute level, sounds of
enemy weapons with which one is unfamiliar is frightening provided
the sounds are associated with a feared weapon or the unknown.

2. (U) Auditory effects have been and still are researched.
Nerve deafness can certainly result from prolonged exposure to
loud sounds. For the purpose of this study it is believed that
the nonauditory effects are just as important when discussing
behavioral alterations. For example, exposure to a siren-generated
sound of 20 kilohertz at 1 watt per square centimeter kills a
variety of insect life in three to four minutes and larger animals
(mice) in about one minute. Human operators, with earplugs, experience
"cool sizzling sensations" in the mouth and an unpleasant tingling
in the nasal passages when near the siren.

3. (U) Sound can be used on controlled groups or in the
field. Sound can produce behavioral changes and the effects of
sound on humans is being investigated in the Soviet Union. For
these reasons, a more detailed discussion can be found later in
this report.

PART F - Electromagnetic Energy

1. (U) Super-high frequency electromagnetic oscillations (SHF)
may have potential use as a technique for altering human behavior.
Soviet Union and other foreign literature sources contain over 500
studies devoted to the biological effect of SHF. Lethal and non-lethal
aspects have been shown to exist. In certain non-lethal exposures,
definite behavioral changes have occurred. There also appears
to be a change in mammals, when exposed to SHF, in the sensitivity
to sound, light, and olfactory stimuli (55).

18

182

ST-CS-01-169-72
July 1972

2. (U)   Because of the possible behavioral changes and reactions
to other important stimuli and the emphasis the Soviet Union has
placed on SHF research, a more detailed discussion of this subject
appears later in this report.

PART G - Deprivation

(U)   The behavior effects on man from the deprivation of food,
sleep, and sensory stimuli have been studied by the Soviet Union.
As mentioned in Section II of this report, certain forms of deprivation to humans is in current use. This area is very important
in the discussion of controlled offensive behavior and it is
clear that the Soviet Union is well aware of this potential. Because
one is able to apply deprivation techniques in controlled situations
as well as in the field, it will be discussed in detail in a later
section of this report. Hahn (56) provides further discussion
on the areas mentioned in this section to include fear phenomena,
anxiety and stress, and cultural background. These specific areas
are not mentioned specifically as separate sections in this report
because they become interlaced with the other areas of major concern.

19

INTENTIONALLY LEFT BLANK

20

UNCLASSIFIED

ST-CS-01-169-72
July 1972

PART II

PARAPSYCHOLOGY IN THE SOVIET UNION

SECTION I - BACKGROUND

1. (U) The science of parapsychology includes special sensory bio-physical activities, brain and mind control, telepathic communications or bioinformation transceiving, bioluminescent and bioenergetic emissions, and the effects of altered status of consciousness on the human psyche. The Soviets prefer the term biocommunications instead of the term para-psychology. Other terms that may appear in the Soviet literature that normally mean parapsychology are: psycho-physiology, psychotronics, psychoenergetics, or biophysical effects. The term parapsychology (biocommunications) as used in this report denotes a multi-disciplinary field consisting of the sciences of bionics, biophysics, psychophysics, psychology, physiology, and neuropsychiatry (57,58).

2. (U) The broad area of biocommunications can be further subdivided into two general classifications: Bioinformation and Bioenergetics. Bioinformation includes paranormal events between living organisms (telepathy, precognition) and events between living organisms and the inorganic world. Bioenergetics denotes those activities such as biological location and indicator techniques, bioenergetic therapy using electromagnetic fields, and psychokinesis, or the influence of mind upon matter. The definitions of the terms Biocommunications, Bioinformation, and Bioenergetics are given in Table III which appeared in the Mankind Unlimited Research report. The basic definitions are based on information provided by Ryzl (59). It should be mentioned that parapsychology was accepted in 1969 as a legitimate field of science and scientific research by the American Association for the Advancement of Science (AAAS).

TABLE III

BASIC TYPES OF BIOCOMMUNICATION PHENOMENA (U)

General: Biocommunications

A new branch of science involved with the human capability of obtaining information from other than the normal senses and the ability to respond to or reasonably interpret such information. Biocommunications, also synonymous with para-psychology, is, however, distinct from other sciences in that it is primarily concerned with researching the exist-ence of a definite group of natural phenomena controlled by laws which are not based on any known energetic influence.

21

UNCLASSIFIED

UNCLASSIFIED

ST-CS-01-169-72
July 1972

TABLE III (Cont)

TYPE I: BIOINFORMATION (U)

Those phenomena associated with the obtaining of information through means other than the normal sensory channels e.g. through extrasensory perception (ESP). There are several forms of ESP, including:

 a. Telepathy, transmission or "reading" of thoughts refers to the extrasensory reception of information about the mental processes of others.

 b. Proscopy or precognition - While the above forms appear to differ only in the nature of the object about which information is received, numerous observations indicate that precognitive ESP involves, under certain circumstances, trespassing the barrier of time to obtain information about future events.

 c. Paragnosia or clairvoyance refers to the extrasensory reception of information about objective events in the outer world.

TYPE II: BIOENERGETICS (U)

Those phenomena associated with the production of objectively detectable effects through means other than the known energetic influences. Seemingly incredible effects have been reported, such as the movement of distant objects without any detectable use of physical force (telekinesis), antigravitational effects, transformations of energy, electromagnetic effects arising without adequate physical cause, and chemical reactions and biological processes occurring through mental concentration.

---

3. (U) Scientists in pre-revolutionary Russia were studying the area of parapsychology as did later such Soviet scientists as V.M. Bekhterev, A.G. Ivanov-Smolensky and B.B. Kazhinsky in the twenties and thirties (60,61). In 1922, a commission composed of psychologists, medical hypnotists, physiologists, and physicists worked on parapsychology problems at the Institute for Brain Research in Petrograd (Leningrad). Work flourished throughout the thirties with research being reported

UNCLASSIFIED

ST-CS-01-169-72
July 1972

in the literature in 1934, 1936, and 1937 (62). After 1937 further
experiments in the field of parapsychology were forbidden. During
Stalin's time, any attempt to study paranormal phenomena might have
been interpreted as a deliberate attempt to undermine the doctrines
of materialism.

4. (U) According to Dodge (63) in 1964, the Aerospace Technology
Division of the Library of Congress reviewed the Soviet literature
in an unpublished bibliography entitled, "Soviet Parapsychology"
(ATD Report U-64-77). At that time, academic opposition to parapsychology in the USSR had reached its zenith which led ATD observers
to the reasonable conclusion that official Soviet support or funds
for parapsychological research were unlikely and that investigation
in this area might be determined.

5. (U) The above conclusion was apparently misguided because
of events that occurred in 1959 and 1960. In 1959 a book entitled
Mysterious Phenomena of the Human Psyche was published in the USSR.
Its author was Professor L.L. Vasilev, head of the Department of
Physiology of Leningrad University and a corresponding member of
the Academy of Medical Sciences of the USSR (64). A year later,
Professor Vasilev was given state funds to establish at the
University appropriately equipped laboratories for the study of
telepathy. The published findings from this laboratory attracted
attention and began to find repercussions in the columns of the
non-specialized periodical press (65-70). This was followed by
a publication in 1962 by Kazhinskiy (71). Following the example
of Leningrad, other cities, including Moscow, Kiev, Novosibirsk
and Kharkov, established similiar laboratories and research centers,
at which not only the phenomena described in world literature
were examined, but a study was made of parapsychic features
displayed by Soviet citizens. The journal Science and Religion (72)
has published many articles on Soviet parapsychology, including
a discussion of whether it was worth-while continuing research
in this field (1965). Affirmative, though extremely cautious,
replies to this question were given by Vice President of the
Academy of Sciences, N.N. Seminov, by Academicians M.A. Leontovich,
A.L. Mints and G.M. Frank, and by Professors A.N. Leontev and
V.F. Asmus (73). This brief survey brings the study of paranormal
phenomena up to the time when studies of a more pertinent nature
to this report have begun.

23

ST-CS-01-169-72
July 1972

SECTION II - SIGNIFICANCE OF PARAPSYCHOLOGY IN THE USSR

1. (U) The Soviet Union is well aware of the benefits and applications
of parapsychology research. In 1963, a Kremlin edict apparently
gave top priority to biological research, which in Russia includes
parapsychology (74). The major impetus behind the Soviet drive
to harness the possible capabilities of telepathic communication,
telekinetics, and bionics is said to come from the Soviet military
and the KGB (57). Today it is reported that the USSR has twenty
or more centers for the study of parapsychological phenomena, with
an annual budget estimated in 1967 at over 12 million rubles
(13 million dollars) and reported to be as high as 21 million
dollars (1,57,75).

2. (U) According to a report by Velinov (76), Soviet interest
in biocommunications was clearly indicated in 1965 when the Department of Bioinformation of the Scientific and Technical Society
of Radio Engineering and Telecommunications was established at
the Popov Institute in Moscow. Its stated objectives are to
discuss physical, biological, and philosophical aspects of bioinformation and to acquaint the Soviet scientific community with biocommunications research conducted outside the Soviet Union.

3. (U) Soviet parapsychology research was actually stimulated
by the 1960 French story (77) concerning the US atomic submarine
Nautilus. The French journalists splashed the now rather infamous
Nautilus story in headlines "US Navy Uses ESP on Atomic Sub!"
Ship to shore telepathy, according to the French, blipped along
nicely even when the Nautilus was far under water. "Is telepathy
a new secret weapon? Will ESP be a deciding factor in future
warfare?" The speculating French sensationalized, "Has the
American military learned the secret of mind power?" In Leningrad
the Nautilus reports went off like a depth charge in the mind
of L.L. Vasilev. In April of 1960, Doctor Vasilev, while
addressing a group of top Soviet scientists stated:

> "We carried out extensive and until now completely
> unreported investigations under the Stalin regime.
> Today the American Navy is testing telepathy on their
> atomic submarines. Soviet scientists conducted a great
> many successful telepathy tests over a quarter of a
> century ago. It's urgent that we throw off our
> prejudices. We must again plunge into the exploration
> of this vital field." (78)

24

ST-CS-01-169-72
July 1972

Although the US Navy subsequently denied the reports of telepathic testing on atomic submarines, the Soviet hierarchy apparently heeded Doctor Vasilev's advice and gave support, both moral and financial, to his dynamic view that: "The discovery of the energy underlying telepathic communication will be equivalent to the discovery of atomic energy (62).

4. (U) Since 1962, Doctor Vasilev has headed a special laboratory for biocommunications research at the University of Leningrad. Major aspects of the work of this laboratory are to conduct research and to develop machines capable of monitoring, testing and studying telepathic communication (79).

5. (U) In 1963, Doctor Vasilev claimed to have conducted successful long-distance telepathic experiments between Leningrad and Sevastopol, a distance of 1200 miles, with the aid of an ultra-short-wave (UHF) radio transmitter. As a result, Doctor Vasilev was convinced that his experiments, and those he conducted jointly with the Moscow-based Bekhterev Brain Institute, offered scientific proof of telepathic communications. His next goal was to identify the nature of brain energy that produces it (59).

Theorizing on the above experiments, one Soviet scientist suggested that telepathic impulses are radiated along the lines of bits of information in a cybernetic system. Another scientist is known to be working on the idea of time as energy, speculating that telepathic transmissions may be propagated through a supposed time-energy system, rather than through the electromagnetic field.

6. (U) Soviet research into biocommunications phenomena does not appear to be earth-bound and limited to inner space, but apparently extends to outer space as well. The so-called Father of Soviet Rocketry, K.E. Tsiolkovsky, stated that:

> "In the coming era of space flights, telepathic
> abilities are necessary. While the space rocket
> must bring men toward knowledge of the grand
> secrets in the universe, the study of psychic
> phenomena can lead us toward knowledge of the
> mysteries of the human mind. It is precisely
> the solution of this secret which promises the
> greatest achievements." (80)

There are reports that the Soviets are training their cosmonauts in telepathy to back-up their electronic equipment while in outer space. One of these back-up schemes is known to involve coded

ST-CS-01-169-72
July 1972

telepathic messages. This method was previously demonstrated
in March 1967, when a coded telepathic message was flashed from
Moscow to Leningrad (81). The involvement of astronauts or cosmonauts
in telepathy experiments is not necessarily unprecedented. In
February 1971, during the Apollo 14 flight to the moon, astronaut
Edgar Mitchell made 150 separate attempts to project his thoughts
from inside the space capsule back to an individual on earth.
The results of the Apollo 14 experiments have been well-documented
in detail and are published in the Journal of Parasychology (82).
Further documentation of Mitchell's experiments can be found in
the University of California Newsletter (83).

7. (U) There are numerous reports on Soviet applications of
clairvoyance, hypotism, dowsing, etc. in military operations.
In the case of dowsing, this is also not unprecedented, since
US forces have employed dowsing in Vietnam for locating enemy
tunnels and caches. With respect to brain and mind control/
conditioning, a recent report indicates that the Soviet Union
has made great strides in emotional training and conditioning.
Soldiers are being taught to set their own emotional tone in
battle and stress situations. Further, astronauts are being taught
through such mental conditioning to distort time and to offset
boredom in outer space (84).

8. (U) Man's sight and hearing are limited to a relatively
small range of wavelengths, other living beings often possess
much wider perceptive capabilities, both with regard to sharpness
of perception and range of stimuli. For example, dogs hear higher
sound frequencies than man; bats and dolphins orient themselves
by means of an ultra-sound radar; bees perceive colors even in the
ultraviolet part of the spectrum; some snakes perceive minute
differences in temperature and orient themselves by means of
thermoreceptors. Certain living beings even react to stimuli to
which man is absolutely insensitive. Some species of fish and
homing pigeons, for instance, react to changes of the electric or
magnetic field in their surroundings (59). In view of these
perceptive processes, it has been difficult to differentiate
between those sensory processes which are merely sharpened or
highly honed and those that are extra or super-normal. Certain
military advantages would come from the application and control of
these perceptive processes. For example, such application and
control could be used in the detection and identification of
animate objects or humans through brainwave interactions, mass
hypnosis or mind control through long-distance telepathy, thermal
receptors, and sensitivity to changes in magnetic/electrical/
gravitational fields.

ST-CS-01-169-72
July 1972

9. (U) According to observations made by Doctor Montague Ullman (M.D.) during a trip to the Soviet bloc countries in the fall of 1970, Soviet biocommunications investigations are effectively combining the use of modern and sophisticated technology with basic pragmatic approaches. This was evident, he states, in their approach to long-distance telepathy experiments where the results were analyzed in physiological (electroencephalographic data) as well as phychological task performance (transmission of data in Morse Code) (85). Doctor Ullman further observed that the Soviet researchers seemed intent on confirming the existence of a new form of energy, referred to as bioplasma, which they maintain is characteristic of life processes and represents matter in the form of an integrated system of elementary charged particles. Such energy, through interaction with other systems, is thought to provide the basis for biocommunications (86).

10. (U) The above commentary documents a clear case for research in the Soviet Union in parapsychology. It is significant because of the energy and resources being allotted for this work in the Soviet Union and because of its military implications especially in mind manipulation and controlled offensive behavior. The more sinister aspects of paranormal research appear to be surfacing in the Soviet Union. Why else would Soviet researchers make the statement:

> "Tell America that the psychic potential of man must
> be used for good." (75)

SECTION III - THE APPORT TECHNIQUE

1. (U) The following discussion on apports and astral projection is not intended to be an endorsement for its scientific verification or even its existence. However, reputable scientists in the USSR and the US are keenly interested in this phenomenon. Areas that appear to have potential must be discussed, even if only briefly.

2. (U) According to Welk (87), a costly weakness in our intelligence system, to a large extent, is an inability to use effectively the resources of the science of parapsychology (there are some definite indicators that the Soviets realize the potential of "psi" which will be reported later in this section). Whenever parapsychology is mentioned, most people are likely to think of ESP. However, there are other types of parapsychological phenomena which are just as important militarily as ESP. Welk claims, based on many Soviet sources, that the so-called "apport" technique is likely to meet valuable intelligence needs. When

ST-CS-01-169-72
July 1972

fully developed, this technique would make possible the abduction
of actual objects (including documents) in enemy territory and
there transfer to friendly territory. Objects so abducted are
known as "apports." They could be returned to the point of origin
without the enemy becoming aware of this temporary abduction.

3. (U) Some of the world's most eminent scientists from the
late 1800's and early 1900's have claimed to have witnessed apport
phenomena. These include Sir William Crookes (1832-1919), British
chemist and physicist, discoverer of the element thallium and former
president of the British Association for the Advancement of Science (88);
Alfred Russel Wallace (1823-1913), British naturalist and co-
discoverer, with Charles Darwin, of the theory of evolution (89);
Johann K.F. Zoellner (1834-1882), professor of physical astronomy
at the University of Leipzig, Germany (90).

4. (U) In the discussion of such an esoteric subject as apports,
it is deemed sufficient to relate only one experience claimed to
have occurred to Sir William Crookes. The interested reader can
consult the non-cited bibliography for further references. The
following account is taken from pp. 87 and 88 of reference 88:

> "Class IX. The Appearance of Hands, either Self-
> luminous or Visible by Ordinary Light."

......"I (William Crookes) will here give no instances in which
the phenomenon has occurred in darkness, but will simply select
a few of the numerous instances in which I have seen the hands
in the light.

.................I have more than once seen, first an object move,
then a luminous cloud appear to form about it, and lastly, the
cloud condense into shape and become a perfectly formed hand.... It
is not always a mere form, but sometimes appears perfectly life-like
and graceful, the fingers moving and the flesh apparently as human as
that of any in the room. At the wrist, or arm, it becomes hazy,
and fades off into a luminous cloud. To the touch, the hand sometimes
appears icy cold and dead, at other times warm and life-like,
grasping my own with the firm pressure of an old friend. I have
retained one of these hands in my own, firmly resolved not to let
it escape. There was no struggle or effort made to get loose,
but it gradually seemed to resolve itself into vapor and faded
in that manner from my grasp."

28

ST-CS-01-169-72
July 1972

5. (U) It is a known fact that the Soviet Union takes the appearance
of luminous bodies very seriously as evidenced by the Kirlian
photography of the human body's aura (91). It appears that the
Soviets may be considering that a hand which appears out of nowhere
and can grasp, "with the firm pressure of an old friend," another
person may have first-rate military possibilities. There has
been some discussion recently about the prospects of being able to
control the apport technique to a point of sophistication where
individuals could control these "luminous clouds." The individuals
who have studied these effects (real or otherwise) have suggested
that since these bodies can travel unlimited distances and are
able to pass through solid material (walls), they might well be
used to produce instant death in military and civilian officials.
It is further conjectured that these bodies could disable military
equipment or communication nets.

6. (U) If one reads the cases and experiments mentioned here,
as well as references two through nine under PART II of the non-cited
bibliography, he can make certain deductions. If any of this
highly questionable material is true then it can be inferred that
organic matter can be transformed into "ectoplasm," that this can
be rendered invisible and impalpable and thus converted into
something which, for all practical purposes, amounts to force.
If organic matter can be converted into such "force-matter," it
seems reasonable to assume that a physical object, if similarly
converted, could travel through space.

7. (U) Two things are certain: (1) that parapsychological
phenomena are due to the little-known faculties of the subconscious
mind; and (2) that the powers of the subconscious mind are vastly
superior to those of the normal consciousness. The fantastic
memory of the subconscious mind (sometimes referred to as
"photographic memory") is a well-established fact. So is its
extraordinary mathematical ability, which has baffled trained
mathematicians no end. It seems probable that some of these
little-understood faculties of the subconscious mind have something to do with its ability to put together again an object
which it had previously disintegrated, and to manipulate the
forces involved in this process. The only way one can learn
more about these little-understood processes is through intensive
study and experimentation. The stakes seem high enough.

29

ST-CS-01-169-72
July 1972

8. (U) While the process by which matter is converted into
"force-matter" (and vice versa) may not be understood, nevertheless, one is faced with the possibility that the human mind can
disintegrate and reintegrate organic matter - a feat which seems
far more complex than the disintegration and reintegration of,
say, a stone, a piece of wood, paper, etc. Experiments show
that a human body which has lost about half its weight can be
reintegrated without loss of normal functions. Since this is
possible, it does not seem safe to exclude - without further
investigation - the possibility that inorganic matter might undergo
a similar disintegration and reintegration. After all, apport
phenomena in which physical objects have passed through solid
walls have been observed and attested to by some of the world's
most eminent scientists as well as by a host of other responsible witnesses. In view of what the human mind has demonstrated
it can do with organic matter, and in view of the very real Soviet
threat in this sector, the science of parapsychology should be
investigated to its fullest potential, perhaps to the benefit
of national defense.

9. (U) According to Pullman (92), Director of the Southeast
Hypnosis Research Center in Dallas, Texas, before the end of the
1970s, Soviet diplomats will be able to sit in their foreign
embassies and use ESP (in this case a form of the apport technique)
to steal the secrets of their enemies. (See also reference 91,
p. 216) Pullman states that a spy would be hypnotized, then
his invisible "spirit" would be ordered to leave his body, travel
across barriers of space and time to a foreign government's
security facility, and there read top-secret documents and relay
back their information. Such "astral projection" already has
been accomplished in laboratory settings, Pullman said, adding
that the Russians are probably now trying to perfect it. Pullman
further states that the Soviets are at least 25 years ahead of
the US in psychic research. According to Pullman, the Soviets
have realized the immense military advantage of the psychic ability
known as astral projection (out-of-the-body travel). In this
reference, details are given for some of Pullman's work in the
US with astral projection. Other scientists and mediums interested
in this work are professor H.A. Cahn of Northern Arizona University (92),
Doctor Charles Tart of the University of Southern California (91,92),
and Doctor V. Inyushin of Alma-ata (91). Sybil Leek, noted astrologer
and author, states, "there is great danger that within the next ten
years the Soviets will be able to steal our top secrets by using
out-of-the-body spies." Further reading, although much older,
can be found in a book by Muldoon and Carrington (93). Suggested
background reading on astral projection can be found in an excellent
article by J. Fraser Nicol in Psychic (94).

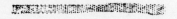

ST-CS-01-169-72
July 1972

SECTION IV - ESP AND PSYCHOKINESIS

1. (U) The reader by this time has realized that it is very
difficult to speak of one area of psychic phenomenon without
overlapping into other areas. There really can be no distinct
separation, for example, between apports and certain aspects
of telepathy; hypnosis also enters into this area. In an attempt
to illustrate the various subjects in parapsychology, however,
artificial sections were established. This is the reason for
a separate part in apports and ESP. Some aspects of hypnosis,
depending on its ultimate use, falls within parapsychology, some
areas into medicine; therefore, hypnosis is presented as a separate
section outside of this parapsychology discussion.

2. (U) Soviet research in ESP was started in the 1920's at
Leningrad University by V.M. Bekhterev. In his early work,
Bekhterev collaborated with V.L. Durov to investigate the effects
of mental suggestion on a group of performing dogs (62). It was
believed that telepathic communication depended on electromagnetic
radiation. Doctor L.L. Vasilev (95-97), shown in Illustration
One, at the Bekhterev Brain Institute set out to identify these
electromagnetic waves that carry telepathy. By 1937, Vasilev
had amassed evidence that known electromagnetic waves do not
carry telepathy. Tests were conducted in electrically shielded
chambers and over extreme distances denying the passage of electromagnetic fields (98). Some of the long range telepathy experiments
have been published (63,99,100) explaining the various techniques
employed including classical tests with Zener cards and more
unique tests with strobe lights and codes.

Illustration One - Professor L.L. Vasilev, pioneer Soviet para-
                   psychologist considered the father of Soviet
                   psychical research.

UNCLASSIFIED

ST-CS-01-169-72
July 1972

3. (U) Professor L. Vasilev died in late 1965 or early 1966
and the task of continuing telepathy research was taken by Doctor
I. Kogan. Doctor Kogan is chairman of the Bio-Information Section
of the Popov Radio and Technical Institute in Moscow. This individual is still trying to wed telepathy to the electromagnetic spectrum
(101,102). Discussion as to the existence of telepathy has been
bandied about the Soviet Union (103) and elsewhere (104) for some time.
For the sake of research the Soviet Union accepts the validity
of ESP even though the argument as to the mode of transmission
continues. Professor E.K. Naumov (105), Chairman of the Division
of Technical Parapsychology at the A.S. Popov Institute mentioned
above, conducted long range telepathy tests from Moscow to
several other cities. Illustration Two is a photograph of Naumov
with associates

Illustration Two - Sender Y. Kamenshi (left), Soviet physicist, and
                    receiver K. Nikolaev, Soviet actor, with para-
                    psychologist Edward K. Naumov (far right).

32

UNCLASSIFIED

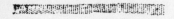

ST-CS-01-169-72
July 1972

4. (U) In 1967, the Soviet Maritime News reported, "Cosmonauts, when in orbit, seem to be able to communicate telepathically more easily with each other than with people on earth. A psi (short for psychic faculty) training system has been incorporated in the cosmonaut training program," but the News provided no further details. Some informal reports relayed to Ostrander and Schroeder (106) indicate that the Soviets are working on psi systems for space use, involving not just telepathy, but also precognition.

5. (U) Kogan's systematic parapsychology research (10?) could also be of potential value to the overall Sovi-' research and development program. Effort   ᴛᴏ optimize sensory inputs in the interest of controlling the quality of human motor activity are well known, as is the ultimate Soviet goal of achieving a perfect cybernetic man. It is of interest that both conventional psychology and parapsychology programs are headquartered in Moscow, although as depicted in the personnel and institute section the trend is decentralization, is probably no coincidence and supports the view that the latter program should not be taken lightly.

6. (U) As mentioned above, the Soviets seem preoccupied with the search for the energy that carries or facilitates telepathy transmission. Is it electromagnetic or not? The search for this unknown energy has led the Soviets to Kirlian photography; named after its inventors Semyon and Valentina Kirlian. The Kirlians developed a technique of photographing with a high frequency electrical field involving a specially constructed high frequency spark generator, tuned up and down between 75,000 to 200,000 electrical oscillations per second. Their first photographs showed turquoise and reddish-yellow patterns of flares coming out of specific channels within leaves. A magnified picture of a finger showed craters of light and flares (Illustration Three). By the 1960s research on bioluminescence revealed by Kirlian photography was going on in many Soviet universities. Perfected techniques of photographing the play of high-frequency currents on humans, plants and animals, as well as on inaminate matter have set the Soviets on some striking discoveries about the energetical nature of man. "Bio-plasma" is a term coined by the Soviets for bio-luminescent phenomenon or energy. Scientists at the Kazakh State University at Alma-ata have found that illnesses tend to show up in advance as a disordered play of flares from the "bio-plasma" long before they manifest in the physical body. According to Ostrander and Schroeder, the Soviets may be attempting to link Kirlian photography with computers, among other things, to instantly analyze the spectra of colors appearing in the vari-colored flares from the living body.

33

ST-CS-01-169-72
July 1972

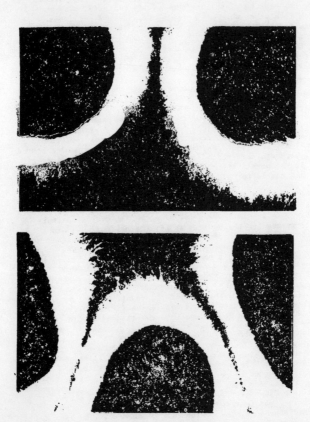

Illustration Three - Upper photograph displays flares of energy from
fingers of the left and right hand of an individual by Kirlian
photography. Lower photograph shows the fingers of three different
people and how the aura of "energy" of each remains intact, yet
interplays in long thread like fibers in the open area between them.

34

ST-CS-01-169-72
July 1972

7. (U)   It is believed that if there is any positive basis for
Kirlian photography and the "bio-Plasma" body of humans, the
Soviets may be closer than is thought on the controlled use of
the apport techniques and possible astral projection phenomenon.

8.   (U) Doctor A. Podshibyakin, an electrophysiologist at the
Institute of Clinical Physiology in Kiev, has found that by charting
acupuncture points a correlation exists between the "bio-plasma"
and changes on the surface of the sun. At the exact moment solar
flares (sun spots) occur, there are changes in the electrical
potential of the skin's acupuncture points. These electrical
charges are measured by a tobiscope (probably a simple wheatstone
bridge device). In some way, the "bio-plasma" of the body is
sensitive to these solar explosions the instant they occur even
though it takes about two days for the cosmic particles to reach
the earth.

9.   (U) The most significant use of Kirlian photography is in the
area of psychokinesis or mind over matter (PK). Doctor Genady
Sergeyev (75) of the A.A. Uktomskii Military Institute in Leningrad
believes Kirlian photography may uncover the mechanism of PK.
Sergeyev is a prominent mathematician for the Soviet military
who works closely with an electrophysiologist from the University
of Leningrad, Doctor L. Pavlova. Sergeyev has devised important
mathematical and statistical methods for analyzing the EEG (107)
which allowed parapsychologists to follow and depict the actions
of telepathy in the brain (108). The type of work reported by
Sergeyev in 1967 and 1968 is just now beginning to appear in the
US efforts to understand the transmission of telepathy (109,110).
Sergeyev has conducted several years of intensive lab research
on the outstanding PK psychic in Leningrad, Nina Kulagina
(pseudonym Nelya Mikhailova). Illustration Four is a photograph of
Doctor G. Sergeyev and Illustration Five is a photograph of
Mrs. Kulagina. Sergeyev registered heightened biological lumi-
nescence radiating from Kulagina's eyes during the apparent movement
of objects by PK. Sergeyev postulates that the "bio-plasma" of
the human body must interact with the environment to produce PK.
Sergeyev emphasizes when target objects are placed in a vacuum,
Kulagina is unable to move them. Barcus (111) in the United
States reports some unusual occurrences during psychic photography
especially of the eyes. Reportedly, Kulagina has caused the
movement of a wide range of non-magnetic objects: (under strict
scientific control) large crystal bowls, clock pendulums, bread,

35

ST-CS-01-169-72
July 1972

matches, etc. In one test, a raw egg was placed in a salt solution
inside a sealed aquarium six feet away from her. Researchers
report she was able to use PK to separate the yoke from the white
of the egg. Observations by Western scientists of Mrs. Kulagina's
PK ability has been reported with verification of her authentic
ability (112,113). These same Western scientists have reported
that as of February 1971, they have not been able to visit or
observe Mrs. Kulagina. A veil of secrecy has been placed on
Sergeyev and Mrs. Kulagina for unknown reasons.

10. (U) Rather than simply observing PK, the Soviets typically
turned to instrumentation. Mrs. Kulagina was subjected to a
number of physiological electronic measuring devices and tested
for important body functions during her PK demonstrations. The
Soviets found that at the moment an object begins to move, all
of Mrs. Kulagina's body processes speed up drastically - heart,
breathing, brain activity - and the electromagnetic fields around
her body all begin to pulse in rhythm. Soviet researchers
postulate that it was these rhythmic "vibrations" that cause
objects to be attracted or repelled to her. Illustration Six
shows a photographic sequence of Kulagina's PK ability.

11. (U) Scientists report (113) that Kulagina has been able
to stop the beating of a frog's heart in solution and to re-activate
it! This is perhaps the most significant PK test done and its
military implications in controlled offensive behavior, if true,
are extremely important.

12. (U) Space does not permit a discussion on other important
parapsychological phenomena such as eyeless sight (75,114-129),
which appeared to be more of a fad than anything else. However
since the mid 1960s, the "eyeless sight" fad has subsided and
serious research has proceeded quietly at the State Pedagogical
Institute in Sverdlovsk, off bounds to foreigners (75). Space
in this report does not permit a discussion of psychotronic generators, devices which are reported to be able to store human bio-plasmic
forces for later use (75). For further reading on ESP, see the
non-cited bibliography; Section V, numbers 12-30.

36

UNCLASSIFIED

ST-CS-01-169-72
July 1972

Illustration Four - Photograph
of G.A. Sergeyev, prominent
scientist at A.A. Uktomskii
Military Institute, Leningrad
with an assistant.

Illustration Five - Nina Kulagina,
who reportedly moves objects by
sheer will (PK).

37

UNCLASSIFIED

201

ST-CS-01-169-72
July 1972

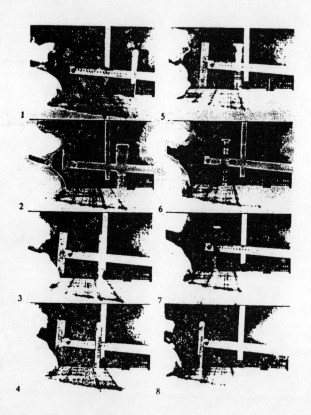

Illustration Six – This series of photos shows Nina Kulagina moving a metallic cigar tube by PK. Scale in background is in centimeters.

38

ST-CS-01-169-72
July 1972

SECTION V - SUMMARY AND MILITARY IMPLICATIONS

1. (U) The following discussion is based on a report by
Ostrander and Schroeder (75). The authors ask the question,
"Is ESP a weapon of war?" All research on ESP in the USSR is
funded by the government. The authors claim that their sources
indicate that psi research with military potential is well-financed
by the Soviet Army, KGB, and other paramilitary agencies. Soviet
scientists doing psi research in nonmilitary areas often have
trouble obtaining funds. Doctor Milan Ryzl (131) reports that secret
psi research associated with state security and defense is going
on in the USSR. Communist state authorities, the military and
the KGB display an unusual disproportionate interest in parapsychology. The Soviets are attempting to apply ESP to both
police and military use (See appendix VI for biographic data
on Ryzl). According to Ryzl, some years ago a project was begun
in the USSR to apply telepathy to indoctrinate and re-educate
antisocial elements. It was hoped that suggestion at a distance
could induce individuals, without their being aware of it, to adopt
the officially desired political and social attitudes. Research
in this field of endeavor will hopefully become clearer in the section
on hypnosis later in this report. Reports of psi research in Soviet
submarines help confirm military involvement in parapsychology.
According to Stone (74), there is clandestine psi research going on at
the Pavlov Institute of Higher Nervous Activity in Moscow, the
Durov Institute, and certain areas in Sibera. Obviously, telepathy
and clairvoyance would make ideal additions to a spy arsenal and
such undercover groups are constantly said to be supporting ESP
research in the USSR. "One conclusion seems justified," says
Doctor Ryzl (130). "Parapsychology in Communist countries and
especially the USSR occupies a strong position. We can expect
it to be developed with determination." According to Ostrander
and Schroeder, the USSR is ahead of the US in certain areas of
technical psi research. The authors report that the USSR is
ahead of the US in discoveries about the physical essence of the
human being and how psi functions in and through us. They are
ahead of the US in uncovering the basic energy behind psi. They
are ahead of the US in attempts to control factors like the influence
of magnetic weather on psi tests. They appear to be ahead of the
US in seeking out and creating conditions that unlock the psi
potential present in every human being.

2. (U) In summary, what is the strategic threat posed by the
current "explosion" in Soviet parapsychological research? Soviet
efforts in the field of psi research, sooner or later, might
enable them to do some of the following:

39

ST-CS-01-169-72
July 1972

a. Know the contents of top secret US documents, the movements of our troops and ships and the location and nature of our military installations.

b. Mold the thoughts of key US military and civilian leaders, at a distance.

c. Cause the instant death of any US official, at a distance.

d. Disable, at a distance, US military equipment of all types including space craft.

3. (U) It is generally conceded that the above four areas sound like science fiction, however, the literature appears to support (b) as being the most possible use of psi phenomena during the time frame of this study. Again from Ostrander and Schroeder who cite Oliver Caldwell, an expert on Soviet affairs and past-acting commissioner for International Education in HEW, as follows:

> "I am amazed at the skepticism and sometimes hostility which I encounter when I try to tell Americans about some of the experimentation which is taking place in the USSR in parapsychology and related fields. I find this strange because there is available documentation in translation which substantiates most of the things I saw in the USSR. I am really disturbed, because if the United States does not make a serious effort to move forward on this new frontier, in another ten years it may be too late."

4. (U) In closing this section on parapsychology a quote from astronaut Edgar D. Mitchell, Jr. is appropriate (131).

> "Extrasensory perception is not a matter of belief. There is a great deal of serious scientific work being done in it, and it has been established over the last thirty years that it is a matter of proba- bility, and the probabilities have been established beyond chance. I think it is an important work. I happen to be curious about it, and thus have been pur- suing it for many years. This happened to be an opportunity (Apollo 14 lunar mission) to do another little step - a piece in the scientific puzzle of what man's all about."

40

UNCLASSIFIED

ST-CS-01-I69-72
July 1972

PART III

MENTAL SUGGESTION AND CONTROLLED BEHAVIOR

SECTION I - HYPNOSIS

PART A - The Use of Hypnosis in Medicine - USSR

1. (U) In the latter half of the nineteenth century, many French and German researchers began to use hypnosis as a therapeutic aid and to study the way in which it worked. In the Soviet Union, pioneer work in hypnosis was undertaken by V. Danilyevski, A. Tokarski, and V. Bekhterev (see Part III, Section IV).

2. (U) V. Danilyevski discovered that the major characteristics shown by man in a state of hypnosis such as lower sensitivity, "wax-like" flexibility of muscles and joints, and suppressed movements, were also typical of animals in a similar state. This led him to assert that hypnosis in man was identical in nature to hypnosis in animals. A. Tokarski proved that hypnosis and suggestion, like other psychical phenomena were determined entirely by the influence of the environment on man. He wholeheartedly supported the view that hypnosis was an effective treatment for a wide variety of disorders. V. Bekhterev applied hypnosis widely for treatment. He maintained that verbal suggestion played a big role in developing a state of hypnotic sleep; physical stimuli merely facilitated the achievement of this state. I. Pavlov advanced a scientifically based theory of the nature of hypnosis and its potential use as a method of treatment. In 1935 he described hypnosis as "the standard method in the physiological struggle against the pathogenic agent." Pavlov's school gave experimental support to the view that hypnosis was a specific variety of sleep, long before that view had been arrived at empirically. This view had already been advanced in the last century by most doctors and scientists who were concerned with the theory of hypnosis and its application to therapeutic practice. On the basis of experiments on animals and later on humans, the phasic suppression theory developed into a firm physiological foundation for understanding hypnosis and suggestion and the way in which they work. The theory held that hypnotic sleep is a transitional stage between wakefulness and sleep and that there is an active "watch" point in the cerebral cortex of both hemispheres (rapport).

3. (U) The three generally recognized stages of hypnosis are sleepiness, hypotaxia, and somnambulism or, respectively, light, medium and deep hypnosis. At the first stage of hypnosis, the

41

UNCLASSIFIED

ST-CS-01-169-72
July 1972

unconditioned responses in most cases hardly differ from the
responses in wakefulness. At the second stage, altered unconditioned vascular responses begin to prevail over normal vascular
responses to stimulation, and thus give evidence of hypnotic
phases in the cortex of both hemispheres. The suppression process
is most obvious with regard to extent and intensity at the third
stage, the deep stage of hypnosis known as somnambulism. Since
there is no vascular response to most of the unconditioned stimuli,
this means that complete suppression prevails. The rare unconditioned
vascular reflexes are of small magnitude, are extended in time and
are characterized by a prolonged latent period.

4. (U) Soviet psychotherapists believe that hypnosis is one of
the leading methods for the treatment of mental disorders. The
Soviets concentrate on the "word" as an adequate stimulus for the
development of the hypnotic state. The tremendous role played
by the emotional message carried by the word should not be overlooked. The psychotherapist will achieve results depending on
the emotional content of the entire system of contact with the
patient. The greater the emotional content the better the results.
Soviets recommend that the psychotherapist takes into account not
only the meaning of what he is trying to achieve through suggestion,
but also the emotional content of his work, his contact with the
patient, his confidence in his own abilities, and the effectiveness
of psychotherapeutic treatment in general.

5. (U) The Soviets believe that the hypnotic state offers the
researcher the means of penetrating into the physiological fundamentals
of human thought and behavior. The Russians conceive of no other
state (hypnosis) which would enable the scientist to simplify
human thought by splitting it into its component parts thus permitting
him to get to the root of this most complex of nature's phenomena,
to control and subordinate it for purposes of research. K. Platonov,
the patriarch of Soviet psychotherapists said (132): "I still
maintain that hypnotherapy is the main stem of psychotherapy.
Hypnotherapy helps us understand better the mechanisms of all
other forms of psychotherapy and, therefore, to master them better."

6. (U) The Soviets stress the use of hypnosis in patients
suffering from disorders of the gastrointestinal tract especially
if neurotic symptoms accompany such disorders. They further stress
the use of hypnotherapy in surgical cases thus providing for a decrease
in anesthetic and drug usage. Hypnosis is also being studied for its
effectiveness in treating alcohol addiction. At first they approached
this problem with the idea of developing an emotionally negative

42

TIM RIFAT

ST-CS-01-169-72
July 1972

nauseous reflex to the taste and smell of alcoholic drinks; this
method was later abandoned for lack of positive results. The method
now employed is to instill in the patient the view that excessive
drinking will inevitably lead to physical and mental destruction.
The Soviets seek to change the patient's mental outlook on alcohol
and to convince them that drinking is impermissible for moral and
ethical reasons. In other words, mental manipulation or behavior
alteration.

PART B - Hypnosis and Controlled Behavior

1. (U) The possible military uses of hypnotism has many rather
bizarre applications. Although there is no concrete proof that
hypnosis will play an important role in controlling behavior
in military situations, some uses will be mentioned. Biderman and
Zimmer (133) discuss hypnosis and other possible alternatives for
defense against brainwashing.

2. (U) The following discussion is based on a report by Estabrooks
(134). According to the author, the facts and ideas presented
are, so to speak, too true to be good, but no psychologist of
standing would deny the validity of the basic ideas involved.
Of interest to this discussion are some of the more unfamiliar
facets of hypnotism which make it of use in warfare. If hypnotism can be used to advantage, we can rest assured that it will
be so employed.

3. (U) One in every five adult humans can be placed into the
hypnotic state - somnambulism - of which they will have no memory
whatsoever when they awaken. From the military viewpoint there
are a few facts which are of great interest. Can this prospective
subject be hypnotized against his will? Obviously no POW will
be cooperative if he knows that the hypnotist is looking for
military information, nor will any ordinary citizen if he suspects
that the operator will use him to blow up a munitions plant. The
answer to this vital question is yes though hypnotists prefer
to say "without his consent" instead of "against his will." There
are disguised techniques available for hypnotizing an unsuspecting
or unwilling subject. The Soviets believe that telepathy may be
one such method.

4. (U) Multiple personality can be caused by hypnotism. One
could deliberately set up a condition of multiple personality
to further the ends of military intelligence and in the development of the "super spy." In his normal waking state which is called
Personality A, or PA, this individual will become a rabid communist.

43

ST-CS-01-169-72
July 1972

He will join the party, follow the party line and make himself as
objectionable as possible to the authorities. Note that he will
be acting in good faith. He is a communist, or rather his PA
is a communist·and will behave as such. Then develop Personality B
(PB), the secondary personality, the unconscious personality.
This personality is rabidly American and anti-communist. It has
all the information possessed by PA, the normal personality, whereas
PA does not have this advantage. The proper training of a person
for this role would be long and tedious, but once he was trained,
one would have a super spy compared to any creation in a mystery
story. The super spy plays his role as a communist in his waking
state, aggressively, consistently, fearlessly. But his PB is a
loyal American, and PB has all the memories of PA. As a loyal
American, he will not hesitate to divulge those memories, but be
sure he has the opportunity to do so when occasion demands. Here
is how this technique would work. Let us choose the Cubans as
examples. One could easily secure, say, one hundred excellent
hypnotic subjects of Cuban stock, living in the United States, who
spoke their language fluently, and then work on these subjects.
In hypnotism one would build up their loyalty to our country; but
out of hypnotism, in the "waking" or normal state, one would do
the opposite, striving to convince them that they had a genuine
grievance against this country and encouraging them to engage in
fifth column activities. So one builds up a case of dual personality.
They would be urged in the waking state to become fifth columnist
enemies to the United States, but also point out to them in hypnotism
that this was really a pose, that their real loyalty lay with
this country, offering them protection and reward for their
activities. Through them one would hope to be kept informed of
the activities of their "friends," this information, of course,
being obtained in the trance state. They would also be very useful
as "plants" in concentration camps or in any other situations
where it was suspected their services might be of use to our
intelligence department. Once again these people would have a
great advantage over ordinary "informers." Convinced of their
own innocence, they would play the fifth column role with the
utmost sincerity. This conviction of innocence would probably
be their greatest protection. Again, if suspected, no one could
obtain from them any useful information. Only a very few key
people could throw them into the trance and, without this, any
attempt to get information would be useless. There are some
difficulties that would be encountered in building up an organization of such personnel. Hardly one somnambulist in ten or even
a hundred according to Estabrooks would be suitable for such spy
work; and the determining of this suitability would be a difficult
task. But, Estabrooks reports, it could be done, and once accomplished would repay amply for all the trouble.

44

ST-CS-01-169-72
July 1972

5. (U) The possibility of creating assassins through hypnotic
techniques on POWs exists. As was pointed out above, the subject
does not need to be willing to enter into such a condition. Once
the captive has been placed in a suitable hypnotic state then
one need only to establish the post-hypnotic suggestion or plan
for the assassination. After the prisoner is released and returned
to his organization, he will carry out his assignment through his
unconscious state, while appearing perfectly rehabilitated in his
wakeful state. The main problem in the assassin plan is in the
area of post-hypnotic reinforcement. There have been some ideas
mentioned that suggest one needs to establish the reinforcement
pattern during initial hypnosis; some object that will reinforce
his goal whenever he looks at it, hears a certain sound, etc.
The real problem for the friendly forces is the detection of
these mentally altered individuals. At the present time there
is no fool proof method of detection. There is no test by which
one can discover these agents. Blood pressure, heart rate, electroencephalograph, psychogalvanic reflex, all these devices which
one can use to detect the most subtle bodily changes are worthless
for there are no bodily changes. Drugs, at least for the present,
appear to be of no value. Further, there are certain safeguards
that the hypnotic method provides for the enemy. Most important
is the conviction of innocence which the man himself has. He
would never "act guilty" and if ever accused of seeking information
would act quite honestly indignant, the conviction of innocence
on the part of the agent is perhaps his greatest safeguard under
questioning by our authorities. The Soviets are aware of the
above mentioned possibilities and appear to be using certain aspects
of psi research in order to manipulate an individuals mental
behavior toward these activities.

PART C - Artificial Reincarnation Through Hypnosis

1. (U) Vladimir L. Raikov, M.D., a Soviet psychiatrist, has
claimed that hypnotic phenomenon can be utilized for what he claims
to be "artificial reincarnations." For example, Raikov claims
that it is possible to hypnotically suggest to a girl who studies
violin that she is the virtuoso violinist Fritz Kreisler. It
is interesting to note, says Raikov, that her manner of playing
at this time is reminescent to that of Kreisler. If so desired,
it is also possible to create this capacity in an awake state.
Raikov has converted persons who have no desire to paint, invent
complex machines, or to play music into masters through hypnosis.
Raikov reports that he is able to evoke this mental alteration
only when the subject is in an exceedingly deep trance which is

45

ST-CS-01-169-72
July 1972

a new form of an active trance. Existence in a state of hypnosis and simultaneous perception of individual moments of reality is usually characteristic of light, superficial hypnosis, however, as mentioned above, Raikov claims that he uses deep hypnosis. As opposed to normal hypnosis, the new found talents of Raikov's subjects retain in part of their conscious equipment the ability gained by this technique. Raikov explains, "The student is thinking, forming relationships and judgments, acquiring his own experience during reincarnation. Consequently the creative potential he develops, draws out, becomes his own." (75)

2. (U) Raikov has used the EEG to prove his supposition that the trance of reincarnation is a new phenomenon. The usual passive trance of deep hypnosis shows via the EEG alpha rest rhythm. In reincarnation the alpha disappears completely and the EEG shows a pattern like that normally recorded in high wakefulness (135). Reincarnation appears to be the antithesis of sleep.

3. (U) Raikov has worked closely with V. Adamenko, a physicist who reportedly has invented the CCAP (Conductivity of the Channels of Acupuncture Points) device. This machine, it is claimed, registers energy flow in the body using as check points for its electrodes the acupuncture points of traditional Chinese medicine. Adamenko reportedly detects changes in body energy caused by alterations of consciousness and varying emotional states. With subjects attached to the CCAP, Raikov put them through various forms of hypnosis. At the end of many sessions the graphs from the CCAP were checked by Raikov and Adamenko. They claim to have found a pronounced difference between the different forms of hypnosis. They now claim to be able to chart objectively the physical activity of the mind in states of somnambulism and various levels of hypnosis. They report that these states are very hard to measure by any other method. Apparently there is even more activity in the mind during reincarnation than there is when a person is wide awake. This corroborates the EEG findings that reincarnation is a state of "super wakefulness" and that it is a very different animal from regular, passive hypnosis, according to Raikov.

4. (U) Raikov's methods are thought to have great possibilities for treating ailments such as alcoholism and certain neuroses. His experiments are the subject of a film "Seven Steps Beyond the Horizon." (136)

46

TIM RIFAT

ST-CS-01-169-72
July 1972

5. (U) Where the Soviets are going to go with Raikov's work is
open to conjecture. There is some indication that the Soviets
believe that Raikov's work and the CCAP device may unlock many
of the mysteries behind ESP and other psi phenomena. If any
of the above is true, this work may be a new way of looking inside
and catching the subtle interplay between thought and body, psyche
and soma. The CCAP device may have a much wider use than charting
the mental states of reincarnated artists.

PART D - Telepathic Hypnosis

1. (U) According to Ostrander and Schroeder (75), the ability
to put people to sleep and wake them up telepathically from a
distance of a few yards to over a thousand miles became the most
thoroughly tested and perfected contribution of the Soviets to
international parapsychology. It is reported that the ability
to control a person's consciousness with telepathy is being further
studied and tested in laboratories in Leningrad and Moscow. The
work was started in the early 1920s but was not publicized until
the early 1960s. The work was begun by K.O. Kotkov, a psychologist
from Kharkov University, in 1924. Kotkov could telepathically
obliterate an experimental subject's consciousness from short
distances or from the opposite side of town. The work was documented
by Vasilev (62) who conducted research of his own but could not
reveal it under Stalin's regime. The reality of telepathic sleep-
wake, backed by columns of data, might be the most astonishing
part of Vasilev's experiments in mental suggestion. See reference
62, pages 75 through 88.

2. (U) Parapsychologists in Leningrad and Moscow are involved
in the telepathic manipulation of consciousness, now recording
successes with the EEG. Doctor V. Raikov (see PART C of this
section) is involved in this EEG research as well as E. Naumov.
Naumov reports that mental telepathy woke up a hypnotized subject
(by telepathy) six of eight times. Naumov remarked that as soon
as the telepathic "wake up" is sent, trance becomes less and
less deep, full consciousness returning in twenty to thirty
seconds (137). In the Leningrad laboratory of Doctor Paul Gulyaiev
(Bekhterev Brain Institute), friends of subjects have been trained
to put them to sleep telepathically (138).

3. (U) Why are the Soviets again hard at work on the telepathic
control of consciousness? Doctor I. Kogan, like Vasilev, is
probably doing it for theoretical reasons; still trying mathe-
matically to prove that an electromagnetic carrier of telepathy
is possible. Why other scientists may be delving into control

ST-CS-01-169-72
July 1972

of consciousness by ESP is another question. During telepathic
sleep is an individual simply dreaming his own private dreams
or does someone else hold sway? The current Soviets have not
divulged the psychological details about their telepathic manipulation of consciousness. Vasilev describes some revelations in
his book (62) but little else has been reported. Doctor Stefan
Manczarski of Poland predicts that this new field of telepathy.
will open up new avenues for spreading propaganda. He feels
that the electromagnetic theory is valid and believes, therefore,
that telepathy can be amplified like radio waves. Telepathy would
then become a subtle new modus for the "influencers" of the world
(139). Doctor Manczerski's wave ideas are still very debatable,
but what about telepathy someday becoming a tool for influencing
people?

4. (U) Hypnotizing someone telepathically probably comes over
as a more eerie, mystifying, almost diabolical act in the US
than it does in the Soviet Union. The US is really just becoming
adjusted to some of the aspects of hypnotism. Since the turn of
the century, the Soviets have been exploring and perfecting the
various advantages that hypnotism provides. In the Soviet Union,
hypnotism is a common tool like X-rays, used in medicine, psychotherapy,
physiology, psychology, and experimental pedagogy.

5. (U) The Soviets have been reportedly working on the effects
of drugs used in combination with psychic tests. Vasilev used
mescarine in the early days and more recently M.S. Smirnov, of
the Laboratory of Vision, Institute of Problems of Information
Transmission of the USSR Academy of Science, has been obtaining
psychic success with psilocybin (140).

6. (U) The tests that Vasilev had perfected may have a more
interesting future in them than the developer had imagined. Manipulating someone else's consciousness with telepathy, guiding him
in trance.....colorful uses are too easy to conjure. The ability
to focus a mental whammy on an enemy through hypnotic telepathy
has surely occurred to the Soviets. In espionage, one could
telepathically hypnotize an individual with the post-hypnotic
suggestion to steal classified documents or detonate important
military equipment. The mission is accomplished and the individual does not even know that he has done anything. Ryzl (see
appendix VI) stated in Psychic (141), "The bulk of recent telepathy
research in the USSR is concerned with the transmission of behavior
impulses - or research to subliminally control an individual's
conduct." Visiting Soviet psi labs in 1967, Doctor Ryzl says

48

ST-CS-01-169-72
July 1972

he was told by a Soviet, "When suitable means of propaganda
are cleverly used, it is possible to mold any man's conscience
so that in the end he may misuse his abilities while remaining
convinced that he is serving an honest purpose." (140) Ryzl
continues, "The USSR has the means to keep the results of such
research secret from the rest of the world and, as practical
applications of these results become possible, there is no doubt
that the Soviet Union will do so." What will ESP be used for?
"To make money, and as a weapon," Ryzl states flatly.

SECTION II - CONDITIONING THROUGH SUGGESTION

PART A - Hypnopedia

1. (U) The subject of hypnopedia or sleep-learning has been
openly discussed in the Soviet literature for the past decade
(142-161). One of the most thorough Soviet reports has been
prepared by Bliznichenko (162) in 1966. Dodge and Lamont (163)
have published a report that covers the field of hypnopedia in
the Soviet Union through 1968. Further elucidation of this subject
in this report, with the exception of a discussion of possible
trends in this area since 1969, is believed to be redundant and
unnecessary.

2. (U) The last decade of Soviet hypnopedia research has led
them into new concepts of memory improvement. It is believed
that areas such as subliminal perception and subconscious learning
with hypnosis were borne from the basic research involved in
hypnopedia training. The most recent indication of new Soviet
interest in utilizing the subconscious as a reserve for the retention
of facts is a booklet written by L.I. Kuproyanovich (164). This
book describes the equipment and technical means used for improving
memory as well as the prospective uses of cybernetics for memory
retention. One of the more interesting features of this book
is a discussion on subliminal acquisition of facts. This is an
area of concern when one is speaking of conditioned behavior or
mental alteration. It is also an area seldom discussed in open
Soviet literature. PART B of this section will briefly discuss
some Soviet work in subliminal perception and possible uses for
this technique.

3. (U) The following discussion on memory and hypnopedia is based
on Kuproyanovich's report. The author states that the subconscious
is one of the unused reserves for the retention of facts. Memory
operation on the subconscious level takes place without our realizing

49

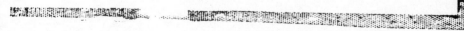

ST-CS-01-169-72
July 1972

it, and a man - without noticing it - has better retention or proceeds
to a solution of a complex problem even when he does not specifically
think of it, such as when he is out for a stroll. And, although
information processing on the subconscious level is widely separated
from the process that takes place in the conscious state, the
transfer from the subconscious to the conscious is carried out
instantaneously. This is why a solution or recollection occurs
unexpectedly after the memory operates on the subconscious level.
There is one other interesting property that is characteristic of
the subconscious: the simultaneous processing of several parallel
streams of information. This fact is extremely important, because
when it occurs, there is a wider circle of associations and analogies
that can become the stimuli and sources of new, unexpected recollec-
tions and decisions. And, finally, the subconscious operation of
memory is more subject to the influence of emotions and feelings.
Hypnopedia with automatic tracking (biological feedback as with
the use of an electroencephalogram), in which - with the aid of
the brains biocurrents - information transmission is carried out
at the most favorable moment for retention and the sleep level
is regulated by the biocurrents, is, in the opinion of the author
more promising than the generally accepted methods of sleep learning.
Experiments in instructing while in a semisleep state artifically
induced in the daytime show good results. These methods have
begun to be used both in the USSR and in non-US countries (Bulgaria,
for example). Before each training session, a suggestion is
received from the tape recorder that puts the student into a semi-
sleeping state. After this, as in hypnopedia sessions, the information
to be retained is given. The new method is as effective as hypnopedia,
insofar as the quantity of information retained is concerned, but
has the advantageous difference that it can be used in the daytime.

4. (U) Hypnosis is an effective means for improving perception
and retention of information. However, hypnosis can be used only
by people with medical training, and under certain conditions.
The use of equipment that automatically induces and regulates
hypnosis has made the problem of using it somewhat simpler. The
most advantageous use of it will be made by an automatic device
for hypnosis during the simultaneous instruction of a large number
of students in hypnotic training classes specially created for
this purpose. Some institutes in Japan and the United States
are already instructing students under hypnosis according to
Kuproyanovich.

50

ST-CS-01-169-72
July 1972

5. (U) The important feature of Soviet hypnopedia research is believed to be the conclusions that the Soviets are now arriving at in regards to the manipulation of the subconscious area of the brain. Much of the early work that is described by Dodge and Lamont (163) provide the foundation for a much broader understanding of the various methods available for conditioning the human mind. Hypnopedia research has produced an interest in the Soviet Union for the use of the psychology of memory and the subconscious in order to create conditions and functional states for improving memory operation. The areas that grew out of basic hypnopedic research include hypnosis, autogenic training and subliminal perception. It is believed that these newer areas of endeavor bear more scrutiny than the more mundane area of hypnopedia.

PART B – Subliminal Perception

1. (U) The use of subliminal perception in the advertising industry gained some notoriety in 1958 when an article appeared in the New York Times uncovering the technique developed by the New York firm known as the Subliminal Projection Company, Inc (165). Subliminal perception is a psychological belief that persons can be stimulated below (sub) the threshold (limen) of consciousness. Another interpretation, more commonly used, is that persons can supposedly be stimulated without being aware of it. Hypnopedia, for example, might be considered a form of subliminal perception.

2. (U) In the late 1950s there was much debate as to the moral and ethical use of subliminal advertising. There was in the US a strong moral repugnance to the use of subliminal perception in TV advertising. The furor raised by the public and the press concluded when the Federal Communications Commission entered the picture in 1957. An excellent overview on the subject of subliminal stimulation was prepared by McConnell et al in 1958 (166). The authors attempt to clarify the issues surrounding the application of subliminal perception. The article examines the levels of behavior that may be influenced by subliminal stimulation as well as the ethical questions that naturally arise. The article contains an extensive bibliography.

3. (U) The distinction between subliminal and supraliminal perception cannot always be clearly made. Because of the statistical nature of thresholds, it is possible that many subjects may receive some cues from stimuli even though they are supposedly below threshold. Also, what may for one person, at a particular

UNCLASSIFIED

ST-CS-01-179-72
July 1972

time with a particular stimulus, be below threshold may for another
person, or the same person in another situation, be above threshold.
Insofar as subliminality is crucial for motivational or security
reasons, stimuli of such low intensity may be required that little
effect could be obtained. As one review of literature in this
area concluded: "There does not appear to be substantial evidence
for subception (subliminal perception) as a distinct phenomenon." (167)
Another review of literature in this area (168) concluded that
most effects that suggest discrimination without awareness can be
attributed to imperfections in measurement techniques or other
shortcomings of experimental methodology and cannot be clearly
demonstrated to be related to perceptual variables. Other research
in the communications field suggests that research on reactions
to propaganda might more profitably focus upon other factors than
upon intensity of stimulation.

4. (U) There is strong moral repugnance to the use of subliminal
perception in propaganda. This was made evident a few years ago
when some efforts were made (169) to introduce subliminal stimulation
into TV as an advertising technique. Insofar as the US is trying
to project abroad an image of itself as a nation encouraging individual freedom, it would seem extremely inappropriate to risk being
detected employing propaganda techniques which appear to invade
human privacy. It is highly doubtful that the American public
would condone such use abroad, just as broadcasters have been
reluctant to use this technique for fear of hostile reactions on
the part of their audiences. While the risks of national public
and international condemnation may be run for worthwhile objectives,
if no great advantage accrues the risky approach would be inappropriate.

5. (U) The possibility of utilizing subliminal perception for
military purposes may have been realized by the Soviets. As
mentioned earlier, there is a distinct lack of open literature
from the USSR dealing with this subject. However, there is mention
of it in Kuproyanovich's recent book (164). The author states
that the showing of movie films and slides, along with being
an additional retention source, has yet another important value
that aids in revealing the subconscious reserves of memory. Earlier
in the author's text he describes the showing of movies where
additional frames, of an advertising nature, were inserted between
the film's basic frames. It was shown that, because of their
brief but sufficiently frequent appearance, this technique acted
on the subconscious (similar to US work in the 1950s). The Soviet

52

UNCLASSIFIED

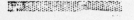

ST-CS-01-169-72
July 1972

technique, when it is necessary to strengthen memory or to create
an emotion, utilizes supplemental frames at the rate of one per
25 basic frames. These supplemental frames, according to the
Soviets, should contain explanations amplifying the memory of the
basic film or creating some mood. Thus whether the movie watcher
wishes it or not, the information filtering through his subconscious
will create an overall background mood supplementing the basic one.
According to Kuproyanovich, these films, which enlist both the
conscious and subconscious memory functions, are very promising.

6. (U)   According to a French expert in the field of
electrosleep and electroanesthesia, the Soviets used a motion
picture technique to interrogate prisoners (170). The French
expert described the method as follows:

> "A movie film which shows what you want the
> individual to do is flashed on a screen at
> double the normal running speed. A speed of 24
> frames per second was considered critical to the
> success of the method. While the movie is being
> shown, a 35mm slide projector is used to flash a
> written statement of what you want the person to
> do. The slide is interposed between each frame
> of the movie projection. The net effect of the
> operation is that neither the movie scene nor
> the slide can be read, but the subconscious picks
> up the information. As the individual becomes
> disorientated, he then responds to questions.
> Apparently there are no long term or residual
> effects as a result of the procedure. It was
> described as being particularly useful for
> interrogating hostile prisoners."

With the above description, Kuproyanovich's work and the Soviets
knowledge in all areas of human behavior, it is not unlikely
that they may be in a position to militarily threaten their
enemies with sophisticated mind manipulation techniques in
controlled situations or in the field.

PART C - Suggestology

1. (U) Suggestology is a new "ology" defined by the communist
countries as the scientific study of suggestion. It is reported
to be a method of reaching and making use of the unknown reserves,

53

ST-CS-01-169-72
July 1972

powers, and abilities of the human mind. In some areas it over-
laps with parapsychology. One individual responsible for
many of the claims for success in the field of suggestology is
Doctor George Lozanov, head of the Institute of Suggestology and
Parapsychology in Sofia, Bulgaria. Through extensive research
he has discovered laws of suggestion which he has applied in
many fields from medicine to education. The Bulgarian methods
of suggestion are mentioned in this report because some of the
theories have been adopted by the Soviets in their work on autosuggestion.

2. (U) Suggestology is not hypnosis. With this method of
conditioning, the individual is always in the waking state. It
has been reported that suggestology has been used successfully
in medicine especially in functional disorders of the nervous
system. The healing is based on the positive suggestion that
nothing is wrong; it is a type of mind over body phenomenon.
Sanatorium officials in Bulgaria testify that many patients are
cured after a few sessions of positive thought patterning (171).
Suggestology has been reported to be successful in replacing
anesthetics in surgical cases as well as aiding the patient in
decreasing his own blood flow. It is further claimed that with
suggestology the incisions from surgical operations heal much
faster than usual (172). The Bulgarians believe the technique
of waking suggestion (not hypnosis) will continue to find a wider
and very useful place in the practice of medicine (173).

3. (U) The possibility for upgrading the memorizing process and
for accelerating the automation of habits, discovered through
suggestological experimentation, offers possibilities for the
development of a new science: suggestopedagogy (suggestopedy).
The suggestopedic method of mastering a foreign language is not a
variety of the current methods (audio-visual, audio-linguistic,
conscious-practical, hypnopedic, etc.), but a qualitatively new
training process in terms of its content, structure, and results.
This method uses suggestion not as a means for some kind of mystical
influence, not as some kind of abstract, "vague" factor, but as
a specific method for directly influencing the emotional world and
intellectual activities, the entire personality, of the student.
Practical experience has revealed that a suggestion is not a sort
of "third grade, marginal factor." Controlled and used purposefully,
it creates conditions for upgrading considerably the capacity to
memorize and to assimilate knowledge faster. In the training process
usually suggestive methods are used spontaneously, intuitively.

54

TIM RIFAT

UNCLASSIFIED

ST-CS-01-169-72
July 1972

Quite frequently, a number of hindering factors are present in
the course of the training process, preventing the spontaneous
adoption of the new material, its energizing and retention. The
new aspect of the suggestopedic training process is that all means
of suggestion - authority, complexity, intonation, music, etc. -
have been scientifically selected and organized in a way as to
achieve the memorization and creative assimilation of a considerable
volume of data without student tension. Creating a favorable psychological climate in class, suggestopedy converts the training process
into an emotion of joy, into pleasure for the student and the
teacher. Under these circumstances the personality of the student
is freed from various hindering complexes. It is "liberated."
New intellectual and memory reserves are discovered. It is this
new psychological system and concept of the training process
that is one of the major features of suggestopedia (174).

4. (U) According to Doctor Lozanov, the suggestopedic method
allows an individual to learn five to fifty times faster. It
is based on the yoga technique of relaxation - "Savasanna." Using
suggestion and autosuggestion, muscle tension is relaxed and the
brain is relieved of the usual anxieties and stresses. During
suggestopedic sessions the alpha rhythm of rest predominates in
the brain. The Soviets were among the first to seize on Bulgaria's
suggestopedia. The Moscow Foreign Lanugage Pedagogical Institute
has claimed resounding success with Lozanov's method (175).

5. (U) The Soviets, although they adopted some of Lozanov's
teaching techniques, have appeared to search for more conclusive
results in the use of autosuggestion. Early work was carried
out under the direction of Professor A.M. Svyadoshch, of the
Karaganda Medical Institute's Department of Psychiatry. It was
reported in 1965 that as a result of a special four month training
session, 40 out of 50 people learned how to produce, at will a
significant change in their own skin temperature. To raise or
lower the temperature they simply repeated to themselves for a
short period of time the appropriate autosuggestion formula:
"hand warm" or "hand cold." The Soviets found that the use of autosuggestion during a state of muscular relaxation, known as autogenous
training, makes possible a hypnotic state similar to that which
is observed during hypnotic sleep. Moreover, a person is able to
maintain control over his emotions and carry on further autosuggestion.
Using ordinary verbal formulas, one can subject various organ systems
to arbitrary effects during such a state (176). Autogenic training
has been reported by the Soviets to be useful in the elimination

UNCLASSIFIED

219

ST-CS-01-169-72
July 1972

of pain and in the treatment of neuroses and other functional
disturbances (177). Professor Svyadoshch believes that autosuggestion
may be used with success in cosmonaut training. In his opinion,
autosuggestion can be of great value to those whose occupation
makes particularly great demands on self-control, in particular,
space crews. Svyadoshch reports that it takes five or six months
of special exercises to master the autosuggestion technique. This
makes a person "immune" to fear, worry, and emotional instability (178).

6. (U) The Soviets have shown interest in the ability of humans
to alter their psychophysiological state by autogenous and exogenous
suggestion. A study was conducted to determine the possibility
of changing the activity of individual organs and systems of the
human body by autogenous and exogenous suggestion. Six test
subjects were exposed to 70-day bed rest. Three of the subjects
served as controls, and the other three were trained for the
first ten days to arbitrarily strain or relax individual muscular
groups, with subsequent sleep. Myotonometric data showed that different
muscle tonus indices could be reduced 5-25%. ECG, EEG, myotonometric,
and actographic data showed that sleep occurred by the 7 to 15th
minute during the second to third weeks of the experiment. By the
fourth week the test subjects were able to arbitrarily achieve a
state of relaxation and sleep at any time, regardless of the emotional reaction background. At such times arterial pressure and
pulse rate were significantly lowered. By the fifth week the
test subjects attained similar results, although somewhat less
effectively, by self-suggestion. Thus it is possible, by autogenous conditioning, for a subject to attain deep refreshing
sleep at a scheduled time even with a background of different
stress factors. Most effective changes in the psychophysical
state occurred during direct contact of the test subject with
the instructor, but exogenous suggestion was performed almost
as well by means of a radio or tape-recorder (179).

7. (U) The possibility of being able to predict suggestibility
in man prior to engaging him in long term trials has intrigued
the Russians. E.F. Mordinov and A.A. Genkin (180) have shown
that the electroencephalogram may serve as one of the objective
quantitative measures of suggestibility in man in the wakeful
state. Thirty-nine subjects in quiet wakefulness were subjected
to two EEG parameters: (1) average level of asymmetry of
oscillations and (2) average period of activity. Significant
differences were reported in the average level of asymmetry of

56

ST-CS-01-169-72
July 1972

oscillations in the readily suggestible group (20 subjects) compared to the resistant group (19 subjects). Suggestibility
difference effects existed in the hypnotic state and during wakefulness. The test of suggestibility was the classical one wherein
the inability to unlock interlocked fingers of the two hands is
suggested.

8. (U)   The field of suggestion provides a further means
for controlling or altering mental behavior. From the available
Soviet literature it can not be determined to what extent it might
be used for changing or manipulating behavior of their enemies.
A possible application for US military forces is in the area of
establishing defenses against hostile interrogation. The ability
to control one's own emotions through autogenous suggestion might
be most useful in PW situations. This, in turn, might provide
the US with a clue as to why the Soviets seem so interested in the
field of suggestion. On the other hand, the Soviets may have the
ability to directly influence the emotional and intellectual
activity of a prisoner, without his knowledge, by using Lozanov's
techniques employing subtle conditions of seemingly relaxing
and unmolesting environments.

57

221

ST-CS-01-169-72
July 1972

PART IV

PROPAGANDA AND MASS MEDIA

1. (U) It is difficult, if not impossible, to assess the Soviet's
potential for controlling or manipulating the behavior of their
enemies through the use of propaganda. One can survey the Western
literature and be able to make some rational judgments on the
effects of mass media, for example, on the mental behavior of
its audiences. Walter Weiss of Hunter College in New York has
published an excellent study (181) on the relationships between
mass media of communication and social change. The author also
reports on the roles of the mass media in the development of
modernized countries. In another report (182), Weiss surveys
the significant literature on the mass media from January 1967-
December 1969. Unfortunately these surveys deal primarily with
the free world.

3. (U) A report prepared by Goure (183) further depicts the
emphasis that Soviet authorities place on propaganda. The report
relates the all out effort that Soviet authorities are using in
order to indoctrinate their own people on the importance of civil
defense. Included in their attempts to create fear of nuclear,
chemical, and biological attack are direct assaults on the US.
This certainly represents a method of behavior change or control.
In an effort to propagandize civil defense in the Soviet Union intensive use is being made of all media of mass communication: the press,
television, radio, movies, exhibits, and lectures. Pamphlets and books
are published and disseminated on a wide scale. All the national
and major provincial newspapers, including Pravda, Izvestiya,
and Red Star, have published articles on civil defense, often
by prominent party or government officials (184). The basic
pamphlet for the instruction of the general public, Everyone
Should Know This, first published in 1968 has been issued to
most families. The following are a few select examples of the
intensity and scope of Soviet civil defense propaganda activities:
In 1969, the Belorussian SSR local newspapers printed 1,200

59

ST-CS-01-169-72
July 1972

articles on civil defense, one district (rayon) alone publishing
700 of them, and there were 45 television broadcasts and over
1,000 radio talks and reports on civil defense (185,186). In
Novosibirsk, 2,000 lectures were given on civil defense subjects
by the "Znaniya" (Knowledge) Society (187). In the Georgian SSR
over 7,000 propagandists of the Ministry of Culture are promoting
information on civil defense (188). Forty civil defense movies
are being shown throughout the country in regular movie theaters
and in various clubs, which were said to have been seen in 1969
by about 90 million persons (185). In the town of Orel, one city
district alone had 179 civil defense exhibits (189). In the
Azerbaidzhan SSR, in one month there were nine television broadcasts
and 300 items in the local press dealing with civil defense, while
in a district in Belorussia in one month there were held 120
public lecture sessions, 75 showings of civil defense movies and
numerous broadcasts (190,186). Many factories broadcast weekly
or biweekly talks on civil defense over their public address
systems. Soviet civil defense authorities also have tried to
expand civil defense propaganda by bringing to it writers,
journalists, painters, movie producers and other persons from the
creative arts. As part of this effort, arrangements were made with
the Union of Writers to send groups of their members to attend two-
week seminars at the Higher Central Officer Course on Civil Defense
of the USSR. Meetings and conferences of writers and other artists
with civil defense officials were also held in a number of the
major cities (191,192). Soviet civil defense leaders argue that
the population must be well prepared in a morale-psychological
sense if it is to withstand the shock of a nuclear war and its
aftermath. Consequently, in addition to reassuring the population
about the effectiveness of civil defense measures and the strength
of the Soviet Armed Forces, the propaganda and training programs
are also used to instill in the population "hatred for the enemies."
It is noted that:

> A rise in the importance of indoctrinating hatred of
> the imperialist aggressors is also due to the objec-
> tive pattern of a further rise in the role of morale
> in modern war (193).

This is accomplished by stressing the alleged US plans to attack
the Soviet Union and other "peace-loving" peoples. It is noted
with some satisfaction that Soviet soldiers "like all honest
people in the world, detest Americans and all other imperialists."
The literature emphasizes the importance of teaching the youth

60

223

UNCLASSIFIED

ST-CS-01-169-72
July 1972

to hate all enemies of the Soviet Union, since unlike its elders
it has not passed through the harsh experience of revolution and war.
This indoctrination, of course, also serves the political purposes
of the Soviet leadership and tends to facilitate its control over
the population. In this respect the civil defense program con-
tributes to strengthening the Soviet citizen's loyalty to the
leaders and the Communist system.

4. (U) It is evident from the information provided above and
in Appendix V that the Soviet Union has a well polished and sophisticated system of utilizing propaganda and the mass medium for its
own advantage. It is thought to be very possible that with the
knowledge gained in utilizing their system on their own people,
and other communist countries, this system of control could be un-
leashed on military forces confronting Soviet or allied Soviet
units.

61
(Reverse Blank)

UNCLASSIFIED

224

UNCLASSIFIED

ST-CS-01-169-72
July 1972

PART V

PSYCHOPHARMACOLOGY IN THE USSR

SECTION I - GENERAL

1. (U) Since ancient times, men have been aware of the fact that plant and animal products can induce desirable or undesirable psychological effects. For example, a primitive faith in the psychological effects of drugs is evident in the continued use of philters and potions to induce love and hate. Hippocrates proclaimed that the brain was the organ of the mind, a view still not held by those of dualistic persuasion.

2. (U) Before the twentieth century, when little was known about the pathophysiology of somatic disease and even less about mental disease, remedies were largely effective on a psychological basis. However, substances long known to have true psychopharmacological actions were opium and wine. These were employed not only to treat disease but also to make life more bearable. During the nineteenth century, the development of the science of chemistry made possible the discovery of agents with relatively selective effects upon the central nervous system. The nineteenth century saw the development of nitrous oxide, diethyl ether, sedatives, and hypnotics. However, until the mid-1950s there was little real progress in clinical psychopharmacology. The development of the phenothiazine drugs in the 1950s saw the augmentation of synthetic agents for therapy in psychotic disorders. The phenothiazines as a class, and especially chlorpromazine (Thorazine), are among the most widely used drugs in the practice of medicine today. From 1955 to 1965 at least 50 million patients received chlorpromazine and more than 10,000 publications have dealt with its actions (195).

3. (U) The use of psychopharmacologic agents is of keen interest throughout the world including the Soviet Union. Investigations on psychotherapeutic agents can no longer be overlooked in the Soviet literature. In the pharmaco-therapeutic reference work by Aronovich (196), four phenothiazines - aminazine (chlorpromazine), propazine, dinezin, and mepazine - and also reserpine (serpasil) are listed: but reports of clinical experience with phenothiazines (Rauwolfia derivatives play a smaller role altogether) refer almost exclusively to aminazine (approximately 127 references available-USSR). Most of the aminazine studies follow standard clinical research techniques however, some uses as mentioned in PART I of this report appear to be for more sinister purposes. Based

63

UNCLASSIFIED

ST-CS-01-169-72
July 1972

on the wealth of Soviet literature, the popularity, for whatever
reasons, of aminazine therapy in the Soviet Union cannot be disputed.
(114 references available on psychopharmacology-USSR).

SECTION II - MAIN PSYCHOTROPIC SUBSTANCES - USSR

1. (U) According to Guseynov (197), modern Soviet medicine
is devoting special attention to the development of psychopharmacology. At the present time (1971), Soviet scientists are conducting
intensive investigative work on the study and introduction into
medical practice of new psychotropic substances. The most important
Soviet psychotropic agents are as follows:

   (1) Diethylamide lysergic acid -- LSD-25
   Disrupts the psyche, causes hallucinations, but consciousness
is maintained. Used to diagnose schizophrenia, and also to create
a model of psychosis in animals.

   (2) Mescaline -- Mescalinum
   Under its influence a dimming of consciousness takes place,
and hallucinations and psychosis develop. Used to diagnose certain
mental illnesses and to create a model of experimental psychosis.

   (3) Harmine -- Harminum
   Calms the central nervous system, disrupts the psyche, causes
hallucinations, eliminates spasms. Used in parkinsonism. Prescribed for internal use.

   (4) Indian cannabis
   The active ingredient is a tar used under various names --
hashish, marijuana, bhang, dagga, and others. This tar is smoked,
chewed, and added to food and drink as a stupefacient. Cannabis
disrupts the psyche, causes hallucinations and euphoria, and
subsequently psychoses and schizophrenia develop. It has no
medicinal significance.

   (5) Iprazide -- Iprazidum (Marsilid)
   Stimulates the mental sphere, eliminates states of depression.
The effect comes on gradually over 12 to 16 hours and lasts 7
days. It is used for schizophrenia, psychoses, states of depression,
and hypertonia.

   (6) Imizine -- (Tofranil)
   Has a thymoleptic effect, eliminates states of depression.
Used in cyclophrenia and other mental disorders. Prescribed for
internal use or is introduced intramuscularly.

64

TIM RIFAT

UNCLASSIFIED

ST-CS-01-169-72
July 1972

(7) Transamine — (Parnate)
By blocking the enzyme monoaminoxidase (MAO), it increases
the content of biogenic amines in the brain and by so doing
eliminates states of depression. Used for mental disorders accompanied by severe depression. Prescribed for internal use.

(8) Phenamine — (Benzedrine)
Sharply stimulates the central and sympathetic nervous systems.
Increases blood pressure, dilates the pupils, quickens pulse,
relieves fatigue and somnolence. Perception is facilitated in
people who have taken phenamine, thinking and memory are improved,
motor activity and speech are increased, and mental and physical
efficiency are improved. Us. n narcolepsy, alcoholic psychoses,
psychogenic depression, and po. nings by narcotics and somni-
facients. Prescribed for intern   e.

(9) Phenatine — (Nicotinamide)
Stimulates the central nervous system; in contrast to phenamine,
it does not increase, but rather lowers blood pressure. Used for
mental and physical fatigue, and also for hypertonia. Prescribed
for internal use and is introduced subcutaneously.

(10) Piridrol — (Meratran)
Intensifies higher nervous activity, eliminates states of
depression. Used in narcolepsy and psychoses accompanied by
depression and apathy. Prescribed for internal use.

(11) Meridil -- (Ritalin)
Stimulates the central nervous system, eliminates states of
depression. Used in psychoses and states of depression. Prescribed
for internal use.

(12) Aminazine -- (Chlorpromazine)
Calms the central nervous system, lowers blood pressure and
body temperature, halts vomiting, slows down pulse, eliminates
the effect of histamine. Successfully used in schizophrenia,
psychoses, neuroses, delirium tremens, and hypertonia, toxicoses
of pregnancy, dermatoses, and in surgery to create artificial
hypothermy. Prescribed for internal use or introduced intramuscularly.

(13) Meprotan -- (Equanil)
Eliminates internal anxieties and feelings of fear and alarm,
calms the central nervous system. Used in physchoses, neuroses,
epilepsy, insomnia, and moderate hypertonia. Prescribed for
internal use.

65

UNCLASSIFIED

227

ST-CS-01-169-72
July 1972

(14) Amizil -- (Diazil)
Calms the nervous system, eliminates spasms and the effect of
histamine, restores disrupted pulse. Used in psychoses, neuroses,
and states of depression and phobia. Prescribed for internal use.

(15) Reserpine -- (Serpasil)
Main alkaloid of the plant Rauwolfia serpentina. Calms the
central nervous system, eliminates feelings of fear, longing,
and alarm, lowers blood pressure, and slows down pulse. Widely
used in schizophrenia, psychoses, neuroses, hypertonia, tachy-
cardia, thyrotoxicoses, and others. Prescribed for internal use
or introduced intramuscularly.

SECTION III - PSYCHO-WARFARE AGENTS

PART A - Diethylamide Lysergic Acid (LSD) and Psilocybin

1. (U) Psycho-warfare agents may be defined as those chemical
warfare agents whose effects rest on changes of the psyche (198).
These materials have the advantage over other warfare agents in
that the efficiency of the victim is impaired even with minimal
doses. Ordinary methods applicable in combat cannot afford detection of these agents, and for this reason warning cannot be sent
out in time when these psychotropic poisons are used. Only the
abnormal behavior of the victim may afford the first indication
that such compounds have been given. In effective concentrations,
these agents are odorless and tasteless and they can be utilized
both on the battlefield and in sabotage for contamination of
drinking water and food. For this reason the military medical
team needs to inform themselves on the effect of these weapons
and their symptoms.

2. (U) Lysergic acid diethylamide (LSD) is almost a "classic"
representative of psycho-warfare agents. A. Hofmann synthesized
this compound in the course of his investigations on the composition of the ergot alkaloids. Even minimal amounts of this substance,
about 30 to 60 micrograms, are evidenced by psychological-emotional
changes in man, which may last from six to eight hours. There is an
association of motor uncertainty, unsure and swaggering walk, poor
prehension and dragging speech with vivid color hallucinations,
disturbances of spatial and temporal sense, attacks of crying and
laughing, fear and delusions and sometimes severe phenomena of
depersonalization. The behavior of the victim is comparable to
that of the schizophrenic. LSD is effective in doses that are
one-ten thousandth of mescaline doses, and it is much more readily
handled in the form of easily water-soluble tartrate. After the

66

TIM RIFAT

ST-CS-01-169-72
July 1972

LSD psychosis wears off, the victim experiences no after effects,
however it has been reported that part of the hallucinations are
subject to recall and flashback reactions have occurred. Psilocybin
exerts a qualitatively similar effect in man, but about 100 times
weaker than LSD. This material is known as the psychotropic subtance
of the Mexican magic mushroom (Psilocybe mex. Heim). The more effective compound is psilozine which occurs in the organism through
dephosphorylation of psilocybin. As shown by animal experiment,
just 20 minutes after i.p. injection of psilocybin, dephosphorylation is observed, indicating a rather high content of psilozine
in brain and other organs of the animals. The two substances
are identical with respect to their psychotropic effect, and at
the start of the psychosis there are changes in physical feelings
(weakness, dizziness) as predominant symptoms. Only later do the
optical and acoustic hallucinations start. Anxiety, restlessness,
nausea and difficulty in speech are characteristic of the further
symptoms of intoxication. In the later course of the psychosis
there is extensive loss of ability to concentrate or think, and
there is also loss of sense of space and time. After the psychosis
wears off the victim complains of exhaustion, fatigue and headache,
but these symptoms disappear after a while. LSD, psilozine and
psilocybin are biochemically correlated to serotonin. It is
not yet clear to what extent this correlation is based in enzyme
chemistry. However, similar structures in the molecules of these
substances suggest pharmacodynamic interpretations. Since brain
function is closely related to serotonin metabolism it can be
assumed that this substance is replaced by structurally very
similar psychotoxins that are built up, namely by substances of
the tryptamine group, e.g., LSD. These poisons do not take over
the functions of the serotonin, however, and this leads to disturbances in the CNS. The comparison of the above named materials
with other tryptamine derivatives such as dimethyltryptamine
and bufotenine, which is an isomer of psilozine, also fits into
the framework of pharmacodynamic interpretation. Both derivatives are psychotropically active substances, effective in man
in doses of about 70 mg.

3. (U)   Several institutes in the Soviet Union have been
identified where LSD research has taken place since 1969. The
Institute of Physiology in Tbilisi was reported to be doing work
on the effects of LSD on baboon behavior. No specific experimental
work is known (199). A group at the Institute of Molecular Biology,
Academy of Sciences, Moscow, has been working with LSD in experiments with inhibitors (200). It is difficult to judge what the
Soviets are doing, but the work with inhibitors might indicate
research efforts in the area of medical defense against the use

67

229

ST-CS-01-169-72
July 1972

of LSD on Soviet troops. There is a group at the Institute of
Physiology in Novosibirsk. No details on their work is available.
The relationship between LSD, serotonin, and motor components
of behavior reactions is being studied at the Donetsk Medical
Institute (201). The Soviet research in the area concerned with
the action of bioamines, e.g., adrenaline, serotonin, and noradrenaline, which the Donetsk group is studying, will be discussed
later in this report. Studies concerned with the reversibility
of pathomorphological changes in the brain of rats after chronic
administration of LSD were going on in 1971 at the Moscow Medical
Stomatological Institute (202). The First Medical Institute
imeni I.M. Sechenov has reported their work on the search for
antagonists for hashish and LSD (203). Kudrin reported that
Haloperidol (a butyrophenone tranquilizer) injection in combination with Phenitron (a propiophenone adrenolytic) prevents cats
from the development of LSD-induced psychosis and catatonia. This
is an important aspect of Soviet LSD research as it indicates
their possible interest in military medical defense against psycho-
warfare agents. Popova has reported on the effect of LSD on the
structure of neurons and interneuronal connections. The author
states that her observations suggest that the central effects
of LSD may be related to changes both in synapses and in the
cell body (204).

4. (U)   This study has attempted to establish the possibility
that the Serbsky Institute of Forensic Psychiatry in Moscow may
be one of the main Soviet facilities for studying controlled
offensive behavior (see PART I). I.P. Anokhina of the Serbsky
Institute reported in 1970 on the effect of LSD on the neurotransmitter systems of the brain. The experiments brought
evidence that the site of action of LSD is in the midbrain reticular
formation and in the limbic system. Anokhina also believes that
LSD inhibits monoamineoxidase (MAO) activity (205). The experiment reported in the open literature is scientifically genuine,
of course, but the important fact is that the Institute is studying
LSD and other psychotropic agents. Since most of the Soviet
LSD literature is from institutes in Moscow, it might be conjectured that there is a concentrated effort in the USSR to determine
the basis of action and uses for LSD and other possible psycho-
warfare agents.

5. (U)   Until March of 1968, there were three chemical
plants located in Czechoslovakia conducting independent research
on CW compounds. As late as March 1968, they were working on
super-active compounds based on materials such as LSD and mescaline.

68

ST-CS-01-169-72
July 1972

At that time, the work was supported by the Soviet Union but
conducted by the Czechs, with the final product going into
Czechoslovakian stockpile. The Soviets furnished formulas, specifications, production guidance, test procedures, and animal data.
They may have also provided some precursor chemicals. The Czechs
were working on aerosols as one method of applying the gaseous
materials developed from this program. It is stated that LSD
experiments had been disappointing but that other materials
similar to LSD had been quite successful. The compounds were
being developed to be dispersed over a wide area from the air.
The agents were designed to make the population lose its will
to resist for anywhere from two hours to two days, depending on
the compound used and the nature of the mission. Damage would
be limited to the brain (206).

PART B - Piperidyl Benzilate and Piperidyl Glycolate

1. (U) In the course of the search for anticholinergic substances,
it was found that methylpiperidyl benzilate and its derivatives
are extremely active hallucinogens. If we start from the general
formula for piperidyl benzilate and piperidyl glycolate, a series
of highly active psychotropic compounds can be derived from it.
The radicals of the formula below are involved as substituents.
From the piperidyl benzilate series we can mention N-methylpiperidyl
benzilate as a highly active psychotoxin ($R_1=CH_3$; R_2 and $R_3=C_6H_5$).
From the piperidyl glycolate series, Ditran ($R_1= -C_2H_5$; $R_2= -C_6H_5$;
$R_3= -C_5H_9$) can be described as an extremely active compound.

69

ST-CS-01-169-72
July 1972

2. (U) Poisoning with piperidyl glycolates is hardly to be
distinguished from LSD poisoning at the beginning, because also
in the first mentioned class of materials the first psychic effects
occur after 45 to 60 minutes. They consist of confusion, speech
difficulty, disorientation and hallucination of optical and
acoustic type. It is to be noted that in piperidyl glycolate
psychosis the victim can still describe his condition relatively
clearly after a dose of 0.5 to 2.0 mg. At doses of 10 mg and above,
however, contact with the environment and insight into the arti-
ficiality of the condition is lost. The victims react only to
their hallucinations, or they present a stupor syndrome. At
still higher doses (15 mg) there is generally a severe disturbance
of consciousness with almost complete lack of consciousness. The
effect of Ditran, for example, lasts for about 24 hours, and sometimes as long as 36 hours. Other toxic phenomena are not to be
anticipated at the indicated doses. At the most nausea and emesis.

PART C - Countermeasures

1. (U) In the use of psychotropic warfare agents, the enemy
sets himself the task of weakening the will and fighting capability
of the opponent, or to bring about his complete inability to act
or fight. For this reason, only well-timed application of protective equipment and measures for guaranteeing indubitably uncon-
taminated drinking water and food can afford flawless protection.
This condition in this case has so much the greater significance
because a timed alarm is questionable in dealing with psychotropic
agents. Certain medicaments are available to the physician for
the treatment of those already poisoned to offset the worst effects.
As antidotes there are:

    (1) Azacyclonol (Frenquel) in an i.v. or oral dose of 200 mg
    (2) Succinic acid, infusion in a 5% phosphate buffered solution
(5ml/min)
    (3) Tetrahydroaminacrin, 30 mg i.v. within 5 minutes
    (4) Chlorpromazine (Thorazine) 25 mg i.m. or orally larger
doses

2. (U) The medicaments under one and two are indicated in poisoning
with LSD, psilozine and psilocybin. The medicament under three is to
be given in poisoning with piperidyl benzilate or piperidyl glycolate.
Chlorpromazine has a favorable effect on most model psychoses
induced by known psychotropic warfare agents.

70

ST-CS-01-169-72
July 1972

SECTION IV - CURRENT RESEARCH INTEREST IN PSYCHOPHARMACOLOGY - USSR

PART A - Bioamine Research

1. (U) Space in this report limits this discussion on bioamine research. There is a vast quantity of literature available on bio-amine research, e.g., serotonin, dopamine, adrenalin, and noradrenalin.

2. (U)   Discarding some elements of sensationalism, acade-mician P.K. Anokhin (relationship to I.P. Anokina unknown; see reference 205) maintains that today's knowledge of the human brain gives grounds to believe that in the next decade some artificial means will be found to influence the intellectual capacities of man (207). Doctor Anokhin is with the Institute of Normal and Pathological Physiology in Moscow (208).

3. (U) A small group of little-known amines, commonly referred to as the biogenic amines, seemed to provide links between behavior and such fields of brain research as neuroanatomy, neurochemistry, and neurophysiology. It seemed possible that advances in the neurochemistry of these amines would greatly enrich one's knowledge of a variety of processes related to brain and mind. This has indeed happened. Although the surface has still barely been scratched, research in the interim has broadened the ideas con-cerning such phenomena as mood, sleep, sexual desires, and appetite -- and such neurological disorders as parkinsonism and chorea. More-over, the whole field of psychopharmacology has become rationalized as relationships between the major psychoactive drugs and amine action have been revealed.

4. (U) It has now been established beyond reasonable doubt that communication between neurons in the mammalian nervous system is by means of chemical agents, or neurotransmitters, which are released from the nerve terminal of one neuron and which cross the synaptic cleft, or interneuronal space, to influence the excitability of the next neuron. The alternative possibility of electrical trans-mission has been ruled out. The existence of these chemical messengers provides a possible way of influencing behavior and mental performance while leaving other aspects of brain function almost completely unaffected. If the transmitters governing the cells associated with such functions as sex, appetite, sleep, or mood turn out to be specific and if chemical methods can be found for selectively interfering with their metabolism, then fairly

ST-CS-01-169-72
July 1972

precise behavioral modifications might be brought about. Unfortunately, the identity of neurotransmitters associated with most cells is unknown. However, a few neurotransmitters have been identified, and an exciting flood of research has always accompanied their discovery. Bridges are built between the often separated fields of pharmacology, physiology, and biochemistry, and a new level of understanding of the nervous system is achieved. So it was when acetylcholine and noradrenaline were found many years ago to be the transmitter substances for the parasympathetic and sympathetic parts of the autonomic nervous system. And so it has been in the past few years as evidence has built up in favor of dopamine, noradrenaline, serotonin, and acetylcholine playing neurotransmitter roles in the visceral brain.

5. (U) Two groups of workers have recently reported that cholinomimetic stimulation of the brain produces aggressive behavior and killing in rats. Cholinergic blocking agents reverse the effect. The areas involved are the lateral hypothalamus (Smith, King, and Hoebel 1970), septal area and amygdala (Igic, Stern, and Basagic 1970). Pathological aggressiveness is probably the most disagreeable of all human traits. The precise identification of circuits of violence and a definition of their means of control would be of inestimable social value. That pathologically agressive behavior can be triggered without discernible provocation in susceptible individuals is as well known to the courts as it is to the medical profession (209).

6. (U) The discussion above was included as important background information on the brain, biogenic amines and theories for controlling behavior. The author mentions that the precise identification of the mental pathways for aggression in humans would be of inestimable social value. However, if one does learn and identify these pathways and ways of initiating aggressive behavior as in the rat experiment above, it may be used for antisocial effects as well.

7. (U) A.R. Luria of the University of Moscow has been studying the functional organization of the brain for several years. In a recent article, Doctor Luria describes some recent Soviet advances in the mapping of the brain (210). The lengthy article is concluded by Luria stating that neuropsychology has put us (the Soviets) on a new path in the investigation of how the brain functions. Luria feels that this is likely to lead the way to substantial changes in the design of psychological research in the future.

72

UNCLASSIFIED

ST-CS-01-169-72
July 1972

8.   (U) An interesting research report in 1968 appeared in the
Soviet press which related biogenic amines with psychotropic
drugs (211). The type of mental disturbance produced by psycho-
pharmaceuticals was investigated in human volunteers. The volunteers received a variety of compounds (not named) in 20—150 mg
doses. Psychic disturbances were of two types: anxiety depressive
and deep depressive. The first group reported more phobias,
while the second group exhibited general lassitude, and hypochondriac symptoms. Adrenalin and noradrenalin were given by injection.
DOPA and serotonin were also given. Creatine levels in the urine
were determined after treatment. Other metabolites were detected
chromatographically or by paper electrophoresis. Before treatment,
group I patients excreted higher than normal levels of creatines,
their metabolites and precursors. In the second group, excretion
of catecholamines, precursors and metabolites was higher (up to
2 times) than in the controls. The administration of tranquilizers
(Librium) accompanied the reduction in excretion of abnormal
metabolites. This study is important because it illustrates
Soviet interest in not only biogenic amines, but also in the
mode of action of psychotropic substances. Once the parameters
are understood, then the development of highly sophisticated
mood altering chemicals should follow.

9.   (U) Of interest was the symposium on Mechanisms of Regulation
of the Biogenic Amines Level in the Tissues held in Lodz, Poland
in August of 1971. No data is available but the abstracts of the
papers is to be published in Acta Medica Polonica in April of 1972.
The main aim of the symposium was for the comparison of data
on the mechanisms of regulation of the biogenic amines level
in the tissues with special emphasis on the role of enzymes responsible for synthesis, catalysis, and storage of amines.

10. (U) The relationship of psychoactive drugs to amine activity
is shown in Table IV below.

TABLE IV

Relation of Psychoactive Drugs to Amine Activity (209)

A. Drugs which impair amine synaptic activity

    1. Tranquilizers
       a. Inhibitors of vesicle binding: rauwolfia alkaloids--
         e.g. reserpine
       b. Blockers of receptor sites: phenothiazines,
         butyrophenones--e.g. chlorpromazine and halo-
         peridol

73

UNCLASSIFIED

ST-CS-01-169-72
July 1972

 2. Amine synthesis inhibitors
  a. Inhibitors of catecholamine synthesis: e.g.
   alpha-methyl-p-tyrosine
  b. Inhibitors of serotonin synthesis: e.g. p-
   chlorophenylalanine

B. Drugs which enhance amine synaptic activity

 1. Psychic energizers
  a. Inhibitors of monoamine oxidase: hydrazines
   and monoamine analogs--e.g. iproniazide,
   tranylcypromine, amphetamine
  b. Inhibitors of amine uptake: dibenzazepines
   and miscellaneous derivatives--e.g. imipra-
   mine, amitriptyline, cocaine, amphetamine
  c. Amine releasers: amine analogs--e.g. amphetamine, tyramine

 2. Amine synthesis stimulators
  a. For dopamine and noradrenaline: L-dopa
  b. For noradrenaline: L-dihydroxyphenylserine
  c. For serotonin: L-5-hydroxytryptophan

PART B - Other Areas of Soviet Research in Psychopharmacology

1. (U) Barkov and Gurovich (212) reported on the effects of
tripthazine (stelazine) and aminazine (thorazine) on emotional
behavior. The compounds were found to inhibit aggression but
prolong the fear reaction in rats.

2. (U) The Soviets have conducted experiments which use an
automatic, multichannel register of motor activity. The instrument
independently records all the movements of the animals located in a
special chamber and transmits the signal to 40 counters. Kruglov is
using a modern radio-electronic device which can record the signals,
of milli-second duration, by which neurons transmit information
to each other. Kruglov and his colleagues have established that
morphine, aminazine, and similar substances inhibit the signaling
rhythm of nerve cells. These experiments yielded many new tranquilizers and stimulants. None of these "new" substances were
described. The Soviets claim that neurotropic drugs are now
making it possible to intervene in the most important processes
taking place in the organism. No description of what important
processes taking place is mentioned (213).

74

 S.-CS-01-169-72
July 1972

3. (U) Controlling group behavior with drugs has been reported
by I.P. Lapin (214). The study dealt with animals but may have
some bearing on human behavior reorientation. According to Lapin,
in order to change the behavior of a large group of animals, it
is sufficient to use drugs to control the behavior of the most
active animals (leaders). The article discusses the use of amphe-
tamines and aminazine. Further reference to Lapin can be found
in an article of 23 September 1968 (215).

4. (U) One of the most interesting areas of research into finding
new psychotropic substances may be associated with the gonionemous
jellyfish. Research into the nervous and pychic disorders resulting
from lesions caused by the jellyfish has been reported by the
aforementioned Serbsky Institute (216). It appears that literature
on Soviet research in this field is extremely limited. Mikhalev
and Vatskov studied 260 cases of lesions by poisonous gonionemous
jellyfish. General and local disturbances are distinguished
according to their severity and symptoms of intoxication in the
clinical picture. In cases of a severe course of the affection
(18 patients), except for polymorphic somatic symptoms, there
were distinct neuropsychiatric deviations. They were expressed
in tormenting headaches, convulsions, paresis, disturbances of
statics, sacral posterior radicular pains. Vegetative symptoms
were in the form of hyperhydrosis, acrocyanosis, hypersalivation,
and red demographism. Mental disturbances proceeded with an
increasing fear of death, sometimes with speech and fugiform
excitation, altered consciousness of the delirio-amentive or
oneiroid type with illusions, hallucinations, psychosenory and
delusional symptoms. The psychotic symptoms of an acute exogenous
reaction subsided during the following two to five days. This research
might have significance in the Soviets attempts to arrive at suitable
means for controlling or altering behavior.

5. (U) A noteworthy book from Czechoslovakia that discusses
some of the present problems of some militarily important psychoactive
substances has been published (217). The book discusses the history
of natural psychotomimetics used in religious rituals. There are
mentioned two possibilities for the application of presently known
psychoactive drugs for the purpose of military gain:

   a. Controlling stress situations in special military units
in combat to include means for treating mass psychoses in extraordinary situations.

   b. The use of temporary incapacitating agents for disrupting
and capturing enemy personnel.

75

ST-CS-01-169-72
July 1972

The problems associated with military misuse of drugs is discussed.
The classification of psychotomimetic drugs relating to their
effects, either on higher nervous activity or in producing temporary
disorders, mainly in somatic functions is outlined. The authors
also mention some characteristics of the piperidyl glycolate group
of psycho-warfare agents. Structural analogy of psychotomimetic
derivates to the particular neurotransmitters is considered together
with a hypothesis of competitive antagonism on receptors. The
authors state that competitive antagonism seems to be one of the
most acceptable possibilities of hallucinogenic effect mechanisms
as well as a good base for the investigation of potential means
for the effective prevention and treatment of hallucinogen intoxi-
cations. The influence of stress and conventional weapons on
the eventual result of pschotomimetic drugs effect in exceptional
situations is taken into account.

6.   It must be concluded, based on the Soviet literature
on psychopharmacological research, that the USSR has the ability
and knowledge to develop and produce a sophisticated arsenal of
incapacitating or mind altering weapons in the form of chemical
agents.

76

ST-CS-01-169-72
July 1972

PART VI

LIGHT AND COLOR AS A MEANS OF ALTERING HUMAN BEHAVIOR

SECTION I - PSYCHO-OPTICS

PART A - Background

1. (U)   According to Dodge (218), there have been persistent
reports of unusual flashing or bright lights emanating from Soviet
naval vessels and long range aircraft (BEAR, BADGER, BISON).
Such activities have coincided with US and NATO surveillance
operations conducted from interceptor aircraft and naval vessels.
In some cases, surveillance personnel have been temporarily blinded
and disoriented by various intensities and colors of continuous
or intermittently flashing lights during nocturnal missions.

2. (U)   Dodge further relates that in 1968, a night watch
officer aboard the HMS Valiant was temporarily blinded by what
appeared to be a bright blue light situated slightly below the
mast of a KOTLIN destroyer. When his night vision recovered,
he reported perceiving red lights which appeared to be situated
above and behind the blue light. Both sources of light appeared
to be portable. In 1970, an aircraft was tracked by a spotlight
trained from a Soviet naval vessel. Several pinpoint bursts of
amber and amber-green light were noted aft of the spotlight and
shined in concert with it.

77

239

text had already been deleted from this page
when document was made available to author

4.   (U)   Again in 1968, another F-102 pilot reported that a
steady brilliant white light was shined from a hand-held aldis-
type lantern situated in the tail blister of a BEAR B aircraft.
In late 1968, still another F-102 pilot reported a blinding light
in concert with a pulsating (1.5 flashes/second) red strobe light
from a BEAR aircraft. In 1970, an F-102 pilot reported that a
BEAR C aircraft shined a hand-held light of brilliant intensity
from its left rear tail blister. The light was trained on the
pilot from 15 to 20 times with a flash duration of two to seven
seconds (218).

78

ɔ1-US-01-169-72
July 1972

5. (U) A report that appeared in 1971 discusses some US air personnel
problems when encountering Soviet aircraft over the Mediterranean
Sea (220). "By far, the most dangerous encounters occur after
dark. For safety's sake, both the BADGERS and the PHANTOMS usually
turn on their navigation lights (which they would never do in
a combat situation), but sometimes the Russians come in blacked
out, or shine searchlights in the eyes of the PHANTOM pilots -
causing a temporary loss of night vision - or trickily switch
their navigation lights on and off."

6. (U)   Some of the nocturnal incidents described above
suggest that the Soviets have not overlooked the possibility of
utilizing bright and flashing lights as a means of altering
behavior. It is interesting to note that the period of active
research in Soviet laboratories, as will be discussed in PART B
below, coincides with the reports of their employment of unusual
flashing lights against US and NATO personnel.

PART B - Soviet Research in Photic-Flicker

1. (U) A series of conclusions were drawn on the effects of
flicker at a symposium held in the US in 1957 (221). Although
the meeting and papers presented are fifteen years old, the facts
presented appear to be relevant to this discussion. The conclusions reached by the group at Tulane were as follows:

     (1) There appears to be general agreement that flicker has
the potentiality of causing considerable interruption of the normal
functions of the human nervous system.

     (2) One manifestation of such interruption may take the form
of sleep, unconsciousness, hypnotic states, or other forms of
interference with consciousness. Another manifestation of interference consists of annoying or irritating sensations such as
queasiness, discomfort referable to the eyeball and caused by
excessive pupillomotor activity, headaches, or general sensations
of apprehension. A third type of manifestation concerns visual
illusions including color sensations, patterns of movement and
development of odd shapes. These may interfere with visual recognition of any objects which actually are in the visual field.

     (3) Those flicker effects which interfere with consciousness
appear at frequencies related to the alpha rhythm of the EEG,
or at 10 Hz. Annoying or irritating sensations seem to occur
with aperiodic flashes or with rhythmic flashes at 3-5 Hz. Visual
illusions appear to be produced by frequencies above 10-12 Hz.

79

241

ST-CS-01-169-72
July 1972

(4) The EEG appears to be a reliable indicator of consciousness but not of sleep or wakefulness...

(5) Not every subject shows truly periodic EEG activity...

(6) Photic driving of the EEG by periodic flicker is a well known phenomenon although many subjects do not show the effect...

(7) The ease with which photic driving can be produced has not yet been correlated with emotional patterns or with sleep-wakefulness cycles. However, the visual illusions which result from flicker may be the basis for a highly predictable method of measuring anxiety.

(8) The production of flicker effects is not limited by the retina but appears to be limited by some process in the central nervous system which converts discontinuous activity to continuous activity (i.e. flicker to fusion)...

(9) Flickering of other sensory modalities may influence the ease of production of the desired effects of visual flicker. Auditory flicker is particularly promising in this regard.

(10) Stress, comparable to that produced in actual combat, may be needed to completely elucidate the practical effects of flicker as far as military applications are concerned.

(11) It appears likely that high intensities of light will be more effective in producing the desired effects of flicker although much remains to be done to determine the optimum light and dark intervals, background contrasts, and effects of stray light.

As will be depicted later, the areas above where no definite conclusions were drawn (4,7, and 10) is the exact area of high Soviet interest. L.I. Kuproyanovich (164) describes in some detail Soviet efforts in relating EEG with sleep and memory as well as the areas of photic drive and the synchronization of flicker frequency and alpha wave rhythm. At the University of Leningrad work has been done on the effects of strobe lights flashing at a different rate for each eye. One rhythm for the left eye and another for the right eye brings on measurable brain wave patterns. Lights flickering at different rates on each eye cause a sensation of rotation and a very unpleasant feeling in the viewer. It might be mentioned that the Soviets are thinking of using the "seasickness" application of flashing lights in a telepathic mode (222).

80

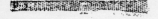

242

ST-CS-01-169-72
July 1972

2. (U)   The most recent conference on flashing lights
was held during the period of 19 through 22 April 1971 in London.
It was the "International Symposium on the Perception and Application of Flashing Lights." From the sources available, it has
been determined that no Soviet or East European personnel attended;
further, no one at the conference discussed the possible use of
flashing lights for military purposes (223).

3. (U) Among the varied research interests in the Soviet Union
dealing with flashing lights is the relationship of the vestibular
to the visual systems. Electrophysiological data on the effect
of the vestibular apparatus on the optical system has been published
in the Soviet Union (224,225). It has been reported that stimula-
lation of the vestibular apparatus (polarization of the labyrinth
by a direct current) causes an increase in neuron reaction to
light stimulation and an increase in the critical frequency of
flashes. The Soviets also conclude that the interactions of
visual and vestibular analyzers is brought about mainly because
of their cortical levels. Studies were carried out with deaf
individuals to provide further evidence of this. If these studies
are all valid, this could lead to the possible development of
systems that combine vestibular stimuli with photic-flicker capability in order to achieve a degree of mental disorientation and
confusion. The Soviets conclude by stating that functional variations of the cortex of normal subjects caused by vestibular stimula-
tions result in a disruption of cortical-subcortical relationships,
which in turn alters the functional states of the retina. Further
work in the relationship of visual perception, auditory stimuli,
and the cerebral cortex have been reported (226-228). Studies
have been conducted on rabbits, cats, and Moscow school children.
It was found that repeated stimulation with sound resulted in a
complete extinction of neuronal response.

4. (U) The reaction to prolonged rhythmic photic stimulation
has interested the Soviets. In experiments with rhythmic light
flashes at different frequencies, monkeys exhibited individual
sensitivity to certain rhythms. Some animals recruited and transformed the lower frequencies better (7.9 flashes per second),
while others responded to the higher frequencies (18 and 25 per
second). The following variations in the cortical and subcortical
responses to the stimuli were distinguished: (a) simultaneous
recruitment of the given rhythm by cells of the motor and visual
cortex and subcortex; (b) recruitment of the rhythm only by the
visual cortex; (c) recruitment of the rhythm by the visual cortex

81

ST-CS-01-169-72
July 1972

and its transformation in the subcortical structures; (d) recruitment only by the subcortex and motor cortex; (e) transformation in the visual cortex and recruitment by the deeper structures of the brain and motor cortex; (f) simultaneous transformation of the rhythm by all the structures recorded; (g) transformation by the visual cortex. All or a combination of these variations in brain activity could occur in the same experiment (30 to 60 min) (229). A study was reported on non-rhythmic prolonged photo stimulation (230) and on the characteristics of sensory afterdischarge of the human brain to photic stimulation (231). A conclusion was drawn that the specificity of processes in the upper parts of the visual analyzer under a prolonged action of light depends on the inhibitory influences from the visual cortex.

5. (U) The Soviet literature contains reference to experimental work in the effect of high brightness on the rate of eye adaptation to darkness. Kartsev (232) reports that the rate of adaptation of central vision of both eyes to the darkness after light exposures of various durations (1.5,3,6 minutes) after illumination (20,000 to 80,000 lux) was studied in four test subjects in the age group 18-30. A white barium screen illuminated by direct sunlight was used as a light source. During adaptation to the darkness the central vision response time was proportional to the quantity of illumination during disadaptation. A value of approximately 8×10^6 lux per sec was used. Apparently the Soviets feel that they have determined the upper limits to the effects of brightness because Kartsev reports that central vision response remained unchanged with any further stimulus increase. Other researches have prepared curves for the computation of restoration to light sensitivity after exposure to superbright light flashes (233-235). Visual perception in aircraft pilots has also been studied (236).

SECTION II - COLOR AND LIGHT

1. (U) The Soviets have reported that low intensity red light creates an irregular alpha rhythm in humans (237). Another study was conducted on the effects of low intensity red, green, and yellow light on humans (238). Physiological tests were administered to 412 females working in a film processing plant under red, green, or yellow light of low intensity 25 watt bulbs. Complex shifts were found in the central and autonomic nervous system which included marked increases in optical rheobase and chronaxy and lengthening of the latent period of visual and motor reactions

82

ST-CS-01-169-72
July 1972

during the course of the day. The EEG was characterized by an
irregular alpha rhythm, frequently followed by more rapid low-
amplitude oscillations, an indication of decreased reactivity
of the cortical processes. The condition of the autonomic nervous
system was judged from shifts in skin temperature and arterial
pressure, both of which were much lower at the end of a work shift
than at the beginning. The physiological data were supported by
the results of a neurological examination which showed a large
number of functional shifts. In general, the adverse effects
were most pronounced in those who worked in soft red light. Yellow
light was less irritating than green.

2. (U) Further evidence of Soviet interest, especially in red
light, is provided by research emanating from Soviet military
institutes. The dynamics of work capacity of healthy human subjects
during adaptation to colored lights was evaluated from the rate
and quality of sensorimotor reactions of varying complexity. The
subjects, seated at a specially designed control board, were required
to press buttons to switch off the lights at appropriate signals during
a two hour adaptation period. Adaptation resulted in changes in
the rate and quality of the reactions in relation to the color
of the light source and the adaptation time. An increase in wavelength increased reaction speed but impaired quality, while a
decrease in wavelength had the opposite effects. Red light produced
tension and irritability. Yellow light induced a good mood characterized by "increased motor readiness" and sustained attentiveness.
Sluggishness and sleepiness were the characteristic reactions to
blue light. Green light did not seem to produce any emotional
reaction (239).

3. (U) The effect of colored illumination on monkeys has been
studied at the Kirov Military Academy. The work reported above
also was done at the Kirov Academy. The work as one can see
involves not only monkeys but humans. The relationship between
agressiveness and color type is of interest especially since the
work comes from a known military establishment. An abstract
of the work on monkeys follows:

"In order to determine the psychophysiological specificity and the emotional working capacity as influenced
by different colors of the visible spectrum -- so
important in technical esthetics in submarines, mines,
planes, and light and heavy industries -- the authors
used two rhesus monkeys. Sultan, four years old, was rather
immobile and aggressive with a big appetite. Generally
he sat at the screen and in the case of a mistaken choice

83

245

ST-CS-01-169-72
July 1972

became aggressive and chewed on the screen. Kahn, three
years old, was lively, emotionally responsive but suspicious, was roused by food less than Sultan, and was conditioned by surroundings. He ran about the cage almost
continously and seldom sat at the screen to wait for
the signal. Food was placed in sight of the monkeys in
one of two feeding troughs shut off from the cage.
After 30-60 minutes of adaptation to light (red, yellow,
green and blue) at different periods, the monkeys were
tested for delayed reaction. After red light the animals were restless, they made many wrong choices, and
emotionally they were tense. After yellow light there
were fewer mistakes. The optimum was green light.
Blue light produced definite sedative effects on the
body and thought, especially so with Kahn, who sat
quietly in the corner and responded to signals with
deliberation or indifference." (240)

4. (U) Other research on color thresholds of lights (241), color
vision (242-243) and the development of visual color perception
(244) have been published. One final paper is of separate interest
because it gives an indication of possible Soviet interest in the
relationship of anticholinergic drugs and photic stimulation with
colored light. The effect of amino glycolates, hydroxypiperedyl-
benzylate, benactyzine, and glypin (unknown), in doses of 0.1 to 5 mg.
per kg., and of the amino acetates, adiphenine and tropacin, in doses
of 1 to 10 mg. per kg. on discrimination of light flashes by
the retina was studied in intact rabbits. In photostimulation
with white, yellow, green, and blue light, 1 to 25 flashes per
second were percieved both before and after the administration
of all doses of the anticholinergic drugs. S.A. Kalning (245)
reports that rhythm perception proceeded undisturbed even when
the intensity of the light was increased after the introduction
of the drugs. It is not known if the Soviets have done similar
studies employing red light; it would appear to be of interest
since it has been shown that red light tends to increase aggressiveness and produce EEG alterations.

SECTION III - CONCLUDING REMARKS AND COUNTERMEASURES

ST-CS-01-169-72
July 1972

2.   (U)   The use of flashing lights to alter or affect
human behavior or one's mental state has not received very much
research attention. Laboratory tests, however, have revealed
some interesting effects which might be worthy of further investigation. At close distances, light of high intensity can alter
the alpha rhythm of the brain to bring it into phase with the
lights (see Kuproyanovich - 164). It has been noted that a person
in hypnosis is more likely to be in the alpha state. Laboratory
tests have been devised so that a subject's brain waves can be
visually displayed on a wall thus teaching him when he is generating alpha waves. These tests have all been conducted in darkened
laboratories. To reproduce such conditions in the field would
require lights of very high intensity. The tests could probably
only be conducted at night. Such a test would probably require
high intensity lights flashing at about ten cycles per second
(cps), which is the approximate cycle rate for the alpha waves.

tion of flashing lights operating at ten cps could indicate experi- Observa-
ments (218, 219) intended to alter or control alpha waves or
could merely indicate coincidence. The color of the lights would
seem to be of no importance or significance. Another explanation
for flashing tungsten filament lights could be linked to an attempt
to interfere with an observers perception of motion (218,219).
Short intense light flashes tend to impede the ability to detect
motion. The eye detects motion by observing an object traveling
from one position to another. If flashing lights were present,
the observer would only be able to observe the object for such
a short period of time between flashes so it would appear to be
stationary. Only prolonged observation and comparison to other
objects would enable the detection of movement. Even a short
period of indecision could be of importance in the detection of
a torpedo for example. Experiments have been conducted in the
laboratory which demonstrate that high intensity flashing lights
operating at ten cps and conducted for a prolonged period of time
result in nausea on the part of the observer. Such flashes could
be particularly effective against someone feeling the effects of
seasickness.

3.   (U)   It is interesting to note that the expert above
mentioned that color would seem to be of no importance or significance. The Soviets have shown a high interest in the effects
of color on human behavior, especially red colored lights. The

85

ST-CS-01-169-72
July 1972

reports from US Air Force personnel also describe the use of
bright red strobe lights that pulsate so rapidly that it almost
gave a stop-motion appearance that one of the Soviet's aircraft
engines was feathered. It might be concluded that, at least
to the Soviets, color is a very important consideration.

4. (U)   The following information is based on a discussion
by   Two
Canadian scientists who are long standing psycho-optic researchers
of the highest rank and who also are oriented towards their military
establishments are Doctor Douglas Pearce and Doctor C.E. Mackinnon.
The two doctors have specialized in psycho-optic research dating
back to the early 1950s. About 1962, they became associated with
the Canadian Ministry of Defense in Toronto, Canada. Doctor Pearce
and Doctor Mackinnon have been experimenting with human subjects
since 1952. Some of their work includes studies on the effects
of light and other stimuli on aircraft pilots; it is believed
that this research was military oriented. It is felt that their
work (and future work) should be studied and watched because of
their expertise in the area of light stimuli.

5. (U)   Very little literature has appeared on countermeasures or defense against flashing lights. One US expert (246)
suggests that perhaps the most simple means of protecting against
the adverse effects of flickering light would be a series of
filters fitted to eye glasses or goggles, but the wearer would
have to be absolutely cognizant of the exact wavelength employed
against him to get the desired results. A variable and selective
filter for eye glasses could be manufactured. Also, there is
optical glass that would limit the field of vision to a few degrees.
Based on the discussion of the use of a tungsten light to conceal
a laser source, it would be of interest to see if any discernable
eye damage had occurred to any of the air crew that was subjected
to Soviet red strobe lights. It appears to be imperative that
eye examinations must be given to all personnel who report exposure
to Soviet flickering lights.

86

ST-CS-01-169-72
July 1972

PART VII

ODOR AND THE ALTERING OF HUMAN BEHAVIOR

SECTION I - BACKGROUND

1. (U) Man has just begun to research the areas of odor and
olfactory phenomena. An increasing amount of evidence implicates
olfactory mechanisms in communication between the sexes in prosi-
mians and also in their social organization, but to date there
is only scant information that olfaction plays a similar role
in higher primates (247).

2. (U) Do pheromones operate also in people? There is no evidence
that they do not, and some evidence that they do. Many psychiatrists
have believed that odor is among the "cues" which operate in the
transference situation, while schizophrenic patients, who are
receptive to unorthodox ideas and have their sensory gain-control
turned right up, claim to "smell" hostility. Some psychiatrists
themselves have long claimed to be able to "smell" schizophrenia--
the substance involved has now been identified as trans-3-methylhexanoic
acid. Olfactory sensitivity varies greatly in humans--a perfumer
can smell the differences between skin and hair colors, and many
unskilled observers have noted the unique, pleasant skin odor of
redheaded women (248).

3. (U) Pheromones control ant behavior and much insect mating.
An artificial pheromone (gyplure) can be synthesized to attract
gypsy moth males into an insecticidal trap. They are also widespread in mammals. Some mammalian odors, like the n-butylmercaptan
of the skunk, or the labeling of territory with urine, are straight-
forward signals. These influence behavior in the same way as a
display of threat, dominance or attraction. The action of a true
pheromone is more direct; it is a signal, but its action is more
like that of a hormone--the distinction is not total, but it is
perceptible, in that many pheromonal odors, at least in mammals,
have a chemical shape rather like that of a steroid molecule,
and might have been derived from one.

4. (U) Insects take advantage of their keen, specialized olfactory
organs (usually the antennae) to guide them to food, the opposite
sex, or mark the place to lay eggs. Sense of smell is particularly

87

ST-CS-01-169-72
July 1972

important to the social insects, which manufacture a variety of
scents to coordinate the activities of their colonies; they employ
odors to warn their kind of impending danger, to recognize intruders,
to mark trails leading to food, to move their nests, and to enlist
the help of other colony members. Because of this phenomenon,
man may be able to control insects through the use of different
chemical attractants (249). It may some day be possible for men to
control other men by using pheromones.

SECTION II - Behavioral Altering Possibilities

1.   (U)   A paper presented at the Ciba Foundation Symposium
on Mechanisms of Taste and Smell in Vertebrates by M.G.J. Beets
is of interest because of the implications of possible chemical
warfare use (250). The paper by Beets reports a new line of synthetic odor producing substances with odors closely related to
those of some of the steroids. The steroids are very complex,
expensive to produce, naturally-occurring substances with strong
odors which are quite important in controlling behavior, particularly in lower animals. Steroids are used in contraceptive medicaments, and perfumers have been looking among them for years for
a substance to insert into perfumes as an aphrodisiac. Beets and
his group have come up with a very simple artificial product
which is easy to synthesize chemically and which has the identical smell of the natural substance it mimics. Instead of having
a large, complicated chemical structure with, say four rings,
Beets has produced a structure with a single ring but with so many
groups attached to it chemically that it is the same shape of
molecule as the natural substance. The accomplishment supports
the theory that odors of chemicals depend upon the shapes of
their molecules (251).

2.   (U)   Beets' paper reports an innocent development, but
the principle of the development applies in chemical warfare with
regard to the search for "mind benders." In fact, Beets observed
that the basic idea of his accomplishment could be extended to drugs,
hormones and some other substances, making their synthesis much
easier by simplifying the steps of production while retaining
the overall shape of the molecule (251).

3.   (U)   There are at least two problems in using this
synthetic mimicry for a placating or confusing effect in chemical
warfare. One is getting the substances sufficiently volatile for
dispersal in the air. The natural substances are generally not

88

250

ST-CS-01-169-72
July 1972

volatile, but a way may be found to make them so. Moreover, we
are just at the beginning of a knowledge of the chemical contro-
lers that are produced in the body, and it is not unlikely that
some of these substances are small-moleculed and thus replaceable
by a synthetic substance which could be readily distributed through
the air. There is also the possibility of distributing the non-
volatile substances through the water system, which is probably
more efficient for some purposes.

4. (U)   The second problem has to do with whether odor—
that is, the chemical traces entering the body which produce the
effect we call odor—can have a substantial behavioral effect upon
human beings. There is the ancient idea of the aphrodisiacal
odor in perfume. Certain food odors can start one to salivate and
make one hungry. Certainly, most of the lower animals and insects
do have strong odor-responsive systems. A bitch in heat will
attract male dogs from half a mile or a mile around. Many insects
use similar systems for attracting a mate or for knowing where
to lay their eggs. Ants produce a smell warning other ants of
danger. In the animal world the phenomenon of pheromone—of
odorous signaling substances—can be powerfully controlling, and
it would be very surprising if the human being is exempt from this.

5. (U)   Many of the secretions of the endocrine glands
have profound effects in signaling changes in the basal metabolism
and changes in the whole operation of the body. It is probable
that more and more substances will be found that are put into
the blood stream by the endocrine glands, or by the brain, which
control whether we feel awake, or sleepy, or active, or sexy,
or hungry or whatever else. So there is a very definite possibility of an eventual chemical warfare application of these substances
synthetically reproduced or mimicked. And just conceivably, Beets'
principle is the way to go (251).

6. (U) There appears to be a very definite lack of Soviet literature
on the subject of pheromones and odor. However, in 1968, Klimenko (252)
authored a book entitled "Live Radio Electronics." There are
some enticing chapter titles but unfortunately no translation was
available at the time of this report. The titles are as follows:

    a. Organs of Sense, Special Devices and Analyzers in
        Animate Organisms.
    b. Olfactory and Gustatory Organs
    c. Use of Odors

ST-CS-01-169-72
July 1972

It is further believed that the book, since it contains a chapter
on biocommunication, deals with parapsychological phenomena.

7. (U) Suffice it to say that the Soviets have been working with
the synthesis of various mercaptan compounds. Apparently they
are looking for oil and water soluble mercaptan compounds with
sharp odors (253). The only reason this is mentioned is because
the work comes from a pharmacology and toxicology laboratory
and not a pure chemistry or industrial laboratory. This suggests
that the Soviets are interested in the effects of these compounds
on living organisms.

8. (U) Another area of interest is the Soviet work on the
influence of carbon tetrachloride on the human body. Belkov (254)
reports that small concentrations (8 mg. per cubic meter) decreases
the light sensitivity of the eye. The threshold of reflex action
of this sensitivity was 6 mg. per cubic meter. Thus concentrations
of carbon tetrachloride undetectable by its odor can change the
light sensitivity of the eye. This fact has possible application
in chemical warfare use as a behavioral control mechanism.

9. (U) Pheromone phenomena has interested researchers in Poland.
A 1969 review article with 88 references was written by J. Kwiatkowska.
The article deals with pheromones and communication in the animal
kingdom (304). A 1970 review by Malicki discusses physical and
chemical attractants for insects (305).

10. (U) One approach to behavior alteration in humans is
through the possible use of the olfactory sensitivity of insects
or animals. One can use a pheromone or other odor-producing
agent to create a condition that will cause insects for example
to gather to a specific location, e.g. on an enemy troop camp. Another
pheromone could be released that could cause aggressive behavior
in the insects, this in turn would disrupt the military unit
and render them ineffective. The Soviets have been working with
attractants for the *Aedes* mosquitoes. They have shown that solutions
of lysine and alanine are useful as *Aedes* attractants (306). It
might be mentioned that these aqueous solutions would probably
be adaptable to aerosol dissemination.

11. (U) Shamshurin et al have claimed that they are able to
synthesize the sex attractant of *Pectinophora gossypiella* (307).
Burtsev and Gladilin have reported on the isolation and testing
for biological activity of the attractant for the butterfly *Danus
gilippus* (308).

90

252

UNCLASSIFIED

ST-CS-01-169-72
July 1972

PART VIII

SOUND AS A MEANS OF ALTERING BEHAVIOR

SECTION I - GENERAL

1. (U) The psychological and behavioral effects of infrasound
and the low ranges of audible sound (those frequencies in the
range of 1 to 100 cycles per second, i.e. Hertz (Hz) are poorly
documented, especially Soviet work. There is some sketchy data
available on sonic (20 to 20,000 Hz) and ultrasound (usually
any frequency greater than 20,000 Hz).

2. (U) The Soviets are, however, aware of the biological effects
of sound and seem to be interested in establishing protective measures
for humans. The Soviets believe that the fact that human beings
are not biologically adapted to the rapid tempo, noise, and pressures
of an urban industrial society accounts for the increase in cardiovascular and nervous disturbances. Therefore, the Soviets are
experimenting with a concept they call "The Zone of Health." One
such zone has been established in Baku. The facility includes
parks and seashore with provisions for 28 kinds of natural therapy
including climatotherapy, kinestherapy, diet therapy, phototherapy,
psychotherapy, etc. During 1969, 142,000 "patients" were treated
with some 98 percent going home "healthy" (255). Apparently the
zone is a form of rest and relaxation with complete absence from
excessive sound stimuli. This would appear to be an expensive
project and therefore illustrates the Soviet concern for the
effects of excessive noxious stimuli on its people.

3. (U) A 1964 book written by G.N. Krivitskaya (256) appears
to be of extreme interest; unfortunately only the preface and
the table of contents is available in translated form. For readers
interested in behavior modifications through sound, it seems that
a full translation is a must. Below is described the purpose
and coverage of the text and the abridged form of the table of
contents. The book is entitled "Effect of Intense Noise on the
Brain; Experimental Research." This book covers the problem of
change in morphological structures (nerve cells, fibers, synapses,
ganglia and vessels) in the neuron systems using different analyzers
for the effect of noise stimulants such as an electric bell with
a strength of 80-130 decibels (db) of mixed frequency used from one
to 44 times. The material is divided into three parts. The
first part describes the harmful effect of sound irritants on
living organisms. The second deals with experimental data
(producing convulsive attacks in a rat in response to sound
irritants). In both chapters, further references are cited.

91

UNCLASSIFIED

UNCLASSIFIED

ST-CS-01-169-72
July 1972

In the third chapter results of studies are compared with data
from references. This book is recommended for neuropathologists,
otolaryngologists, therapeutists and pathomorphologists.

SECTION II - INFRASONIC NOISE

1. (U) The following discussion on the effects of infrasound
is based on a report by Maire (257). Due to the lack of appropriate
Soviet literature, this discussion is based upon references from
other countries.

2. (U) Observed psychological and physiological effects have
included significant impairment of compensatory tracking ability,
choice-reaction time, foot pressure constancy and peripheral
vision. Other effects were greater error increases in reaction
times and performance at 5 Hz than at 2 Hz, increased initial
reaction time and an increasingly detrimental effect on visual
performance as frequencies were increased above 8 Hz, with maximum
effect occuring between 40 and 50 Hz. Gavreau (258) observed that
high intensity infrasound caused sensations of panic and the
impression that the head would burst. Infrasound at a frequency
of 7 Hz (emitted by a faulty industrial ventilator) caused difficulty in the performance of mental activities and precision work.
Other studies (259, 260) have shown that at exposures to stimuli
of 15-17 Hz, at SPL's (sound pressure level) of approximately 104 dB,
subjects experienced feelings of apprehension. During initial
exposures to intense sound fields, many individuals presented symptoms
typical of generalized stress reactions, particularly in cases where
sufficiently effective ear protectors were not in use. Severe storm
activity in North America was compared with the automobile accident
rate and the rate of absenteeism among school children in the
area of Chicago, Illinois during May 1967. The results suggested
that a correlation may exist between the presence of infrasonic
disturbances in the area and changes in selected patterns of
human behavior (261).

UNCLASSIFIED

ST-CS-01-169-72
July 1972

3. (U) Very little information is available on animal reactions
to infrasound at this time. According to Maire, it has been
reported that a frequency of 7 Hz caused "epileptic fits" and
the subsequent death of rats at some distance from the laboratory
in which the generator was located. There is a newspaper article
claiming that during experiments with a frequency of 7 Hz, all
dogs in a nearby apartment building "went completely insane with
fear" (262).

SECTION III - SONIC NOISE

1. (U) There have been several pertinent Soviet reports on the
psychological effects of noise in the 20 to 20,000 Hz range.
Among these was a report by Korotkin et al (263) that showed
changes in auditory thresholds as a result of suggestion during
hypnosis. In 14 of 16 subjects, the deterioration or improvement
in audibility of sound signals suggested during hypnosis produced
a significant change in auditory sensitivity in accordance with
the suggestion of the hypnotist. More substantial changes in
auditory sensitivity (up to 60 db) followed the suggestion of
poor audibility. The range of changes in sensitivity following
the suggestion of good audibility was narrower (up to 21.4 db).
The lowering of the auditory thresholds in response to a suggestion
of good audibility was largely dependent on their level on the day
of the experiment. The higher the original levels, the more they
dropped as a result of suggestion. The considerable individual
variations in auditory sensitivity caused by suggestion were
obviously related to the degree of suggestibility of the subjects.

2. (U) Rudenko reports that canine death can be caused by strong
acoustic stimulation (264). Prolonged attempts (for six weeks)
to evoke neurosis in a dog possessing exceptional strength and
equilibrance of nervous processes by using super-strong acoustic
stimuli failed to produce any appreciable disturbances of its
nervous activity. Then to increase the excitability of the dog's
nervous system and raise its working capacity to the limit, a
loud tone (120 decibels) was combined with the administration
of caffeine in 0.5, 1.0, and 1.5 grams doses 30 minutes before
the experiment. Ten minutes after a 1.5 gram dose of caffeine
was administered, there was a drastic tonic convulsion of the
entire body and a few seconds later the animal died. This indicates
that this type of animal has strongly pronounced protective mechanisms and that destruction of these mechanism may lead to a breakdown of higher nervous activity or to even graver consequences.

93

ST-CS-01-169-72
July 1972

3. (U) Alekseyev and Suvarov (265) studied the speed and intensity
of acoustic and visual reactions in subjects exposed to noise from
thirty minutes to four hours. Using 70 to 90 db noise intensities
in a soundproof chamber, the investigators recorded vocal and motor
reaction response times after varying exposure durations. Prolonged
(3-4 hour) testing at either db level caused fatigue of the central
nervous system, reduced effective response, and disturbed relationships between motor responses and strength of stimulus. Noise of
70 db produced no essential changes in responses within the first
hour of testing, while 90 db noise caused changes in vision dependent
reactions and slowing of reaction times.

4. (U) Strakhov (267) has investigated the effect of high intensity
noise (95-100 db, 1500-3000 Hz) on EEG patterns. In human subjects
a gradually increasing desynchronization of cortical rhythms was
noted together with the appearance of slow waves. In rabbits and
cats, both desynchronized and synchronized rhythms occurred. The
general character of noise induced changes, the considerable after
effect of noise, accompanying changes in respiratory function, and
the presence of a cardiovascular reaction suggested that subcortical
brain structures (especially the reticular formation of the medulla
oblongata) were primarily responsible for the genesis and development
of these changes. This hypothesis was confirmed by electrophysiological studies with potentials taken directly from subcortical
structures. In addition, histological examination showed pronounced
changes in medullary nerve cells. In a later report (267), Strakhov
reported that a generalized alpha rhythm depression develops during
a period of several minutes as a result of exposure to 95-100 db
noise, but that if photic stimulation were applied at the beginning
of the noise, alpha rhythm bursts appeared which weakened, then
completely disappeared as the noise action continued. Discontinuation
of the noise first brought about new bursts of alpha rhythm in response
to photic stimulation, and subsequently led to its complete restoration.
The administration of scopolamine delayed the development of the
changes. The results were regarded to be due to development of an
inhibitory state in the cerebral cortex due to the activation by
noise of the reticular structures of the inferior parts of the brain
stem and the release of inhibitory mechanisms of the nonspecific
thalamus. Other EEG work has been reported by Korzh (268) and by
Doroshenko et al (269).

5. (U) On a more subjective psychological level, Vogel (270),
classifies effects into three categories: gross, annoyance, and
subtle, arranged roughly according to decreasing sound intensity.
Subtle involves sounds used to instill fear, anxiety, confusion,
panic, etc., examples of which would be the bugles played by

94

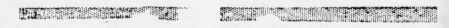

ST-CS-01-169-72
July 1972

the Communist Chinese in the Korean War and the Confederate "yell"
of the Civil War. Annoyance sounds would be sounds used to interfere
with work performance such as the ability to learn and retain.
Gross psychological damage would be the complete loss of the ability
to function, destroying or "muddling" of the conscious to such a
degree that the ability of all but involuntary actions (breathing,
heart beat) would be destroyed. Vogel states that nowhere in the
scientific literature could there be found a documented incident
where high intensity sound caused a gross psychological effect,
or any closely related effect, on a man.

6. (U) The intense noises associated with aircarft may in many
ways be similar to those that might be purposely generated under
combat conditions. In this respect the work of Terent'yev, Sheludyakov
and Sviridova (271) may be quite relevant to assessment of the psychological effects of noise on highly motivated, trained personnel. These
investigators observed 90 people from an aviation engineering technical staff, who, in the course of their work, were subjected to the
influence of noise with an intensity of 100-102, 110-112, 118-120,
and 130-136 db daily, or two to three times a week for one to six
hours at a time. The majority of the technicians exposed to 130 db
and more, complained of general fatigue, reduced work capability,
headache, unpleasant sensations in the region of the heart, noise
and ringing in the ears after each day's work, less frequently of
itching over the entire body, pains in the front wall of the abdomen,
and sometimes nausea and vomiting. In some, sleep was irregular and
appetite lowered. In a majority, these phenomena disappeared after
a nights sleep; in others after 2-3 days if work under noise conditions was not repeated. Analysis of case data showed that the
frequency, expression and duration of unfavorable sensations were
determined by both intensity and noise duration. Individual characteristics of those examined were also important. The symptom complexes
described developed more frequently and earlier in people in whom
head trauma, hyperthyroid, neurocirculatory dystony and other
illnesses had been noted. In order to validate the observations
made under work noise conditions, fifteen healthy volunteers were
tested under laboratory conditions. After exposure to noise with
an intensity of 100-102 db for one hour, some subjects complained
of noise in the head and sleepiness; after three hours, five of
eleven complained of general fatigue and one, of sleepiness; after
six hours, all examinees complained of noise and ringing in the
ears, headache and general fatigue, reduced appetite, nausea,
sleepiness and general irritability. After exposure to an intensity
of 110-112 db for up to three hours, all subjects complained of
headache, fatigue, sleepiness, and a sensation of deposits in the
ears; one subject complained of nausea and reduction of work capability..

95

ST-CS-01-169-72
July 1972

Under daily six hour exposure to noise of 110-112 db for five days,
the changes increased from day to day: fatigue, headache and general
malaise. After the third day the symptoms did not disappear by the
beginning of the following work day. With noise of 118-120 db,
a single exposure elicited the same changes as at lower levels, but
the degree of expression increased significantly and the aftereffects
lasted longer. Especially strong reactions were observed in three
and six hour exposures. All volunteers complained of noise and
ringing in the ears, general fatigue and heaviness of the head. In
some subjects, paleness of the skin, involuntary twitching of face
muscles, apathy or irritability, perspiration, or tremors of the
eyelids and fingers appeared. One general observation of considerable significance was that the effects of prolonged noise exposure
are cumulative.

7. (U) Mikhaylova and Byshevskiy report that 2000 Hz for various
periods of time (from 30 minutes to 10 days) on exposed rats may
contribute to inhibition of the anticoagulation process (272).
Further studies on rats exposed to 2000 Hz for various time limits
showed a reduced transketolase activity (273).

8. (U) Yuganov et al (274) have suggested that there be a standardization for admissible limits for high intensity sound. The effect
exerted on humans by noise of 114-116 and 125-126 db with an acoustic
energy of 500 Hz was studied. The auditory thresholds, blood
pressure values and time of response to light stimuli were measured.
Sixty-four healthy male test subjects were used in 152 experiments.
Adverse changes in the acoustic analyzer, cardiovascular system
and locomotor analyzer were detected during an exposure to 125-126
db noise. Taking into account the changes in the thresholds of
skin vibrosensitivity when the ear was protected, it is concluded
that the skin becomes a second gauge for acoustic energy beginning
with 125-126 db. Noise of 114-116 db is considered admissible during
powered stages of spaceflight.

SECTION IV - ULTRASONIC NOISE

1. (U) Various psychological effects to exposure to ultrasound
(greater than 20,000 Hz) has been reported in the Soviet literature.
Mel'kumova and Koroleva (275) reported psychological-subjective
findings based on clinical observations of 104 individuals exposed
to ultrasound in an industrial environment. The main complaints
of the examinees were headache, extremely pronounced fatigability,
tiredness and a general weakness. The onset of fatigue in most
of the subjects began as early as two to three hours after starting
work with simultaneous development of headache, with the latter

96

ST-CS-01-169-72
July 1972

increasing progressively in intensity until the midday break.
For some, the 30 minute break at noon restored work capacity and
lessened the severity of the headache. Considerable exhaustion
was experienced by most subjects by the end of the workday. Besides
the marked fatigability and tiredness the examinees complained of
a constant feeling of general weakness and vertigo with dimming of
vision occurring by noon, at the end of the workday, under physical
or mental strain and in stuffy rooms. These sensations caused loss
of consciousness in some individuals.

2. (U) Another effect of ultrasound was disturbances in sleeping
patterns. The need for sleep was felt by one group during actual
work, before the noon break, or toward the end of the work day.
Some individuals were overcome by drowsiness during short pauses
in work and in longer pauses, fell asleep standing up or in other
normally uncomfortable positions. In rare cases daytime drowsiness
was of the nature of a hypnagogic state, during which the individuals
continued to be oriented in their surroundings, hear speech, follow
the industrial process, and at the same time, sleep with clear
dreams. Changes in nocturnal sleep were also reported. Thirty-
eight per cent of the workers complained of drug-like heavy, dreamless sleep, while another group (18%) slept superficially and intermittently with difficulty in falling asleep and, in some cases, with
oppressive dreams.

3. (U) Other reported effects were morbidly sharpened perception
of ordinary sounds during off-duty hours, leading to sleeplessness
and the opposite extreme, in which one worker reported the sensation of "wanting to sleep day and night," even during the workday.
Heightened irritability was detected in 30 persons, while in 15
others, intellectual impairments were found. These included pronounced loss of memory (especially for current events), decreased
perception, and inability to master new material.

4. (U) During clinical examination of this group of workers the
investigators noted lassitude, apathy and retardation of movements
and reactions. The examinees rarely expressed their complaints
themselves, but more often had to be prodded verbally in order to
elicit information. Replies to questions were monsyllabic and
conversational initiative was lacking.

5. (U) In other studies conducted by the Institute of Hygiene
imeni Erisman, Yefimov (276) reported findings including weakening
of the sense of smell and decreased taste sensations as well as
certain disturbances in digestion. Of the gastrointestinal symptoms, the most frequently noted were poor appetite, nausea and a
tendency toward constipation. In some cases these symptoms were

ST-CS-01-169-72
July 1972

combined with pains in the stomach which radiated into the right
subcostal region. Menstrual disturbances (dysmenorrhea and prolonged
amenorrhea) were detected in several women workers, but gynecological
examination revealed no inflammatory or proliferative disease in
any of them. Many men among the examinees complained of reduced
sexual capacity. Two men, aged 46 and 48, with long work exposure
on ultrasonic installations displayed sexual impotence.

6. (U) The organ and cellular effects of ultrasound have also
been documented. Gorshkov (277) cites studies by Wolf in which
small aquatic animals were exposed to varied durations and intensities
of 800 kHz ultrasound. The results suggested that a species specific
relationship may exist for sensitivity to ultrasonic irradiation.
Gorshkov also cites experiments by Buchtala who described spontaneous bone fracture in a young dog after ultrasonic irradiation,
and Majno, who exposed the extremities of a rabbit to ultrasound
at 960 kHz, 6 watts/cm^2, for 30-120 minutes. Edemas of soft tissues,
ulceration, periosteal separation from the bone, and subendosteal
hemorrhages resulted. Necrotization of the bone eventually followed,
although the joint cartilage and epiphyseal growth plates remained
completely unchanged.

7. (U) Klupp (278) et al exposed the kidney region of animals
to 2 MHz ultrasound at intensities greater than 5 watts/cm^2. Morphological changes were found in the primary convoluted tubules, the
loops of Henle, the secondary convoluted tubules, and the descending
arms of the loops of Henle. The connective tissue elements and
collecting tubules of the medullary layer were found to be more
resistant to ultrasound. Other investigators have observed dila-
tation of the renal blood vessels, hemorrhages in the medullary
and cortical layers, and degenerative changes in the epithelium of
the urinary tubules following exposure to high intensity sonic waves.

8. (U) The behavioral effects of ultrasound on animals have been
examined to a limited extent.

9. (U) Wood and Loomis (279) exposed fish to ultrasound. The
fish showed initial disquietude, then rushed from side to side in
the tank, swam to the surface and attempted to gulp greedily for
air. Some, after as little as one minute of exposure, became
sluggish, motionless, or showed symptoms of disturbed equilibrium
and weak, irregular respiration. At times, sporadic attacks of
renewed frenzied activity followed, with rapid respiration and
cardiac activity. Subsequent increase in intensity killed the fish.

98

TIM RIFAT

ST-CS-01-169-72
July 1972

10. (U) In chronic experiments with ultrasound of moderate
intensity, Onanov (280) observed changes in animal behavior (apathy,
lassitude, refusal of food, emaciation, trophic ulcers and loss
of fur). Death due to stress with adrenal failure has been reported
in sheep subjected to ultrasonic irradiation at high intensities
similar to those used in the treatment of human auditory disease.
Stress due to ultrasound of lower intensities has also been claimed (281).

SECTION V - CONCLUSION

1. (U)   Although the above discussion on Soviet research in
the areas of biological (psychological) properties of sound was
brief, it expresses an awareness on the part of the Soviets of
the potential harmful effects on humans. Some Soviet research
has indicated that the behavioral changes in man and animal are
of prime importance.

2. (U)   According to Maire (257) scientists from Warsaw
Pact countries have evinced interest in French sonic and ultrasonic sirens and pneumatic compressors for acoustic wave generation.
Therefore, the Soviets may be expected to continue research on small
siren powered emitters for mob control and on larger acoustic arrays
for area denial and anti-infiltration application.

99
(Reverse Blank)

261

UNCLASSIFIED

ST-CS-01-169-72
July 1972

PART IX

SENSORY DEPRIVATION

1. (U) A relatively recent development in experimental psychology has been the study of the effects upon human behavior of
a severe reduction in the level and variability of visual, auditory,
and tactual-kinesthetic stimulation. The experimental attempts
to achieve such a non-changing sensory environment are often
referred to by such terms as stimulus deprivation, sensory or
perceptual deprivation, or sensory and perceptual isolation. Whatever the terminology, this condition can produce marked behavioral
and physiological changes. It has been demonstrated that a varied
and patterned sensory environment is essential to the maintenance
of normal human behavior. If a person is required to live for
many days in a monotonous, non-changing sensory and perceptual
environment, his physiological and psychological processes may
operate in extraordinary ways (282).

2. (U) The following discussion is excerpted from a report by
Zubek (282). According to Zubek, the first experimental work on
perceptual deprivation began in 1951 at McGill University. Its
purpose was to further the understanding of the mechanisms underlying "brainwashing" (e.g. Korean War) and of the lapses of attention noted under monotonous environmental conditions, such as
watching a radar screen for a prolonged period of time. The
results of the McGill research were very enlightening. The subjects,
who were paid to do nothing except lie alone in a semi-soundproofed
chamber for several days, wear translucent goggles and listen to
a constant masking sound of low intensity, reported a variety of
unusual subjective phenomena e.g. vivid and highly structured
hallucinations, delusions, and gross changes in the appearance
of the perceptual environment upon emerging from isolation. In
addition to these introspective reports, objective test data
were obtained which indicated an increased susceptibility to
propaganda material, impairments in cognitive and perceptual
functioning, and a progressive slowing of occipital alpha frequencies with increasing duration of isolation.

3. (U) The results described above, together with several other
post-World War II developments, soon started worldwide interest in
the effects of sensory isolation and confinement. One source of
interest came from the highly publicized "confessions" extracted
by communist interrogators (e.g. the Cardinal Mindzenty case).
What little information was available suggested that the results
were obtained by techniques which often employed solitary confinement

101

UNCLASSIFIED

ST-CS-01-169-72
July 1972

and the deliberate impoverishment of the prisoner's perceptual
environment (283). Drugs and physical torture were apparently
not used. Another development was the arrival of the space age
in 1967. Other advances, as reflected in increased use of submarines, isolated radar and meteorological stations, and of auto-
mated equipment in general, also provided considerable impetus
to the initiation of research programs dealing with reactions to
restricted sensory and social environments.

4. (U) Despite the recounts of the Mindzenty case, the Soviets
did not publish reports on sensory deprivation until the mid 1960s.
The Soviet data is usually published in their aerospace or related
literature. Hinkle in 1969, however, has reported that under
prison isolation, as this has been carried out by Soviet and
Eastern European state police, most prisoners developed symptoms
of disorganization within three to six weeks; but some have been
known to endure this for many months, and some have succumbed
within days (284). Based on Hinkle's statement and numerous
other accounts on the treatment of prisoners in the Soviet Union
and other communist countries, it seems safe to say that they have
had some experience with the effects of sensory deprivation prior
to their acknowledgment of actual research in this field.

5. (U) The Soviets are quick to point out that the Canadians
and the Americans were the first to report and maintain research
efforts in the field of isolation and sensory deprivation (SD). Perhaps
to detract attention from the prison reports, Kosmolinskiy reports
that from the mid-fifties, sensory deprivation experiments attracted
increasingly greater attention in scientific investigation centers
of the Army, Air Force, and Navy of the United States and Canada (285).
In another section of Kosmolinskiy's report, he mentions, however,
that the question of sensory deprivation was already established in
the USSR in the twenties by I.P. Pavlov. The distinction between
Pavlov's work and research by Galkin in 1932 (286) as compared to
Western work is that the Soviet efforts were more humane. Kosma-
linskiy states that abroad, crueler forms of isolation were imposed
and that sensory limitations were created by the most severe means
e.g. plaster cast usage.

6. (U) Western literature on sensory deprivation deals with many
of the psychic manifestations that appear during or after the
experiment. Many investigators noted significant changes in the
emotional sphere of subjects in sensory deprivation (50) experiments: the appearance of varying degrees of apathy, melancholy,
anxiety and fear (287). Sometimes, apathy and dulled consciousness
of the subjects become so profound that one of the most important

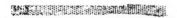

ST-CS-01-169-72
July 1972

instincts is destroyed - the instinct of self-preservation - and
the person contemplates suicide (288). The Soviets contend that
serious psychological disorders in subjects as described above
are evidently related to the exessive burden of the severe experimental conditions on the physiology of the subjects. The Soviets
continue by stating that in the above studies it is not only a
matter of the action of isolation and SD factors, but also a
number of supplementary factors complicating the circumstances
of the experiment (restraint with straps, plaster casts, uncomfortable postures, and occasional painful sensations). The Soviets
further believe that Western experimental work does not appear to
be a true model of human life and work conditions, especially in
space flight simulation SD studies.

7. (U) According to Kosmolinskiy, experiments on the limitation
of stimuli and conditions of isolation carried out by Soviet
scientists showed that a healthy person with greater will power
can remain in a soundproof chamber for an extended period of time
without any psychic changes threatening the condition of his
health. The various specific sensory illusions which appear are
not of a morbid nature. This form of sensory illusion pertains
to illusions associated with incorrect perception of stimuli,
the information characteristic of which is insufficient (289).
The illusions themselves do not appear to be a sign of psychic
disease and often are encountered in healthy persons, especially
in those instances when something interferes with the distinct
perception of visual and auditory images; for example, poor
lighting. Baseline psychological status, fatigue, distraction,
states of expectation and fear are of great significance. O.N.
Kuznetsov and V.I. Lebedev (289) in describing the presence of
illusions involving recognition errors in subjects under investigation in the soundproof chamber as a consequence of insufficient
information, of a feeling of the extraneous presence of eidetic
images, ideas of relationship and over evaluations, do not consider
these phenomena to be pathological, and propose calling them
pseudopsychopathological. According to the data of F.D. Gorbov
(290), psychopathological phenomena were absent in the experiments
of Soviet cosmonauts in a soundproof chamber.

8. (U) Soviet scientists assume that the isolation factor must
be studied in conformity with conditions which can occur on space
flights. In this regard, the most important factor appears to
be that a person believe in the necessity of the work which he is
to accomplish, and that he have a clear conception of the objects
of a given experiment. Each experiment in the soundproof chamber
is a moral and volitional examination for future cosmonauts, for
example, which prepares them for the performance of complex tasks.

103

ST-CS-01-169-72
July 1972

9. *(U)* Most Soviet literature, as was mentioned previously,
dealing with SD experiments is related to the space effort. The
purpose for discussing some of the Soviet views above was to
illustrate the rather mundane work that they report in the open
literature. The more interesting aspect is their awareness and
apparent concentration on Western literature as is evidenced by the
Kosmolinskiy report. The Soviets don't go so far as to condemn
the Western approach, but seem to be quick to point out the
differences from their approach which is reported to be not as
severe. Based on early reports on "confessions" and "brainwashing"
in communist countries, it would be naive not to assume that the
Soviets do not have a clear conception of the effects of sensory
deprivation. Based also on their work in certain areas such as
the biological and mental effects of light and sound it should be
assumed that the capability for the application of SD in field
situations exists. Perhaps Kosmolinskiy gave himself away when
he stated that experiments show that isolation and sensory deprivation create complex physiological and psychological reactions
in the human organism. Measures must be developed to prevent
these disorders, which can involve several physiological systems
and lead to a decrease in his capacity for work and other psychological manifestations. Zubek's (282) work of 1969 indicated
that a prolonged period of perceptual deprivation and confinement
can produce, in most cases, a considerable disturbance of brain-
wave activity. Zubek in concluding his report said, "In the
light of these results, one can only wonder about the possible
physiological and psychological state of prisoners of war and
others who, in the past, have been isolated for months or even
years."

ST-CS-01-169-72
July 1972

text had already been deleted from this page
when document was made available to author

INTENTIONALLY LEFT BLANK

106

ST-CS-01-169-72
July 1972

PART X

ELECTROMAGNETIC EFFECTS

1. (U) Over a span of years which exceeds that of a century, numerous researches and observations have been conducted and published on the physiological and psychological effects of electric fields. As Davis (293) has stated in his exhaustive review of the subject, not much of substance has derived from all the attention which has been paid to the physiological effects on living organisms of placing them in environments which have been changed by manipulating one or more electromagnetic parameters. Somewhat more in the way of positive findings has been published as they relate to the psychological effects. There appears to be more literature from Soviet sources than from Western sources concerning the effects of electromagnetic fields on the central nervous system.

2. (U) A question was raised concerning the possible hazard to personnel working with a device which generated very high field density electromagnetic pulses. Of particular concern was the possibility that people working on an object which was to be subjected to the pulse might themselves receive the energy by virtue of a premature triggering or some other mischance. The generator created an electromagnetic field in the form of a pulse which had a duration of 3×10^{-9} sec, at a voltage of 1.0 megavolt. In essence, a Van de Graaf generator was used to charge a bank of high capacity condensers. The condensers were discharged into a load consisting of an array of aerial wires so that a high potential difference was caused to exist between them and a grounded metal mesh plate beneath. With the breakdown of the air dielectric an intense pulsed field was created. On one occasion when the generator was being tested after its erection, a bird flew under the aerial wires just as it was pulsed. The bird fell from the sky and flopped about in a rather disorganized way for a minute or so. It then appeared to regroup all those things which birds must have in order to fly, and flew off about its avian business apparently none the worse for the experience. This incident was unsettling to those working with the generator, so a search was made in the literature for something germane which would indicate whether or not a hazard to operating personnel existed. This literature search was reported by Hirsch et al (294). According to Hirsch, not very much was found except for a paper by Salvingnac et al (1967) which related to the psychomotor disturbances in air crews when their airplanes were struck by lightning. The density of the electromagnetic fields to which these people were exposed

107

ST-CS-01-169-72
July 1972

was probably of the same order of magnitude and duration as was
that associated with the EMP generator, since a lightning bolt
generates a cylindrical electromagnetic field of about 10 mega-
volts at its center with the density decreasing toward the periphery.
The duration is about 6 microseconds. Salvingnac described the
psychomotor disturbances as a "slowing of thought processes and
psychomotor reactions" from which the people recovered within a
brief period apparently without permanent damage.

3. (U) The above information concerning pulsed electromagnetic
energy could have behavior implications just as the photic-flicker
"experiments" described in PART VI could have. The "slowing of
thought processes and psychomotor reactions" could lead to behavioral
changes effecting the ability of an individual to perform a critical
task such as piloting an aircraft. It cannot be determined if
the report mentioned above initiated or accelerated Soviet
research in the area of the psychological or behavior effects of
electromagnetic energy. Since the early 1960s, the Soviets have
been publishing reports on the effects of electromagnetic and
magnetic fields on the central nervous system of animals. Although
the Soviet reports do not contain specific reference to effects
on humans, the data would give one the impression that they have
extensive knowledge of the subject as it might apply to humans.

4. (U) One of the more outstanding publications from the Soviet Union
is a book prepared by Yu. Kholodov (295). The book is a compilation
of Soviet and Western work in the area of electromagnetic effects
on the central nervous system. The bibliography to the book contains
455 entries. A large portion of the text directs itself to the
subject of the changes in conditioned reflexes and sensitivity
to light in birds, rabbits, and fish. The effects of ultrahigh
and superhigh frequencies on the electrical activity of the rabbit
brain is extensively discussed. A report on constant magnetic
fields is also presented. Although the book addresses physiological
responses, it points out that the Soviets have considerable knowledge
and a keen interest in the field of electromagnetic energies.

5. (U) The UCLA Brain Information Service in Los Angeles is
a bibliographic collector of information which is pertinent to
this discussion. The service has compiled an extensive bibliographic list on the biological effects of electromagnetic fields
(below visible frequencies) especially on the central nervous system.
The list contains many Soviet references. However, the list is
constructed around research that addresses the physiological
aspects and not the psychological or behavior effects (296).

108

ST-CS-01-169-72
July 1972

6. (U) A Soviet review article concerning the effects of superhigh
frequency (wavelength of from one millimeter to one meter) on the
central nervous system is worth incorporation into this report.
Although the work is primarily physiological, it is meaningful
because it contains some of the important areas of interest to the
Soviets and could be correlated to Soviet work with other frequencies. Kholodov (297) reports that the effect of SHF on the functions
of the central nervous system is of particular interest. So far,
few studies have dealt with this subject. Kholodov contends that
foreign investigators (chiefly American) use an SHF field with an
intensity on the order of tens of watts/sq cm, which results in
a considerable heating of the brain (above 40 degrees C). Depending
upon the duration of the radiation, mice and rabbits have stopped
eating for some time, or have made spasmodic movements, and even
died. Post-mortem examination of the animals have shown that the
action of the powerful SHF field has resulted in destruction of
the brain cells. Especially extensive destruction has been observed
in the inter-brain and mid-brain. When the head of a monkey is
exposed to a strong SHF field, the animal behaves normally for
the first minute or two, and then covers his eyes and starts to
go to sleep. But a minute later he wakes up; the rate of respiration increases; the pupils dilate despite the bright illumination;
and there is a heavy secretion of saliva. After some time the
monkey begins to shake with convulsions and utter cries. If the
radiation is discontinued, by the following day the monkey in no
way differs from other monkeys who have not been exposed to radiation.
If exposure is continued, the animal dies after a few minutes.
Experiments have shown that when men or animals are exposed to
radiation, there is a change in the sensitivity to sound, light,
and olfactory stimuli. A study of the receptors in the skin, the
gastrointestinal system, and the circulatory system has shown
slight changes in them after exposure to the action of SHF. Consequently, the SHF field can act on the first link in the reflex
arc. At the same time, SHF may act directly on the central nervous
system. On the other hand, the appearance of slow waves in the
record of the biological currents of the cerebral cortex, the
inhibition of reflex activity, and the appearance of various
vegetative reactions indicate action of the SHF field on the inter-
brain, where the higher vegetative centers are located. The data
from physiological experiments check very well with the results
from morphological investigations. After exposure to SHF, reversible structural changes were observed in the cerebral cortex and
in the inter-brain. It may be assumed that those areas of the
brain are the most sensitive to the action of an SHF field, although
if the intensity or duration of the action is increased, other

109

TIM RIFAT

ST-CS-01-169-72
July 1972

parts of the central nervous system will also participate in the
reaction. Kholodov concludes by stating that only further experiments will help us to explain the mechanism of the direct action
of an SHF field of nonthermal intensity. But it can already be
stated that these effects can be produced by an electromagnetic
field other than one of super-high frequency.

7. (U) Although Kholodov's article is early 1960, it points out
the interests the Soviets had over a decade ago; for that matter,
Vasilev was working with electromagnetic radiation in the 1930s
in his investigations of the transport methods for ESP. It is
evident that the effects of electromagnetic frequencies below
visible light on man are of interest to the Soviets. Kholodov
states that there is a change in the sensitivity in man to sound,
light, and olfactory stimuli. One can only make certain guesses
as to the possible relationship in Soviet research between electromagnetic radiation effects and behavioral responses to other
stimuli that they are working with.

8. (U) Christian (298) reports that the Soviet use of infrared
to cause gross damage to human targets is conjectural. However,
Christian in his report states that studies are being conducted
in the USSR which would lead one to conclude that infrared is
being considered as an anti-personnel weapon. Temporary blindness,
even of long duration, does not endanger the eye and yet is quite
serious when it alters the behavioral response of pilots or sentries
to their mission. Despite an extensive review of Soviet literature
on the effect of infrared radiation on humans, Christian could
find no reports on psychological effects. There was only one
report on behavior effects of infrared radiation. A report by
Dul'dier (299) states that a temporary loss of work capacity among
workers in hot shops, such as foundries, is directly related to
the dose of infrared received. He found somewhat surprisingly,
that temporary loss in working capacity is found more frequently
with younger workers, those on the job less than five years, than
the more experienced workers.

9. (U) One report has appeared in the Soviet literature relating
to the behavior effects of ultraviolet radiation. A study by
Al'bitskaya (300) seems to show that ultraviolet radiation can
show a decrease in the latent period of speech reaction during
association testing. Al'bitskaya studied the effect of 136-400nm
ultraviolet radiation on 15-16 year-old technical school students
as measured by their response in a conditioned reflex situation
and the length of the latent period in motor and speech reactions.

110

ST-CS-01-169-72
July 1972

She concludes that the response system based on speech is more excitable than the response system based on sensory perception since it can be stimulated by ultraviolet radiation.

10. (U) Low frequency electromagnetic fields have been found by Kevanishvili and Zhgenti to generate sonic and ultrasonic oscillations in living organisms (301). These oscillations produce elastic deformations in the organism. If the frequency of the outside field corresponds to the oscillation frequency of the cells, the latter deteriorate as the result of the mechanical resonance.

11. (U) More recently, research at the Riga Medical Institute has shown that high-tension static electrical fields affect the neurohumoral regulatory systems (301). Work is now apparently underway that is investigating the possibility of an effect of strong electrical fields as the energy balance of living objects at this institute.

12. (U) Sweeney (302) has prepared a study on the biological effects of electromagnetic radiation in the range of 3 to 300,000 mHz. The study covers research in the Eurasian communist countries. This exhaustive report again contains primarily information on the effects of electromagnetic radiation as it applies to physiological responses, not psychological or behavioral.

13. (U) Since almost all of the Soviet data on electromagnetic radiation (below visible) applies to physiological response, one can only imply that they have substantial knowledge of the psychological effects. Even if psychological or behavioral research is under way in the USSR, it is doubtful that they would publish it. There have been certain indications in the past that the Soviets may be actively engaged in weapons research employing electromagnetic radiation. Doctor V.V. Meriakri, the Director of the Institute of Radio Engineering and Electronics of the Soviet Academy of Sciences stated during an early 1969 visit to the United States, that he is studying the radiation absorption properties of biological fluids.

It is impossible to assess the truth of this assertion on the basis of ths information alone. Much more information about Meriakri and his research organization is needed.

111
(Reverse Blank)

ST-CS-01-169-72
July 1972

APPENDIX I

PERSONNEL AND INSTITUTES

CURRENT EVENTS

PART A - Affiliation Known

Serbsky Central Scientific Research Institute of Forensic Psychiatry,
Moscow, USSR

      LUNTS, D.R. (possible KGB Colonel)
      MALTSEVA, M.M.
      MARTYNENKO (fnu)
      MOROZOV, G.V. (Director)
      PECHERNIKOVA (fnu)
      TABANOVA (fnu)
      TALTSE (fnu)
      TUROVA, Z.G.

The Republican Hospital of the City of Riga, Latvian SSR

      KRASNYANSKY, O.A.
      MARKIS, L.A.
      RUSINOVA, Z.G.

Skvortsov-Stepanov Psycho-Neurological Hospital Number Three,
Leningrad, USSR

      BROVERMAN, L.B.
      SHCHERBATOV (fnu)
      SVETLANOVA, N.K.

KGB

      BERYOZOVSKY (fnu)

Chernyakhovsk Hospital (Chernyakhovsk, formerly the East Prussian
town of Insterburg)

      BELOKOPYTOV (MAJOR) Prison Commandant (fnu)

113

ST-CS-01-169-72
July 1972

PART B - Affiliation Unknown

      ALEKSEYEVNA, T.
      DETENGOF, F.F. (Tashkent, Uzbek SSR)
      KUZNETSOVA, E.I.
      NIKOLAYEVICH, L.

PART C - Important Institutes - No Personalities Available

      VLADIMIR PRISON (100 miles east of Moscow)
      ORYOL PSYCHIATRIC HOSPITAL (170 miles southwest of Moscow)
      BUTYRKA PRISON (Hospital Section), Moscow, USSR

SOVIET PSYCHOLOGY AND PSYCHIATRY - RESEARCH

PART A - Affiliation Known

Department of Psychology, Moscow State University

      KONOVALOV, V.F.
      KRINCHIK, E.P.
      LURIA, A.R.
      TIKHOMIROV, O.K.
      VASILYEVA, V.M.
      VORONIN, L.G.

Military Medical Academy (Leningrad)

      BODROV, V.A.

Naval Medical Academy

      SHASTIN, N.R.

Sechenov Institute (Leningrad)

      FADAYEVA, D.K.
      TRAUGOTT, N.N.

Pavlov Institute of Physiology (Leningrad)

      ANOKHIN, P.K.
      KOLTZOVA, M.M.
      ROGOVENKO, Ye.S.
      ROKOTOVA, N.A.

TIM RIFAT

UNCLASSIFIED

ST-CS-01-169-72
July 1972

Leningrad State University

GALUNOV, V.I.
GUBINSKIY, A.I.
LIVSHITS, V.A.

USSR Academy of Medical Sciences (Leningrad)

BEKHTEREVA, N.P.
BUDASHEVSKY, B.G.
ORLOV, V.A.

Institute of Higher Nervous Activity and Neurophysiology (Moscow)

ALEKSEYEV, M.A.
ASLANOV, A.S.
ARATYIAN, E.A.
LIVANOV, M.N. (Chief)
NAPALKOV, A.V.
RUSINOV, V.S.
SIMONOV, P.V.
YERSHOV, P.M.

USSR Academy of Sciences (Moscow)

BASHKIROV, O.A.
BOGACHENKO, L.S.
BRIKS, Z.N.
FELBAUM, A.I.
FUFLYGINA, T.P.
GERASIMCHUK, V.A.
IVANOV-SMOLENSKY, A.G.
KORBATOV, B.M.
MASLENNIKOVA, V.M.
MUCHNIK, I.B.
NARODITSKAIA, G.D.
NOVIK, I.B.
SEREDINA, M.I.
SHITL'MAN, E.V.
STROKHINA, T.V.

Institute of Psychology, Academy of Pedagogical Sciences (Moscow)

BOYOKO, E.I.
CHUPERIKOVA, N.I.
EL'KONEN, D.B.'
ISTOMINA, Z.M.

115

UNCLASSIFIED

275

ST-CS-01-169-72
July 1972

> LEONT'YEV, A.N.
> LOMOV, B.F.
> NEBYLITSYN, V.D.
> OSHANIN, D.A.
> SAMOKHVALOVA, V.I.
> SHVARTZ, L.A.
> SMIRNOV, A.A.
> TEPLOV, B.M.
> USHKOVA, T.N.
> ZAPOROZHETS, A.V.

Pavlov Hospital (Leningrad)

> LEBEDEN, B.A.

Soviet Academy of Medicine, Institute of Psychiatric Research

> SHCHIRINA, M.G.
> SNEZHNEVSKIY, A.V.
> VARTANIAN, M.

PART B - Affiliation Unknown

> SVYADOSHCH, A.M. (Karaganda)

PARAPSYCHOLOGY - USSR

PART A - Affiliation Known

Department of Physics, State Instrument Engineering College of Moscow

> NAUMOV, E.K.
> VALUS, N.A.

Bio-Information Section, A.S. Popov All-Union Scientific and Technical Society of Radio Technology and Electrical Communications, Moscow

> KOGAN, I.

Physiology of Labor Laboratory, University of Leningrad

> PAVLOVA, L.

A.A. Uktomskii Physiological Institute, Leningrad

> SERGEYEV, G.A.

116

UNCLASSIFIED

ST-CS-01-169-72
July 1972

Department of Theoretical Physics, Moscow University

TERLETSKY, Ya.

Bekhterev Brain Institute, University of Leningrad

GULYAIEV, P.

Research Institute of Psychology, Ukrainian SSR Academy of Sciences

GUBKO, A.
LEONTOVICH, M.A.
LEONTOVICH, A.V.

Moscow Institute of Aviation

ZIEGEL, F.U.

Laboratory of Vision, Institute of Problems of Information Transmission of the USSR Academy of Science

BONGARD, M.
SMIRNOV, M.S.

Pavlov Institute, Moscow

KOZAK, V.A.

Pulkovo Observatory, Leningrad

KOZYREV, N.

Filatov Institute, Laboratory of the Physiology of Vision, Odessa

SHEVALEV, A.

Geology Department of Moscow State University

OGILVY, A.A.

Kazakh University, Alma-ata

GIBADULIN, F.
GRISHCHINKO, V.
INYUSHIN, V.
SHOUISKI, N.
VOROBEV, N.

117

UNCLASSIFIED

UNCLASSIFIED

ST-CS-01-169-72
July 1972

Institute of Clinical Physiology, Kiev

    PODSHIBYAKIN, A.

PART B - Affiliation Unknown (1972)

    ADAMENKO, V. (Moscow)
    ARLASHIN, A.G. (telepathic tests vs distance)
    BOGATYREV. V.A.
    BULAVIN, G.I.
    DOBRONRAVOV, S.N. (Sverdlovsk)
    EFIMOV, V.
    FIDLEMAN, V.Ye.
    GULEVSKIY, V.V.
    HOLODOV, Y.A.
    IVANOVA, M.R.
    KAMENSKIY, Yu.I. (Physicist - ESP)
    KHOLODOV, Yu.A.
    MONIN, A.I. (telepathic tests vs distance)
    OSHCHEPKOV, P.K.
    PRESMAN, A.S. (Physicist - ESP)
    RAIKOV, V.L. (Moscow)
    SEROV, S. (Sverdlovsk)
    SOCHEVANOV, N. (Leningrad)
    TROSKIN, A. (Sverdlovsk)
    ZAKAROV (Leningrad)

MENTAL SUGGESTION AND CONTROLLED BEHAVIOR

PART A - Affiliation Known

Serbsky Central Scientific Research Institute of Forensic Psychiatry,
Moscow, USSR

    ROZHNOV, V.

The Institute of Suggestology and Parapsychology, Sofia, Bulgaria

    LOZANOV, G.

Psychiatry Department, Karaganda Medical Institute

    SVYADOSHCH, A.

118

UNCLASSIFIED

UNCLASSIFIED

ST-CS-01-169-72
July 1972

PART B - Affiliation Unknown

> GENKIN, A.A.
> GURVICH, G.I.
> KHVOGNOV, B.S.
> MARISHCHUK, V.L.
> MORDINOV, E.F.
> TISHCHENKO, M.I.
> YEFIMENKO, G.D.

PSYCHOPHARMACOLOGY IN THE USSR

Affiliation Known

Serbsky Institute of Forensic Psychiatry, Moscow

> ANOKHINA, I.P.
> GORDOVA, T.N.
> MIKHALEV, P.V.

Institute of the Brain, Academy of Medical Sciences, Moscow

> POPOVA, E.

First Medical Institute imeni I.M. Sechenov, Moscow

> KUDRIN, A.N.
> MENSHIKOV, V.V.

Moscow Medical Stomatological Institute, Moscow

> MATVEYEV, V.F.

Donetsk Medical Institute

> KOMISSAROV, I.V.
> TALALOYENKO, A.N.

Institute of Molecular Biology, Academy of Sciences, Moscow

> BRAUNSHTEYN, A.Ye.
> ENGELGARDT, V.A. (Head)
> SEVERIN (fnu) (son of Severin, S.Ye.)

119

UNCLASSIFIED

ST-CS-01-169-72
July 1972

Institute of Physiology, Tbilisi

      BACKURADZE, A. (Director)

Laboratory of Psychopharmacology, Bekhterev Scientific Research
Psychoneurological Institute, Leningrad

      LAPIN, I.P.

Laboratory of Pharmacology of the Nervous System, Institute of
Pharmacology, USSR Academy of Medical Sciences

      RAYEVSKIY, K.S.
      ZAKUSOV, V.V.

Institute of Normal and Pathological Physiology, Moscow

      ANOKHIN, P.K.

LIGHTS AND COLOR AS A MEANS OF ALTERING HUMAN BEHAVIOR

Affiliation Known

Military-Medical Academy imeni S.M. Kirov, Leningrad

      KOZHEVNIKOV, Ye.P.

Medical Institute imeni S.V. Kurashov, Kazan

      AMIROV, N.Kh.
      KALPINA, G.A.
      KAMCHATNOV, V.P.
      MENDELEVICH, D.M.
      ZUBAIROVA, G.O.

Institute of Higher Nervous Activity and Neurophysiology, USSR
Academy of Sciences, Moscow

      BAGDONAS, A.
      DAUROVA, F.K.
      LALAYAN, A.A.
      POLYANSKY, V.B.
      SOKOLOV, E.N.
      'VALTSEV, V.B.

UNCLASSIFIED

ST-CS-01-169-72
July 1972

Institute of Experimental Medicine, Academy of Medical Sciences, USSR, Leningrad

     DANILOV, I.V.
     KUDRYAVTSEVA, N.N.

Institute of Child and Juvenile Physiology, USSR Academy of Pedagogical Sciences, Moscow

     FRID, G.M.

ODORS AND THE ALTERING OF HUMAN BEHAVIOR

PART A - Affiliation Known

Scientific Research Institute of Pharmacology and Toxicology, Kiev

     NEDOPEKIN, T.K.
     PORTNYAGINA, V.A.
     STOLYARENKO, L.G.
     VASILYEVA, Ye.V.

PART B - Affiliation Unknown

     BELKOV, A.N.
     KLIMENKO, A.I.

SENSORY DEPRIVATION (non-aerospace)

Institute of Medical and Biological Problems, Moscow

     IL'IN, Y.

Laboratory of Sensory Processes, Scientific Research Institute of Psychology, Moscow

     LOMOV, B.

ELECTROMAGNETIC EFFECTS

Scientific Research Institute of Traumatology and Orthopedics, Riga

     KIKUT, R.

121

UNCLASSIFIED

ST-CS-01-169-72
July 1972

Division of Clinical Biophysics, Medical Institute, Riga

PORTNOV, F.

Ivanovo-Frankovsk Medical Institute

LAZAROVICH, V.G.

Institute of Higher Nervous Activity and Neurophysiology, Academy of Sciences USSR, Moscow

KHOLODOV, Yu.A.

Institute of Radio Engineering and Electronics of the Soviet Academy of Sciences

MERIAKRI, V.V.

ST-CS-01-169-72
July 1972

APPENDIX II

INTELLIGENCE GAPS

1. (U) More information, in the form of update data, is needed on Soviet parapsychological research. Before early 1971, Western psi scientists were allowed unusual access to Soviet institutes and personalities for the purpose of exchanging scientific results. As of February 1971, this practice came to an abrupt halt. Very little parapsychology literature has appeared since from the USSR.

2. (U) The lack of information on the parapsychological work of G.A. Sergeyev of the A.A. Uktomskii Laboratory (military) in Leningrad represents a definite intelligence gap.

3. (U) More information is needed on the Soviet experimental work on subliminal perception. The research on the use of motion pictures and other photographic techniques to alter behavior and to create conditions of weakened resistance in humans to interrogation has been reported in only one document.

4. (U) More information is required on the Soviet propaganda machine. Who runs it? Who is involved and numbers of people working within the propaganda framework? Is there an institute or school where the techniques of human manipulation thru mass media and/or terror manipulation principles are researched and taught?

5. (U) More information would be desirable on Soviet odor and pheromone research. Little is known about the chief laboratories and personalities involved. Little is known concerning the Soviet ability to synthesize pheromone compounds. No information is available concerning possible military uses of pheromones (animal, insect, or human) to create conditions that are conducive to disruption of military missions.

6. (U) More information is needed on the Serbsky Institute of Forensic Psychiatry in Moscow. It appears that this institute is involved, among other things, in the development of psychotropic drugs that may have possible psycho-warfare applications.

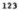

123

ST-CS-01-169-72
July 1972

8. (U) More information concerning V.V. Meriakri of the Institute of Radio Engineering and Electronics of the Soviet Academy of Sciences is needed. There is one report suggesting his involvement in anti-personnel weapons development based on electromagnetic principles.

9. (U) More information is needed concerning the work of V.L. Raikov, a physician with expertise in hypnotism.

124

ST-CS-01-169-72
July 1972

APPENDIX III

FUTURE TRENDS

1. (U)   It is now apparent that the ideological stigmas
attached to parapsychological phenomena have been breached in
the Soviet Union. Although serious studies of psi have been
going on in the USSR since the 1920s, it has only been since
1962 that researchers such as L. Vasilev have been allowed to
publish their work. In 1971, however, the open literature and
the open exchange of ideas between the USSR and the West
halted. During the next fifteen years it is expected that the
Soviets will energetically pursue all aspects of parapsychology.
With party approval and with the large sums of money allocated
in the late 1960s, it is inconceivable that the work has stopped.
It is believed that certain military applications have been discovered and that by 1980, the Soviets will have mastered some
aspects of psi phenomena in order to alter human behavior.

2. (U)   The Soviets are concentrating on the development
of psycho-warfare agents. One of the more recent areas appear
to lie in the development or isolation of marine toxins. The
Serbsky Institute of Forensic Psychiatry in Moscow is one such
facility shown to have interest in psychotropic substances to
include LSD, tranquilizers, and marine toxins. It is believed
that the search for new "mindbending" agents will continue in
the USSR. Close scrutiny of the literature, etc., especially
in marine toxin research is imperative.

3. (U)   Based on exhaustive searches of Soviet literature,
it is now apparent that the USSR has initiated research into the
behavior of insects and animals (possibly human) that is related
to pheromones. The technological base is available in the USSR
(and elsewhere) which could allow immediate behavioral exploitation
of certain insect and animal populations. The use of certain
pheromones that cause a gathering of animals to a certain location
and release of their aggressive behavior would cause immediate
disruption and confusion, and depending on the insect or animal,
even death to military units at the focal points of infestation.
It is extremely likely that given five to ten years of further
research, the Soviets will have the means as well as countermeasures
for the military employment of pheromones.

125

ST-CS-01-169-72
July 1972

4. (U)   The Soviets, it appears, have already experimented
with the use of flashing lights and colored lights for the
purpose of eliciting behavioral change in human targets. There
is literature available that reports on Soviet work involved in
the interactions of sound, light, and olfactory stimuli in humans.
The possibility already exists that the USSR has systems for the
use of flickering lights in the field. It can now be assessed
that in the next 15 years, they may develop a system that alters
behavior by combining two or more systems e.g. sound and light
together, to mask the use of the principal weapon e.g. the administration of a pheromone or a psychotropic compound.

126

286

ST-CS-01-169-72
July 1972

APPENDIX IV

THE "1961 DIRECTIVES" (U)

<u>Directives on the Immediate Hospitalization of Persons Mentally
Ill Who are a Social Danger</u>, Practice of Forensic Psychiatric
Diagnosis, Research Handbook No. 6, under the editorship of G.V.
Morozov, Ministry of Health of the USSR, Serbsky Central Research
Institute of Forensic Psychiatry of the USSR, Moscow, 1962.

<u>Confirmed</u> by the deputy minister of health of the USSR,
I Kochergin, October 10, 1961. Number 04-14 32.

<u>Affirmed</u> for Procurator of the USSR, by Deputy General Procu-
rator of the USSR, A. Mishutin, October 10, 1961.

<u>Affirmed</u> for the Ministry of Internal Affairs of the RSFSR,
by the Deputy Minister of Internal Affairs of the RSFSR,
P. Romashkov, October 9, 1961.

In a number of instances the necessity for prevention of dangerous
actions of persons mentally ill requires their immediate hospitalization in psychiatric institutions. In accordance with this:

1. If there is a clear danger from a person mentally ill to
those around him or to himself the health organs have the right
(by way of immediate psychiatric assistance) to place him in
a psychiatric hospital without the consent of the person who
is ill or his relatives or guardians.

2. In the psychiatric institution within 24 hours the sick
person hospitalized must be examined by a special committee composed
of three doctor-psychiatrists, which considers the question of
correctness of hospitalization and determines the necessity for
further presence in the hospital. The closest relatives are
informed of the hospitalization of the sick person.

3. The basic indication for obligatory hospitalization is
the social danger of the sick person as conditioned by the following
particular features of his sick condition:

a. Psychomotor excitation with a tendency towards aggressive
actions;

b. Deviant conduct accompanied by psychiatric disorder
(hallucinations, deliriums, a syndrome of mental automatism,

127

ST-CS-01-169-72
July 1972

syndromes of disordered consciousness, and pathological impulsiveness),
if it occurs in a condition of sharply expressed affective tension
and a tendency to pass into action;

c. Systematic delirious syndromes with a chronic deteriorating
course, if they determine the socially dangerous conduct of the
sick person;

d. Hypochondriac delirious conditions causing incorrect,
aggressive attitudes of the sick person towards particular persons,
organizations and institutions.

The morbid conditions enumerated above, tending within themselves
to undoubted social danger, may occur with externally correct
conduct and dissimulation. In this connection special care must
be used when assessing the mental condition of such persons, so
that the indications for immediate hospitalization are not
stretched to fit the case, and, at the same time, the possibility
of socially dangerous behavior on the part of the mentally sick
can be prevented by means of timely hospitalization. The indications for immediate hospitalization enumerated above are not
exhaustive, but are only a list of the more frequently occurring
illnesses which present a social danger.

4. Simple, although acute, alcoholic intoxication is not
an indication for immediate hospitalization in a mental institution, as is not also intoxication brought about by other narcotic
compounds (except serious intoxicational psychosis and psychotic
variations of abstential conditions), and affective reactions
of persons who are not suffering from mental illness.

5. Doctor-psychiatrists effect the immediate hospitalization
directly, but in districts where there are no psychiatric institutions doctors belonging to the general medical service do so,
as the ill person must be immediately conveyed to the nearest
psychiatric hospital.

6. When immediate hospitalization is indicated, the doctor
committing the sick person to the hospital is under obligation to
give full details of the medical and social grounds for his
decision, and in the conclusion of his report on the case, to
mention his place of work, the post he occupies, his name, and
the time when the decision on immediate hospitalization had been
reached.

128

ST-CS-01-169-72
July 1972

7. Local organs of the police in cases of necessity (if
relatives or guardians of the ill person object or offer resistance) are obliged to offer assistance to medical workers in the
hospitalization of persons mentally ill upon the request of the
persons mentioned in paragraph five of the present Directives.

8. Sick persons hospitalized in psychiatric institutions
are placed in the department appropriate to their mental condition
for carrying out actual treatment, and are subject without exception (no less than once a month) to examination by a special
commission composed of three doctor-psychiatrists for consideration
of the question of further stay in the hospital. Upon improvement
of the mental condition of the sick person, or such changes in
the clinical picture of the illness as to eliminate the social danger
on the part of the sick person, the commission of doctors issues
an opinion on the possible release of the sick person. Release
of such an ill person is carred out by handing him over to relatives or guardians.

9. If a sick person who is due, according to medical indications to be released from the hospital, is in a condition where
he may not be left on his own and does not have a permanent place
of residence or persons able to take care of him, he may be
released from the hospital only through transfer to patronage.
In cases of necessity the hospital takes measures for the official registration of guardianship over the sick person.

10. Upon release of the sick person the psychiatric hospital
informs the relatives of the sick person and the psychoneurological
clinician as to where such sick persons must attend for particular
check-ups, if they are subject to regular prophylactic treatment.

ST-CS-01-169-72
July 1972

APPENDIX V

text had already been deleted from this page
when document was made available to author

131

290

ST-CS-01-169-72
July 1972

---

text had already been deleted from this page
when document was made available to author

The science of mass manipulation plays a major role in modern
warfare - at least theoretically. In past wars, a hostile confrontation between two parties was a diplomatic duel, or a military
battle which was based on and regulated, in general, by classical
concepts of acceptable military conduct (e.g., international
agreements on the status of POWs, unarmed civilians, etc.). But
this concept has changed. In modern warfare, there is a powerful
third force which has, perhaps, the most decisive bearing on
the outcome of any diplomatic and/or military confrontation today.
This third force is the manipulated mass - individuals who, by
modern mass communications media, have been welded into a solid
front, holding the same, or very similar, opinions. This third
force conflicts with, and ultimately controls the hostile confrontation by appling its criteria rather than the older criteria

132

ST-CS-01-169-72
July 1972

of acceptable diplomatic and military conduct. The study of these
criteria is also the task of opinionology. Source again cited, as
a case in point, the war in Vietnam. According to older, classical
concepts of warfare, the Vietnamese (including the North Vietnamese),
should have sided with the Americans who are fighting in Vietnam to
liberate the Vietnamese from the threat of Communist oppression and
mass terror. Instead, the Vietnamese masses have been welded
opinionologically (i.e., deceived by Communist manipulation), into
believing that they are fighting for their freedom and national
independence against a "foreign (American) invader, whereas in
reality they are fighting the Americans to be eventually enslaved
by the Communists. Source believes that this situation is an
obvious result of American ignorance in manipulating mass media.
By ignoring mass opinion (both American and world), the Americans
have maneuvered themselves into the position of an "invading
foreign power," in the eyes of the opinionologically indoctrinated
Vietnamese.

2.   General

The study of the pattern of mass manipulation and mass resonance
is based on the new scientific approach to psychology known as
structural psychology. This psychology, which is also taught in
the West, rejects the classical psychology which devotes itself
exclusively to the individual. According to structural psychology,
the individual is conceived as a derivative of the hierarchic groups
which condition and mold his existence. These groups are:

The Intimate micro-group (family);

The social micro-group (environment);

The social molding group (LORENZ, Praegungsgruppe); and

The basic structuring group (ethnic group).

According to structural psychology, the phenomenology of the individual
is considered to be a reflection of the phenomenology of these four
groups. The study of mass resonance is concerned with the fourth
group. Of the different methods of investigating the pattern of
this group, opinionology is one of the most rewarding and most
commonly used.

a. Glossary of Terms

Source furnished the following glossary to define the
psychological and psychiatric terminology used in this report:

133

292

ST-CS-01-169-72
July 1972

(1) <u>Opinionology</u>: This term is understood as the theory dealing with the unstructured reaction of the masses, and/or the reaction of the unstructured masses. NOTE: Opinionology is not identical with cemoscopy; i.e., PO (public opinion) research which represents statistical evaluations of social data (mainly pseudo data).

(2) <u>Unstructured mass</u>: An unstructured mass consists of large numbers of individuals whose standards of value have been disturbed to a point approaching disintegration, so that the values have become ambiguous as a result. In other words, the reactions governing individuals are not homogeneous to the mass and, therefore, cannot weld the mass into an integrated whole.

(3) <u>Structured mass</u>: A structured mass is one in which certain affective behavior manifestations are constant based on certain laws governing the individuals comprising the mass.

(4) <u>Mental structure of an individual</u>: The mental structure of an individual is composed of certain affective behavior manifestations which remain constant; hence the mental structure of the individual is a repetitive phenomenology.

(5) <u>Structuralization</u>: This is the process of persuading individuals comprising a mass to accept a certain system of values (i.e., a "structure").

(6) <u>Unstructuration</u>: This term has the same definition as item (2) above (unstructured mass).

(7) <u>Structuration</u>: Defined under item (3) above (structured mass). This term can also be defined as the structural form of a mass; i.e., of the individuals comprising the mass.

(8) <u>De-structuration</u>: This is the process of depriving a mass of individuals (structured or structurized), of its values (i.e., its structure).

(9) <u>Engrammation</u>: A permanent effect produced in the psyche as a result of stimulation. It serves as the basis for memory.

(10) <u>Chronaxia</u>: The mimimum time necessary to excite.

(11) <u>Cybernetics</u>: A science dealing with the comparative study of complex electronic calculating machines and the human nervous system in an attempt to explain the nature of the brain.

134

293

ST-CS-01-169-72
July 1972

(1) The factors of mass de-structuration and of unstruc-
turation; that is, the circumstances under which groups of individuals
(masses), become unorientated (not disorientated) masses. Studies
show that these masses can be manipulated 100 percent, as a result
of de-structuration.

(2) The factors governing the unstructured mass resonance;
i.e., public opinion (PO); the excitement threshold of public opinion,
its latency period and, as a link between the two, its chronaxia
(latency period of the double excitement threshold). See Figure 1.

(3) The types of unstructured mass resonance (public opinion),
which range from latent undemonstrated sympathy and/or antipathy,
to extreme turbulence and, in the final degree, to massive demonstrations of violence.

(4) The short-term and long-term memory of public opinion
(PO), in relation to events, and its engrammation.

135

ST-CS-01-169-72
July 1972

text had already been deleted from this page
when document was made available to author

136

ST-CS-01-169-72
July 1972

text had already been deleted from this page
when document was made available to author

137

ST-CS-01-169-72
July 1972

text had already been deleted from this page
when document was made available to author

ST-CS-01-169-72
July 1972

text had already been deleted from this page
when document was made available to author

139

298

ST-CS-01-169-72
July 1972

text had already been deleted from this page
when document was made available to author

ST-CS-01-169-72
July 1972

text had already been deleted from this page
when document was made available to author

141

ST-CS-01-169-72
July 1972

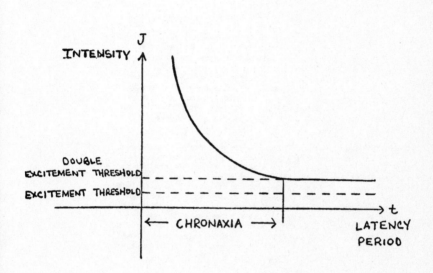

Figure 1 (C) Chart of Public Opinion Resonance

142

UNCLASSIFIED

ST-CS-01-169-72
July 1972

APPENDIX VI

MILAN RYZL
Biocummunications (Parapsychology) Scientist

1. (U) Doctor Milan Ryzl is an international authority on parapsychology, who has lectured widely both in the United States
and in Europe. Doctor Ryzl, educated in Czechoslovakia, was a
member of the Czechoslovak Academy of Sciences in Prague and
was a leading figure in the application of scientific methods
to the study of parapsychology. After he arrived in the United
States, he worked with Doctor J.B. Rhine at the Institute of
Parapsychology in Durham, North Carolina. There Doctor Ryzl
was especially noted for his original research on the influence
of hypnosis on ESP.

2. (U) Doctor Ryzl has taught parapsychology at San Diego State
College and is currently a professor of parapsychology at San
Jose State University. He is a member of and has founded parapsychological and psychical research groups in Europe and in the
United States. Doctor Ryzl's primary efforts in this field have
been to document a case for parapsychology by means of highly
refined and systematized scientific methods. He published his
results in, Parapsychology: A Scientific Approach (Hawthorn Books,
1970). In his work, Doctor Ryzl presents indisputable and thoroughly
documented evidence that psychic phenomena exist and scientifically
examines the full range of psychic phenomena by evaluating experimental evidence derived from laboratory controlled testing.

3. (U) Doctor Ryzl is also well-known as a reviewer and analyst
of parapsychology developments and trends in Eastern Europe. He
has frequently published reviews and commentaries on parapsychological works from behind the Iron Curtain. One such is Telepatie
A Jasnovidnost (Telepathy and Clairvoyance), by Doctor Z. Rejdak.
Doctor Ryzl's review of this book was published in the July-August
1971 edition of the Parapsychology Review.

143
(Reverse Blank)

UNCLASSIFIED

UNCLASSIFIED

ST-CS-01-169-72
July 1972

BIBLIOGRAPHY

1. Congressional Record, 92nd Congress of the United States, Volume 117, Number 176, 17 November 1971, Washington, DC. (U)

2. Shallice, T. and Wall, P., Interrogation Question, New Scientist, UK, Volume 52, Number 773, p. 67, 9 December 1971. (U)

3. Psychologist Says Detainees in Ulster Undergo Torture, The New York Times, 9 January 1972. (U)

4. Biderman, A.D. and Zimmer, H., The Manipulation of Human Behavior, John Wiley and Sons, Inc., New York-London, 323 pp., 1961. (U)

5. Medvedev, Z.A. and Medvedev, R.A., A Question of Madness, The New York Times Magazine, 7 November 1971. (U)

6. Department of State Airgram, CA-5185, 15 November 1971. (C)

7. Reddaway, P., Plea to West on Soviet "Mad-house" Jails, The London Times, 12 March 1971. (U)

8. Ibid, Save Ex-Soviet General, The London Times, 2 May 1971. (U)

9. Ibid, Soviet Group's Plea to Psychiatrists, The London Times, 23 October 1971. (U)

10. Jensen, H., Soviet Dissenter Speaks Out, The Washington Post 17 May 1970. (U)

11. Shabad, T., Two Dissidents in Soviet Prison Hospital Charge Drugs are Used to Change Beliefs of Political Prisoners, The New York Times, 18 March 1971. (U)

12. Reston, R., Russian Use of Drugs to Curb Dissent Told, The London Times (no date). (U)

13. Goodman, L.S. and Gilman, A., The Pharmacological Basis of Therapeutics, 4th edition, The Macmillian Company, New York, pp. 155-170, 1970. (U)

14. Brumberg, A., How Russia Uses Asylums to Kill Dissent, The Washington Post, 18 October 1971. (U)

145

UNCLASSIFIED

ST-CS-01-169-72
July 1972

15. Directives on the Immediate Hospitalization of Persons Mentally
Ill Who are a Social Danger, Practice of Forensic Psychiatric
Diagnosis, Research Handbook Number Six, Morozov, G.V., Editor
Ministry of Health, USSR, Serbsky Central Research Institute of
Forensic Psychiatry of the USSR, 1962. (U)

16. Chalidze, V.N., Concerning Compulsory Commitment to Psychiatric
Hospitals, Moscow (in samizdat), May-June 1970, MIO Number Five,
ST-CS-01-169-72. (U)

17. Outpatient Forenic-Psychiatric Examination of Yakhimovich,
I.A., The Neurological Center of the City of Riga, 1 April 1969,
MIO Number Three, ST-CS-01-169-72. (U)

18. Report Number 96, Inpatient Forensic-Psychiatric Examination
of Yakhimovich, I.A., Psychiatric Section of Investigation Department,
Number One, City of Riga, 3 June 1969. (U)

19. Report Number 33, Inpatient Forensic-Psychiatric Examination
of Yakhimovich, I.A., Central Scientific Research Institute (Serbsky
Institute) of Forensic Psychiatry, 12 January 1970. (U)

20. Volpin, A., Novoye Russkoye Slovo, New York, 10 June 1968. (U)

21. Report Number 575, Skvortsov-Stepanov Psycho-Neurological
Hospital, Leningrad, 14 October 1969. (U)

22. Conclusion of a Commission Presided Over by the (Moscow)
City Psychiatrist I.K. Yanushevsky, 19 November 1969, MIO Number
Two, ST-CS-01-169-72. (U)

23. Report Number 28/S, The Forensic-Psychiatric Examination
of N.E. Gorbanevskaya, 6 April 1970. (U)

24. Gorbanevskaya, N.E., Letters from the Butyrka Prison (Moscow),
1970, MIO Number One, ST-CS-01-169-72. (U)

25. Fainberg, V., Appeal to Human Rights Organization, July 1970,
MIO Number Four, ST-CS-01-169-72. (U)

26. Report Numbe 40, The Outpatient Forensic-Psychiatric Diagnosis
of P.G. Grigorenko, KGB Report, 18 August 1969. (U)

27. Report Number 59/S, An Inpatient Forensic-Psychiatric Diagnosis
of P.G. Grigorenko, Serbsky Scientific Research Institute,
19 November 1969. (U)

146

ST-CS-01-169-72
July 1972

28. Kallistratova, S.B., Petition to the Tashkent City Court in Defense of P.G. Grigorenko, 2 February 1970, MIO Number Six, ST-CS-01-169-72. (U)

29. Whom the Gods Wish to Destroy, The Economist (International Report), 31 July 1971. (U)

30. Pisarev, S.P., From the Russian Underground, The New York Times, 6 July 1971. (U)

31. Shabad, T., Soviet Denies Charges on Dissidents, The New York Times, 24 October 1971. (U)

32. Izvestiya, Moscow, 24 October 1971. (U)

33. Ortiz, F., Snezhnevskiy Interviewed at Psychiatric Meeting, Excelsior, Spanish, pp. 1, 14, 1 December 1971 (JPRS 54842, 3 January 1972). (U)

34. Gonzales, S., Interviews with Delegates to the Fifth World Psychiatric Congress, Excelsior, Spanish, pp. 1, 15, 16, 18, 30 November 1971 (JPRS 54778, 23 December 1971). (U)

35. Noble, C.E., Current Psychological Research in the Soviet Union and Sovbloc Countries: Recent Developments in the Theory of Learning and Performance, p. 7, AMD-CR-01-1-70, 15 December 1971. (U)

36. Information Report 00-B-321/14973-66, 14 October 1966. (C/CD/NDA)

37. Information Report 00-B-321/15621-66, 14 October 1966. (C/CD/NDA)

38. Noble, C.E., Current Psychological Research in the Soviet Union and Sovbloc Countries: Recent Developments in the Theory of Learning and Performance, p. 27, AMD-CR-01-1-70, 15 December 1970. (U)

39. Persic, N., Psychiatry in the Soviet Union, Lijecnicki Vjesnik (Serbo Croatian), Volume 85, Number 7, pp. 747-758, 1963, (FTD-TT-64-259/1). (U)

40. Fry, J., Medicine in Three Societies, American Elsevier Publishing Co., Inc., New York, 249 pp., 1969. (U)

UNCLASSIFIED

ST-CS-01-169-72
July 1972

41. Dyachenko, M.I. and Fedenko, N.F., Military Psychology, Moscow, 259 pp., 1967. (U)

42. Tyurnev, P.T., Moral-Psychological Training of Rear-Zone Troops, Tyl I Snabzhiniye Sovetskikh Vooruzhennykh Sil, Number 8, pp. 19-23, 1969, (J-7296). (U)

43. Psychoprophylaxis In the System of Troop Morale-Psychological Preparation, Voyenno-Meditsinkiy Zhurnal, Number 9, pp. 16-19, 1969, (J-7524). (U)

44. Stolyarenko, A., Psychological Training of Servicemen in the Process of Military Training, Moscow, Kommunist Vooruzhennykh Sil, Number 2, pp. 72-76, January 1970 (JPRS 50030, 10 March 1970). (U)

45. Information Report 2-218-1866-70, 17 February 1970. (C/NFD EXCEPT UK)

46. Fulton, J., A Textbook of Physiology, 17th edition, Saunders, Philadelphia, 1955. (U)

47. Johnstone, R.T. and Miller, S.E., Occupational Diseases and Industrial Medicine, Saunders, Philadelphia, 1960. (U)

48. David, Th. A., Derau, J.V., Kornblueh, I.H., McGurke, C.J., and Minehart, J.R., Ionization of the Air; The Sedating Effect of Polarized Air; International Biometeorology Conference, Proceedings of the Second Conference, Volume II, 1962. (U)

49. Ludwig, H.W., A Hypothesis Concerning the Absorption Mechanism of Atmospherics in the Nervous System, International Journal of Biometeorology, Volume 12, Number 2, pp. 93-98, 1968. (U)

50. Hamburger, R.J., On the Influence of Artificial Ionization of the Air on the Oxygen Uptake During Exercise, International Biometeorology Conference, Proceedings of the Second Conference, Volume II, 1962. (U)

51. Bachman, C.H., McDonald, R.D., and Lorenz, P.J., Some Effects of Air Ions on the Activity of Rats, International Journal of Biometeorology, Volume 10, Number 1, pp. 39-46, 1966. (U)

52. Carlson, A.J., Johnson, V., and Cavert, H.M., The Machinery of the Body, 5th edition, Chicago, University of Chicago Press, 1961. (U)

148

UNCLASSIFIED

306

ST-CS-01-169-72
July 1972

53. Davson, H. and Eggleton, M.G., Starling's Human Physiology, 14th edition, Philadelphia, Lea and Febiger, p. 1417, 1968. (U)

54. Bartley, S.H., The Psychophysiology of Vision, Stevens, S.S., editor, Handbook of Experimental Psychology, New York, Wiley, pp. 921-984, 1951. (U)

55. Kholodov, Yu.A., The Effect of an Electromagnetic Field on the Central Nervous System, Priroda, Number 4, April 1960, (JPRS 14447, 12 July 1962). (U)

56. Hahn, C.P., Psychological Phenomena Applicable to the Development of Psychological Weapons, ATL-TR-65-98, American Institutes for Research, Silver Spring, Maryland, December 1965. (U)

57. Unsolicited Proposal for Special Research Services and Technical Analyses, Mankind Research Unlimited, Inc., Washington, DC, MRU Proposal Number 101, 5 January 1972. (U)

58. Teodorovich, N., Soviet Studies of Parapsychic Phenomena, Review of Soviet Medical Sciences, Volume 4, Number 1, 1967. (U)

59. Ryzl, M., Parapsychology: A Scientific Approach, Hawthorn Books, Inc., New York, 1970. (U)

60. Bekhterev, V.M., Experiments on "Mental" Influencing of the Behavior of Animals, Voprosy Izucheniya i vospitaniya lichnosti, Petrograd, Number 2, 1920. (U)

61. Ivanov-Smolensky, A.G., Experiments in Thought Transmission Carried out on Animals, Ibid. (U)

62. Vasilev, L.L., Experimental Research of Mental Suggestion, Leningrad Press, Leningrad, 1962. (U)

63. Dodge, C.H., STIC-CP-17-3-68. (S/NFD)

64. Vasilev, L.L., Mysterious Phenomena of the Human Psyche, Moscow, 1959, 2nd edition, 1963; 3rd edition, 1964. (U)

65. Komsomolskaya pravda, 15 November 1959. (U)

66. Nauka i zhizn, Number 11, p. 46, 1960. (U)

67. Znaniye-sila, Number 12, pp. 18-23, 1960. (U)

149

ST-CS-01-169-72
July 1972

68. Znaniye-sila, Number 7, p. 22, 1961. (U)

69. Smena, 15 January 1961. (U)

70. Tekhnika molodizhi, Number 1, 2 and 3, 1961. (U)

71. Kazinskiy, B.B., Biological Radio Communications, Izdatil-stvo Akademii Nauk Urainskay SSR, Kiev, 168 pp., 1962. (U)

72. Nauka i religiya, Numbers 7 through 11, 1965. (U)

73. Ibid, Number 9, pp. 41-45, 1966. (U)

74. Stone, W.C. and Growning, N.L., The Other Side of the Mind, Prentice-Hall, Englewood Cliffs, N.J., 1964. (U)

75. Ostrander, S. and Schroeder, L., Psychic Discoveries Behind the Iron Curtain, Prentice-Hall, Englewood Cliffs, N.J., 1970. (U)

76. Velinov, I., Recent Soviet Experiments in Telepathic Communication, Foreign Science Bulletin, Volume 4, Number 8, p. 13, 1968. (U)

77. Messadie, G., Du Nautilus, Science et Vie, Number 509, February 1960. (U)

78. Soviet Review, Volume 2, Number 6, June 1961. (U)

79. Popovkin, V., Le Congress de Moscow sur la Telepathie, Planete, Paris, July-August 1968. (U)

80. Ryzl, M., Review of Biological Radio, Journal of Parapsychology, Volume 35, Number 2, June 1971. (U)

81. Kolodny, L., Wireless Telegraph, Number 2, Moscow, Pravda, 9 April 1967. (U)

82. An ESP Test from Appollo 14, Journal of Parapsychology, Volume 35, Number 2, June 1971. (U)

83. The University Explorer, ESP - The Extrasensory Puzzle, Newsletter of the University of California, (U.E. 2156), 23 May 1971. (U)

84. Science News, Volume 99, Number 16, 17 April 1971. (U)

85. Newsletter, American Society for Psychical Research, Number 10, Summer 1971. (U)

ST-CS-01-169-72
July 1972

86. Vaughan, A., Interview: Montague Ullman, MD., _Psychic_,
Volume II, Number 6, June 1971. (U)

87. Welk, G.A., Proposed Use of the Apport Technique as a Means
to Strengthen the U.S. Intelligence System   , 15 October 1970,
MIO Number Seven, ST-CS-01-169-72. (FOUO).

88. Crookes, W., Notes of an Enquiry into the Phenomena Called
Spiritual, During the Years 1870-73, _The Quarterly Journal of
Science, and Annals of Mining, Metallurgy, Engineering, Industrial
Arts, Manufacturing, and Technology_, London, Volume Number XLI,
January 1874. (U)

89. Wallace, A.R., Buchanan, J.R., Lyman, D., and Aargent, E.,
The Psycho-Physiological Sciences and their Assailants, Boston,
Colley and Rich, 1878. (U)

90. Zoellner, J.K.F., _Transcendental Physics_, 2nd edition, Boston,
1881. (U)

91. Ostrander, S. and Schroeder, L., _Psychic Discoveries Behind
the Iron Curtain_, Prentice-Hall, Englewood Cliffs, N.J., pp. 196-
209, 1970. (U)

92. Dick, W., Russians Perfecting ESP for Spying, _National Enquirer_,
p. 8, 9 January 1972. (U)

93. Muldoon, S. and Carrington, H., _The Projection of the Astral
Body_, London, Psychic Book Club, 1929. (U)

94. Nicol, J.F., Old Light on "New" Phenomena, _Psychic_, Volume
II, Number 6, pp. 26-28, 36, June 1971. (U)

95. Information Report 00-B3261161, 15 May 1963. (C/CD/NDA)

96. Information Report 00-B3904092, 4 June 1964. (C/CD/NDA)

97. Information Report 00-B321/02171-64, 3 August 1964. (C/CD/NDA)

98. Mutschall, V., The Present Status of Research in Telepathy
in the Soviet Union, _Foreign Science Bulletin_, Volume 4, Number
8, 1968. (U)

99. Popovkin, V., Thought Transference Between Moscow and
Novosibirsk, _Komsomolskaya pravda_, Moscow, p. 3, 7 July 1966,
(JPRS 36911, 9 August 1966). (U)

151

ST-CS-01-169-72
July 1972

100. Scientists Investigate Results of Telepathic Experiments,
Literaturnaya gazeta, Moscow, p. 12, 5 June 1968 (JPRS 45922,
18 July 1968). (U)

101. Kogan, I.M., Telepathy, Hypotheses, and Observations, Nauka
i Tekhnika, Riga, Number 4, pp. 35-36, 1967 (JPRS 43028, 19 October
1967). (U)

102. Kogan, I.M., The Information Theory Aspect of Telepathy,
paper presented at the Symposium entitled "A New Look at Extrasensory Perception," 7-8 June 1969, University of Southern California at L.A. (U)

103. Simonov, P., Pros and Cons of Existence of Telepathy, Nauka
i Zhiza, Moscow, Number 4, pp. 54-58, April 1966, (JPRS 37313,
29 August 1966). (U)

104. Rejdak, Z. and Rosinsky, T., Psychotronics - Trojan House
of Irrationality, Kulturny Zivot, Bratislava, Number 16, 21 April
1967, (JPRS 41122, 23 May 1967). (U)

105. Information Report 00-B321/10424-68, 22 April 1968. (C/CD/NDA)

106. Ostrander, S. and Schroeder, L., Psychic Enigmas and Energies
in the USSR, Psychic, Volume II, p. 14, May-June 1971. (U)

107. Telepathy and Electronic Machines, Moscow, Pravda, 22 March
1967. (U)

108. Segeyev, G.A., Pavlova, L., and Romanenko, A., Statistical
Method of Research of the Human EEG, Leningrad: Academy of Science
USSR, Science Publishing, 1968. (U)

109. The Parapsychological Association, Fourteenth Annual Convention,
Durham, N.C., 9-11 September 1971. (U)

110. The American Association for the Advancement of Science,
138th Meeting, Philadelphia, Pa., 26-31 December 1971. (U)

111. Barcus, L., Stevenson, I., and Pratt, J.G., Inferences
about Processes Derived from Unusual Occurrences during "Psychic
Photography," Farrand Optical Co. of N.Y.C. and University of
Virginia, paper presented at the 14th Annual meeting of the Parapsychology Association, Durham, N.C., 9-11 September 1971. (U)

152

UNCLASSIFIED

ST-CS-01-169-72
July 1972

112. Pratt, J.G. and Ransom, C., Exploratory Observations of the Movement of Static Objects without the Apparent Use of Known Physical Energies by Nina S. Kulagina, Ibid. (U)

113. Ullman, M., Some Observations on Mrs. Kulagina, Ibid. (U)

114. Vera Sees Through Walls, Moscow, Selskaya Zhiza, p. 4, 6 June 1964. (U)

115. Novomeyskiy, A.S., The Nature of the Dermo-Optical Sense in Man, Voprosy psikhologii, Volume IX, Number 5, pp. 99-117 (JPRS 23068). (U)

116. Teplova, L. and Nyuberg, N.D., Finger Seeing, Piroda, Number 6, 1964. (U)

117. Nyuberg, N.D., Sight in the Fingers, Piroda, Number 5, 1963. (U)

118. Baratyants, M., Second Case of Skin Vision Phenomenon Demonstrated in USSR, Trud (USSR), p. 3, cols., 2-6, 8 May 1964. (U)

119. Seeing Without Eyes, Moscow News, p. 4, 22 August 1964, (U)

120. Second Case of Seeing Hands, Moscow News, p. 14, 8 February 1964. (U)

121. Bongard, M.M. and Smirnov, M.S., Skin Vision of R. Kuleshova, Biofizika, Volume 10, Number 1, pp. 148-154, 1965. (U)

122. Snyakin, P.G., The Problem of the Development of the Relationship Between Optic and Skin Perception of Light in Man, Bulletin of Experimental Biology and Medicine, Moscow, Volume XXIX, Number 8, pp. 16-20, 1964. (U)

123. Dobronravov, S.N. and Fishelev, Ya.R., Skin Vision, Ibid. (U)

124. Dozens of Persons in USSR with "Touch Sight," Zycie Warszawy, p. 2, cols. 5-6, 29 March 1963. (U)

125. Skin Vision, Meditsinskaya gazeta, Number 4, cols. 6-7, 15 February 1963. (U)

126. FBIS Report 63, 29 January 1963. (FOUO)

127. FBIS Report 63, 6 June 1963. (FOUO)

153

UNCLASSIFIED

ST-CS-01-169-72
July 1972

128. Salnikov, Ye., The Effect of the Seeing Hands, Trud, Moscow, p. 4, 21 May 1967. (U)

129. Information Report 1-561-0033-63, 24 October 1963. (C/NFD)

130. Ryzl, M., Parapsychology in Communist Countries of Europe, International Journal of Parapsychology, Volume 10, Number 3, 1968. (U)

131. Mitchell, E.D., Jr., The David Frost Show, 16 March 1971. (U)

132. Roshnov, V., Treatment by Hypnosis, Soviet Science Review, July 1970. (U)

133. Biderman, A.D. and Zimmer, H., The Manipulation of Human Behavior, John Wiley and Sons, Inc., New York-London, 323 pp., 1961. (U)

134. Estabrooks, G.H., Hypnotism, E.P. Dutton and Co., Inc., 1959. (U)

135. Raikov, V., Reincarnation by Hypnosis, Science and Religion, Number 9, 1966. (U)

136. Melenevskiy, I., Psychiatrists' Work with Hypnosis, Trud, Number 259, P. 3, Cols. 4-7, 3 November 1971. (U)

137. Naumov, E. and Fesenko, R., What We're Working on Now, Science and Religion, September 1966. (U)

138. Theta, Number 15, Durham, N.C., 1966. (U)

139. Borzymowski, A., Parapsychology in Poland, International Journal of Parapsychology, Volume 4, Number 4, 1962. (U)

140. Ryzl, M., Parapsychology in Communist Countries of Europe, International Journal of Parapsychology, Volume 10, Number 3, 1968. (U)

141. Ryzl, M., ESP in Eastern Europe and Russia, Psychic, Volume 1, Numbers 1-2, 1969. (U)

142. Information Report 1-502-0003-69, 6 January 1969. (C/NFD)

154

ST-CS-01-169-72
July 1972

143. Zavalova, N.D., Zukhar, V.P., and Petrov, Yu.A., The Problem of Hypnopedia, Voprosy Psikhologii, Number 2, pp. 98-102, 1964. (U)

144. Zukhar, V. and Pushkina, I., Learning While You Sleep, Moscow News, 25 July 1964. (U)

145. Torzhevskaya, G., Sleeping With Sound, Nauka i Tekhnika, Number 9, 1966. (U)

146. Kulikov, V.N., The Problem of Hypnopedia, Voprosy Psikhologii, Volume 10, Number 2, pp. 87-97, 1964. (U)

147. Zukhar, V.P., Kaplan, Ye.Ya., Maksimov, Yu.A., and Pushkina, I.P., An Experiment on Collective Hypnopedia, Voprosy Psikhologii, Number 1, pp. 143-148, January 1965. (U)

148. Korinteli, I., Hypnopedia Without Sensation, Zarya Vbstoka, p. 4, 26 May 1965. (U)

149. Svyadoshch, A., Hypnopedia, Meditsinskaya gazeta, p. 3, 10 July 1964. (U)

150. Puskina, I. and Sukhar, V., Hypnopedia in the USSR, Literaturnaya gazeta, p. 2, 27 February 1965. (U)

151. Hypnopedia, Its Limits and Possibilities, Truth and Fiction Surrounding It, Tekhnika-Molodizhi, Moscow, Number 11, pp. 26-28, November 1965. (U)

152. Town's Citizens Learn English While Asleep , 24 December 1965, FBIS Number 251, 30 December 1965. (FOUO)

153. Smarokova, M., A Thorough Study of Hypnopedia is Recommended, Meditsinskaya gazeta, p. 3, 2 November 1965. (U)

154. Vladziyevskiy, A., Komsomolskaya Pravda, p. 4, cols. 1-5, 11 December 1965. (U)

155. Zheleznov, N., Sovetskaya Moldaviya, p. 4, cols. 3-6, 4 January 1966. (U)

156. Svyadoshch, A.M., On the History of Hypnopedia, Voprosy Psikhologii, Number 3, 1965. (U)

155

ST-CS-01-169-72
July 1972

157. Balkhashov, I., Concerning Hypnopedia and the Rapid Learning of a Foreign Language, Voprosy Psikhologii, Number 4, 1965. (U)

158. Khilchenko, A.Ye., Moldavskaya, S.I., Kolchenko, N.V., and Shevko, G.N., The Effect of Hypnopedic Teaching Methods on the Efficiency of the Cerebral Cortex, Voprosy psikhologii, Number 4, 1965. (U)

159. Ryzhonok, B., Experiment in Teaching During Sleep, Volennyy vestnik, Number 11, 1966. (U)

160. Hypnopedia - Pros and Cons, Moscow News, Number 14, 1967. (U)

161. Nikitin, L., Trends and Discoveries, Rabochaya gazeta, 1 December 1966. (U)

162. Bliznechenko, L.A., Introduction and Retention of Information in the Human Memory During Natural Sleep, Naukova Dumka, Kiev, 1966, (FTD-HT-23-1630-67). (U)

163. Dodge, C.H. and Lamont, E., Sleep Learning in the USSR, 7 February 1969, (ATD Report 68-91-108-6). (U)

164. Kuproyanovich, L.I., Reserves for Improving Memory, Moscow, 143 pp., 1970 (JPRS 54449, 10 November 1971). (U)

165. Talese, G., Most Hidden Persuasion, The New York Times, 12 January 1958. (U)

166. McConnell, J.V., Cutler, R.L., and McNeil, E.B., Subliminal Stimulation: An Overview, The American Psychologist, 1958. (U)

167. Naylor, J.C. and Lawshe, C.H., An Analytical Review of the Experimental Basis of Subception, Journal of Psychology, Number 46, pp. 75-96, 1958. (U)

168. Goldiamond, I., Indicators of Perception, Psychological Bulletin, Volume 55, Number 6, 1958. (U)

169. Corrigan, R.E., Becker, H.C., and Moor, A.B., Subliminal Perception: A Positive Asset to its Field of Communication, An Address to the Federal Communications Commission and National Association of Broadcasters, Washington, DC, 13 February 1958. (U)

156

UNCLASSIFIED

ST-CS-01-169-72
July 1972

170. Information Report 00-B-321/23027-71, 13 August 1971. (S/CD/NDA)

171. Radeva, M., Psychotherapy Heals and Fortifies, Evening News, Sofia, Bulgaria, 14 August 1965. (U)

172. Unusual Case in Medical Practice, Sofia Pravda, Bulgaria, 27 August 1965. (U)

173. Operating Through Suggestion in Awakened State, Rabot-nichesko Delo, Sofia, Bulgaria, 25 August 1965. (U)

174. Novakov, A., Pashmakova, K., Staleva, L., Dimcheva, M., Petrunova, S., Metsova, R., Chukova, M., Bavieri, B., and Stoykova, Z., Doubtful Methods or Doubtful Information, Sofia, Vecherni Novini, Bulgarian, p. 4, 3 August 1971 (JPRS 53960, 1 September 1971). (U)

175. Simurov, A., Is It Possible to Learn a Language in a Month?, Pravda, 27 July 1969. (U)

176. Autosuggestion Experiments in Karaganda, Krasnaya Zvezda, Moscow, p. 4., 7 March 1965, (JPRS 30083). (U)

177. Autogenic Training - A New Method of Autosuggestion, Zarya Vostoka, p. 4, cols. 3-8, 29 August 1966. (U)

178. Space-Conditioner, Spaceflight, Volume 9, Number 1., P. 10, January 1967. (U)

179. Gurvich, G.I., Marishchuk, V.L., Tishchenko, M.I., Yefimenko, G.D., and Khvognov, B.S., Changing the Psychophysiological State of the Organism by Autogenous and Exogenous Suggestion, Kosmicheskaya biologiya i Meditsina, Volume 1, Number 4, pp. 73-76, 1967. (U)

180. Mordinov, E.F. and Genkin, A.A., On the Possibility of Predicting Suggestibility in Man Through Use of Data of the Spontaneous Electroencephalogram, Zhurnal Vysshii Nerunoi Deyatil nosti, Volume 19, Number 6, pp. 1022-1032, November 1969. (U)

181. Weiss, W., Mass Media and Social Change, Technical Report Number 16, Hunter College of the City University of New York, August 1970, (AD 711338). (U)

157

UNCLASSIFIED

ST-CS-01-169-72
July 1972

182. Weiss, W., Mass Communication, Technical Report Number 15, Hunter College of the City University of New York, July 1970, (AD 710773). (U)

183. Goure, L., Recent Developments in Soviet Civil Defense 1969-1970, Center for Advanced International Studies, University of Miami, Coral Gables, Florida, May 1971, (AD 724150). (U)

184. Voennye Znaniia, Number 8, pp. 14-15, August 1970. (U)

185. Red Star, 2 July 1970. (U)

186. Voennye Znaniia, Number 12, p. 14, December 1970. (U)

187. Voennye Znaniia, Number 2, p. 13, February 1970. (U)

188. Voennye Znaniia, Number 10, p. 13, October 1970. (U)

189. Voennye Znaniia, Number 5, p. 15, May 1970. (U)

190. Voennye Znaniia, Number 1, p. 15, January 1970. (U)

191. Voennye Znaniia, Number 9, pp. 10-11, September 1970. (U)

192. Voennye Znaniia, Number 11, p. 24, November 1970. (U)

193. Demin, V., Hate for the Enemy - An Inseparable Aspect in the Patriotism of Soviet Soldiers, Kommunist Vooruzhennykh Sil, Number 13, July 1969, (JPRS 541, 28 August 1969). (U)

194. Kommunist Vooruzhennykh Sil, Number 9, October 1970, (JPRS 657, 13 November 1970). (U)

195. Goodman, L.S. and Gilman, A., The Pharmacological Basis of Therapeutics, 4th edition, The Macmillian Company, New York, p. 155, (1970). (U)

196. Aronovich, G.D., Farmakoterapeuticheskij spravochnik nervropatologa, Leningrad, 1959. (U)

197. Guseynov, D.Ya., Main Psychotropic Substances, Azerbaydzhanskiy Meditsinskiy Zhurnal, Baker, Number 4, pp. 40-41, April 1971. (U)

198. Trapmann, H., Psycho-Warfare Agents - A Problem of Military Medicine, Wehrmedizinische Monatsschrift, German, Volume 14, Number 4, pp. 89-92, (J-8482). (U)

158

ST-CS-01-169-72
July 1972

199. Information Report 00-B-321/30644-69, 27 October 1969.
(C/CD/NDA)

200. Information Report 00-B-321/36622-69, 21 November 1969.
(C/CD/NDA)

201. Komissarov, I.V. and Talaloyenko, A.N., An Analysis of
Receptive Structures Participating in the Behavior Reactions
of Cats Induced by Catecholamines and Serotonin, Byulleten Eksper,
i Biol. Medits., Volume 70, Number 9, pp. 42-45, 1970. (U)

202. Matveyev, V.F., Character of Reversibility of Changes in
the Brain of Experimental Animals Caused by Prolonged LSD Administration, Byulleten Eksper, Biol. Medits., Volume 71, Number 1,
pp. 45-48, 1971. (U)

203. Kudrin, A.N., Search for Antagonists of Hashish and LSD,
C.I.N.P. Congress, Prague, p. 256, 11-15 August 1970. (U)

204. Popova, E., Effect of LSD-25 on the Structure of Neurons and
Interneuronal Connections, C.I.N.P. Congress, Prague, p. 348,
11-15 August 1970. (U)

205. Anokhina, I.P., LSD Effect on Neurotransmitter Systems of
Brain, C.I.N.P. Congress, Prague, p. 7, 11-15 August 1970. (U)

206. Information Report 00-K-323/06371-70, 23 March 1970. (S/NFD)

207. Kiyanskiy, D., Brain Research, Rabochaya gazeta, Number
290, p. 4, cols. 2-5, 15 December 1970. (U)

208. Information Report 00-B-321/34591-68, 16 December 1968.
(C/CD/NDA)

209. McGeer, P.L., The Chemistry of the Mind, American Scientist,
Volume 59, March-April 1971. (U)

210. Luria, A.R., The Functional Organization of the Brain,
Scientific American, Volume 222, Number 3, March 1970. (U)

211. Berezin, F.B., Bolshakova, T.D., Bassalyk, L.S., and
Lukicheva, T.I., Metabolism of Biogenic Amines and its Changes
in Hypothalamic Disorders Caused by Psychic Breakdown, Under
the Influence of Psychotropic Substances, Sovremennyye psikhatropnyye
sredstva, Number 2, 1967. (U)

159

ST-CS-01-169-72
July 1972

212. Barkov, N.K. and Gurovich, I.Ya., Experimental and Clinical Studies of the Effects of Trepthazine and Aminazine on Aggressiveness and Withdrawal, Sovremennyye psikhotropnyye sredstva, Number 2, 1970. (U)

213. Sokolov, S., What is Neuropharmacology?, Frunze, Sovetskaya Kirgiziya, p. 4, 17 March 1970. (U)

214. Lapin, I.P., Controlling Group Behavior with Drugs, Nauki i Tekhnika, Number 7, pp. 12-15, 1968. (U)

215. Information Report 00-B-321/23373-68, 23 September 1968. (C/CD/NDA)

216. Mikhalev, P.V. and Yatskov, L.P., Nervous and Psychic Disorders Resulting from Lesions by the Poisonous Gonionemous Jellyfish of the Primorye, Zhurnal Neuropatologii i Psikhiatric, Volume 68, Number 3, pp. 436-440, 1968. (U)

217. Fink, Z. and Kabes, J., Present Problems of Some Military Important Psychoactive Compounds, Vojenke Zdravotnicke Listy, Number 5, 1970. (U)

218. Dodge, C., The Soviet Potential for Visual Countermeasures Operations (S/NFD), NAVSTIC Draft, Medical Intelligence Office Number 215112, 29 September 1971. (S/NFD)

219. Information Report 6-062-0083-68, 26 December 1968. (S)

220. Honan, W.H., Playing "Chicken" Over the Mediterranean, Condensed from the New York Times Magazine, Readers' Digest, pp. 71-81, March 1971. (U)

221. Bach L.M.N., Tulane Symposium on Flicker, New Orleans, Louisiana, 6 April 1957. (U)

222. Naumov, P., On the Question of Wordless Transmission of Information, 24th All Union Scientific Session, Published, A.S. Popov Scientific Technical Society, Moscow, 1968. (U)

223. Information Report 00-E-324/32031-71, 9 November 1971. (C/CD/NDA)

224. Medvedeva, N.G., On the Problem of the Interaction Mechanisms of the Visual and Vestibular Analyzers, Medical Intelligence Office Translation Number 13, (no date available). (U)

160

318

UNCLASSIFIED

ST-CS-01-169-72
July 1972

225. Gorgiladze, G.I. and Smirnov, G.D., Electrophysiological Investigation of the Interaction of the Vestibular and Visual Afferent Systems, Medical Intelligence Office Translation Number 12, (no date available). (U)

226. Frid, G.M., Influence of Orienting Reaction on Visual Evoked Potentials in EEG of School Age Children, Zhurnal Vysshey Nervnoy Deyald'nosti, Volume 20, Number 5, pp. 1016-1021, 1970. (U)

227. Daurova, F.K., A Study of Cortical Evoked Responses to Photic Stimulation, Ibid, Number 4, pp. 529-536, 1970. (U)

228. Sokolov, E.N., Polyansky, V.B., and Bagdonas, A., Dynamics of the Single Unit Reactions in the Visual Cortex of the Unanesthetized Rabbit, Vision Research, Volume 10, Number 1, pp. 11-28, 1970. (U)

229. Danilov, I.V. and Kudryavtseva, N.N., Dynamics of Inter-central Relations in the Monkey Brain During Prolonged Rhythmic Photic Stimulation, Fiziologicheskiy Zhurnal SSSR, Leningrad, Number 8, pp. 1089-1098, 1971. (U)

230. Valtsev, V.B. and Lalayan, A.A., On the Mechanism of Functional Reorganization of Different Links of the Visual Analyzer in Conditions of Prolonged Photic Stimulation, Zh, Vys, Nervnoy, Deyatel nosti, Volume 19, Number 5, pp. 853-861, 1969. (U)

231. Kudinova, M.P. and Myslobodskiy, M.S., Some Characteristics of Sensory Afterdischarge of the Human Brain to Photic Stimulation, Zh, Vys, Nervnoy, Deyatel nosti, Volume 20, Number 1, pp. 89-94, 1970. (U)

232. Kartsev, V.I., Effect of High Brightnesses on the Rate of Eye Adaptation to Darkness, Kosmicheskaya Biologiya i Meditsina, Volume 5, Number 4, pp. 47-49, 1971. (U)

233. Shostak, V.I., Certain Features of the Action of Short Term Superbright Light Flashes on a Background of Total Dark Adaptation, Izdatilstvo Nauka, Volume 15, p. 144-146, 1969. (U)

234. Khitun, V.A., Korzun, P.A., Shostak, V.I., and Obukhova, E.A., Restoration of Visual Acuity After a Bright Light Flash of Short Duration, Ibid, pp. 142-143, 1969. (U)

UNCLASSIFIED

UNCLASSIFIED

ST-CS-01-169-72
July 1972

235. Shostak, V.I. and Obukhova, E.A., Effect of Intensity
of the Desadapting Photic Stimulation of Restoring the Light
of the Visual Center in Humans, Fiziologicheskiy Zhurnal SSSR,
Volume 56, Number 4, pp. 558-562, 1970. (U)

236. Davydov, V.V., Psychophysiological Features of the Perception
of Instrument Information by the Pilot After Diverting His Attention
to Features Outside the Cockpit, Voenno Meditsinskiy Zhurnal,
pp. 50-53, November 1970. (U)

237. Amirov, N.Kh., Zubairova, G.O., Mendelevich, D.M., and
Kalpina, G.A., EEG Changes in Persons Working Under Low-Intensity
Red Light and in Complete Darkness, Gigiyena Truda i Professionalnyye
Zabolevaniya, Number 1, pp. 13-16, 1971 (JPRS 53509, 1 July 1971). (U)

238. Kamchatnov, V.P. and Kalpina, G.A., Physiological and
Hygienic Evaluation of Working Conditions of Persons Who Work
in Low-Intensity Light, Ibid, Number 9, pp. 16-19, September
1970, (JPRS 52753, 30 March 1971). (U)

239. Kozhevnikov, Ye.P., Human Work Capacity During Adaptation
to a Bright Light Source of Varying Spectral Composition, Ibid,
pp. 12-16, September 1970. (U)

240. Ibid, The Effect of Colored Illumination on Delayed Reactions
in Lower Monkeys, Doklady Akademii Nauka SSSR, Volume 189, Number
4, pp. 917-919, 1969. (U)

241. Folb, R.L. and Voronina, S.V., Light and Color Thresholds
of Lights on a Background of Different Brightness, Izdatilstvo
Nauka, Volume 15, pp. 49-53, 1969. (U)

242. Lobanova, N.V., Possible Forms of Color Vision, Ibid, pp. 39-42,
1969. (U)

243. Makashova, E.V., Condition of Peripheral Field of Color
Vision in Healthy Persons of Different Age Groups, Vestn Oftalmol,
Volume 5, pp. 55-57, 1969. (U)

244. Makarov, P.O., Microinterval Analysis of the Development
of Visual Perceptions, Izdatelstvo Nanka, Volume 15, pp. 57-60,
1969. (U)

162

UNCLASSIFIED

UNCLASSIFIED

ST-CS-01-169-72
July 1972

245. Kalning, S.A., Effect of Amino Glycolates and Acetates on
the Discrimination of Rhythms of Light Flashes by Rabbit Retinas,
Farmakol Toksikol, Volume 33, Number 2, pp. 173-178, 1970. (U)

246. Information Report, 00-E-324/23772-71, 14 September 1971.
(S/CD/NDA)

247. Michael, R.P., Keverne, E.B., and Bonsall, R.W., Pheromones:
Isolation of Male Sex Attractants from a Female Primate, Science,
Volume 172, Number 3986, 28 May 1971. (U)

248. Comfort, A., Communication May Be Odorous, New Scientist
and Science Journal, UK, 25 February 1971. (U)

249. Beroza, M., Insect Sex Attractants, American Scientist,
Volume 59, May-June 1971. (U)

250. Beets, M.G.J., Odour Similarity Between Structurally Unrelated
Odorants, Paper presented at the Ciba Foundation Symposium on
Mechanisms of Taste and Smell in Vertebrates, London, 23-25 September
1969, (International Flavors and Fragrances, Hilversum, The Netherlands). (U)

251. Information Report 00-B-321/03044-70, 13 February 1970.
(C/CD/NDA)

252. Klimenko, A.I., Live Radio Electronics, Moscow, Znaniye
Publishing House, 128 pp., 1968. (U)

253. Portnyagina, V.A., Stolyarenko, L.G., Vasilyeva, Ye.V.
and Nedopekin, T.K., 1,3, Dimercaptopropyl, 2, thiopyrimidines,
Akademiya Nauka Atviyskoy, Number 5, pp. 605-610, 1970. (U)

254. Belkov, A.N., Action of Small Concentrations of Carbon
Tetrachloride on the Human Body, Tr. Tsent. Ins. Usoversh Vrachei,
Volume 135, pp. 90-96, 1969. (U)

255. Gasanov, SL.M., "The Zone of Health" - A New Type of Medical
Establishment for Large-Scale Improvement of Public Health,
Azerbaydzhanskiy Meditsinskiy Zhurnal, Baker, Number 4, pp. 43-48,
April 1970. (U)

256. Krivitskaya, G.N., Effect of Intense Noise on the Brain;
Experimental Research, Akademiya Meditsinskikh Nauka SSR, 157 pp.,
1964. (U)

163

UNCLASSIFIED

UNCLASSIFIED

ST-CS-01-169-72
July 1972

257. Maire, L., Biological Hazards of Infrasonic, Sonic and
Ultrasonic Noise of Military Significance - Warsaw Pact (U),
ST-CS-01-103-71, June 1971. (C/NFD/CD/NDA)

258. Gavreau, V., Condat, R., and Saul, H., Infrasound: Generators,
Detectors, Physical Properties, Biological Effects, Acustica,
Volume 18, Number 1, pp. 1-10, 1966. (U)

259. Mohr, G.C., et.al., Effects of Low Frequency and Infrasonic
Noise on Man, AD 627420. (U)

260. Wever, E.G. and Bray, C.W., The Perception of Low Tones
and the Resonance Volley Theory, J. Psych., Volume 3, Number 101,
1936. (U)

261. Dunn, F., UHF Acoustic Attenuation and Research in Biological
Accoustics, AD 674519. (U)

262. De Telegraaf, Amsterdam, The Netherlands, 15 June 1967. (U)

263. Koratkin, I.I., Pleshkova, T.V., and Suslova, M.M., Change In
Auditory Thresholds as a Result of Suggestion During Hypnosis,
Moscow, Zh. Vysshey Nervnoy Deyatelnosti, Number 1, January 1968. (U)

264. Rudenko, L.P., Canine Death Caused by Strong Acoustic
Stimulation, Ibid, Volume 15, Number 1, 1965. (U)

265. Alekseyev, S.V. and Suvarov, G.A., Substantiation of
Procedures for Studying Higher Nervous Activity Under the Action
of Noise, Giyiyena truda i professional'nyye zabolevaniya, Number
5, pp. 35-39, 1967. (U)

266. Strakhov, A.B., Some Problems of Action of Noise on the
Organism, paper presented at the Conference of Problems of
Space Medicine, Moscow, 1966. (U)

267. Ibid, Dynamics of Cortical Electrical Responses to Photic
Stimulation Under the Influence of Noise, Zh. Vysshey Nervnog
Deyatel'nosti, Volume 18, Number 5, pp. 873-879, 1968. (U)

268. Korzh, N.N., Soholov, Ye.N., and Cole, M.L., Mechanisms of
Detection of Acoustic Signals by Man, Moscow, Voprosy Psikhologii,
Number 2, pp. 126-131, 1969. (U)

269. Doroshenko, V.A., Muranyev, V.I., and Pudovkin, A.I., Changes
in the Amplitude of the Main EEG Rhythms in Man in Response to
Acoustic Stimulation, Zh Biologiya, Number 9, September 1969. (U)

164

UNCLASSIFIED

ST-CS-01-169-72
July 1972

270. Vogel, H.H., The Applicability of Acoustic Energy as a
Battlefield Weapon, AD 451239. (U)

271. Terentyev, V.G., Sheludyakov, Ye.Ye., and Sviridova, Ye.S.,
The Reaction of the Human Nervous and Cardiovascular Systems
to the Influence of Aviation Noise, Military Medical Journal,
pp. 55-58, June 1969. (ACSI translation J-6902.) (U)

272. Mikhaylova, L.V. and Byshevskiy, Possible Mechanism
Governing Inhibition of the Physiological Anticoagulation System
in a Long-Term Effect of Sound, Byull Eksp. Biologii i Meditsiny,
Volume 69, Number 2, pp. 28-32, 1970. (U)

273. Maydanova, N.V., Rat Liver Transketolase and Erythrocytes
Activity Under the Effect of Sound, Ibid, pp. 47-49, 1970. (U)

274. Yuganov, Ye.M., Krylov, Yu.V., and Kuznetsov, V.S., Standardization of Admissible Limits for High Intensity Noise, Kosmichiskaya
Biologiya i Meditsina, Moscow, Volume 4, Number 1, January-February
1970. (U)

275. Melkumova, A.S. and Koroleva, V.A., Effect of Combined
Ultrasound and High Frequency Noise on the Central Nervous System,
(JPRS 36613 21 July 1966). (U)

276. Yefimov, N.A. and Lukyanov, V.S., Effect of Ultrasound
on the Organism (Clinical Observations), (JPRS 36613, 21 July
1966). (U)

277. Gorshkov, S.I., Gorbunov, O.N., and Antropov, G.A., Biological
Effects of Ultrasound, Moskova, 1965 (JPRS 36924, 10 August
1966). (U)

278. Klupp, H., Vyslonzil, E., and Wachtinger, B., Arch. Phys.
Ther. (Leipzig), Volume 4, p. 44, 1952. (U)

279. Wood, K. and Loomis, A., Physical Rev., Volume 29, p. 379,
1927. (U)

280. Ovanov, A.N., in the book Collection of Works of the Clinic
of Diseases of the Ear, Nose and Throat, Tbilisi Medical Institute,
Tbilisi, Number 1, p. 113, 1957. (U)

281. Goldstein, N. and 'Sinskey, A.J., Health Hazards from Ultrasonic
Energy, Department of Nutrition and Food Science, Massachusetts
Institute of Technology, PB 185963. (U)

UNCLASSIFIED

ST-CS-01-169-72
July 1972

282. Zubek, J.P., Behavioral and EEG Changes During and After 14 Days of Perceptual Deprivation and Confinement, Readings in General Psychology: Canadian Contributions, McCelland and Stewart, Toronto, 1970. (U)

283. Brownfield, C.A., Isolation: Clinical and Experimental Approaches, Random House, New York, 1965. (U)

284. Hinkle, L.E., The Physiological State of the Interrogation Subject as it Affects Brain Function. In A.D. Biderman and H. Zimmer (Eds), The Manipulation of Human Behavior, Wiley, New York, 1961. (U)

285. Kosmolinskiy, F.P. and Schiubina, Z.D., Sensory Deprivation in Space Flight, MIO translation Number 21. (U)

286. Galkin, V.S., Arch. Biol. Nauka, Volume 32, Number 2, 1932. (U)

287. Heron, W., Science, Volume 196, Number 1, pp. 52-56, 1957. (U)

288. Cunningham, G., Journal of British Interplanetary Society, Volume 17, Number 9, pp. 311-313, 1960. (U)

289. Kuznetsov, O.N. and Lebedev, V.I., Zhurn. Neuropatol i Psikhiat, Volume 65, Number 3, pp. 59-64, 1965. (U)

290. Gorbov, F.D., Myasnikov, V.I., and Yazdovskiy, V.I., Zhurn. Vyssh. Nervn. deyat., Volume 13, Number 4, pp. 585-592, 1963. (U)

291. Information Report 1-670-0256-70, October 1970. (C)

292. Information Report 00-B-321/16078-70, 11 June 1970. (S/CD/NDA)

293. Davis, J.B., Review of Scientific Information on the Effects of Ionized Air on Human Beings, Aerospace Medicine, Volume 34, pp. 35-42, 1963. (U)

294. Hirsch, F.G., McGiboney, D.R., and Harnish, T.D., The Psychologic Consequences of Exposure to High Density Pulsed Electromagnetic Energy, International Journal of Biometeorology, Volume 12, Number 3, pp. 263-270, 1968. (U)

295. Kolodov, Yu.A., Effect of Electromagnetic and Magnetic Fields on the Central Nervous System, Moscow, 1966, (NASA TT F-465). (U)

166

UNCLASSIFIED

324

UNCLASSIFIED

ST-CS-01-169-72
July 1972

296. Biological Effects of Electromagnetic Fields (Below Visible Frequencies) Especially in the Central Nervous System, University of California at Los Angeles, School of Medicine and Biomedical Library, 1964-1970. (U)

297. Kolodov, Yu.A., The Effect of an Electromagnetic Field on the Central Nervous System, Priroda, Number 4, April 1960, (JPRS 14447, 12 July 1962). (U)

298. Christian, J.G., Electromagnetic Radiation Biological Effects (Infrared, Ultraviolet and Laser) - Eurasion Communist Countries (U), ST-CS-01-74-71, May 1971. (S/NFD/CD/NDA)

299. Dul'dier, A.N., Effect of Infrared Radiation on the Morbidity of Workers in Hot Shops, Vrach Delo, Volume 2, pp. 98-100, 1969. (U)

300. Biological Effects of Magnetic Fields, Vyshka, Number 24, p. 3, cols 2-3, 29 January 1971. (U)

301. Portnov, F., Meditsinskaya Gazeta, Number 2, p. 3, cols. 1-5, 5 January 1972. (U)

302. Sweeney, S.A., Electromagnetic Radiation - Biological Effects, (3 - 300,000 MHz and Laser) - Eurasian Communist Countries (U), MIO-CS-01-9-68-INT, 1968. (S/NFD)

303. Information Report 00-B-321/04285-69, 10 March 1969. (C)

304. Kwiatkowska, J., Pheromones and the Problem of Communication in the Animal Kingdom, Postepy Hig. Med. Dosev., Volume 23, Number 4, 1969. (U)

305. Malicki, J., Attractants: The Agents Attracting Insects, Postepy Nauk Roln, Volume 17, Number 3, pp. 69-75, 1970. (U)

306. Funnikova, S.V. and Krivova, M.I., Attractant Properties of Lysine and Alanine for Aedes Mosquitoes, Uch. Zap. Kazan. Vet. Inst., Volume 102, pp. 333-335, 1969. (U)

307. Shamshurin, A.P., Kovalev, B.G., and Donya, A.P., New Synthesis of Trans, 1, Acetoxy, 10, Propyl, 5, 9, Tridecadiene, Propylure, Sex Attractant of Pectinophora Gossypiella, Dokl. Akad. Nauk. SSSR, Volume 190, Number 6, pp. 1362-1364, 1970. (U)

308. Burtsev, A.L. and Gladilin, K.L., Attractant, Priroda, Moscow, Volume 3, p. 114, 1970. (U)

UNCLASSIFIED

ST-CS-01-169-72
July 1972

NON-CITED BIBLIOGRAPHY

PART I

SECTION III

1. Pearce, R.M., The Insurgent Environment, ARPA, RM. 5533, The Rand Corporation, California, May 1969. (U)

2. The Institute of Contemporary Russian Studies, Medical Reports, Volume 6, Number 1, Fordham University, January-March 1964. (U)

PART II

1. Information Report 00-B-321/11572-70, 12 May 1970. (C/CD/NDA)

2. Lombroso, C., Researches on Hypnotic and Spiritualistic Phenomena, Truin, Italy, 1909. (U)

3. Dingwall, E.J., Very Peculiar People, London, 1950. (U)

4. Bramwell, J.M., Hypnotism, London, 1903. (U)

5. Wallace, A.R., Miracles and Modern Spiritualism, London, 1875. (U)

6. Aksakof, A. (ex-prime minister of Russia), A Case of Partial Dematerialization of the Body of a Medium, Boston (translation) Banner of Light Publishing Co., 1898. (U)

7. Crawford, N.J., The Psychic Structures at the Goligher Circle, New York, E.P. Dutton and Co., 1921. (U)

8. Ibid, Experiments in Psychical Science, New York, E.P. Dulton and Co., 1919. (U)

9. Doyle, A.C., The Edge of the Unknown, New York, G.P. Putnam's Sons, 1930. (U)

10. Leek, S., Guide to Telepathy, New York, The Macmillian Co. (U)

11. Information Report 00-B-321/07499-65, 11 May 1965. (C/CD/NDA)

12. Kazhinskiy, B.B., Biological Radio Communication, Publishing House of the Academy of Sciences, Ukrainain SSR, 169 pp. 1962. (U)

UNCLASSIFIED

ST-CS-01-169-72
July 1972

13. Information Report 00-B-321/07022-68, 28 March 1968. (C/CD/NDA)

14. Information Report 00-B-321/10422-68, 22 April 1968. (C/CD/NDA)

15. Telepathy Research Trud, Moscow, p. 4, 27 December 1966. (U)

16. Kogan, I.M., New Telepathy Research Section, Znaniya sila, Number 1, p. 51, 1966. (U)

17. Kogan, I.M., Is Telepathy Possible?, Radiotekhnika, Volume 21, Number 1, pp. 8-14, 1966. (U)

18. Psychologists Experiment in Mental Telepathy, Moscow, Tass International Service, 9 October 1966. (U)

19. Parapsychology Laboratory, Komsomolskaya pravda, p. 4, 9 October 1966. (U)

20. Thought Transference or Telepathy, Moscow News, Number 13, p. 11, 1967. (U)

21. The Voice of the Brain, Rabochaya gazeta, 8 January 1967. (U)

22. FBIS Report Number 188, 27 September 1967. (FOUO)

23. Kogan, I.M., Informational Analysis of Experiments in Telepathic Communication, Radiotekhnika, Volume 23, Number 3, pp. 87-92, 1968. (U)

24. Presman, A.S., Parapsychological Investigations, Izd-vo Nauka, pp. 238-242, 1968. (U)

25. Akhlibininskii, B.V., Psychocybernetics and Parapsychology, Lenizdat, Leningrad, 144 pp. 1966. (U)

26. FBIS Report Number 56, 21 March 1963. (FOUO)

27. Soviets Serious About Telepathy, Columbus Dispatch, 6 May 1962. (U)

28. Faddeyev, Ye.T., What is this Telepathy?, Nauka i Zhizn, Number 6, pp. 60-63, 1961. (U)

29. Telepathy, Tekhnika molodezhi, Number 1, pp. 28-32, 1961. (U)

30. Information Report 00-B-321/14531-66, 13 September 1966. (C/CD/NDA)

170

UNCLASSIFIED

ST-CS-01-169-72
July 1972

31. Information Report 00-B-321/00671-69, 14 February 1969. (C/CD/NDA)

32. Leontyev, A.N., Is Parapsychology a Science? Moscow, Priroda, Number 1, p. 122, 1970. (U)

33. Dobronrovov, S.N., Ivanova, N., and Zakharov, N.V., Detection of Photosensitivity of the Skin by Forming Conditional Defense Reflexes to Light Stimuli, RZN-Biologiya, Number 9, September 1969. (U)

34. Sergeyev, G.A., Romanenko, A.F., and Guryev, A.V., Filtration of Random Processes, Radiatekhnika, Volume 19, Number 1, pp. 63-70, 1964. (U)

35. Sergeyev, G.A. and Romanenko, A.F., Evaluating the Error in Determining the Correlation Interval, Radiotekhnika, Volume 9, Number 4, pp. 741-743, 1964. (U)

36. Sergeyev, G.A., Sukhodolskiy, G.V., and Bodlozerov, V.M., Investigation of the Statistical Characteristics of a Human Operator for the Case of Nonstationary Input Signals, Izd-vo Nauka, p. 185, 1965. (U)

37. Sergeyev, G.A. and Romanenko, A.F., Hybrid Computer for Statistical Data Processing, MIO Number Ten, ST-CS-01-169-72, (no date). (U)

38. Sergeyev, G.A., Experimental Investigation of Self-Adjustment Functions of the Human Operator, Moscow, Izd-vo Nauka, pp. 222-232, 1966. (U)

39. Sergeyev, G.A., Pavlova, L.P., and Prodan, V.T., Frequency Characteristics of Electroencephalograms of the Active Human Brain, Problems of Neurocybernetics, Rostov-on-Don, 1967. (U)

40. Sergeyev, G.A., Romanenko, A.F., and Pavlova, L.P., Statistical Methods for Studying Reliability Mechanisms of the Human Brain, Voprosy Bioniki, 1967. (U)

41. Sergeyev, G.A. and Romanenko, A.F., Operative Methods for Monitoring the Efficiency of an Operator in a - Man and Automation - System, Voprosy Bioniki, 1967. (U)

42. Sergeyev, G.A. and Romanenko, A.F., Use of Stochastic Simulation Concepts in Studies of the Reliability of the Human Operator, Problems of Engineering Psychology, Moscow, pp. 180-190, 1967. (U)

171

ST-CS-01-169-72
July 1972

43. Sergeyev, G.A. and Romanenko, A.F., Equipment for Investigating Human Coordination Functions, Izo Prom Ob Tov Znaki, Number 24, 1968, (Patent Number 223253). (U)

44. Sergeyev, G.A. and Romanenko, A.F., Device for the Running Statistical Processing of Biopotentials, Izo Prom Ob Tov Znaki, Number 30, 1968 (Patent Number 227496). (U)

45. Information Report 00-B-321/10281-69, 29 April 1969. (C/CD/NDA)

46. Fidelman, V.Ye., Gulevskiy, V.V., Bogatyrev, V.A., Ivanova, M.R., and Bulavin, G.I., Procedure for and Results of Experimental Checking of the Possibility of Telepathic Communication Radiotekhnika, Volume 25, Number 7, pp. 109-110, 1970. (U)

47. Annual Report of Communist Country Psychological Research in Support of the Soviet Manned Space Flight Program (U), MHR 67 6A, Project Have Eagle. (S)

48. Vega, J.W. and Gruenke, R.A., Soviet Interest in Mental Telepathy (S), FTD-TA-63-16/5. (S/NFD)

49. Sweeney, S.A., Electromagnetic Radiation Biological Effects (3 through 300,000 MHz and Laser), Eurasian Communist Countries (U), MIO-CS-01-9-68-INT. (S/NFD)

50. Information Report 00-B-321/33929-67. (C/CD/NDA)

PART III

SECTION I

1. Raikov, V. and Adamenko, V., Questions of Objective Research of Deep Hypnotic States, Therapy of Mental Disease, Moscow: Sechenov Medical Institute, 1968. (U)

2. Rozhnov, V., The Mechanisms of Hypnosis, Meditsinskaya gazeta, p. 3, 24 September 1965. (U)

PART III

SECTION I1

Hypnosis without Hypnosis, Pravda Vostaka, Number 140, p. 4, col. 4, 18 June 1968. (U)

ST-CS-01-169-72
July 1972

PART IV

SECTION II

Lustig, B., Therapeutic Methods in Soviet Psychiatry, I.C.R.S.
Medical Reports, Fordham University, Number 3, 1963. (U)

PART VI

SECTION I

1. Orlansky, J., The Use of Flashing Light to Perturb Human Behavior,
Institute for Defense Analysis, Research and Engineering Support
Division, Research paper, p. 172, March 1965. (U)

2. Churchill, A.V., An Annotated Bibliography of Reports 1951–
1970, Human Factors Wing, Defense Research Establishment Toronto,
Downsview, Ontario, DRET Report Number 769, September 1970. (U)

3. Dahlke, A.E., Palmer, J.D., and Page, M.M., A Study of the Effects
of Visual Flicker and Auditory Flutter on Human Performance, University
of Oklahoma Research Institute, Norman, Oklahoma, AF-08(635)-5257,
February 1967. (U)

4. Christner, C.A., Austen, B.G., Cress, R.J., Hassfurther, M.E.,
McFarland, R.R., and Roppel, R.M., State-of-the-Art Study of the
Pulsed-Light Phenomenon, Remote Area Conflict Information Center,
Battelle Memorial Institute, Columbus, Ohio, Report Number,
BAT-171-6, 4 December 1964. (U)

5. Alexander, H.S. and Chiles, W.D., Prolonged Intermittent
Photic Stimulation, U.S. Armed Forces Medical Journal, Volume 2,
pp. 1156–1161, 1960. (U)

PART VIII

1. Barrett, A.M., Personality Characteristics Under the Stress
of High Intensity Sound, Unpublished Ph.D. dissertation, 1950,
Penn State College, State College, Pennsylvania. (U)

2. Broadbent, D.E., Effects of Noise in Behavior, Handbook of
Noise Control, Harris (Ed.), Chapter 10, McGraw-Hill, New York,
1957. (U)

3. Plutchik, R., The Effects of High Intensity Intermittent Sound
on Performance, Feeling, and Physiology, Psychol. Bull., Volume 56,
pp. 133–151, 1959. (U)

Appendix II

Defence Intelligence Agency Document: Soviet and
Czechoslovakian Parapsychology Research – USSR, April
1975

A complete table of contents and selected sections are reproduced here. The numbers refer to sources, which are listed at the end of the document.

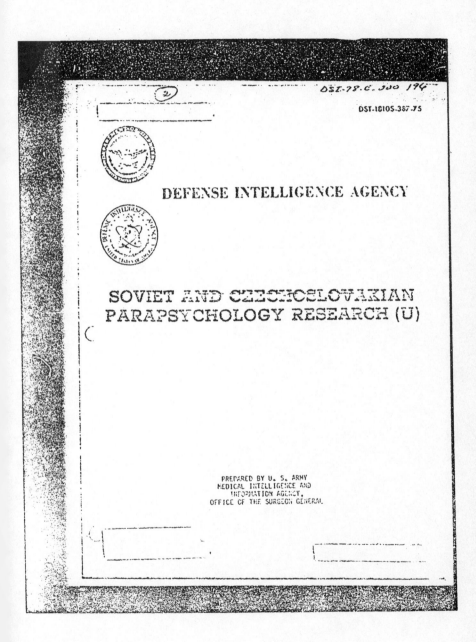

DST-1810S-387-75

DEFENSE INTELLIGENCE AGENCY

SOVIET AND CZECHOSLOVAKIAN PARAPSYCHOLOGY RESEARCH (U)

PREPARED BY U. S. ARMY
MEDICAL INTELLIGENCE AND
INFORMATION AGENCY,
OFFICE OF THE SURGEON GENERAL

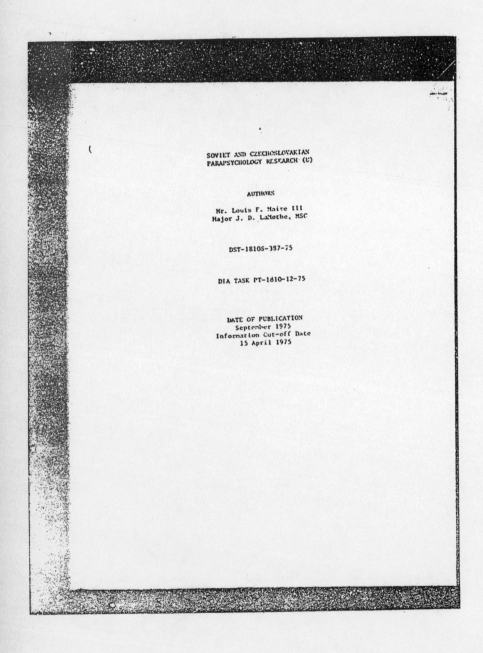

SOVIET AND CZECHOSLOVAKIAN
PARAPSYCHOLOGY RESEARCH (U)

AUTHORS

Mr. Louis F. Maire III
Major J. D. LaMothe, MSC

DST-1810S-387-75

DIA TASK PT-1810-12-75

DATE OF PUBLICATION
September 1975
Information Cut-off Date
15 April 1975

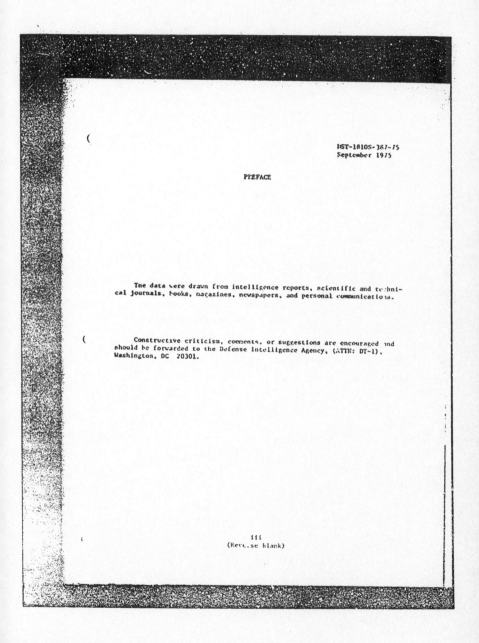

IST-1810S-387-75
September 1975

PREFACE

The data were drawn from intelligence reports, scientific and technical journals, books, magazines, newspapers, and personal communications.

Constructive criticism, comments, or suggestions are encouraged and should be forwarded to the Defense Intelligence Agency, (ATTN: DT-1), Washington, DC 20301.

iii
(Reverse blank)

DST-1810S-387-75
September 1975

TABLE OF CONTENTS

v

336

DST-1810S-387-75
September 1975

vi

DST-1810S-387-75
September 1975

SUMMARY

During the past 25 years, Soviet and Czechoslovakian parapsychologists have reported that paranormal phenomena such as extrasensory perception (ESP), telepathy, and psychokinesis (PK) have been demonstrated under rigorously controlled laboratory conditions. Skeptics in both nations have attacked the study of such phenomena on both scientific and political – ideological grounds. Criticism based on political ideology has stemmed from the fact that such past research has been non-materialistic in the sense that results have not been reported in terms of contemporary conventional science. Thus the critics feel that parapsychology has fostered continued belief in mysticism, occultism, and religion.

In order to rebut the skeptics' contentions that psychic phenomena do not fit accepted scientific and political thought, Soviet and Czech scientists now argue that there are many well established "facts" which remain as anomalous to scientific paradigms as extrasensory perception (ESP). ESP refers to information which is not received via the usual senses, and as a general term, includes telepathy (the Soviet "biocommunication") and psychokinesis or PK (the Soviet "bioenergetics"). Communist parapsychologists argue that after decades of research, conventional science still has no satisfactory neurophysiological explanation of memory, nor is there any appropriate model for explaining how raw data impinging on man's senses are transformed into a conscious experience. They also point to the dematerialized character of contemporary physics, a science filled with such bizarre components as advance potential (waves of electrons perceived before they are generated), tunneling effects (electrons penetrating barriers which, by the laws of probability, should be impenetrable), and tachyons (particles traveling faster than light, and thus implying the possibility of a backward flow of time). In short, they conclude that "hard" science no longer offers a secure rationale for the denial of the possibility of any noncausal event.

vii

338

DST-1810S-387-75
September 1975

PART I

EXTRASENSORY PERCEPTION (ESP)

SECTION 1 - BACKGROUND

Parapsychology is a field involving research on the informational and energetic possibilities of the psychic and biophysical activities of living organisms. Parapsychology investigates the complex of phenomena relating to the interaction of living organisms with each other and with the surrounding environment without the mediation of the known sense organs or of presently identified energy transfer mechanisms. Western parapsychologists refer to this complex of phenomena as extrasensory perception (ESP) and psi phenomena.[1]

The Soviets prefer the term biocommunications instead of parapsychology, psi phenomena, or ESP. Other Soviet terms which are equivalent to the term parapsychology include psychophysiology, psychotronics, psychoenergetics, and biophysical effects. The Soviet term biocommunications can be further subdivided into two general classifications: bioinformation and bioenergetics. Bioinformation includes paranormal events between living organisms (telepathy, precognition) and events between living organisms and the inanimate world. Bioenergetics denotes activities such as biological locator and indicator techniques (dowsing), bioenergetic therapy using electromagnetic (EM) fields, and psychokinesis, or the influence of bioenergy on matter. Definitions of the terms biocommunications, bioinformation, and bioenergetics are as follows:[2]

BASIC TYPES OF BIOCOMMUNICATION PHENOMENA (U)

General: Biocommunications

A branch of science involved with the human capability of obtaining information from other than the normal senses and the ability to respond to or reasonably interpret such information. Biocommunications, also synonymous with parapsychology, is, however, distinct from other sciences in that it is primarily concerned with determining the nature of a definite group of natural phenomena controlled by laws which are not based on any presently known energetic influence.

1

339

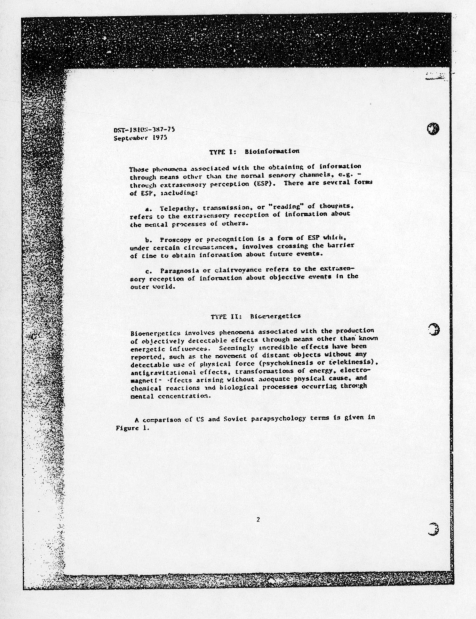

DST-1810S-387-75
September 1975

Fig. 1 Comparison of US and Soviet Parapsychology Terms (U)

US				Soviet
Parapsychology	)		(	Biocommunications
PSI Phenomena	)		(	Psychophysiology
ESP	)	Equals	(	Psychotronics
			(	Psychoenergetics
			(	Biophysical Effects

Biocommunications

A. Bioinformation
B. Bioenergetics

Telepathy	)	Equals Bioinformation
Precognition	)	

Dowsing	)	Equals Bioenergetics
Psychokinesis	) .	

In recent years, Czechoslovakian parapsychologists have begun using the term "psychotronics" in reference to all aspects of their paranormal phenomena research. They define psychotronics as the study of those borderline phenomena and signs of human existence that have a psychosomatic base, but manifest themselves in such a way that they more or less exceed the framework of this base. Such phenomena include autosuggestion, hypnosis, telepathy, psychokinesis, and other paranormal effects and phenomena. The Czech term does not encompass the study of stigmata, levitation, etc., since these are considered to be hallucinatory states or processes and, as such, areas of investigation and treatment more appropriate for psychology or psychiatry.[3] In general, however, the Czech science of psychotronics includes the study of all phenomena presently being investigated by Soviet and Western parapsychologists.

3

DST-1810S-387-75
September 1975

Current Soviet and Czech parapsychological terms and objectives have evolved in a climate of fluctuating political pressure. Scientists in pre-revolutionary Russia studied parapsychology as did later such Soviet scientists as V.M. Bekhterev, A.G. Ivanov-Smolensky, and I.B. Kazhinsky in the twenties and thirties.[4] In 1924, A.V Lunakharsky, Commissar for Education, took the initiative in forming a Soviet Committee for Psychical Research. As a result of Academician V.M. Bekhterev's enthusiasm for the subject, extensive work was financed at the University of Leningrad Institute for Brain Research. L.L. Vasilev, a former student of Bekhterev's demonstrated to his own satisfaction that telepathic influence at a distance may indeed occur. Work flourished throughout the thirties with research being reported in the literature in 1934, 1936, and 1937. After 1937 further experiments in the field of parapsychology were forbidden. During Stalin's time, the study of paranormal phenomena was interpreted as a deliberate attempt to undermine the doctrines of materialism. Telepathy was treated as a mystical and antisocial superstition and nothing further was heard of parapsychology in the Soviet Union until the late 1950s. Then, as a result of French newspaper articles, rumors began to circulate that American researchers had disproved the "brain-radio" theory as a result of ship-to-shore telepathy experiments involving the US atomic submarine Nautilus. The Nautilus "experiments" probably were mythical, but the claims had one tangible consequence: the Soviet authorities permitted Vasilev, then Professor of Physiology and holder of the Order of Lenin, to publish his own earlier work in which decades previously he had proven to his own satisfaction that radio-type brain waves did not mediate telepathy. Vasilev was also allowed to open a unit for the study of parapsychology at the Institute for Brain Research. His work first reached the West with an English translation of his monograph "Experiments in Mental Suggestion" in 1963. The result was instant international interest. Numerous Western researchers traveled to the Soviet Union and found a fair amount of activity and interest in the paranormal, although the research approaches were frequently different from those in the West. Soviet workers tended to be far more preoccupied with whole-body physical and biological effects rather than with the "mental" phenomena with which Western researchers had long been preoccupied.

Some of the first parapsychologists to visit the Soviet Union after the publication of Vasilev's work described the differences in atmosphere pervading two conferences in 1963 and 1968. During the first, free and cordial exchange of views was possible; the second was overshadowed by an article in Pravda attacking parapsychology which largely wrecked the formal plans for the program. Most of the Soviets declined to speak, Western visitors were pressed to deliver impromptu lectures, and the House of Friendship in Moscow withdrew its invitation to hold further meetings or allow films to be shown there. From this time onwards, with certain

4

DST-1810S-387-75
September 1975

fluctuations, official hostility towards parapsychology increased in the
Soviet Union. For example, Soviet authorities took the strongest possible
exception to a best-seller in the West, Ostrander and Schroeder's "Psychic
Discoveries Behind the Iron Curtain."[5] Edward K. Naumov, then Director of
the Institute of Technical Parapsychology, Moscow,[6] was cited throughout
as the journalists' guide and mentor. Unfortunately, the Voice of America
beamed a radio program into the Soviet Union discussing the Schroeder and
Ostrander book, a broadcast that was construed as a politically motivated
attack using parapsychology as a weapon. Apart from this episode, it is
not entirely clear why Soviet officialdom should have taken such fierce
exception to a frankly popular, sensational, and rather chaotic book, which
was not taken seriously by many Western scientists. The most plausible
interpretation seems that the Soviets were worried that they might be
believed by the world's scientific community to be self-proclaimed champions
and leaders of parapsychology. In fact, Soviet scientists are just as divided among themselves concerning parapsychology as scientists elsewhere and
since 1972, a number of openly critical publications concerning parapsychology research have appeared in the Soviet Union. A few examples of such
open attacks follow.

In 1972, V.M. Bleykher (a reputable Soviet neurophysiologist) published a book titled "Parapsychology - Science or Superstition." In an
annotation to this book (and, in fact, as the lead paragraph) Bleykher
stated, "this book is designed (sic) to debunk parapsychology." The
book began with such arcane and archaic topics as phrenology (headbump
reading) and ended with a chapter prefaced by a cartoon showing a broom
sweeping the Russian word "parapsychology," out of the picture. The
entire bias of the book was to make a direct link between 19th century
"spiritualism" and 20th century parapsychology.

In 1973, Kazakhstanskaya Pravda (Alma-Ata) carried an article by
Doctor of Medical Science V. Fudachin, titled "Careful: Paramedicine!"
In his article Fudachin openly attacked "unproven telepathic transmission of information over distances from one person to another on the
basis of their neuropsychic states," and criticized parapsychologists
"for claiming to obtain results that are completely unrelated to the
cause-and-effect principle."

In October 1973 a long and detailed paper entitled "Parapsychology:
Fiction or Reality?" was published in Questions of Philosophy, an
official publication of the Soviet Academy of Pedagogical Sciences, by
four eminent members of the Moscow Academy of Pedagogical Sciences, V.P.
Zinchenko, A.N. Leontiev, B.F. Lomov, and A.R. Luria. They explicitly
set out "to express the viewpoint of the USSR Society of Psychologists

5

343

DST-1810S-387-75
September 1975

towards parapsychology." "Obviously," they wrote, "some so-called parapsychological phenomena do happen; however, the main obstacle to the acceptance of their existence is ignorance of the basis of their operation." It is not clear from this paper just which parapsychological phenomena "obviously do happen;" the only ones which the authors unambiguously supported as authentic were Kirlian photography (radiation field photography by means of which the biological energy fields of plants and animals may be visualized) and "dermal-optical vision" (the alleged ability to see colors through opaque shielding by touch alone). Paradoxically, Kirlian photography is probably based on known forms of energy, while dermal-optical vision has no known basis in fact. A large portion of the paper was in fact devoted to a denunciation of "militant parapsychologists," popular credulity, fraudulent practices, physicists who quite unnecessarily change their jobs to investigate paranormal phenomena, sensationalistic journalists, and institutions such as the Institute for Technical Parapsychology (which was cited by name). Apparently, the objective of the paper was to discredit as myth any idea of a "parapsychological movement" in the Soviet Union, and to insure that the science of parapsychology should not continue to exerge. To quote the authors, "there is no need for parapsychology to exist as a separate discipline."

There is additional evidence that the official attitude toward parapsychology in the Soviet Union may have changed. In the 1960's, Moscow parapsychologist Edward K. Naumov was recognized internacionaliy as the unofficial Soviet spokesman for the science. In March of 1974, Naumov was arrested and sentenced to two years hard labor. In January 1975, parapsychologist Larissa Vilenskaya, who had previously been permitted to visit Naumov in jail, was herself arrested. The reason for her arrest is not known, but Naumov was apparently convicted of taking fees for his lectures without the permission of the appropriate authorities. According to reports from the Soviet Union, the fees seem to have been collected in the normal way by the club's director or his assistant. However, both were subsequently declared psychologically unfit to testify, certified schizophrenic, and referred for some unspecified form of involuntary treatment at the Serbskiy Institute of Forensic Psychological Expertise. This Institute's director, Dr. Andrej Snezhnevsiy, is widely known for his psychiatric zeal on behalf of ideological orthodoxy and for his opposition to parapsychology. At the trial Snezhnevsky himself gave evidence to the effect that parapsychology was a pseudoscience based on idealism and mysticism. Although 40 witnesses said they had bought their tickets from the club's director or his representative, Naumov was found guilty and sentenced to two years in a camp. According to Lev Regelson, a Moscow physicist, Naumov's offense was twofold: first, despite reiterated warnings from the KGB he had "maintained free, personal, human contacts with foreign scholars..." and made use of the material he received

6

344

DST-1810S-387-75
September 1975

for disseminating information on parapsychology in the USSR. Naumov's second fault is ideological. Up to most recent times parapsychology has been looked on in the Soviet Union as "mysticism" and "pseudoscience," sharing the fate of the theory of relativity, quantum mechanics, cybernetics, genetics, etc.

Naumov's trial and the dismissal from their posts of others who had been active in parapsychology in the Soviet Union in the 1960's may mark the end of a phase during which free and indeed spirited discussion of parapsychological topics was permitted throughout the Soviet Union, and during which a fair amount of informal and unofficial East-West contact was at least tolerated.[8]

Despite apparent shifts in the official attitude toward the science, 49 out of the 91 papers presented in 1973 at the First International Conference on Psychotronic Research in Prague, Czechoslovakia, were authored by Soviet or ECC researchers. In addition, the Moscow publication "Zhurnalist," published a lengthy editorial[9] in 1974, in which readers were assured that "all energy fields existing in nature are not known to contemporary physics" and "that because various phenomena cannot as yet be explained does not mean that they do not exist." The name of the science may be changed in the future, but the research will continue.

During the past decade parapsychology has undergone many changes in the Soviet Union and Czechoslovakia. In a sense, this is a question of changing generations. The elder generation of researchers, who actively investigated the problems of psychotronics, regarded it predominantly as philosophy and psychology. To a certain extent, this concept determined their approach to the problems: in most cases they concluded that very complex psychic processes were involved, processes that were difficult to control and hence were not always reproducible. This elder generation of researchers had as their primary objective the proof of psychic processes and the defense of their theories. They confined themselves to their own specifics and problems. In terms of the quantity of accumulated facts and performed experiments their work was considerable and often awe-inspiring.

Researchers of the younger generation in the USSR and Czechoslovakia are beginning to regard this concept as one-sided, a straitjacket. They are not satisfied with the constant proving and description of the phenomena. They also want to model, amplify, formulate and compute. A desire to conclusively master the problems has compelled them to abandon the previous concept and to define parapsychology for the time being, as a border-line interdisciplinary science. To the unipolar philosophical-psychological concept there is now added another pole, the technical-physical concept. Between these two poles there is sufficient room for parapsychology to comprehend all the phenomena that it investigates, in their complexity.

7

DST-1810S-387-75
September 1975

Present-day Soviet parapsychologists are recruited from practically all scientific disciplines, not as individual enthusiasts but as members of coordinated interdisciplinary teams of specialists. In 1967 the Czechs established the Coordination Group for Psychotronic (parapsychological) Research. They intentionally set as one of their principal objectives the description of the undetermined properties of the energy bound to man and to animate nature. They appear to be convinced, for example, that de Broglie's dual concept, in which the electron may appear as a mass of inertia or as electromagnetic radiation, requires a third aspect (the vehicle of which would not necessarily be de Broglie's electron but possibly the mental ion or "mention" presupposed by Professor F. Kahuda), and that only then will it be possible to completely express the animate and inanimate world of matter in motion. By defining the parameters of the undefined form of energy the concept of matter in motion could gain a third aspect, and matter in motion would be defined by laws far more complex and comprehensive than at present. It is interesting to note the increasing validity of Professor L.L. Vasilev's statement that "...discovery of the laws of the as yet unknown form of energy bound to man will be of no less significance than the discovery of atomic energy." Therefore it is no coincidence that theoretical physicists and plasma physicists in the Federal Republic of Germany believe that understanding of the psychical-physical interactions of living organisms will add something basically new to physics and biology. The Czechs believe that as soon as science begins to understand the properties of this new form of energy, questions of its mastery and utilization will rise to the forefront. Robert Pavlita's work, which is discussed in detail in Part II, is no small contribution in this direction. Whereas in the past parapsychology operated predominantly by the method of exceptional individual performance, psychotronics presupposes a new model: the living organism (man)—processing of energy—performance.

In 1982, a century will have elapsed since the foundation in England of the first Society for Psychical Research. Zdenek Rejdak, internationally renowned parapsychologist of the Czechoslovak Scientific and Technical Society, Section for Psychotronic Research has stated, "we are convinced that psychotronics will mark this centennial with significant results in practical, applied, and basic research, in the knowledge that it will become an essential new anthropological science, one that will enhance primarily man's integrity."

8

DST-1810S-387-75
September 1975

SECTION II - TELEPATHY (ENERGY TRANSFER) IN ANIMALS

Soviet and Czechoslovakian parapsychologists have not reported "telepathy" in animals in recent years; instead, they have emphasized research on biological energy transfer. Soviet parapsychology research is multidisciplinary and indistinguishable from conventional Soviet physiological research. Both disciplines are presently involved in attempts to identify the sources of internally generated and externally imposed stimuli underlying physiological processes.

Soviet research on telepathy in animals in the 1920's and 1930's was devoted largely to proving that telepathy between man and animals did indeed exist. A good example of the early Soviet approach was research conducted by V.M. Bekhterev of Leningrad University, in collaboration with a circus performer, V.L. Durov. Bekhterev reported that Durov's trained dogs successfully solved arithmetic problems and identified or retrieved objects solely on the basis of their trainer's mental suggestion.[10] The results of these tests were controversial, since the dogs' performances were good when Durov was present and supplied the "suggestions," but deteriorated markedly when he was absent and another individual attempted to mentally control them.

Bekhterev's original objective was to demonstrate that telepathy between man and animals was mediated by some form of electromagnetic radiation (EMR), but by 1937, he and other Soviet parapsychologists had concluded that no known form of EMR was the carrier of thought transmission. The EMR theory of information transfer is still unresolved by the Soviets, but is still the major basis underlying much of their research.

In 1962 B.S. Kazhinskiy advanced the theory that animals are capable of visual and aural perception and reflex understanding of the behavior of other animals or humans.[1] He postulated that this ability resulted from the capacity of one animal to detect (via its nervous system), analyze, and synthesize signal-stimuli given off by another animal. According to Kazhinskiy, the signals were transmitted in the form of a "bioradiational sight ray" and analyzed by the percipient animal as a result of its Pavlovian conditioning. The term "bioradiational rays" is still used by some Soviet and Czech parapsychologists to refer to focusing and concentration of biological energy by the brain and the optical neural channels.

Present day Soviet and Czech parapsychology research with animals is devoted almost exclusively to investigation of sources of biological energy involved in physiological processes, the interactions of such energy with external fields, and the effects of externally generated fields on animal physiology. Reference to telepathy in the sense of communications by transmission of total, conceptual, mental formulations is seldom made.

9

DST-1810S-367-75
September 1975

A significant advance toward identification of the EMR source of
biological energy transfer was gained from recent research conducted at
the University of Novosibirsk. Scientists there investigated the release
of energy during cell division and during cellular damage and repair
resulting from viral infection or toxic chemicals. In over 5000 experiments with cell cultures and animal organs it was shown that damaged cells
radiated some form of energy and that the energy released was capable of
causing damage in adjacent control preparations of organs or cells.
Further investigation revealed that a uniform pattern, code, or rhythm of
radiation was emitted by normal cells. This pattern was disturbed when
cellular damage occurred, becoming quite irregular. It was also found
that the patterns were transmitted from experimental to control preparations only when the cells or organs were cultured in quartz containers.
Since quartz transmits ultraviolet (UV) radiation and standard laboratory
glassware does not, the Soviets concluded that UV radiation mediated
cellular information transfer. The researchers subsequently correlated
given irregularities of emission with specific diseases and are now
attempting to develop techniques for diagnosis and therapy by monitoring
and altering cellular radiation codes.[6]

Czechoslovakian research on energy transfer between animal muscle
preparations, from animals to man, and from man to man, has also demonstrated EMR as the vehicle of biological energy transfer. In experiments
conducted between 1948 and 1968 at the Okres Institute of Public Health,
Kutna Hora, Czechoslovakia, Dr. Jiri Bradna demonstrated contactless
transfer (myotransfer) of stimuli between frog neuromuscular preparations.
Bradna placed identical preparations side by side; stimulation of one
preparation with electric pulses at frequencies between 10 and 30 pulses
per second caused contraction and a recorded electromyographic response
in the other. In other experiments, stimulation of muscle preparations
influenced the oscillations of a pendulum and increased the muscle tension
of a human subject. Bradna obtained objective proof that energy in the very
high frequency (vhf) range mediated the stimulus transmission. He also
demonstrated that myotransfer could be blocked with ferrous metal filters
and aluminum, could be deformed with magnets, ferrites and other conductors,
could be reflected and transmitted over waveguides, and shielded with grids.
Bradna concluded that primary perceptual and informational pathways between
animals are based on metabolic processes at the macromolecular level and
that the magnitude of energy transfer depends on muscular adenosine
triphosphate (ATP) energy release.[12]

Bradna has reported successful application of myotransfer in physio-
therapy. It has been found to be effective for both individuals and groups.
In the latter case, the summation of stimuli has been shown to enhance the
neuromuscular responses of individual within the group. Bradna feels
that such stimuli influence the herd behavior of animals and may also
be a factor in altering human behavior under conditions of isolation or
overcrowding.

10

DST-1610S-387-75
September 1975

In the Soviet Union, Doctor Y.A. Kholodov has investigated the effects of a constant magnetic field (CMF) on rabbits.[13] Whole-body exposures to fields between 30 and 2000 oersteds resulted in nonspecific changes in the electroencephalogram, but no other directly measurable physiological responses. Kholodov showed that weak magnetic as well as other externally generated radiation fields have a direct effect on nerve tissue, and for this reason he feels that natural and artificial fields in man's environment may have an influence on health and behavior via the nervous system and the hypothalamus. Kholodov's research is representative of current Soviet efforts to explain paranormal phenomena on the basis of known physical and biological parameters.

Another Soviet scientist, A.S. Presman, feels that biological energy and information exchange between living organisms is the result of electromagnetic field (EMF) interactions between individuals or between the individual and the environment.[14] He and other Soviet scientists have recorded EMF's from man, frogs, and insects of various species at ranges from several centimeters to several meters from the body surface. The frequencies of the EMF's were found to correspond to various biorhythms of organs, rhythms of movement and acoustic signals, and bioelectric rhythms. Presman thinks that in groups of animals, electromagnetic oscillations are synchronized by frequency matching and that the cumulative intensity may grow in proportion to the square of the number of individuals. Such cumulative emission is also thought to be possible as the result of synchronization of the emissions of many cells in animals in a highly excited state.

Presman, like Kholodov, feels that the effects of subthreshold stimuli are mediated through the hypothalamic region of the midbrain. The hypothalamus regulates diverse physiological processes in the organism (pulse, body temperature, oxygen consumption, carbon dioxide liberation, urine volume, urine nitrogen concentration, etc.) and these are the functions most commonly disturbed by changes in EMF's.

Presman believes that electromagnetic signalling is universal between animals, but not between humans who may have lost the capability for such communication as a result of evolution and the development of verbal and artificial communication channels. He does not rule out the possibility that "spontaneous telepathy" may occasionally occur, but regards such occurrences as rare cases of atavism. Consequently, he regards man as the least suitable animal for studying electromagnetic communication.

It is important that the increased degree of sophistication which has occurred in Soviet ESP or telepathy research since 1960 be understood. At present the terms "ESP" and "telepathy" are seldom used. It is possible that the newer terms "biocommunication" and "psychotronics" will vanish in the near future only to be replaced by conventional high-energy physics

11

DST-1610S-387-75
September 1975

terminology, or terms such as "interpersonal subconscious reactions" or "mention" forces. In any event, the classical ESP experiments with animals are no longer of interest in the USSR. The typical Vasilev experimentation from 1920 to 1955 has been replaced with sophisticated research protocols which study complex interactions between man, animals and plants.

Dr. Pavel Naumov, who bears no relation to the now imprisoned Edward Naumov, conducted animal biocommunication studies between a submerged Soviet Navy submarine and a shore research station; these tests involved a mother rabbit and her newborn litter and occurred around 1956, three years prior to the U.S.S. Nautilus disclosure. According to Naumov, Soviet scientists placed the baby rabbits aboard the submarine. They kept the mother rabbit in a laboratory on shore where they implanted electrodes (EEG?) in her brain. When the submarine was submerged, assistants killed the rabbits one by one. At each precise moment of death, the mother rabbit's brain produced detectable and recordable reactions. As late as 1970 the precise protocol and results of this test described by Naumov were believed to be classified. Many examples can be found in Soviet literature dealing with dogs, bears, birds, insects, and fish in conjunction with basic psychotronic research. The Pavlov Institute in Moscow may have been involved in animal telepathy until 1970.

pages 13 and 14 of
document not provided

12

DST-1810S-387-75
September 1975

SECTION III - TELEPATHY (ENERGY TRANSFER) IN MAN

PART A - Classical Theories and Experiments

Over the past 25 years, Soviet scientists have reported that abilities such as extrasensory perception, clairvoyance, and telepathy have been demonstrated in the laboratory under rigorously controlled conditions. Many of these claims have been published in the Soviet technical and popular literature. Just how far the Soviets have really gone in their efforts to learn about the mechanisms of human telepathy is not known. If the Soviet reports are even partly true, and if mind-to-mind thought transference can be used for such applications as interplanetary communications or the guiding of interplanetary spacecraft, the Soviets have accomplished a scientific breakthrough of tremendous significance.

For many years, any attempt to study telepathic phenomena was denounced in the Soviet Union as mysticism and idealism. From 1922 to 1959, however, this attitude gradually changed. Official recognition of parapsychology as a legitimate science was prompted to a considerable extent by the Party's recognition of other disciplines which had previously been rejected as bourgeois idealism (quantum mechanics, the theory of relativity, and cybernetics). In 1959 Professor L.L. Vasilev published his "Mysterious Phenomena of the Human Psyche," followed in 1962 by his "Experiments in Mental Suggestion." These two publications caused some surprise among Western scientists, but the possible military implications were apparently overlooked in the West. The first attempt to illustrate the possible military and intelligence impact of Soviet research in telepathy and psychokinesis was published in 1972. [15]

The publication of Vasilev's first book in 1959 was followed by the appearance of countless studies by other Soviet researchers and numerous articles in the Soviet periodical press. Soviet parapsychology research gained impetus and sophistication, growing from a single laboratory into a coordinated USSR-wide effort; laboratories were also established in Czechoslovakia. Funds for research (reported at 20 million rubles in 1973) are believed to be primarily from military sources. This high level of support advanced Soviet research on human telepathy far beyond that of the West and the USSR became the leader in sponsoring and participating in international parapsychology symposiums. Such international meetings have served Soviet interests by allowing them to benefit from Western research.

After 1959 large numbers of Soviet scientists began investigating telepathic communication. In 1965, a bioinformation department was formed

15

DST-181C3-387-75
September 1975

at the Moscow section of the Scientific-Technical Society of Radio
Engineering and Telecommunications imeni A.S. Popov, with the purpose
of furthering scientific research on information transmission "in the
living part of nature." The early Soviet objectives which were made
public were: (1) to study and organize relevant materials from the
world literature; (2) to record and systematize observed occurrences
of "spontaneous" telepathy; and (3) to develop and organize experiments
on artifically initiated telepathic occurrences.

At a meeting of the Bionics Department of the Presidium of the
Academy of Sciences of the USSR in 1965, I.M. Kogan raised the following
three questions: (1) is telepathy possible in principle; (2) does it
contradict natural laws; and finally, (3) do the observed facts agree
with the concept of electromagnetic fields?[16] To answer these questions,
the following hypotheses have been advanced in the USSR:

(1) The electromagnetic hypothesis (1892), advanced as a result of
the discovery of electromagnetic waves in 1888. By the mid 1960s this
hypothesis had been subjectd to considerable criticism. The entire range
of the electromagnetic spectrum from gamma rays to radio waves had been
studied; throughout this range there was not a single sector in which
telepathic communication could be established. Experiments with reliable
forms of metallic shielding had not prevented the percipient from receiving messages transmitted to him (also verified in the West). Moreover,
the effectiveness of "signals" transmitted over hundreds or thousands of
kilometers should, according to the theory, diminish in proportion to the
square of the distance; this has never been established in relevant experimentation. The electromagnetic hypothesis has not been rejected and some
evidence indicates that there may be electromagnetic waves of some unknown
length emitted by the brain which are capable of penetrating metallic
obstacles.

(2) The metaethereal hypothesis, borrowed from French parapsychology.
This presupposes the existence of some unknown methaethereal energy, the
oscillations of which can be detected only by special organs of "crypto-
aesthetic sensitivity," possessed by persons endowed with parapsychic
abilities.

(3) The psychic energy hypothesis. According to this theory, bioelectrical charges in the "working" brain of the inductor are transformed
into psychic energy which is transformed back again into bioelectric charges
in the "receiving" brain of the percipient.

(4) L. Vasilev proposed the gravitational hypothesis, first formulated
by the German physicist Pascual Jordan and Einstein's former collaborator
Dr. B. Hoffman. Vasilev suggested that an interaction between the

16

352

DST-1810S-387-75
September 1975

gravitational field and some existing but unexplained factor, possibly produced by the cerebal matter itself, might be involved in telepathic communication. He also suggested that thought transmissions might be connected with the laws of cybernetic systems. Vasilev also referred to the action of neutrino particles formed during nuclear reactions.[17] If it could be established that such particles (which have no electric charge, move with a speed approaching that of light and are capable of penetrating obstacles of enormous mass) are generated during the neuropsychic activity of the brain, it might conceivably be shown that these particles serve as the medium for telepathic transmissions.

The Soviets' renewed interest in the problem of parapsychology during the 1960s constituted, to a certain extent, another aspect of the trend away from doctrinaire control which had previously dominated all areas of intellectual effort in the USSR. The easing of intellectual control was exemplified by a quote from Laplace's "Essai Philosophique sur les Probabilities" used by Professor Vasilev:

"We are so far from knowing all the forces of nature and their various modes of action that it would be unworthy of the philospher to deny phenomena simply because they are inexplicable at the present state of our knowledge. The more difficult it is to acknowledge their existence, the greater the care with which we must study these phenomena."[18]

Vasilev himself said:

"It has happened more than once in the history of science that the establishment of new facts that were unexplainable by what was already known gave us a glimpse of unforeseen aspects of existence."

Such was the climate of Soviet parapsychological research in the early 1970s; Soviet science, for all its characteristic pragmatism, had apparently begun to free itself gradually from the restraints of an outworn materialistic foundation which on more than one occasion had shown its flimsy bases when faced with new discoveries. However, as noted in Section I, there may now once again be a fairly concerted effort on the part of some highly placed Soviet scientists in other disciplines to undermine parapsychology on political-ideological grounds.

In 1966, F. Zigel, a renowned Soviet astronomer, concluded that telepathy is the science of the future. In order for it to become a service to mankind, research in telepathy must be organized on a statewide basis. Otherwise, after a short while, "reproaching ourselves for past mistakes, we again would have to catch up with foreign countries. If the insulting remarks addressed to scientists engaged in telepathic

17

DST-1810S-387-75
September 1975

studies were made privately they could simply be ignored. Such criticisms, however, are aired publicly in the press by people of incontestable authority in other fields. What happened to genetics and cybernetics is now being repeated again and again. One can no longer remain silent, but must take the full responsibility of stating that "criticism" of telepathy is tantamount to militant obscurantism."[19] Zigel's words did not go unheeded because by 1968 the Soviets already had: (1) established several research centers specializing in telepathic experiments on an academic and scientific level; (2) organized teams of scientists—physiologists, physicists, psychologists, mathematicians, cyberneticians, neurologists, and electronic engineers—to investigate telepathy, find out how it works, and devise means of practical application; and (3) conducted experiments involving long-range thought transference (Leningrad-Moscow (600 km); Moscow-Tomsk (4,000 km)).

Without actually taking an unequivocal stand on the controversial issue of telepathy, Ye. Parnov,[20] in 1966, cited at least three paradoxes: (1) telepathic communication is independent of distance; (2) telepathic communication is achieved without the use of the known senses and has no apparent relation to electromagnetic waves; (3) some cases of spontaneous telepathy and clairvoyance contradict the law of causality. It should be mentioned that if Parnov had stated his third paradox a few years sooner it would have meant certain scientific and intellectual exile. However, Parnov attempted to ascertain the extent to which these paradoxes might fit into the fundamental laws of natural science, and thereby remained somewhat within the bounds of traditional dogmatic, materialistic principles.

Parnov felt that the first paradox might be resolved if: (a) the material carrier of the telepathic effect is some type of energy unlikely to dissipate in space, or (b) all people are linked together by a special "telepathic field." In the first case, the material carrier could conceivably be the neutrino which, at least within the earth's biosphere, is not absorbed by matter. In the second case, it might be surmised that, in addition to the inductor and percipient, telepathic phenomena involve an unspecified number of people for amplification of the telepathic signal, just as a photomultiplier amplifies light.

A similar explanation was applied to the second paradox; the "neutrino hypothesis," however, has its drawbacks. It is not quite clear, for instance, which type of neutrino is responsible for the transmission of telepathic signals. It is possible that all people are interlinked by a neutrino field, and this would support the amplification theory.

The third paradox is the least palatable to traditional scientists and the most susceptible to criticism by opponents of telepathy. Its explanation requires, by implication, the breakdown of well-established concepts regarding time and space. One of the ideas advanced by some

18

354

DST-1810S-387-75
September 1975

theoreticians is that of "closed time" in which such notions as past and future become relative even beyond the theory of relativity. By accepting such an idea, it must be assumed as a matter of fact that the human brain can somehow "locate" the future by means of the neutrino. Parnov observed that other theoreticians had hypothesized that the neutrino's peculiar behavior is due to the fact that this particle moves from the future into the past rather than the other way around. Such a concept would do justice to the third paradox. It is interesting to note that these paradoxes were expressed before theoreticians began extensive discussions on tachyons (particles said to have a velocity greater than that of light). Mental ions ("mentions"), having similar velocities of propagation, have also been postulated. They are discussed further in Part B of this section.

Another theory which could help explain the third paradox is based on the law of conservation of combined parity, advanced by L.D. Landau. According to that law, symmetry is preserved in any system whenever the "left" is substituted by the "right" and a particle by an antiparticle. It then appears that all relationships are invariant with respect to time inversion. Thus, Parnov concluded, the third paradox may contradict the letter, but not the spirit of modern physics.

I.M. Kogan, referred to earlier, was the first to publish experimental results in human telepathic communication in the post-Vasilev era.[18,21,22] Only the qualitative and quantitative results will be presented here; the interested reader can peruse the above references for Kogan's research protocol. Kogan arranged his experiments in four groups (excluding experiments involving the use of hypnosis which can be found in an excellent article by Velinov);[23] the four groups included: (1) mental suggestion of an act involving objects at short distances; (2) mental suggestions of the image of an object and selection of a given object at short distances; (3) mental suggestion of object images over long distances; and (4) mental transmission of object images over long distances. None of the experiments reported by Kogan were inconsistent with the Soviet electromagnetic hypothesis. An analysis of the results revealed certain qualitative and quantitative characteristics common to all experiments. They were: (1) the rate of telepathic information transmission varied between 0.005 and 0.1 bit/sec.; (2) the rate of information transmission depended upon the distance the information had to travel, ranging from 0.1 bit/sec for a distance of several meters to 0.001 bit/sec for a distance of 4,000 km; (3) in telecommunications, the percipient did not take cognizance of the logical concept of the type of object being transmitted; normally, only qualitative images eliciting some kind of sensation (shape, color, hardness) were perceived; and (4) the best perception of telepathic information occurred when the messages were short (up to one minute). Transmission of simple, brief, coded combinations of elements (images, emotion) appeared to be the proper way of handling coded telepathic information.

19

355

DST-1810S-387-75
September 1975

Numerous Soviet experiments in human telepathic communication followed Kogan's work. Rapid Soviet advances in electronics, cybernetics, tionics, and neurophysiology brought new techniques to the study of telepathic phenomena. By 1970 the prime objective of Soviet telepathic research was reproducibility of results and Soviet scientists now say that in the future they will be able to make ample use of telepathic resources and to develop, direct, and control telepathic processes as well.[24]

PART B - Current Soviet/Czech Theories and Research Objectives

The most obvious trend of current Soviet and Czech telepathy research is that it is now causally oriented rather than directed toward pragmatic attempts to apply observed but little-understood phenomena. The previous "cart-before-the-horse" approach was not, however, an illogical one, since it led them to theorize that telepathic effects may be based on subtle, unidentified forms of energy or non-energy interactions.

In 1973 Peter Rezek of Prague stated that telepathy may be conceived of as transfer realized by means of some known or unknown type of energy, or is made possible by some non-energy factor that accompanies the functioning of the brain. Rezek questions G.A. Sergeyev's dedication to the interpretation of electroencephalograms (EEG) and wave measurements to uncover the carrier of transfer and feels that Sergeyev's approach is directed primarily toward the application of the investigated phenomena and not towards an understanding of them. He questions attempts to regulate or control psychic phenomena before their underlying causes are understood.[25] According to Rezek, ESP research and research on sense perception are similar since scientists in both fields are investigating the composition and structure of the apparatus by which transfer takes place. Perception, as such, in the natural science approach, is actually incomprehensible; nevertheless, the advocates of this approach are unable to accept telepathic phenomena because proof of energy transfer is lacking. Rezek feels that if the natural-science approach, which is unable to explain perception as such, were applied to ESP, this would make ESP doubly incomprehensible. Even if a wave motion is found to be associated with ESP, this phenomenon as such will again be incomprehensible. Rezek concludes that when ordinary sense perception become comprehensible, it may open the way to the understanding of telepathy. On the other hand, ESP could become the basis for an understanding of perception in general.

page 21 missing
from document

356

TIM RIFAT

DS1-1810S-387-75
September 1975

(U) The trend towards the theoretical development of models for cybernetic systems incorporating psychotronic phenomena has been augmented by
a psychotronic model of man proposed by Josef Wolf of Prague. As an
integral part of the psychosomatic picture of human existence, a psychotronic model of man is an entirely unique contribution to the study of
the concept of man. From an anthropological viewpoint as well as from
broader aspects that cover the comprehensive investigation of human
existence, such a model is needed within the framework of other human
sciences, particularly anthropology and psychology. A psychotronic model
of man based on present knowledge of psychology, anthropology, and the
medical sciences, not only offers an entirely new concept of man as an
individual and as a species of living beings, but also permits new
approaches to the solution of human psychosomatic disturbances and defects.

The experimental psychotronic model of man, which Wolf presents in
rather simplified and schematic form (see Figure 2) may serve this purpose.
The concept of this model is universal, i.e., it applies not only to man
(regardless of sex, age, etc.) but to any living being as well, whether
terrestrial or extraterrestrial.

The model includes the principal spheres of man: (1) the somatic or
biological sphere, denoted by a triangle against the base; (2) the psychic
or mental sphere, designated by a circle inscribed in the somatic triangle;
and (3) the psychotronic or parapsychic sphere, designated by a circle
circumscribing the psychosomatic triangle. Because psychotronic coupling
in man usually occurs on the basis of communication between at least two
individuals, the principal types of such connections are also presented.

Type 1 or the ego, for example, is the psychotronic model of man as an
individual, i.e., a sort of psychotronic unit, a basic element or initial
point. Type 2, called identical, is the ideal type of psychotronic and
psychosomatic identification between two individuals. Type 3, called
platonic, is the ideal type of purely psychic and psychotronic connection.
Types 4 and 5 can be called telepathic, with minimal to maximal psychosomatic coupling. Here, a different theoretical interpretation based on
the assumption that there exist two different modes of telepathic transfer
is also feasible. Types 6, 7, and 8 are characterized by some genetic or
psychosomatic coupling among several individuals (relatives, etc.).
Types 9 and 10 can be regarded as examples of higher psychotronic coupling
involving many individuals; applications of such models will be feasible
only with perfect mathematical-physical tools and a corresponding system
of psychotronic knowledge.

22

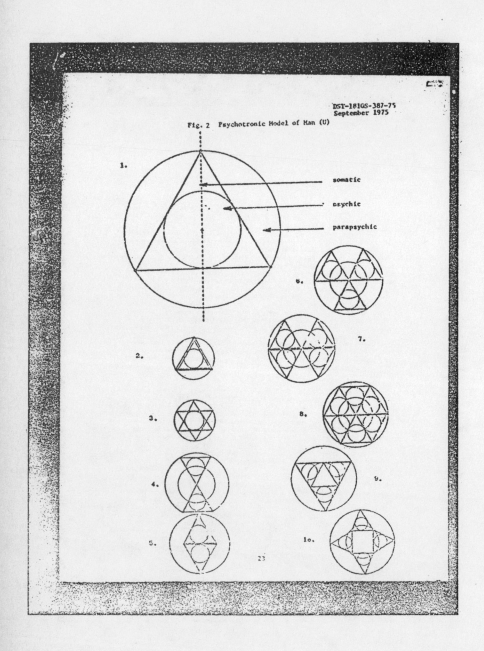

DST-181GS-387-75
September 1975

Fig. 2   Psychotronic Model of Man (U)

somatic

psychic

parapsychic

358

DST-1810S-387-75
September 1975

Recently the most important source of new questions concerning man has arisen from the need to humanize the technical sciences, where man is often subordinated to the operation of machinery and to the technocratic apparatus, rather than the other way around. Specifically, where the human factor is completely relegated to the background and where human activity remains only on the fringe of human existence, human shortcomings, defects and failures are the most frequent; technological dehumanization may have affected not only individuals but entire groups, and perhaps even all of society. Wolf thinks that the primitive peoples — i.e., the ethnic groups of aborigines who still live at the lowest cultural and economic level in the world, and who belong to so-called primitive, preliterate and preclass societies — might be one of the most rewarding sources for studying psychic phenomena and for modeling the psychotronic profile of man, since they have not been culturally dehumanized by technology.[29]

Czech investigator M. Cernousek of Prague[30] suggests that primitive levels exist in all human minds and that there is a regressive nature to telepathic phenomena. By regression he means some "primitivization" of behavior, a return to older psychic functions on the ontogenetic plane. This behavior change is characterized by an abandonment of and withdrawal from, the rational components of the human psyche – a complete detachment from reality or from the perceived environment. The end effect of this detachment from reality is a spontaneous sinking into a state that can be characterized as one of primary, primordial empathy. Although Cernousek describes the parameters for obtaining certain levels of regression in modern man, his theory does not encompass any of the concepts of biological energy transfer. Instead, he appears to accept the theory that the human brain is analogous to a highly sophisticated data bank in which all of life's experiences and impressions, consciously perceived or subliminally registered, are stored. Cernousek's idea of telepathic communication involves a high level of empathy between individuals; when such empathy exists, he feels that information transfer occurs as a result of nearly instantaneous and simultaneous processing of similar stored information bits by both sender and receiver. The net result is a coincidence of opinion concerning the telepathic message's content.

Cernousek's theory is based on a great deal of research. The Soviet and Czech literature on psychology, creativity, and the evolution of human existence is extensive. A huge volume of data has been compiled on the brain's memory capacity. The Czechs claim that 1973 experiments employing LSD have lead them to the conclusion that all of man's activities and experiences whether perceived intensively or less intensively, are stored. They are now investigating the quantity of information the brain can process per unit of time, its bit capacity, and how this becomes manifest at the level of the conscious and the unconscious. The objective of this research is to make the process of cognition more economical. Czech scientists have likened the neuron to an integrated modular element that contains a resistor, a capacitor, and perhaps as many as 1,000 times seven

24

DST-1810S-387-75
September 1975

billion, or seven trillion semiconductor elements in operation, and another
seven trillion in reserve. The brain has about 14 billion nerve cells.
If only 10 billion are able to receive information at any one time, and the
transmission capacity of a nerve fiber is 14 bits per second, then this
means that the brain is able to receive 140 billion bits of information
per second. Thus the memory capacity of the brain seems to be a million
times greater than that of current computers. For ordinary perception
and deliberation, 14 to 16 bits/second are adequate. But for more complicated perception and deliberation, such as the solution of a mathematical problem, etc., about 20 bits per second are needed. The brain's great
reserve bit capacity may indicate that unconsciously and subliminally, man
may be perceiving far more information than what has been assumed previously.
Experiments with known telegnostics seem to confirm this, since they apparently process and evaluate a huge quantity of information within an un-
imaginably short time.

Czech theoretical cyberneticians are proposing the construction of
computers that will "create" and possess at least a degree of intuition.
However, the Czechs admit that this concept is somewhat premature, because
they do not yet understand these processes in man and are unable to describe
them adequately.   Parapsychology may eventually provide such essential
knowledge about these processes and thereby help cybernetics in solving
the problem of teaching computers to create. The point is not merely to
build more-perfect computers, but to design computers with qualitatively
new functions. Work is now underway on a fourth generation of computers,
and a fifth generation is being planned. The Czechs believe that parapsychology is already capable of offering cybernetics fruitful models.[31]
In the opinion of some cyberneticians,[32] the present prostheses that replace
missing parts of the body are foreign bodies within the organism, regardless
of how perfect they may be. Once the technology of molecular circuits is
mastered it will be possible to integrate perfectly a prosthesis and the
central nervous system's information system. From there it will be only a
short step to direct man-machine communication. Understanding of molecular
circuits will also clarify the mechanisms of extrasensory communication
between people.

The Soviet-Czech team approach to parapsychology research, not widely
used as yet in the West, will advance them into direct man-machine communication, creative computers, and eventually into cyborgs, i.e., human
inductors coupled with physical psychotronic instrumentation.

Frantisek Kahuda of Charles University, Prague has expanded on the
original "neutrino" theory proposed in 1966 by Ye. Parnov of the Soviet
Union. Kahuda and other Czech researchers have demonstrated that space
(mental horizon) and time (mental time) in the world of mental processes
have characteristic properties that should be in accord with the properties

25

360

TIM RIFAT

DST-1810S-387-75
September 1975

of the particles that are the material vehicles of such processes. These
are particles that in man's internal relativistic mental process may have
a velocity v = c (c equals the velocity of light in vacuum) without vio-
lating in the external physical world Einstein's postulate that the
maximum feasible velocity is v < c. Such particles, essential to mental
processes, have not been discovered to date. Kahuda calls them mental
ions or "mentions."

For physical microparticles other than luxons, which have a velocity
v = c (photons and neutrinos), Olexa-Myron Bilaniuk and F.C. George
Sudarshan introduced in 1969 the concept of tardyons for subliminal particles traveling at velocities v < c, and the concept of tachyons for
physical superliminal particles traveling at velocities v > c. The actual
existence of tachyons with an imaginary rest mass, has not been proven so
far. Thus, the predicted tachyons correspond to Kahuda's mentions traveling at velocities v > c; the tardyons and luxons correspond to the mentions
traveling at velocities v ≤ c. However, the essential difference between
tachyons and the Czech mentions is that tachyons are supposed to be particles of the physical microworld and hence also of inanimate nature,
whereas mentions are particles formed by living organisms, specifically
by their nervous systems, that represent matter on the highest level of
organization, with the most complex and finest structure. Moreover,
Kahuda's theory does not require the introduction of imaginary rest mass
as in the case of tachyons; it predicts the real existence of mentions,
based on fairly accurate laboratory measurements of the physical time and
mental time of the investigated mental material motions.

In agreement with the laws of the electron's quantum field theory,
Kahuda assumes that an entire conglomerate of elementary mention fields,
specific to the individual mentions, forms through interaction and trans-
mutation, a single common mention field in which the mental material
motions take place - a sort of metaetheric environment that is linked to
man's living organism and exists in nature independently of the will of
all human beings. During the mental process of thinking one mental particle "changes" into another, however Kahuda does not designate any
particle as primary and another particle as secondary. These constant
changes and mutual transmutations reflect the psychic world's material
homogeneity. The basis of this homogeneity is the motion of mentions as
universal material particles of the human psyche. From the theory based
on the principle of quantum mentiodynamics Kahuda has proposed the following formula for total mention energy:

1)
$$E = \frac{E_p(B)}{const} \cdot \frac{m_o c^2}{1 - \frac{uv}{c^2}}$$

26

361

DST-1810S-387-75
September 1975

where Ep(B) is the potential (psychic) energy of the investigated respondent. From this equation it follows that the rest mass of the mention, at the moment when the mental process starts (i.e., when the respondent emits the first mention), and when numerically Ep(B) = E, is expressed by the relationship:

$$2) \qquad m_0 = \frac{const}{c^2 \Omega_c^2}$$

where $f_0 = \frac{1}{\Omega}$ is the rest-time factor of man's mental abilities. Thus, the mental structure (nervous system) of each respondent forms and emits its own mentions whose rest mass, according to experimental results to date, is approximately 10^6 to 19^6 times smaller than the rest mass of the μ-meson, which is $m_0 = 10^{-12}g$ to $10^{-13}g$. The smallest values of total mention energy that were measured indirectly at the moment when the mental process began ranged from $0.384 \cdot 10^{-10}$ to $9.744 \cdot 10^{-10}$ erg, which is approximately the same level as the energy of X-rays; the quotient of this energy range's relative amplitude is roughly 25. Kahuda assumes that after the commencement of the mental process, in the course of its formation, the velocities of the mentions' material motions may increase severalfold, so that the total mention energy according to equation 1 may be considerable, even though the average respondent's initial energy is equal only to the mean energy necessary for the visual stimulation of the human eye ($2.1 \cdot 10^{-10}$ erg/sec). For high velocities Kahuda thinks that it will now be possible to actually develop quantum mentiodynamics as the quantum theory of mention fields.

Mention energy, which may be the essence of the propagating changes and energetic information in mental processes, is an as-yet unknown form of energy in human beings. It occurs in quanta that cannot be measured directly with the instrumentation presently available. Therefore, Kahuda measured the quantitative values of potential energy (Ep(B)) indirectly.

Kahuda's results indicate that electromagnetic processes alone cannot be the vehicles of psychic processes, and that within the framework of the entire complex mental structure there must also exist another carrier of mental processes, one that permits the propagation of psychic reactions and interactions at velocities greater than the velocity of light in vacuum. In Kahuda's opinion, it is indisputable that mentions do exist, but he points out that the discovery and experimental verification of mentions will require a thorough theoretical knowledge of their possible characteristics and the most sophisticated and most accurate measuring equipment that science will be able to develop.[33]

27
(Reverse Blank)

DST-1810S-387-75
September 1975

SECTION IV - TELEPATHIC BEHAVIOR MODIFICATION

Part A - Basic Research

Behavior modification through telepathic means is in itself applied research. The changes or alterations of human activity desired can be either beneficial or detrimental to the percipient. Soviet research in the field of behavior modification by telepathy dating from the early 1920s through the early 1970s has had one major objective — application of techniques. In telepathy research, unlike research in most scientific disciplines, the applied phase preceded the basic phase. To put it simply this is why telepathy is still called a phenomenon, both in the USSR and the West. The phenomenon of telepathy has many applications, one of which is behavior modification. Basic research therefore applies to the phenomenon itself; this is covered in Part I Section II and Part II (Psychotronic Generator Research).

Part B - Applied Research

Between 1920 and 1943, L.L. Vasilev conducted numerous experiments involving telepathic mental suggestion; his first work involved the mental suggestion of motor (muscle) movements. This early work was based in part on the published results of similar experiments conducted by Dr. Joire[34] of Lille, France. Vasilev's human test subjects were asked to perform various muscular movements through the medium of telepathy. For comparative purposes some tests were made with hypnotized percipients, while others were placed only in a relaxed state. During the same time frame (1920-1943), Vasilev also conducted experiments involving the mental suggestion of visual images and sensations with and without hypnosis. Vasilev's results indicated that it was altogether possible to telepathically suggest and produce voluntary, controllable motor acts as well as influence involuntary, uncontrollable movement. He noted that some of the best subjects for the suggestion of motor acts were unsuitable for mental suggestion of visual images and vice versa. Apparently there was no visible positive correlation between these two variants of telepathic susceptibility. Some of the subjects under hypnosis responded more readily to verbal suggestion of a sensory nature while others were more responsive to verbal suggestion of the motor type. This observed variance applied for both mental and verbal suggestive techniques. After a thorough series of experiments, Vasilev concluded that mental suggestion involving hypnosis would provide the most fruitful results.[35]

According to Ostrander and Schroeder,[5] the ability to telepathically produce sleep-wake states (obliteration of one's consciousness) from a distance of a few meters to over a thousand kilometers became the most

29

DST-1810S-387-75
September 1975

thoroughly tested and perfected Soviet contribution to international
parapsychology. Parapsychologists in Leningrad and Moscow demonstrated
the telepathic manipulation of consciousness and correlated it with
systematic EEG recordings. The Naumov-Sergeyev-Pavlova team found that
EEG recordings changed dramatically when the telepathic impulse contained
a message affecting human emotions. Transmission of several successive
emotions of a negative character elicited the appearance of cross-
excitation of the brain. It changed the spontaneous EEG character to
the tired state of the brain, dominated by slow, hypersynchronized waves
of the delta and theta type. Percipients of unpleasant emotions followed
by positive emotions (feelings of calmness or cheerfulness) regained
normalized EEG's within one to three minutes. Other Soviet tests included
sending to the percipient the anxiety associated with suffocation and the
sensation of a dizzying blow to the head. Pavlova, Sergeyev and Naumov
uncovered impressive data on the power of thought and concluded that a
person doesn't have to conjure up his own "nasty" thoughts; someone else
can do it and telepathically transmit them to him. S. Serov and A. Troskin
of Sverdlovsk demonstrated that the number of white blood cells rose by
fifteen hundred after they suggested positive emotion to patients. More
important was the observation that after impressing negative emotion, the
white cell count decreased by sixteen hundred. Since leucocytes are one
of the body's main defense mechanisms against disease, such a telepathically
imposed shift in cell count could be used in altering human health. In
similar research the Czechs found that intense mental activity in the
sender caused, at a distance, a slight change in blood volume in a resting
percipient. Measurements were made with a plethysmograph. Experiments
in the West have verified this phenomenon. Soviet and Czech research in
manipulative telepathic techniques has also included experimental transmission of kinetic impulses, sound, and taste.

Outside of the Soviet and Czech research on the manipulative possibilities of PK and psychotronic generators, the emphasis on manipulation
by means of telepathy still involves the use of hypnotism. Many Soviet
and Czech scientists are using this technique as a means to try to identify the "carrier" of telepathy but others may be conducting such research
for more devious reasons.

Dr. Stefan Manczarski of Poland predicted that the field of telepathy
will open new avenues for spreading propaganda. He feels that the electromagnetic theory is valid and believes, therefore, that telepathy can be
amplified like radio waves. Telepathy would then become a subtle new
modus for the "influencers" of the world. Some Western followers of
psychic phenomena research are concerned, for example, with the detrimental effects of subliminal perception techniques being targeted against
US or allied personnel in nuclear missile silos. The subliminal message
could be "carried" by television signals or by telepathic means.

30

DST-1810S-387-75
September 1975

The potential applications of focusing mental influences on an enemy through hypnotic telepathy have surely occurred to the Soviets. The bulk of recent telepathy research in the USSR has been concerned with the transmission of emotional or behavioral impulses and the study of physiological responses to PK exercises, etc. In their exploration of telepathy, they are seeking the evenual capability to reproduce and to amplify the phenomena so that control is feasible. Control and manipulation of the human consciousness must be considered a primary goal.

31
(Reverse Blank)

DST-1810S-387-75
September 1975

PART II

PSYCHOTRONIC GENERATOR RESEARCH

Psychotronic generators (also called Pavlita generators after the inventor) are small devices said to be capable of drawing biological energy from humans; the energy is accumulated and stored for future use. Once charged with human energy, the generators can do some of the things a psychic subject can do, but, according to the inventor, Robert Pavlita, can be charged by individuals possessing no psychic ability.[5]

The concept of man as a source of unusual energy dates back at least as far as ancient Chinese and Hindu teachings, in which it was called "vital energy" or "prana." Between the 18th and 20th centuries it was called various things (animal magnetism, odic force, motor force, n-rays, etheric force, etc.) by rediscoverers of its existence. In contemporary Soviet and Czechoslovakian parapsychology this energy is called bio-plasmic or psychotronic energy. The Czechoslovakian rediscovery of biological energy is credited to Robert Pavlita, an inventor and business-man from Prague who began work on his devices over thirty years ago.[5]

Some representative examples of Pavlita generators are shown in Figures 3 through 7. No details of their construction have ever been made available to Western observers, possibly because Pavlita eventually plans to seek foreign patents. It has been reported, however, that the devices are fabricated from various metals (steel, bronze, copper, iron, gold) and that their effects are a result of their form.[5]

Pavlita's generators can be charged by direct contact (e.g., rubbing or touching to the temporal region of the head) or by visually directing mental concentration upon them from a distance. The nature of the energy stored is still not understood, but over the years a number of observations about its effects have been reported. It can be reflected, re-fracted, polarized, and combined with other forms of energy. It creates effects similar to magnetism, heat, electricity, and luminous radiation, but is itself none of these. The energy apparently can be conducted by paper, wood, wool, silk, and other substances normally considered to be good insulators. The devices have been tested by commissions of experts from the Czechoslovakian Academy of Sciences and the University of Hradec Kralove in Prague. Static electricity, air currents, temperature changes, and magnetism, were eliminated as possible explanations for the observed effects. In addition, the energy exerted its effect through glass, water, wood, cardboard, or any type of metal and was not diminished.

33

366

DST-1810S-387-75
September 1975

According to both Soviet and Czech researchers, one major advantage of studying psychotronic generators is the reproducibility of their effects; in addition, they can be activated by nearly anyone, with or without any special psychic abilities. The devices may have other practical applications not related to parapsychology. The Czechs claim that irradiation of seeds with the energy enhances plant growth, and that industrial pollutants have been precipitated out of water by its action (Figure 7). These claims may be open to question, since in 1972, Zdenek Rejdak, head of the Psychotronic Research Section of the Czechoslovakian Society for Science and Technology, termed the experiments with plants and water "ineffective."

A recent newspaper article,[36] quoting Pavlita, reported that his generators could serve as weapons; no further details were given. No information is available on Czech efforts to develop psychotronic weapons, but Pavlita has stated that some forms of his devices can exert both favorable and unfavorable effects on living organisms, including man. In experiments with snails exposed to the energy from a generator, a state similar to hibernation resulted. When flies were placed in the gap of a circular generator (Figure 6) they died instantly. In another test, Pavlita aimed a generator at his daughter's head from a distance of several yards. Her electroencephalogram (EEG) changed, she became dizzy, and her equilibrium was disrupted.

In their present form and size, Pavlita's devices could probably exert an effect on humans at only relatively short range. It is possible that their size could be enlarged or their energy amplified, thereby extending their range. If the Czech claims for these devices are valid, biological energy might be an effective antipersonnel weapon. It would be difficult to defend against, since it apparently penetrates most common forms of insulation and its reported effects (changes in brain wave characteristics, disturbance of equilibrium, dizziness) could result in personality changes or physical discomfort which might alter combat effectiveness.

Soviet or Czech perfection of psychotronic weapons would pose a severe threat to enemy military, embassy, or security functions. The emitted energy would be silent and difficult to detect electronically (although the Soviets claim to have developed effective biological energy sensors) and the only power source required would be the human operator.

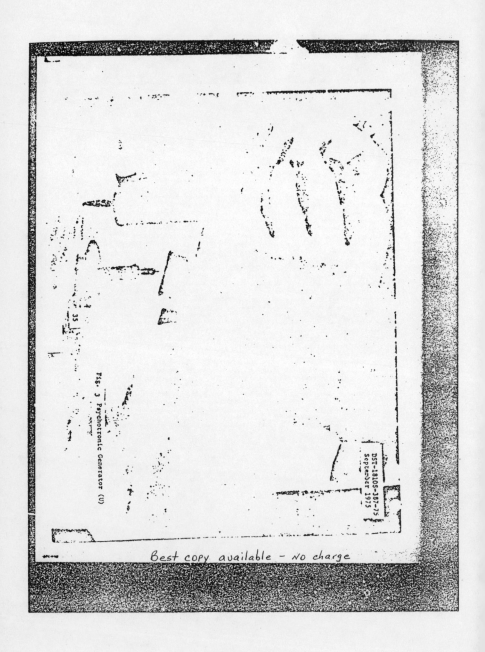

Fig. 3 Psychotronic Generator (U)

DST-1810S-387-75
September 1975

Best copy available - No charge

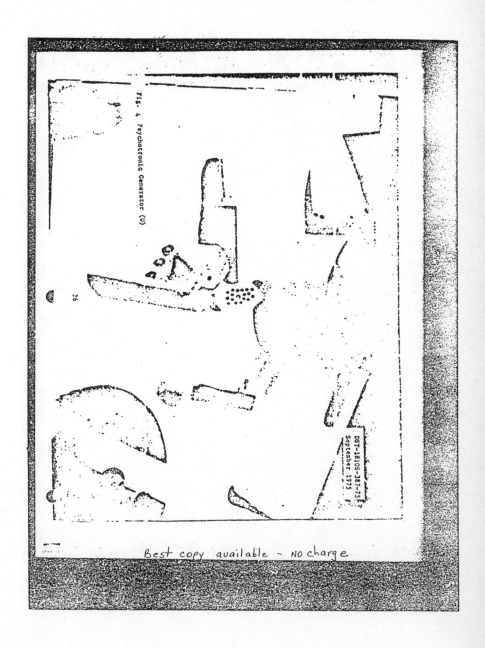

Fig. 4 Psychotronic Generator (U)

DST-1810S-387-75
September 1975

Best copy available - No charge

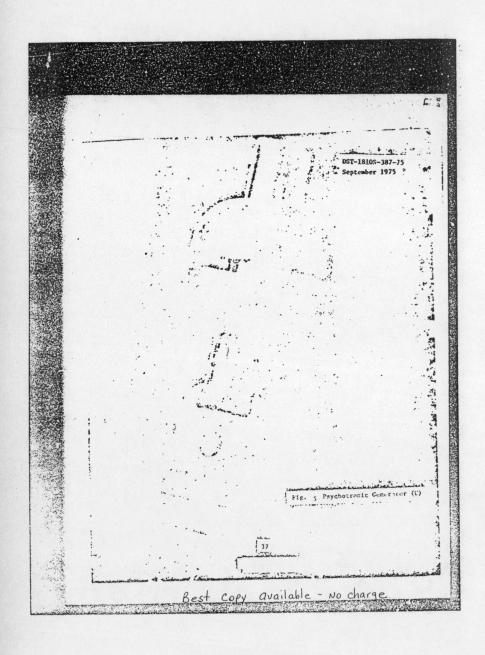

DST-1810S-387-75
September 1975

Fig. 5 Psychotronic Generator (U)

37

Best Copy available - No charge

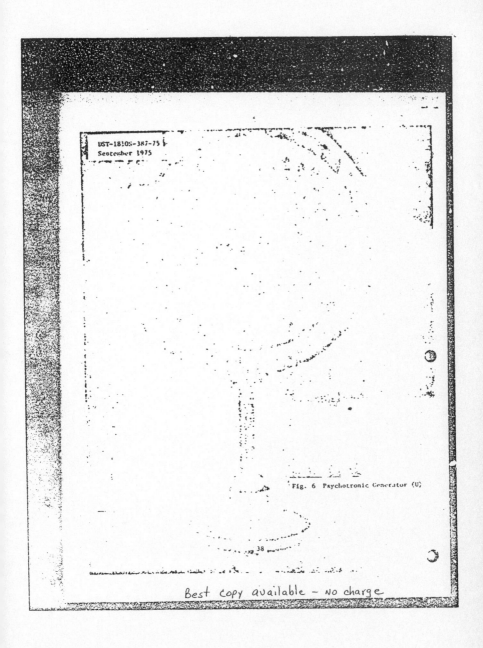

UST-1810S-387-75
September 1975

Fig. 6 Psychotronic Generator (U)

38

Best copy available – No charge

Fig. 7 Psychotronic Generator (U)

(Reverse Blank)

FST-18105-357-75
September 1975

Best copy available – No charge

DST-1610S-387-75-
September 1975

PART III

PSYCHOKINESIS RESEARCH

Psychokinesis (PK), or as it is sometimes called, telekinesis, is the ability to influence animate or inanimate objects at a distance, without physical contact, by means of uncontrolled or controlled biological energy fields. Some, but not all, of the effects of PK include: initiation or cessation of motion in inanimate objects; apparent neutralization of the effect of gravity on inanimate objects (levitation); induction of changes in physiological processes of animate matter; the creation of measurable electric, electrostatic, magnetic, or gravitational fields around target objects; and the imposition of images on shielded photographic emulsions.

Current Soviet and Czechoslovakian parapsychological research emphasis is on identification and quantification of the generated bioenergetic force fields, identification of the physiological processes underlying their origin, and development of practical applications of PK energy.

There are fundamental differences between the Soviet and Czech approaches to PK research. Since paranormal research was granted political respectability in the Soviet Union in the 1950's, Soviet scientists have concentrated their investigations on a relatively few, highly "gifted", psychic individuals, and have attempted to determine what (if any) physiological attributes underlie their capabilities and differ from those of non-psychic subjects. Parallel with these efforts to determine cause(s), the Soviets have concentrated considerable effort on determination of the nature of the energy fields formed and to attempts to determine whether all psychokinetically gifted subjects create the same, or different, energy fields.

Czechoslovakian research is also cause-and-effect oriented, but appears to be governed far more by the belief that PK effects can be produced by a majority of people and that no inherent or highly developed psychic capability is prerequisite to the investigation and demonstration of PK effects.

41

373

DST-1810S-387-75
September 1975

Soviet research has taken several different directions in efforts to develop materialistic explanations for observed PK effects. This research has involved in-depth studies of the characteristics of the electrical field between subject and object, characterization of electrical fields immediately around the subject, study of bioelectrical fields by detection devices, study of subjects' brain wave patterns, and photography of the subjects' bioenergy fields. To date, Soviet scientists are by no means in accord concerning the nature of the forces involved, but all are in agreement that a physical energy is at work.[37]

Dr. Viktor G. Adamenko of the Moscow Institute of Radiophysics, Dr. Viktor Inyushin, of the Kazakh University, Alma-ata, and Dr. Genady Sergeyev of the A.A. Uktomskii Physiological Institute, Leningrad are the leading Soviet theoreticians studying PK. Both Inyushin and Sergeyev have developed theories based on the existence of a new form of energy-a form of biological energy referred to as "bioplasma". They consider PK effects as analogous to lightning accidentally charging a surface and feel that movement in PK occurs as a result of the interaction of the object's electrostatic charge and electromagnetic field with the human operator's field. The biological energy involved is under conscious direction by the subject, who can make a target object start or stop motion, change direction, or rotate. Sergeyev has developed instrumentation which measures changes in the bioplasmic field at distances up to 3 meters (9.9 feet); he has recorded fields of 10,000 volts/centimeter in the vicinity of a target object with no indication of an electrical field in the space between the subject and the object. According to Sergeyev, bioplasmic energy is maximally concentrated in the head region. He attributes PK to a polarization of the bioplasma in a laser-like fashion and refers to this as a "biolaser effect" which acts as a material force upon the object.[37]

Dr. Sergeyev has developed detectors that monitor the energy field during PK demonstrations. Although Western observers have been denied information on the construction of the detectors, (information reported to have been classified by the Soviet military), details may have been published by the Soviet Academy of Sciences. It is possible that the Sergeyev detectors are similar to those developed by an American, David Thomson. Thomson's devices, which have been used in human force field research at the University of Saskatchewan, Canada, consist of two capacitor plates, a preamplifier, and a line recorder like that of an encephalograph. Other Soviet force field detector research has been done at the Laboratory for Biological Cybernetics in the University of Leningrad Physiology Department. There, according to Soviet reports, Dr. Pavel Gulyaev developed extremely sensitive electrodes capable of detecting the electrical force fields of nerves at distances up to 24

42

374

DST-1810S-387-75
September 1975

centimeters (9.46 inches). For more detailed information on Soviet
biological energy detectors, the reader is referred to reference (5),
pages 393-396.

Dr. Adamenko has conducted experiments to ascertain the role of
electrostatic charges on the surface of target objects as the cause of
their movement. Adamenko has advanced the theory that man may be
anisotropic - i.e., man may be able to alter his external energy state
in accordance with his internal energy state, and this ability in turn,
may depend on his physiological processes. According to Adamenko,
humans, animals, and plants probably possess electric fields as a result
of spontaneous tissue polarization, and such fields may interact with
externally imposed or induced charges. He proposes that the observed
properties of living tissue come closest to the properties of electrets.[38]
Electrets are defined as "forcibly" polarized bodies having comparatively
high conductivity and the ability to maintain an external electrical field
after exposure to adverse factors of either the external or internal
environment. Adamenko has shown that the material basis of contactless
interaction between man and objects results from an electrostatic field
whose magnitude depends on man's physiological state. Other Soviet
researchers have observed that when subjects are exposed to various external stimuli, their physiological state varies in both the character and
magnitude of the bioelectret effect. They have formed the hypothesis that
the polarization of living tissue is the explanation for contactless interactions between humans and between humans and objects.

Adamenko has also advanced the concept that, in the thermodynamic
sense, living tissue may not be subject to the same physical laws that
are valid for inorganic matter. He argues that living tissue may
possess "new" properties (in terms of thermodynamics) when compared with
inorganic matter. He believes that if living molecules differ
qualitatively from inorganic molecules, then a distinction may exist
between "living" and "technical" force fields. To demonstrate his
point, Adamenko makes reference to healing by "the laying on of hands"
(in Western terms "faith healing"). The Soviets have measured electrical
fields between "healers" and patients, yet knowing these field potentials
they have not been able to duplicate the beneficial effects obtained from
humans by means of mechanically generated fields.

Aleksandr Dubrov, a biophysicist with the Institute of Earth Physics,
USSR Academy of Sciences, has advanced the concept of "biogravitation"
to explain PK. Biogravitation, as a term, was introduced by Soviet
physicist V.A. Bunin in 1960, and was used to refer to the ability of
living organisms to form and detect gravitational waves. Dubrov bases
his theory on currently accepted concepts of molecular biology and
high-energy physics.

42

DST-1810S-387-75
September 1975

In molecular biology, the capacity of intracellular molecules to alter their spatial structure is recognized. Biomolecules are capable of making the transition from a "liquid" to an orderly crystalline state. Dubrov defines this change as "molecular conformational change"; like present day high energy physicists, he believes that as a result of this change, the molecules are brought so close to each other that tremendous forces of attraction or gravitation emerge; when this occurs, a constant conformational field having a "quasigravitational" nature is formed. In Dubrov's opinion, this means that a vector, or force field, is formed at the subcellular level which is capable of attracting or repelling naturally occurring gravitational forces, or of itself emitting minute gravitational waves.[4]

Dubrov feels that psychic subjects may, in some manner, have the ability to synchronize their subcellular molecular conformational changes and thus generate attractive or gravitational fields of sufficient strength to alter electromagnetic or natural gravitational forces acting on a target object. Dubrov, like some other Soviet and Western parapsychologists, thinks that changes in the space-time continuum may be the basis for observed PK phenomena - i.e., time may be accelerated or decelerated by the psychic subject.

In 1973 and 1974, a Soviet psychic named Boris Ermolayev participated in a series of experiments at Moscow University. Ermolayev is reported to have the ability to levitate (suspend) objects in midair by concentrating psychic energy at a focal point in space.[10] In some of the tests, Ermolayev pressed an object between his hands, then slowly moved his hands apart until they were approximately eight inches from the object, which remained suspended in the air. Soviet scientists claim that all tests were conducted under the strictest controls and that no strings or other devices of any kind were used. Dubrov feels that Ermolayev's levitation powers can be used to prove that space-time and gravitational changes occur in the area between the psychic's hands and the object. He suggests that the transmission of electromagnetic energy of known velocity should be delayed when beamed through the levitation field.

Two female psychic subjects, Nina Kulagina and Alla Vinogradova, have been studied extensively by Drs. Sergeyev and Adamenko. According to Sergeyev, Mrs. Kulagina can control the beat of frog heart preparations, imprint images on shielded photographic emulsions, and move objects weighing one pound or more. In 1970, Dr. Sergeyev conducted experiments in which Mrs. Kulagina was asked to influence, if possible, a living frog heart preparation; such preparations normally continue to beat for several hours after removal from the animal's body. In one experiment, the heart was placed in a glass jar 2½ feet from Mrs. Kulagina. As she

44

DST-1810S-387-75
September 1975

concentrated on controlling its beat, electrocardiograms showed that the rate of contraction increased or decreased at her command. Five minutes after the experiment began, she stoped its beat entirely. When a second preparation was placed in the jar its beat was stopped in 23 minutes.

In other experiments, Mrs. Kulagina imprinted images on unexposed film sealed in black envelopes. During these experiments Sergeyev measured the energy around the psychic's body and found it to be half that of a non-psychic individual. This led Sergeyev to believe that she absorbs, or draws, energy from around her and then discharges it on the target object.

Mrs. Kulagina experiences considerable stress while she is being tested. Her pulse increases, as does her rate of breathing; she develops pain in her upper spine and the back of her neck. At the onset of her "activated" state she feels thirsty and has a taste of iron or copper in her mouth. During the activated state, she experiences occasional periods of dizziness and nausea. Her blood sugar level rises and within one hour following cessation of tests, a loss of weight (1.5 - 2.0 lbs) occurs. She experiences less stress when alone, and claims to respond best in an atmosphere of friendly mutual trust and belief. Her PK ability is mood dependent (her mood and the mood of the observers) and she expends more energy in a hostile or skeptical atmosphere.

The mechanical aspects of Mrs. Kulagina's PK effects are as follows:

    a. Size and shape are more important than the physical structure of the substance she is trying to influence.

    b. Weight and dimensions of objects she is trying to move are important; the weights vary from a few ounces to nearly one pound.

    c. She finds moving a vertical cylinder easier than moving a horizontal one.

    d. She causes no changes in the shape of soft objects during movement.

    e. The direction an object moves depends on her will, and may be either toward or away from her. She can also cause rotational or vertical movements to occur.

    f. Kulagina's optimum field effect occurs at approximately 1½ feet; her distance limit is approximately 3 feet and 4 inches, when the object to be influenced is 3 feet form the edge of the working surface. At these distances she is said to be able to move one object out of many,

45

DST-1810S-387-75
September 1975

depending upon where she centers her concentration.

The electrical aspects of Kulagina's effects are as follows:

a. An electrical field is generated in the vicinity of the object she is attempting to influence; however, there is no measurable field between Kulagina and that object and no sparks are observed.

b. She can exert no effect on an object situated in a vacuum.

c. Electrostatic screening has no effect on her powers, which seem to be better with the object under a dielectric cover, but she is unsuccessful during storms or other atmospheric conditions when there is a greater than normal amount of electricity in the air. She cannot, at any time, exert an influence on an electroscope.

d. She can cause luminescence of crystal luminphors and produce changes in the spectrum of visible light absorbed by liquid crystals.

Dr. Adamenko has found that Alla Vinogradova produces effects similar to those of Nina Kulagina, but undergoes far less physiological stress. In some of his experiments with her in Moscow, during which she moved a variety of objects about on a dielectric surface, a great deal of electrostatic (ES) energy was measured around the objects (supposedly enough to light a small neon glow tube). The measurements detected field pulsations which were synchronous with Vinogradova's respiration rate, heartbeat, and brain alpha rhythm pattern; however, the region between Vinogradova and the object contained no energy fields nor frequencies, and the ES energy increased in intensity as the objects were approached.

The results with Alla Vinogradova have led Adamenko to believe that there may be individuals who have the ability to build up an ES field on the body surface at will and project it as required.[38]

The Czechs, like the Soviets, are attempting to identify the source, or sources, of biological energy, but their research is not centered on psychically gifted individuals. Instead, some leading Czech parapsychologists have developed the theory that most people possess psychic capabilities and that such capabilities may best be demonstrated as observable PK effects. Czech parapsychology research is currently heavily PK oriented, probably as a result of Robert Pavlita's development of psychotronic generators (described in Part II of this study). The Czechs believe that the use of these devices for biological energy collection and concentration may make it possible for nearly anyone to cause PK effects.

46

DST-1810S-387-75
September 1975

Although the design and construction of the generators may be quite complex, they are simple to operate and require only minimal training in their operation. They have two other major advantages, they require no supervision of the subject by an investigator and the observable physical effects (motion, attraction, etc.) serve as positive, encouraging feedback for the subject.

One of Pavlita's devices for demonstrating PK is shown in Figure 8. The usual way of charging the device with psychic energy is to touch the temple area of the head with the hand, then touch the device. The accumulated energy then causes the spoked wheel to revolve. Pavlita claims that with training some individuals can learn to make the wheel turn by visual concentration alone.

Czech physicist Julius Krmessky[41] has experimented with very light foil or paper discs or cylinders enclosed in circular containers; the effect of biological energy on them is generally a slow, but observable, rotation. They have no directly practical applications, but Krmessky feels that they are ideal research tools, since they are simple, inexpensive, and require no special training or psychic talent for their operation. A device similar to Krmessky's is shown in Figure 9. The cylinder is made to rotate by placing the hands above or alongside the device while concentrating ones gaze on the upper strip, or cross-bar. Krmessky recommends isolation of the system from the motion of air and the effect of heat radiation by enclosing it in glass, metal, or other containers with provision for inspection through a glass cover. Motions in such enclosed spaces are slow and hence not too spectacular, but are nevertheless convincing. The slow rate of motion or the occasional immobility cannot be explained by the walls being impenetrable to outside impulses, because the device is able to detect the nearing of a hand, even through a thick layer of lumber, metal, water, etc. The cause lies somewhere else. The reaction of rotational systems in free and enclosed space is highly variable and changes with place and time. Krmessky believes that changes of meteorological or even a cosmic nature may be the cause. Similar cases occur with physics experiments, where even the most carefully prepared electrostatic demonstration may not be successful if a change in weather raises the relative humidity or causes alterations in atmospheric ionization. Magnetic experiments are disrupted by the proximity of magnets, electrical wiring and appliances, and also by the aurora borealis, sunspot activity, or other cosmic causes. The causes of disturbances in PK experiments have yet to be explained. Krmessky feels that no quantitative observations could be made in the privacy of homes, where diverse effects accumulate and overlap. Such effects are various radiations, changes in the conditions of illumination (in the intensity of diffused daylight, for example),

47

379

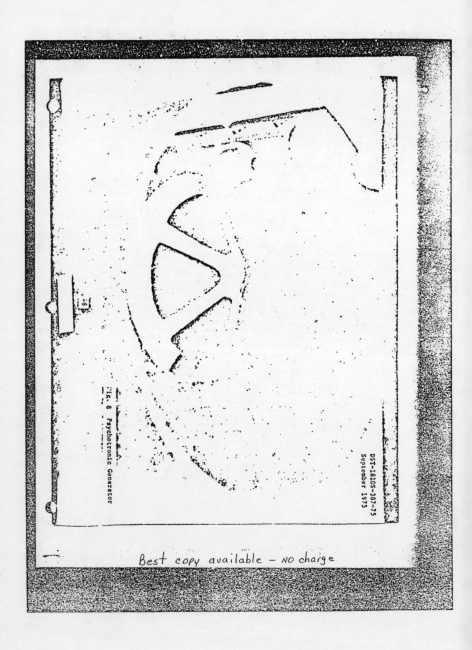

Fig. 8 Psychotronic Generator

DST-1810S-387-75
September 1975

Best copy available – NO charge

LST-1810S-337-75
September 1975

and also the presence and changing positions of objects and persons, perhaps even in the next room or next apartment. Rotational systems enclosed in cylindrical containers are the most suitable for experiments. Angular enclosures are unsuitable for this purpose, since the motions observed in them are too slow and unconvincing. The best devices consist of rods or tubes suspended horizontally by a monofilament thread, foils in the shape of narrow rectangles rotating about their minor axis, or circular planes rotating about their diameter. The angular velocities of the rotational systems are sometimes very noticeable, but more often they are comparable to the velocity of a watch's minute hand. However, such systems are able to exclude other physical causes that could influence rotational motion. Placement in a steel container can form a magnetic shield. A glass jar or cylinder can be packed in a grounded Faraday cage of woven wire, or the space between the walls of two containers, one placed in the other, can be filled with water to shield against electrostatic energy. Despite such measures, the indicators react to changes in radiation from heat and light sources. They react especially sharply to direct sunlight, but they also detect changes in diffused daylight or the narrow beam of a flashlight, even from a considerable distance. Under stable conditions of heat and light, the indicators remain steady in some equilibrium position. A convincing example of this is the fact that when an indicator is permanently located, it settles in the same equilibrium position every night and remains in it until morning. After sunrise, even on a cloudy day, it occupies a new position and maintains it until it is subjected to a further impulse, for example, to a sudden clearing of the sky, to the presence of a person, to a change in the positions of nearby objects, etc. From such observations, Krmensky assumes that successful telekinetic experiments are very demanding in terms of their physical conditions. Such experiments cannot be performed at just any time or place. There are cases when the indicator's plane occasionally rotates without any intervention by the experimenter and without any perceptible cause. If such a case occurs under constant conditions of light and heat, and if its cause cannot be determined in the immediate environment, then Krmensky feels that the effect of distant sources of radiation, perhaps even of cosmic origin, may be the energetic force. The opposite of this seemingly spontaneous motion has also been observed; the rotational system will remain practically immobile, the indicator will not be affected much by either a gaze or the proximity of the hand, and a very slow displacement of only a few degrees is all that can be induced. Thus, a suitable time and place must be chosen for the experiments so that the conditions may be as favorable as possible.

DST-1810S-387-75
September 1975

Kraessky found that the indicators reacted not only to the nearness of a human body, but also to a slightly lesser extent to other animate and inanimate objects. They also reacted to the nearness of plants, vegetables, fruits, flowers, etc., and to subjects made of a variety of materials (metal, glass, etc.) so long as the surface areas were sufficiently large. When the dimensions of the objects were small, their activity was increased by roughing their surface, thus essentially increasing the surface area. Porous or spiny objects, such as sponges or sea urchins were especially suitable for experiments of this type. To insure that the temperature of these objects was the same as that of the movable system, they were placed near the indicators for a sufficient length of time to allow for temperature equilibration. Only then were experiments performed, and the positive results obtained completely eliminated heat radiation as the source of energy.

Kraessky has found that although the hands and other parts of the body are effective in inducing rotational motion, a fixed gaze produces motion of greater magnitude, probably because it condenses the biological energy into a fairly concentrated beam, whereas impulses from the body surface are scattered. The "visual rays" were shown to exert an effect even when reflected or when focused through binoculars.

In Kraessky's experiments with inanimate objects and plants, man's role was of very brief duration and consisted only of placing the objects or plants near the device. In future experiments, Kraessky plans to position such objects by purely mechanical means. He feels that if positive results are still obtained, he will have demonstrated that interactions between objects and objects and humans and objects differ. At the present stage of his research, he supports his hypothesis as follows: the indicator distinguishes the effect of objects from the effects of man in the following manner: after an object has been placed near the indicator, the plane rotates from its original equilibrium position to a new equilibrium position and remains in it or gradually returns to the original position. When man affects the indicator, the final position of the indicator's plane depends on man's will, unless fatigue, that is an accompanying phenomenon of psychic exertion, sets in.

Kraessky believes that he is observing an energy field which is quite similar to magnetism, but a magnetism with some finer structure and a very unstable, fluid field. The poles of this magnetic field may be formed by very easily movable plasma particles that represent elementary magnets which, under the influence of external factors, are never in a completely chaotic state, but rather in a very unsteady state of partial ordering. Probably the occasionally observed fine

50

DST-1810S-387-75
September 1975

oscillations of the indicator's planes at the beginning of rotation are actually the collective effect of the process of aligning the particles. Krmessky has yet to explain why, under seemingly identical conditions and in response to apparently identical stimuli, the rotational indicators of his devices are on one occasion attracted, and on another, repelled. Such erratic responses seem to indicate a double magnetic layer in which the poles are located side by side; this is not feasible if the poles are similar to electric charges. The indicators react as if there are positive, negative, and neutral loci alternately distributed in a relatively small plane. The materials from which the devices are built are such that they should not react to the inductive effect of the earth's magnetic field.

Krmessky has advanced the theory that the hypothetical poles in all objects on the earth's surface are induced by light, or by radiation in general. This "quasimagnetic field," then, could be a resultant phenomenon induced by interaction of plasma and radiation, without having to assume an analogy to the earth's magnetic field. He also accepts the hypothesis that in man's brain the processes of thinking are accompanied by the motion of plasma particles, and that this motion is the source of excitation or, more aptly, the modulator in this hypothetical field of very fine structure, able to transmit much more subtle impulses than the well-known electromagnetic field. But even in this case, he does not disregard the role of the electromagnetic field. Certain phenomena -- the reflection of visual rays by polished surfaces, refraction, the effect of light on the polarity of objects, etc. -- indicate that a common denominator for PK and for the electromagnetic field may eventually be found.

All of the Soviet and Czech research on PK is significant, especially that associated with the spectacular Soviet psychics Kulagina, Vinogradova, and Ermolayev. Kulagina's highly publicized ability to affect living tissues might be applied against human targets; in like manner, Vinogradova's power to move objects, and Ermolayev's levitational ability could possibly be used to activate or deactivate power supplies or to steal military documents or hardware. Robert Pavlita's generators and Julius Krmessky's PK indicators could be (and possibly are now) used to train large numbers of lesser known Soviet and Czech citizens to develop, enhance, and control their latent psychic abilities. Such a cadre of trained, but anonymous individuals could be used for any number of covert activities. Less spectacular, but more significant, is the fact that Soviet and Czech scientists are pursuing an interrelated, unified approach to determining the energy sources and interactions underlying PK and appear to be far ahead of their Western counterparts in reaching this goal. It will be but a short step from understanding to application and there is little doubt that many applications can be directed toward man for whatever purpose, be it good or bad.

51

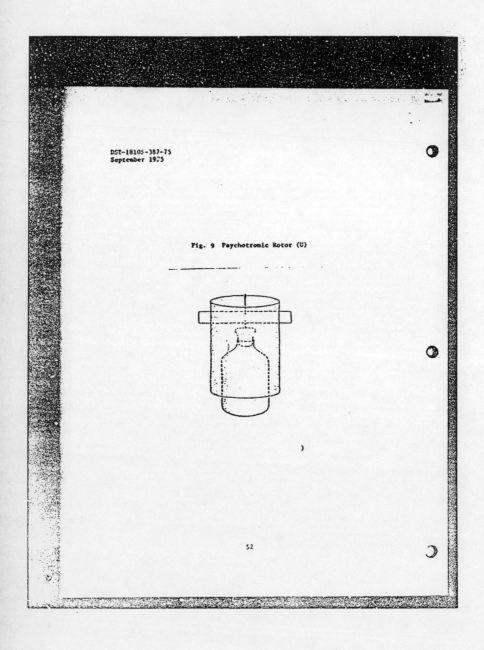

DST-1810S-387-75
September 1975

Fig. 9 Psychotronic Rotor (U)

52

DST-1810S-387-75
September 1975

PART IV

OUT-OF-THE-BODY PHENOMENA

SECTION I - REMOTE VIEWING

Remote viewing refers to the ability of some individuals to project themselves mentally to remote or inaccessible locations and observe and report on details of terrain, structures, and other salient features. This ability is also referred to as astral or mental projection. It differs from telepathy in that the percipient does not piece together information bits to form an image, but rather, has a vivid sense of leaving his body and personally observing the target area in toto.

Remote viewing has been investigated in the US at Stanford Research Institute (SRI), Menlo Park, California. Psychically gifted subjects were tested for the ability by presenting them with map coordinates randomly selected on a double blind basis. The subjects were required to respond immediately with a description of the target area and were tested both with and without feedback as to their accuracy. According to the SRI report on this study, there were at least some categories of information in which the results exceeded any possible statistical bounds of coincidental correlation and precluded acquisition of data by known means.

(C) SRI reports of remote viewing research have not been publicized, but other SRI research on the psychic abilities of an Israeli (Uri Geller) and a British (Ingo Swann) subject has been widely cited in the US news media. Geller has been quoted many times on his avowed ability to transport himself mentally to any place of his choosing. Soviet parapsychologists are aware of Geller's claims (he has, in fact, been invited to the Soviet Union for tests) and continuing US interest in this phenomenon, nevertheless they have reported very little similar research of their own.

53

385

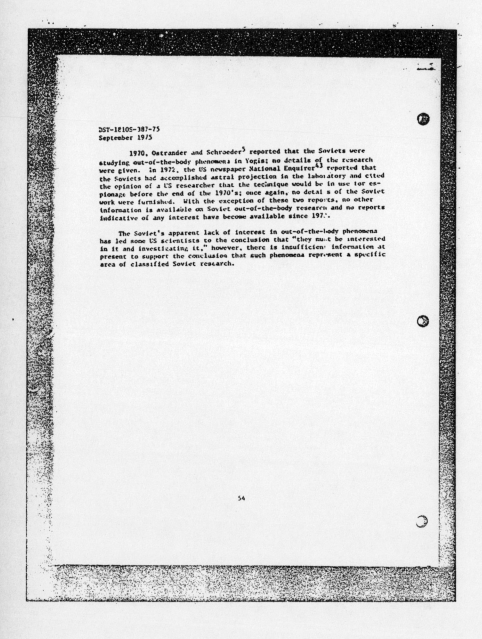

DST-1810S-387-75
September 1975

1970, Ostrander and Schroeder[5] reported that the Soviets were studying out-of-the-body phenomena in Yogis; no details of the research were given. In 1972, the US newspaper National Enquirer[43] reported that the Soviets had accomplished astral projection in the laboratory and cited the opinion of a US researcher that the technique would be in use for espionage before the end of the 1970's; once again, no detai s of the Soviet work were furnished. With the exception of these two reports, no other information is available on Soviet out-of-the-body research and no reports indicative of any interest have become available since 197.'.

The Soviet's apparent lack of interest in out-of-the-body phenomena has led some US scientists to the conclusion that "they must be interested in it and investigating it," however, there is insufficien: information at present to support the conclusion that such phenomena represent a specific area of classified Soviet research.

54

DST-1810S-387-75
September 1975

SECTION 11 - THE APPORT TECHNIQUE

The apport technique is a form of astral projection in which the psychic subject transports his "energy body" to a remote site, dematerializes an object, then transports it back and materializes it. In past reports there has been some very general speculation on espionage applications of the technique but to date no definitive reports, US or foreign, have verified the claims of psychics reputed to have the ability. There have been no Soviet or European Communist Countries' reports concerning research on apport techniques and if such research is being conducted, it is a well-kept secret. Lack of information on Soviet interest in the technique represents a major intelligence gap.

DST-1810S-387-75
September 1975

PART V

CONCLUSIONS

Soviet and Czechoslovakian researchers have accepted the reality of paranormal events and are primarily concerned with the formulation of a unified theory to describe the basic energy transformations involved. The Soviet emphasis on the electrostatic and electromagnetic components of the energy may play an important role in the final determination of the nature of psychical phenomena. This emphasis on energetics or interaction effects has lead to the concept that man must be investigated as a complete, integrated unit.

Soviet and Czech psychotronic research will eventually be applied to human problems. As this occurs, the question will arise whether this knowledge and the equipment developed will be used for the enhancement of human freedom and social development, or for regimentation and enslavement. Psychotronics could conceivably play a role in contributing to the survival of the human species; by emphasizing the interconnections between all living beings, it should help to reduce human aggressive tendencies. By the same token, it could also be applied to increase such aggressive tendencies and it has powerful potential for use as an effective weapon against groups of men and key leaders.

The Czechs claim that a direct transfer of biological energy from healthy to diseased or injured muscle is not only possible, but proven. The Soviets do not restrict the possibility of such energy transfer to any one physiological system, but state that biological energy transfer can be utilized to relieve human functional disorders of the nervous system, the internal organs, and the mind. In all cases, such medical applications of biological energy transfer are officially described as having beneficial results, but this may not necessarily be true. By analogy, conventional medical techniques can be beneficial, but when misapplied, can cause serious damage, or even death. By the same token, there can also be "psychic" malpractice, although the Soviets and Czechs are not likely to publicize this fact.

Both Czech and US researchers have described Robert Pavlita's work with psychotronic generators as possibly the most important contemporary development in the field of parapsychology and as a major contribution to the deeper understanding, mastery, and utilization of biological energy for human advantage. Just as in the example of direct transfer of biological energy for medical purposes, the use of such devices is not

57

388

ST-CS-01-187-75
September 1975

necessarily intended to be beneficial. If Pavlita's devices can kill insects at present, their potential in the future after refinement and enlargement may well be for killing men. If bioenergy can be reliably controlled and focused by such devices, death could be caused by disruption of fundamental brain rhythms, heart control, or biological clock mechanisms.

It should also be pointed out that some of Pavlita's experiments seem to contradict Soviet results obtained with humans. As an example, the effect of his devices on suspended magnets is lessened if the magnets are electrostatically shielded, whereas such shielding has no effect in Soviet experiments with Nina Kulagina and Alla Vinogradova. It would appear that although the Czechs and the Soviets are examining the same phenomena, passage of biological energy through Pavlita's devices alters it in some manner. This raises the question of how well these machines can be controlled, and whether the alteration they induce on bioenergy is beneficial or detrimental.

Soviet research with Kulagina and Vinogradova indicates that energy interchanges, or transfer mechanisms, may be possible between gifted psychics and inanimate objects. There is evidence that Soviet research with these women also involves attempts to influence animate biological systems. In 1972, LaMothe reported that Kulagina had the capability for stopping and starting the beat of an excised, living, frog heart. If true, it supports the contention that Czech and Soviet claims for "beneficial" applications of biological energy transfer are reversible - if a frog heart can be started and stopped, the same effects might be imposed on humans. Such dramatic effects illustrate some of the dangerous potential of controlled biological energy transfer.

58

389

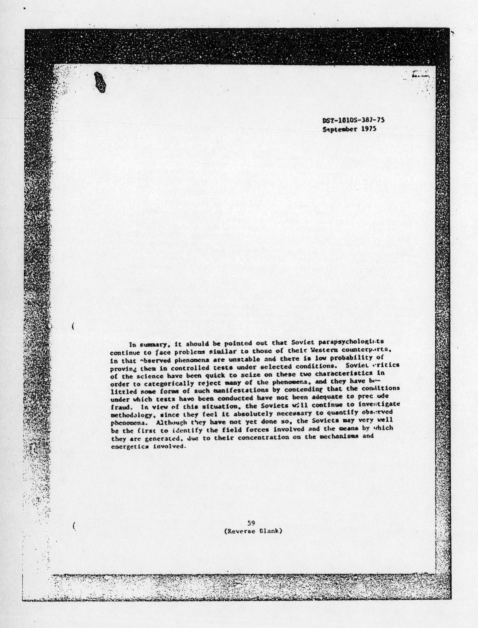

DST-1810S-387-75
September 1975

In summary, it should be pointed out that Soviet parapsychologists continue to face problems similar to those of their Western counterparts, in that observed phenomena are unstable and there is low probability of proving them in controlled tests under selected conditions. Soviet critics of the science have been quick to seize on these two characteristics in order to categorically reject many of the phenomena, and they have belittled some forms of such manifestations by contending that the conditions under which tests have been conducted have not been adequate to preclude fraud. In view of this situation, the Soviets will continue to investigate methodology, since they feel it absolutely necessary to quantify observed phenomena. Although they have not yet done so, the Soviets may very well be the first to identify the field forces involved and the means by which they are generated, due to their concentration on the mechanisms and energetics involved.

59
(Reverse Blank)

DST-1810S-387-75
September 1975

PART VI

TRENDS AND FORECASTS

1. TRENDS

Criticism: All Soviet science is very much influenced by political ideology. Parapsychology, as a result of the fleeting phenomena it deals with, is perhaps more vulnerable to ideological attacks than other science. Soviet critics point out that parapsychology, as a "pseudo-science," makes it enormously more difficult for the Party to eliminate than religious prejudices and superstitions. They claim that parapsychology, if viewed from the standpoint of Lenin, represents a revival of "bourgeois subjective idealism." Soviet critics claim that subsensory, subthreshold perception takes place in the presence of a stimulus and an analyzer and that such perception is subject to the very same physiological laws as is a subjectively registered perception. They admit, however, that the study of these laws is still far from the stage at which it will be possible to explain scientifically a person's subconscious psychological activity.

Concentration on Energetics: Faced with such criticisms, Soviet and Czech scientists engaged in parapsychology research have, more and more, stressed the "biological energy" concept, and are continuing to develop theoretical bases which will provide an integrated approach to paranormal phenomena. In order to bring their science more nearly in line with accepted theories of contemporary physics, they have postulated a "fifth state of matter" consisting of "free charged particles" arranged in organized patterns forming a uniform energy network. They are continuing to emphasize the electrostatic and electromagnetic components of such energy and argue that the eventual definition of this energy will allow them to ultimately integrate psychical phenomena into contemporary theoretical constructs of the universe.

Official Attitude: There are no indications of any organized or officially sanctioned attacks on Soviet/Czech psychotronic research, but such criticisms as have been noted have appeared in State-sanctioned publications. Continued monitoring of the Soviet and Czech press will be required in order to determine whether or not the official attitude toward the science shifts.

2. FORECASTS

In the next 15 years the Soviets and Czechs will continue to emphasize parapsychological research. Such research will, of necessity, involve the further development of appropriate instrumentation for the detection and

61

DST-1810S-387-75
September 1975

identification of the biological energy internal to the human body and
its interactions with living or inanimate objects at a distance. The
cyborg aspects (coupling of human inductors with physical psychotronic
devices) will continue to be emphasized. During this time frame, research will progress from instrumentation development to computer
assisted mathematical modeling of biological energy intera-tions. In
order to establish a basis for such modeling, experimental techniques
which can be controlled and replicated will be developed. This, in turn,
will lead to the eventual improvement of research on paranormal phenomena
since they will be made increasingly more producible and predictable.

The Soviets are known to be involved in development of inferential
measurement and complex systems modelling (IMCSM) techniques.[44,45] IMCSM
is especially adapted for application to the examination and study of many
objects, especially those with many interacting parts, even when the behavior of the objects are partly or mostly determined by features of which
the researcher is unaware or which he cannot observe. Soviet parapsychology
research would probably be an ideal subject for the application of the IMCSM
technique. If IMCSM is applied, the likelihood of a Soviet breakthrough
in parapsychology is greatly increased. The Soviets are leaders in development of this technique and will probably apply it to parapsychology
research.

DST-1810S-387-75
September 1975

PART VII

GAPS

1.   Information is needed on the effects Nina Kulagina, Alla Vinogradova, and other Soviet psychics exert on magnetic tapes.

2.   More information is needed on Robert Pavlita's psychotronic generators. Pavlita was quoted as having stated that he intended to obtain foreign patents on his devices in 1974, after which he would publicly divulge the details of their construction and operation. Information is needed on such patent applications and on Pavlita's explanations of their construction and operation.

3.   More information is needed on the circuitry and response characteristics of current or proposed Soviet or Czech biological energy detection instruments. Such information is needed on instruments utilized for measurements at the cellular level and at the total body level.

4.   Information is needed on the status of Soviet cellular radiation research. Present information indicates that they have identified ultraviolet (UV) radiation as one electromagnetic (EM) carrier or transfer mechanism from cell to cell. More information on this research is needed in order to determine whether it is fortuitous in regard to Soviet parapsychology research, or is an integral part of it.

5. . Information is needed on the extent of Soviet mass-screening for identifying psychic citizens. Does the Soviet military have screening programs, and if so, which branches of service are involved? If such screening programs exist, are they conducted by psychological testing, or by direct observation of abilities to influence simple instruments such as those developed by the Czechs?

6. . There are indications that the official attitude concerning parapsychology is changing in the Soviet Union and Czechoslovakia. Information is needed concerning the basis for the apparent changes in official attitude.

7.   Is there any evidence of clandestine use by the Soviets of apparently electromagnetic or electrostatic devices against personnel, equipment, or radio and television stations?

63

393

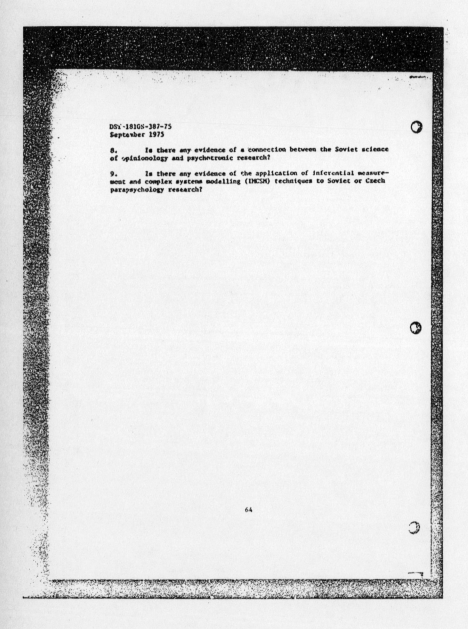

DSI-181GS-387-75
September 1975

8.   Is there any evidence of a connection between the Soviet science of opinionology and psychotronic research?

9.   Is there any evidence of the application of inferential measurement and complex systems modelling (IMCSM) techniques to Soviet or Czech parapsychology research?

64

DST-1810S-387-75
September 1975

APPENDIX

PERSONNEL AND FACILITIES

1.   USSR - Affiliation Known

Adamenko, V.G.; Moscow Institute of Radiophysics

Bleykher, V.M.; Bekhterev Brain Institute, University of Leningrad

Dubrov, A.; Institute of Earth Physics, USSR Academy of Sciences

Gulyaiev, P.; Bekhterev Brain Institute, University of Leningrad

Inyushin, V.; Kazakh University, Alma-ata

Kaznacheyev, V.; University of Novosibirsk

Kholodov, Y.A.; Institute of Higher Nervous Activity and Neurophysiology,
    USSR Academy of Sciences, Moscow

Leontiev, A.N.; Soviet Academy of Pedagogical Sciences

Lomov, B.F.; Soviet Academy of Pedagogical Sciences

Luria, A.R.; Soviet Academy of Pedagogical Sciences

Mikhailova, L.; University of Novosibirsk

Naumov, E.K.; formerly of the Institute of Technical Parapsychology,
    Moscow

Nikolayev, K.; Bioinformation Section of the A.S. Popov All-Union
    Scientific and Technical Society of Radio Technology
    and Electrical Communications, Moscow

Pavlova, L.; Physiology of Labor Laboratory, University of Leningrad

Pushkin, V.; Moscow University

Sergeyev, G.A.; A.A. Uktomskii Physiological Institute

Shchurin, S.; University of Novosibirsk

65

REMOTE VIEWING

DST-1810S-387-75
September 1975

Snezhnevsky, A.: Serbskiy Institute of Forensic Psychological Expertise

Zigel, F.; Moscow Institute of Aviation

Zinchenko, V.P.; Soviet Academy of Pedagogical Sciences

2.   USSR – Affiliation Unknown

Arvashkin, A.; Moscow (psychic subject)

Ermolayev, B.; Moscow (psychic subject)

Kazhinsky, B.B.

Kulagina, N.; Moscow (psychic subject)

Kulin, Ye.T.; Minsk

Naumov, P.

Parnov, Ye.; Sverdlovsk

Presman, A.S.

Serov, S.; Sverdlovsk

Sysoletin, A.; (psychic subject)

Sysoletin, L.; (psychic subject)

Troskin, A.; Sverdlovsk

Vinogradova, A.; Moscow (psychic subject)

3.   Czechoslovakia – Affiliation Known

Bradna, J.; Neurology Department, Okres Institute of Public Health,
    Kutna Hora, Czechoslovakia

Kahuda, F.; Charles University, Prague, Czechoslovakia

Krmessky, J.; Chair of Physics, Pedagogical Institute, Trnava,
    Czechoslovakia

Pavlita, R.; probable affiliation, Hradec Králové University, Prague,
    Czechoslovakia

66

396

DST-1810S-387-75
September 1975

Pavlita, J.; probable affiliation, Hradec Králové University, Prague, Czechoslovakia

Rejdak, Z.; Psychotronic Research Section, Czechoslovakian Society for Science and Technology

4.   Czechoslovakia - Affiliation Unknown

Cernousek, M.; Prague

Miza, M.G.

Rezek, P.; Prague

Wolf, J.; Prague

(

(

DST-18105-387-75
September 1975

SELECTED BIBLIOGRAPHY

1. JPRS 55557, 28 March 1972 (UNCLASSIFIED).

2. ST-CS-01-169-72, July 1972, pp 21-22 (SECRET).

3. JPRS L/5022-2, 6 September 1974, Volume I, p 111 (UNCLASSIFIED).

4. Op. cit. (2), p 4.

5. Ostrander, S. and Schroeder, L., *Psychic Discoveries Behind the Iron Curtain*, Prentice-Hall, Englewood Cliffs, NJ, 1970 (UNCLASSIFIED).

6. Psychic, May/June 1974, p 51 (UNCLASSIFIED).

7. Zinchenko, V.P., Leontiev, A.N., Lomov, B.F., and Lur'a, A.R., *Parapsychology: Fiction or Reality*, Questions of Philosophy, Volume 27, 1973, pp 128-136 (UNCLASSIFIED).

8. New Scientist, Volume 65, No. 936, 13 February 1975, pp 397-398 (UNCLASSIFIED).

9. JPRS 61662, 4 April 1974 (UNCLASSIFIED).

10. JPRS 60883, 28 December 1973, p 71 (UNCLASSIFIED).

11. Kazhinskiy, B.B., *Biologicheskaya Radiosvyaz*, Kiev, 1962 (UNCLASSIFIED).

12. Bradna, J., *Distant Energy Myotransfer*, presented at the 1st Conference on Psychotronic Research, Prague, 1973 (UNCLASSIFIED).

13. Kholodov, Y.A., *Investigation of the Direct Effect of Magnetic Fields on the Central Nervous System*, presented at the 1st Conference on Psychotronic Research, Prague, 1973 (UNCLASSIFIED).

14. JPRS 64228, 4 March 1975 (UNCLASSIFIED).

15. Op. cit. (2).

16. Kogan, I.M., *Is Telepathy Possible*, Radiotekhnika, Volume 21, No. 1, pp 8-14, 1966 (UNCLASSIFIED).

17. Vasilev, L.L., *Telesuggestion*, pp 158-159, Moscow, 1962 (UNCLASSIFIED).

69

DST-1810S-387-75
September 1975

18. Vasilev, L.L., Mysterious Phenomena of the Human Psyche, p 155,
Moscow, 1964 (UNCLASSIFIED).

19. Zigel, F., Telepathy, a Science for the Future, Nauka i Religiya,
No. 3, p 35, 1966 (UNCLASSIFIED).

20. Parnov, Ye., The Neutrino - Why Not, Nauka i Religiya, No. 3,
pp 48-49, 1966 (UNCLASSIFIED).

21. Kogan, I.M., Telepathy, Hypotheses and Observations, Radiotekhnika,
Volume 22, No. 1, pp 95-99, 1967 (UNCLASSIFIED).

22. Kogan, I.M., Informational Analysis of Experiments in Telepathy
Communication, Radiotekhnika, Volume 23, No. 3, pp 87-92, 1968 (UNCLASSIFIED).

23. Velinov, I., Recent Soviet Experiments in Telepathy, Foreign Science
Bulletin, Volume 4, No. 8, pp 17-18, 1968 (UNCLASSIFIED).

24. Mutschall, V., The Present Status of Research in Telepathy in the
Soviet Union, Foreign Science Bulletin, Volume 4, No. 8, p 10, 1968
(UNCLASSIFIED).

25. Rezek, P., The Obvious and Nonobvious Nature of Telepathic Phenomena
in Scientific Investigation, presented at the 1st Conference on Psychotronic Research, Prague, 1973 (UNCLASSIFIED).

26. Mirza, M.G., Nauka i Religiya, No. 1, 1967 (UNCLASSIFIED).

27. Sergeyev, G.A., Some Methodological Problems of Parapsychology,
Telepatie as Jasnovidnost, 1970 (JPRS L/4922, 3 June 1974) (UNCLASSIFIED).

28. Sergeyev, G.A., Problems in the Application of the Analysis of
Random Events, Soviet Radio Publishing House, 1968 (UNCLASSIFIED).

29. Wolf, J., A Psychotronic Model of Man, presented at the 1st Conference
on Psychotronic Research, Prague, 1973 (UNCLASSIFIED).

30. Cernousek, M., Regressive Nature of the Telepathic Phenomenon,
presented at the 1st Conference on Psychotronic Research, Prague, 1973
(UNCLASSIFIED).

31. Rejdak, Z., Psychotronics Reveals New Possibilities for Cybernetics,
presented at the 1st Conference on Psychotronic Research, Prague, 1973
(UNCLASSIFIED).

32. JPRS L/4798, No. 764, 28 January 1974 (UNCLASSIFIED).

70

REMOTE VIEWING

DST-1810S-387-75
September 1975

33. Kahuda, F., Mental Time and Psychotronics, presented at the 1st
Conference on Psychotronic Research, Prague, 1973 (UNCLASSIFIED).

34. Joire, P., De la Suggestion Mentale, Annals des Sciences Psychiques,
No. 4, 1897 (UNCLASSIFIED).

35. Vasilev, L.L., Experimental Studies of Mental Suggestion, 1962
(UNCLASSIFIED).

36. The San Juan Star, Sunday, 20 April 1975, p 25 (UNCLASSIFIED).

37. Ullman, Montague, PK in the Soviet Union, Department of Psychiatry,
Maimonides Medical Center, Brooklyn, NY, Personal Communication (UNCLASSIFIED).

38. Adamenko, Viktor G., Some Problems of Biological Electrodynamics and
Psychoenergetics, presented at the 1st Conference on Psychotronic Research,
Prague, 1973 (UNCLASSIFIED).

39. Dubrov, Aleksandr, Biogravitation, presented at the 1st Conference
on Psychotronic Research, Prague, 1973 (UNCLASSIFIED).

40. National Enquirer, 25 March 1975 (UNCLASSIFIED).

41. Krmessky, Julius, On the Trail of an Unknown Field, presented at the
1st Conference on Psychotronic Research, Prague, 1973 (UNCLASSIFIED).

42. SRI, No. ISH 73-146, 2 October 1973, p 13 (UNCLASSIFIED).

43. National Enquirer, January 1972, pp 8-9 (UNCLASSIFIED).

44. Ivakhnenko, A.G., "Polynomial Theory of Complex Systems," IEEE Trans-
actions on Systems, Man and Cybernetics, Volume 1, No. 4, October 1971,
pp 364-378 (UNCLASSIFIED).

45. Ivakhnenko, A.G., "Kiberneticheskiye Sistemy S Kombinirovannym
Upvaolentyem, (Cybernetic Systems with Combined Control), Izdatel'stvo
Tekhnika, 1967 (UNCLASSIFIED).

71
(Reverse Blank)

Appendix III

Sixth World Congress of the International Ozone Association
22-26 May 1983
Washington DC, USA

Since July 4, 1976 the Soviet Union has been bombarding many parts of the world
with E.L.F. transmitters. - a total of 14 giant transmitters are known to exist
world-wide. It should be pointed out in the 9 years of transmissions by their
government not once has a 79Hz signal been recorded, a frequency that is
beneficial for human biological systems.

Successful treatment of neoplasms in mice with gaseous suproxide anion (2) and
ozone (03), with a rationale for the effect - Paper by Andrija Puharich MD, LLD

When the Soviets went on the air on July 4, 1976 with their 100 megawatt
transmissions of extremely low frequency waves (ELF), the intelligence community
of the US was caught unaware of this new technology. The Soviets- ELF pulses
covered the frequency range of the human brain. No-one knew what the purpose of
this new technology was. I had a hypothesis that this was a new mind-control
weapon that could entrain a human being's EEG. Bob Beck and I designed an
experiment that conclusively proved that the Soviet transmissions could indeed
entrain the human brain, and thereby induce behavioural modification. I reported
this finding to the intelligence community in the US, and my paper was promptly
classified (26). A CIA commission of inquiry reported to President Carter that
there was no substance to our findings. Today, five years later, all of our
findings have been confirmed by various agencies of the US Government. However,
they went one step beyond our findings, and proved that a certain ELF frequency
(Classified) will cause cancer (27). 1 have repeated these experiments, and
found this to be true. The mechanism of this effect is that the ELF frequency
modified the function of the RNA transferases so that amino acid sequences are
scrambled and produce unnatural proteins. The ELF exerts its effect on the
nuclear level, more specifically, the nuclear magnetic resonant property of the
nucleus. The table shows the spin-spin coupling constants of various common
chemical chains. Note the common chemical groupings with coupling constants
around 8Hz. Note that a powerful carcinogen, ethylene dioxide, has coupling
constants around 3 to 5Hz. Note that another powerful carcinogen, formaldehyde,
has a coupling constant around 41Hz. Parrish et al, have found that the
spin-spin coupling constants for water in malignant brain tumours (in humans and
dogs) range from 4.8 to 13.4Hz.Thus malignancy shows a spread of frequencies from low to high
ELF range, i.e. with respect to normal brain EEGs, and carcinogens have a wide
spread from 3Hz to about 41Hz around the center frequency for normalcy of 8Hz.
However, a single ELF frequency can produce cancer.

REFERENCE

(26) The Imminence of ELF Magnetic Global Warfare. Confidential Report by A.
Puharich, submitted March 13, 1977 to
Hon. Pierre Elliot Trudeau, Prime Minister, Canada
Hon. James Carter, President, USA
Hon. Margaret Thatcher, Leader of the Opposition, Great Britain

(Classified) Report warns that the Soviet ELF signals broadcast since July 4,
1976 are psychoactive (in a predatory sense) and can lead to other biological
effects.

(27) Note: 1982, US Navy confirms that Soviet ELF signals are indeed
psychoactive and can cause mental depression at 6.66Hz and at 11Hz can lead to
manic and riotous behavior in humans.

401

Appendix IV

Defense Intelligence Agency document: Biological effects of electromagnetic radiation (radiowaves and microwaves) Eurasian Communist countries, March 1976.

A complete table of contents and selected sections are reproduced here. These DIA documents show that microwave frequencies similar to those of cellular phones can cause health problems in the following areas:

1. Blood
2. Cardiovascular System
3. Cells
4. Central Nervous System
5. Digestive System
6. Glands
7. Metabolism
8. Reproduction
9. Visual System
10. Internal Sound Perception

Microwave phones use 900MHz and 1800MHz. In 1997, Australian scientists found that exposure to radiation of this type causes cancer in mice. The documents show that similar frequencies and intensities as found in mobile phones were used as psychotronic weapons by the Soviets. The document, dated March 1976, shows that the dangers were known about over 20 years ago.

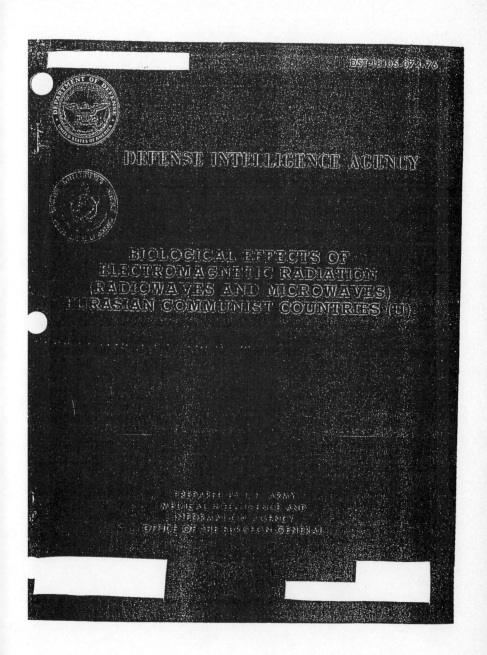

DST-1810S-074-76

DEPARTMENT OF DEFENSE
UNITED STATES OF AMERICA

DEFENSE INTELLIGENCE AGENCY

BIOLOGICAL EFFECTS OF
ELECTROMAGNETIC RADIATION
(RADIOWAVES AND MICROWAVES)
EURASIAN COMMUNIST COUNTRIES (U)

PREPARED BY U.S. ARMY
MEDICAL INTELLIGENCE AND
INFORMATION AGENCY
OFFICE OF THE SURGEON GENERAL

BIOLOGICAL EFFECTS OF ELECTROMAGNETIC RADIATION
(RADIOWAVES AND MICROWAVES) –
EURASIAN COMMUNIST COUNTRIES (U)

DST-1810S-074-76

DIA TASK PT-1810-02-75

DATE OF PUBLICATION
March 1976
Information Cut-off Date
10 October 1975

Supersession Notice
This document supersedes ST-CS-01-74-74, dated March 1974

WARNING

This publication contains information affecting the National Defense of
the United States within the meaning of the Espionage Laws, Title 18,
U.S.C., Sections 793 and 794.   Its transmission or the revelation of its
contents in any manner to an unauthorized person is prohibited by law.

This is a Department of Defense Intelligence Document prepared by the
US Army Medical Intelligence and Information Agency and approved by the
Directorate for Scientific and Technical Intelligence of the Defense
Intelligence Agency.

)

DST-1810S-074-76
March 1976

PREFACE

| The purpose of this review is to provide information necessary to
assess human vulnerability, protection materials, and methods applicable
to military operations. The study provides an insight on the current
research capabilities of these countries. Information on trends is
presented when feasible and supportable.

The study discusses the biological effects of electromagnetic radiation in the radio- and microwave ranges (up through 300,000 megahertz).
It is not within the realm of this study to provide detailed descriptions
of every laboratory experiment. Such data have been purposely omitted in
favor of an analytical approach. An attempt has been made to identify the
principal areas of research and to discuss the significance of experimental
results.

| The information reported in this study has been drawn from scientific,
medical, and military journals, intelligence reports, magazines, news items,
books, and other publications. The information cut-off date for this study
was 1 October 1975.

)

(U) Constructive criticism, comments or suggested changes are encouraged,
and should be forwarded to the Defense Intelligence Agency (ATTN: DT-1A),
Washington, DC 20301.

iii
(Reverse Blank)

)

UNCLASSIFIED

DST-1810S-074-76
March 1976

TABLE OF CONTENTS

v
(Reverse Blank)

UNCLASSIFIED

DST-1810S-074-76
March 1976

SUMMARY

(U) The thermal effects of electromagnetic radiation have been reasonably
well established through experimental investigation. The nonthermal effects,
however, remain a controversial issue between scientists in the West and in
the Eurasian Communist countries. The difficulties encountered in conclusively demonstrating the nonthermal effects of electromagnetic exposure are
likely responsible for differences in exposure standards; some standards are
based largely on the demonstrable thermal effects, while others allow for
possible nonthermal effects at subthermal intensities.

(U) The Eurasian Communist countries are actively involved in evaluation
of the biological significance of radiowaves and microwaves. Most of the
research being conducted involves animals or in vitro evaluations, but
active programs of a retrospective nature designed to elucidate the effects
on humans are also being conducted. The major systems, system components,
or processes currently under study include the blood, the cardiovascular
system, cells, the central nervous system, the digestive system, the
glandular system, metabolic effects, and the reproductive and the visual
systems. Other aspects of exposure are also being studied, but the limited
number of reports uncovered makes assessment of the importance placed upon
this research impossible. These lesser reported research areas include
nonthermal effects, immunological studies, and use of radiowaves for
functional control of organ systems.

No unusual devices or measures for protection from radiowave exposure
were noted, but a continued stress upon personnel protection in occupational situations was apparent. Here, protective goggles and clothing are
recommended when working in regions of microwave radiation. Although some
differences in standards remain between the various Communist countries
and between military and civilian standards, the Communist standards remain
much more stringent than those of the West. An exception to this may be
Poland where a recent relaxation of their standards has occurred. This is
the first significant shift of an East European country away from the
standard first set by the USSR in 1958.

If the more advanced nations of the West are strict in the enforcement
of stringent exposure standards, there could be unfavorable effects on industrial output and military functions. The Eurasian Communist countries
could, on the other hand, give lip service to strict standards, but allow
their military to operate without restriction and thereby gain the advantage
in electronic warfare techniques and the development of antipersonnel
applications.

vii

409

DST-1810S-074-76
March 1976

(U) As may be expected, the bulk of the research being done in this area
is in the USSR. However, a notable volume is also being produced by Poland,
Czechoslovakia, Bulgaria, Rumania, and Hungary.

Western scientists who have followed the Soviet research efforts on the
biological effects of microwaves have expressed a variety of reactions ranging from disbelief to passive acceptance. The overall impact of current
Soviet work is not overly significant, at least on their civilian sector.
One possible exception may be their studies of the central nervous system
where some interesting work is being done. Elsewhere, most of their work
tends to be outdated, some of their experiments cannot be duplicated, and
others are of doubtful credibility. No real new developments or fresh
approaches have been identified. Nevertheless, a large volume of material
continues to be published on the effects of radiowaves and microwaves on biological systems, indicating a fairly high degree of interest and a genuine
desire to pursue these investigations. No significant research and development has been identified that could be related to work in this field in
the People's Republic of China, North Korea, and North Vietnam.

viii

DST-1810S-074-76
March 1976

SECTION I

INTRODUCTION

(U) The effects of radiowaves and microwaves on biological systems have
traditionally been separated into two basic classifications, (1) thermal
effects, and (2) nonthermal effects. The thermal effects are widely recognized and the mechanism of action reasonably well understood. Nonthermal
effects, however, are controversial since the mechanisms involved are not
clearly understood. Soviet and East European scientists believe that biological side-effects occur at power densities that are too low to produce
obvious thermal effects. Such effects have been questioned in the West
because experimental evidence, obtained largely in US laboratories, does
not corroborate occurrence of nonthermal side-effects.

(U) Divergences in opinion between Bloc and Western researchers concerning
the effects of microwave radiation are the result of nonstandardized research
protocols and materials. In addition, mechanisms underlying observed biological effects are at present poorly understood by any of the world's
scientists engaged in microwave research. The exchange of scientific information on microwave hazards has increased greatly since the active partici-
pation of Soviet, Czechoslovak, and Polish scientists in the International
Symposium on Biological Effects and Health Hazards of Microwave Radiation
in Warsaw in October 1973.

(U) It is now generally agreed that biological systems irradiated with
electromagnetic waves in the radiowave and microwave frequency ranges (one
kilohertz to more that 10^5 megahertz) absorb varying amounts of energy
depending on the irradiation frequencies and the physical properties of
the system. Typically, however, 40-50 percent of the incident energy is
absorbed by the biological system and the remainder reflected. In reality,
only the shorter wavelengths represent any appreciable hazard as a result
of thermal heating. Radiation fields in the microwave range vary in wavelength from about one meter to very short wavelengths on the order of a
millimeter. The depth of penetration of the waves is also variable and
again depends on the frequency, wave polarization, and the physical properties of the system (i.e., dielectric and geometric), but typical penetra-
tions are on the order of 1/10 of the wavelength. Therefore, very short
waves are absorbed primarily by the skin, while long wavelengths penetrate
to much greater depths.

(U) The degree of heating appears to be a function of the water content
of the tissue and probably results from oscillations of water molecules or
dipoles. Another possibility is a resonance absorption of energy by protein molecules of the cell. As might be expected, the actual damages
resulting from a given exposure are functions of the thermal regulatory

1

DST-1810S-074-76
March 1976

and active adaptation processes of the organ or animal. Less vascularized
tissues are more susceptible to thermal damage because of a poorer ability
to dissipate the heat, therefore, crystalline lens damage or cataract
formation may be observed.

(U) Many techniques and indices have been employed to study the effects
of irradiation on biological systems. These include:

> Body weight.
> Biochemical studies.
> Cardiovascular studies.
> CNS effects (including conditioned and unconditioned reflexes).
> Electrophysiological measurements.
> Fertility and mutation studies.
> Histology and pathology studies.
> Metabolic studies.
> Temperature.

While these and other experimental studies have been conducted on animal
and cellular models, knowledge regarding human exposure has been almost
exclusively obtained retrospectively. Accordingly, information regarding
the amount and/or portion of the body exposed, field intensities, and
duration of exposure are usually ill defined.

(U) As can be seen from the above, quantitation of the biological responses
to electromagnetic exposure is a very complex problem because of the wide
frequency spectrum, the large number of physical and biological variables,
and the interrelationships of those variables. Factors requiring consideration include the frequency, intensity, waveform, (pulsed, CW, or modulated) configuration of the body, its orientation with respect to the
source, portion of the body irradiated, exposure time-intensity factors,
environmental conditions (temperature, humidity, and air currents), and
shielding. Other complicating factors include the subject's state of health
and previous or concomitant medication. In addition to the above factors,
the animal species used and its comparative relation to man is important.
Accordingly, experimental results from animals cannot easily be extra-
polated and assumed to apply to human exposure because of size differences
relative to exposure wavelength which can markedly influence the system
or organ being damaged.

(U) With these complicating factors in mind, the evaluation contained in
this report was undertaken. The data presented were obtained from the
sources outlined in the preface and sometimes contained insufficient information to make absolute decisions regarding their significance. The sources
were, however, indicative of the types of effects being reported and suggested those areas of research being emphasized, thereby permitting assessment of recent Eurasian Communist attempts to define the biological effects
of radiowaves and microwaves.

2

TIM RIFAT

DST-1810S-074-76
March 1976

SECTION II

BIOLOGICAL SIGNIFICANCE OF RADIOWAVES AND MICROWAVES

PART 1 - BLOOD

(U) Effects of electromagnetic irradiation on the blood include biochemical variations, effects on erythrocytes, changes in coagulation,
and alterations in the blood forming system. As would be expected,
most communist-country reports originate from in vitro or in vivo
animal experiments rather than from human data.

(U) Long-term ultrahigh frequency (UHF) exposure in rats reportedly
reduced the iron and copper content in both the blood and muscle with
a concomitant increase in iron content in the liver. Similar exposure
in chicks caused an increase in total proteins and globulins, but decreased the albumin in the plasma. Rats exposed to 0.04 W/cm^2 for 25
days demonstrated similar shifts. In some studies with dogs, irradiation
with microwaves significantly decreased the lifetime of erythrocytes, while
other studies indicated no changes in the granulocytic system after exposure.
In the lymphocytic system, however, mitotic disturbances and changes of
nuclear structure occurred. Rabbits exposed to "an electromagnetic field"
showed significant increases in the number of monocytes, basophils, and
lymphocytes/mm. Although undesirable, these shifts are not significant
enough to impair the functional performance of humans. However, they are
significant enough to warrant further experimentation. Soviet researchers
will emphasize more experiments with animals and they will continue to try
and relate these experiments to data on human exposure to microwave environments. They will most likely work toward relating such changes in
different species of animals to particular intensities or exposures.

(U) One study involved the observation of several thousand persons working
in microwave-irradiated workshops, as well as animal experiments. In the
human subjects, three kinds of damage were found:

> (1) Lymphocytosis and monocytosis.
> (2) Granulocytopenia, monocytosis, and eosinophilia
>   frequently accompanied by absolute lymphocytosis.
> (3) Moderate neutrophilia.

The degree of changes in the blood could be correlated with exposure and/or
duration of working period. This determination was based on the relative
changes as a function of period of employment, which was felt to indicate a
cumulative effect of microwaves in the human body. The type and intensity
of the exposure was not documented.

3

UNCLASSIFIED

413

DST-1810S-074-76
March 1976

(U) Blood coagulation indices of dogs subjected to high intensity super-
high frequency fields were studied at intervals of ten minutes to thirty
days after irradiation. Initially the coagulation time was prolonged, but
two hours after irradiation it was accelerated as a result of protective
compensatory changes in neurohumoral factors. The protective reaction
was, however, of short duration; the irradiation-induced prolongation of
coagulation time reappeared and the animals' clotting times did not
return to normal until at least fifteen days after exposure. Another
study showed that long-term exposure to microwaves at a power density of
$10mW/cm^2$ decreased the overall activity of butyrylcholinesterase in the
blood serum of rats. Under conditions of whole-body exposure, the microwaves did not exert a consistent effect on the enzyme molecule. The
decrease in the overall activity of butyrylcholinesterase was correlated
with a decrease in its concentration in the blood of the irradiated
animals.

(U) The action of microwaves on human erythrocyte permeability to potassium and sodium ions was also investigated. The mechanism of action appears to be an inhibition of active transport and an altered diffusion
through the pores in the membrane. The latter may be caused by the
influence of UHF energy on the membrane itself or on the hydrated sodium
cation and potassium cation. The microwaves either change the membrane
structure thereby increasing the passive sodium cation and potassium
cation diffusion and reducing the concentration gradient, or somehow
block the mechanism of active ion transport.

(U) The question of stability of microwave-induced changes in blood components was addressed in chronic and acute tests using dogs and rabbits.
The irradiation was at a frequency of 2375 MHz with a field strength of
thirty microwatts per square centimeter. The rabbits were subjected to
between one and ten irradiations of sixty minutes duration each, and the
dogs were subjected to repeated irradiations over a period of more than
a year. The changes in the blood and marrow of rabbits were found to be
unstable and to pass after a period of five to ten days. Changes observed
in the chronically exposed dogs were more stable, but became normalized
over a period of twenty-five days. Investigation of chronic microwave
irradiation on the blood-forming system of guinea pigs and rabbits was
also reviewed. Both continuous wave (CW) and pulsed microwaves were
utilized at an intensity of 3.5 mW/cm^2 and a wavelength of 10 cm. Increases in absolute lymphocyte counts in peripheral blood, abnormalities
in nuclear structure, and mitosis in the erythroblastic cell series in the
bone marrow and in lymphoid cells in lymph nodes and spleen were observed.
The changes appeared to be a cumulative result of repeated irradiations
and were attributed to nonthermal effects. There is limited evidence to
support the belief that these cumulative effects are reversible upon
cessation of exposure. It is still not quite clear if similar results
could be observed in humans since wide species-variations have been
observed by Soviet researchers working with animals.

4

DST-1810S-074-76
March 1976

(U) The primary concern of the present study was with electromagnetic
field effects, but numerous reports regarding the effects of constant
magnetic fields on the blood system were noted during the review. As with
electromagnetic effects, effects on coagulation, biochemical properties,
and formed elements were observed.

(U) To summarize the effects of electromagnetic radiation exposure on the
blood, the following general changes emerge although conflicting reports
are also present:

      (1) General decrease in hemoglobin content.
      (2) Generally reduced coagulation times.
      (3) Decrease in leucocyte count.

These findings are based largely on animal experimentation. While detrimental in themselves, the extent of these changes would not be expected
to be great enough to materially affect an individual's performance or
general health, especially under stress conditions, where other factors
such as physiological protective responses would be far more important.

PART 2 - CARDIOVASCULAR SYSTEM

(U) Heavy emphasis has been placed on investigations involving electromagnetic radiation on the cardiovascular system. Effects on hemodynamics include blood pressure variations and cardiac arrhythmias. Also included are
reports of a slowdown of intraventricular and intra-atrial conduction,
diffuse cardiac muscular changes, and ventricular extrasystole. As with
other effects, animal studies are frequently reported and human reports
are typically retrospective in nature. Many of the variations noted on
the cardiovascular system result from central nervous system effects.

(U) Several reports concerning human cardiovascular effects from super-
high frequency exposure were reviewed. Functional changes were noted,
including a slight increase in the asynchronous contraction phase, a
tension period, as well as other data indicative of moderate dystrophic
changes of the myocardium accompanied by a disruption of its contractive
capacity.

(U) Comparison of a group of engineers and administrative officials who
were exposed to microwaves for a period of years and an unexposed control
group revealed a significantly higher incidence of coronary disease,
hypertension, and disturbances of lipid metabolism among the exposed
individuals. Hereditary predisposition to heart disease was approximately
the same in both groups, but overt disorders developed much more frequently
in the previously exposed group. It was concluded that microwaves may act
as a nonspecific factor which, under certain conditions, interferes with
adaptation to unfavorable influences. Exposure may, therefore, promote an
earlier onset of cardiovascular disease in susceptible individuals.

5

DST-1810S-074-76
March 1976

(U) Hemodynamic indices for thirty men in the 25-40 year age range who had been exposed to UHF exposures for from two to ten years were studied. These men showed a tendency to bradycardia, moderate decrease in the stroke and minute volumes, and a slowing of the rate of blood ejection from the left ventricle. Arterial pressure was essentially normal, but a compensatory constriction of the precapillary bed was noted in response to the decrease in cardiac ejection. There was also an increase in the tone of the large arteries. EKG changes indicated an intensification of vagotonic influences on the heart; possible fluctuations in the potassium-sodium balance were also postulated. In a similar study, it was concluded that hemodynamic changes resulted from disturbances occurring in the structural and functional state of the regulating system.

(U) Morphological changes in experimental mice exposed to short and ultra-short wavelengths were observed. Two series of experiments were conducted using 14.9 MHz and 69.7 MHz waves. In the first series, twelve animals were subjected to single lethal doses of the electromagnetic radiation. Very pronounced vascular dystrophic changes were found throughout the organism. In the second series, 37 mice were given daily 60-minute exposures to nonthermal intensities for five months. Morphological studies of these animals showed slight vascular disorders and compensatory proliferative processes in the internal organs as well as dystrophic changes in brain cells.

(U) In a group of patients suffering from "radio wave disease," cerebral hemodynamic changes were observed. These included reduced intensity of the pulse blood volume and an increase in tonicity of the intra- and extra-cranial vessels. The changes did not, however, appear to be functional in nature.

Personnel exposed to microwave radiation below thermal levels experience more neurological, cardiovascular, and hemodynamic disturbances than do their unexposed counterparts. Some of the cardiac and circulatory effects attributed to exposure include bradycardia, hypotension, and changes in EKG indices (sinus arrhythmia, extrasystole changes in intra-ventricular and intra-atrial conduction, diminished amplitude of EKG deflections, etc.).

(U) The cardiovascular effects have always been of primary interest, therefore, it is likely that research in this area will continue. It is not apparent if cardiovascular effects were first observed in animals or in patients suffering from the so-called "radiowave disease." It is probable that further research will more accurately establish hemodynamic variations in both animals and humans. Greater emphasis will be placed on animal studies which will allow for more precise dose-response quantitations.

6

TIM RIFAT

DST-1810S-074-76
March 1976

PART 3 - CELLS

(U) Histological techniques have been used extensively for evaluating
the effects of electromagnetic radiation on cellular systems. Such studies
have included in vivo investigations of the cellular effects resulting from
whole body irradiation and in vitro studies employing cell cultures.

(U) The most popular cells for study appear to be those of rat or mouse
liver. Nonthermal effects on subcellular structures include the formation
of binuclear cells and irregular thickening of the nuclear membrane. In-
vagination of cytoplasm into the nucleus has also been observed, frequently
accompanied by breaks in the nuclear membrane. Marked changes in the
endoplasmic reticulum and the mitochondria have also been noted. The
available data, although still insufficient and inconclusive, seem to
indicate that the magnitude of these effects is frequency dependent.

(U) The liver cells of rats exposed for three hours to a 1.625 MHz field
showed damage to the protein synthesizing structures. Distinct changes
were seen in the nucleoli or ribosome synthesizing apparatus. The ultra-
structure of mouse liver cells was investigated after exposure to the same
frequency. The mitochondria became swollen and underwent lysis. Some giant
mitochondria also appeared. The cellular reactions observed were largely
the same as those observed after the action of many other environmental
factors.

(U) Phagocytic function has reportedly been increased by exposure to an
electromagnetic radiation field and induction of colicin synthesis has
been observed in E. coli irradiated with a nonthermal intensity.

(U) In many cases, electromagnetic radiation effects occur at the cellular
level, therefore tissue culture techniques provide a well controlled and
accurate method for study of those effects. Ultrahigh frequency exposure
of cultures of rat fibroblasts, monkey kidney cells, and human embryo
fibroblasts led to degeneration of the culture in four to six days. The
earliest degeneration occurred in primary cell cultures. Studies are now
under way on cell permeability, cell interfaces, cell stimulation, and
the electrical characteristics of nerve cells. Other Bloc research will
include study of microwave effects on mitosis, cell differentiation, and
subcellular deoxidation potentials. The data obtained from these studies
of cellular and subcellular responses to electromagnetic stimulation will
be highly significant, since they may lead to the eventual understanding
of basic mechanisms underlying biological changes which occur during and
after microwave radiation.

7

417

DST-1810S-074-76
March 1976

PART 4 - CENTRAL NERVOUS SYSTEM

(U) Research on the effects of radiowaves and microwaves on the central
nervous system of humans was relatively widespread. A number of reports
are discussed in this section, as well as research results regarding
central nervous system effects on animal models and isolated nerves.

(U) Subjects exposed to microwave radiation exhibited a variety of
neurasthenic disorders against a background of angiodystonia (abnormal
changes in tonicity of the blood vessels). The most common subjective
complaints were headache, fatigue, perspiring, dizziness, menstrual
disorders, irritability, agitation, tension, drowsiness, sleeplessness,
depression, anxiety, forgetfulness, and lack of concentration.

(U) Various neurological disorders were investigated by studying the
vestibular and visual analyzer functions in persons exposed to radio
waves of varying types for various periods. Elevation of the threshold of excitability was also accompanied by a lengthening of the time
required for dark adaptation. The magnitude and intensity of the
changes tended to increase with length of exposure. Similar studies
showed increases in the threshold of olfactory sensitivity. EEG automatic
frequency analysis was performed on 80 persons exposed to one meter wavelength radiation and 80 healthy controls. No differences were found between the exposed group and the controls regardless of length of the
exposure, intensity of the field, or frequency. Presumably, all of these
exposures were of a nonthermal nature. Conversely, thirty-seven persons
occupationally exposed to a superhigh frequency microwave field
($10 \ \mu W/cm^2$) over periods of two to eight years, were studied; symptoms
of asthenic and autonomic vascular disturbances, endocrine shifts, and
abnormal EEG's were observed in half of the patients. Their reflexes in
response to light and sound were weak, distorted, or nonexistent and
their skin galvanic reaction to flashing light was abnormally intense
and prolonged. Additional data will be required in order to assess the
significance of these human studies.

(U) Long-term experiments conducted on rabbits demonstrated that irradiation with intermittent or continuous low intensity microwave fields
elicits qualitatively and quantitatively different changes in the EEG.
Intermittent radiation had a more pronounced effect on the recovery time.
It has also been observed that long-term exposure of humans to microwave
radiation results in extremely flattened EEG patterns.

8

)

DST-1810S-074-76
March 1976

/   Exposure of rabbits to low levels of microwave radiation resulted in alteration of brain electrical activity, but caused no detectable macroscopic or microscopic histological changes. Examination of the brains of rabbits sacrificed immediately after exposure to 10 centimeter microwaves at power densities of 20 to 30 mW/cm^2 revealed hyperemia of the meninges, distension of superficial vessels, and small extravasations of blood in deeper brain areas. Some, or all of the observed changes, could have been thermal rather than nonthermal effects, since the power density employed in the experiment was powerful enough to have caused a fairly great temperature rise. The effects noted immediately after exposure were apparently reversible, since no changes in the condition of the brain tissue were found in animals sacrificed on the day following exposure.

(U) Study of the rabbit visual cortex after a one minute exposure of the head to 40 $\mu W/cm^2$ at a wavelength of 12.5 cm revealed changes in the frequency of the background activity of 52 percent of visual cortical neurons. Chronic irradiation (two weeks) of rabbits caused the development of a prevalence of slow, irregular biological currents; this was interpreted as evidence of progressive establishment of an inhibitory state in the cortex of the cerebral hemispheres. Normalization of the electrical shifts required up to two months in some cases. Similar studies with rats indicated apparent decrease in cholinesterase activity in the central nervous system.

(U) Histological examination of the cerebral cortex cells from rats exposed to UHF at 5 to 15 $\mu W/cm^2$ revealed the onset of sclerosis and the formation of vacuoles in some of the cells.

(U) Some excellent studies using biopotential recordings were performed to determine the effect of microwaves on the kinetics of nerve impulse conduction. Frog sciatic nerves were irradiated with 12.5 cm wavelength microwaves for one minute and parallel temperature measurements were made. Calculations showed that the absorption of one calorie of microwave energy per gram of material per minute gave a temperature rise of 1.1 degrees C in the experiment. The effects of microwaves and of direct contact heating (from three to nine degrees) on nerve impulse parameters (the rate of excitation conduction (EC) and the biopotential amplitude (BA)) were measured and compared. For thermal effects alone, one degree increased the values of EC and BA about five percent. Changes in EC were characterized by rapid increases as absorption of microwave energy increased, followed by a fairly sharp drop upon switching off the microwave irradiation and normalization within three minutes. These increases in EC values (higher than values obtained by thermal effects alone) were especially pronounced in a study where the samples were heated three and six degrees. In a series where $\Delta t = 9.1$ degrees, EC was lower, although the temperature did not exceed physiological normal limits. Changes in BA

9

419

DST-1810S-074-76
March 1976

during microwave irradiation were also characterized by a much faster increase, followed by a sharp drop to below the original level after irradiation and essential recovery in three minutes. In a series where the temperature increased to 31°C, the microwave effect at first was the same as the thermal effect; after thirty seconds the BA value was even lower than for the thermal effect alone, possibly due to overlap of ionic currents at such high temperature. This was followed by a substantial drop after irradiation, and very little recovery in three minutes. The differences in results in this series were attributed to different initial conditions of the preparations.

(U) These experiments indicate that microwaves may have a specific effect of a nonthermal nature on EC and BA, causing sharp and reversible changes in these functional parameters of nerve impulse. Further experimentation will be needed before extrapolations of similar functional changes to in vivo conditions, or to humans, are attempted. It is expected that Soviet research on these and other CNS responses will continue during the next five years.

PART 5 - DIGESTIVE SYSTEM

(U) A number of alterations in the function of the gastrointestinal system were observed. Reportedly, exposures of subjects working for long periods of time in the presence of low intensity centimeter and decimeter waves resulted in numerous disorders. These included dyspeptic disorders, edema of the gums, bleeding gums, alteration of the gastric acidity, and a reduction of the tonus and evacuator functions of the stomach.

(U) Numerous animal studies have been conducted on the motor function of the gastrointestinal tract and the secretory function of the stomach. Non-thermal intensities were reportedly used. In general, suppression of the stomach's evacuatory function, with signs of adaptation upon repeated exposure, was found. After partial denervation of the stomach, the opposite occurred. It was concluded that the waves have a dual effect - a mediated action through changes in the function of the CNS and a direct effect on the organ or its local innervation. In general, gastric juices increased and little change in acidity was noted. This work tends to support observations of functional changes in humans and indicates that they may actually result from a CNS interaction. Other animal results are discussed below, but do not relate to the human observations.

10

UNCLASSIFIED

DST-1810S-074-76
March 1976

(U) The effects of high frequency radiowaves on the content of nucleic
acids in the digestive organs of rabbits were studied. The total nucleic
acid content and the individual levels of DNA and RNA were assayed in the
liver, pancreas, stomach, small intestines, and blood. It was found that
the content of nucleic acids in the organs was a function of the power
and duration of exposure. Low doses were found to considerably stimulate
the nucleic acids, while higher doses reduced their content. Significant
shifts in DNA content required very high level exposures. In a similar
study on frogs exposed to microwaves (2307 MHz), the highest nucleic acid
content was found in the pancreas and the lowest in the stomach. Again,
low doses increased the total nucleic acid content while higher doses
induced insignificant increases or reductions in their content.

(U) The effects of microwaves (2307 MHz) on radiophosphorus resorption
in the stomach, duodenum, ileum, and colon were studied in rabbits.
Simultaneously, absorbed radiophosphorus distribution in the liver, lungs,
kidney, and spleen was investigated. It was found that rates of radioactive phosphorus resorption by sections of the alimentary canal differ.
Under microwave exposure, resorptive activity of the stomach is somewhat
decreased, while in the small and large intestines, it is increased. Lower
intensity exposure accelerated the intestine resorptive function to a
greater extent than large doses of lower frequency waves. Radiophosphorus
deposition in the viscera is also a function of the dosage.

PART 6 - GLANDS

(U) Investigations of the effects of radiowaves and microwaves on the
glandular system have been concentrated mainly on the adrenal, pituitary,
and the thyroid. The glandular effects, however, do not appear to be a
high priority area when compared to other systems currently under investigation.

(U) The functional status of the adrenal cortex in shipboard specialists
subjected to the effects of a UHF field was reviewed. Thirty-eight men
were exposed to the field for periods of 24 to 1800 hours and ketosteroids
and oxycorticosteroids (which reflect androgenic function) were monitored.
The results indicated that androgenic, glucocorticoid, and mineral corti-
coid functions of the adrenal gland cortex do not deviate from the normal.
Microwave exposure also increased thyroid function in these subjects. The
increase was attributed to secondary effects of the radiation and was felt
to result from disturbances of the sympathetic nervous system in the
hypothalmic region. In guinea pigs, the weight of the adrenal glands increased after continuous exposure at low levels for fourteen days, but
decreased in animals exposed to interrupted exposures. Modification of
lipid metabolism appears to be the mechanism of action. Similar exposure

DST-1810S-074-76
March 1976

using chicks resulted in increased ascorbic acid content in the cytoplasm
of the adrenal cortex, but other work has produced conflicting results
regarding the effects on the adrenal cortex.

(U) A quantitative assay of the gonadotropic hormones and growth hormones
in the pituitary body of rats exposed to microwave radiation indicated that
for a certain time after exposure, blocking or inactivation of gonadotropin-
releasing agents occurs in the hypothalamus. Both neural-hormonal and
pituitary gonadotropic hypofunctional effects resulted from whole-body
microwave irradiation.

(U) The general conclusion that can be drawn from various (both animal
and human) studies of the anterior pituitary and adrenal cortex is that
exposure to radiowaves and microwaves of thermal intensities results in
suppression of the hormone producing functions but exposure to nonthermal
intensities tends to enhance production.

(U) An increase of the thyroid function indices was found in animals
undergoing microwave irradiation for four months at a power density
of 5 mW/cm^2. In histological sections of the cylindric epithelium covering the thyroid, follicles were seen and electron microscopy revealed
reticulum.

PART 7 - METABOLISM

(U) Electromagnetic radiation exposure has been found to produce disturbances in carbohydrate energy and nitrogen metabolism in the brain, liver,
and muscles. It appears that under electromagnetic exposure, macroergic
compounds become deficient due to disjunction of the oxidative phosphorylation processes and deranged metabolism of carbohydrates. With respect
to nitrogen metabolism, radiation causes an intensification of the ammonia
formation processes in the absence of correspondingly more vigorous processes for its elimination.

(U) Exposure of rats to various intensities of electromagnetic fields
with a frequency of 48 KHz produced an increase of lactic and pyruvic
acids and a decrease in glycogen content in brain tissue. The changes
depended on the field intensity and exposure duration and one month
after cessation of the exposure the titer of lactic acid in the rat
brain had not returned to normal.

(U) The role of metabolic disturbances of the heart in development of
functional and structural changes under the influence of low frequency
impulse electromagnetic fields was studied. Test animals were rats
and it was found that exposure decreased ATP and creatinphosphate by

12

422

TIM RIFAT

)

DST-1810S-074-76
March 1976

causing disturbances of the oxidative changes of carbohydrates and diver-
gence of conjugation of oxidation and phosphorylation processes. It was
concluded that changes in carbohydrate energy and nitrogen metabolism
preceded the inception of structural changes in the myocardium.

(U) While these animal studies indicated an upset of some metabolic
pathways, the degree of functional impairment was relatively small and
probably not a significant factor. No human metabolic variations were
noted and meaningful extension of these animal studies to the human is
not possible. Research in this area is likely to remain low key and
will be conducted mostly on animals.

PART 8 - REPRODUCTION

(U) The effects of electromagnetic radiation on reproductive systems
have been the subject of numerous animal studies. Experiments with
female white mice revealed changes in the estrus cycle. During the five-
month study, the mice were irradiated twice daily for one hour, using a
10 cm wavelength of low intensity (10 mW/cm^2). Although the average
number of normal cycles was unchanged, normal cycle duration increased.
Prolonged diestrus and metestrus, along with a shortened estrus period,
resulted in a decrease in the reproductive function of the ovaries. A
weight loss was found to occur starting at about two weeks, reaching
a maximum loss after four months.

(U) The fertility of female white mice was also investigated. The
animals, irradiated as above, were mated during proestrus or early estrus
with nonirradiated males. Conception in fifty-eight control animals was
94 percent, but only 75 percent in irradiated animals. Long-term nonthermal microwave irradiation of male mice evoked diffuse changes in the
testes. Subsequent mating of the animals resulted in reduction in the
size of litters.

(U) Microwave radiation at 10 and 50 mW/cm^2 intensity was administered
for twenty and fifteen minutes respectively at various stages of the
twenty day gestation periods. The progeny showed reduced viability,
poor development, and anomalies. Changes in rate of postnatal development
and disturbances of higher nervous system activity were also observed.

(U) Female white mice were irradiated twice daily for one hour with 10 cm
waves of low intensity (10 mW/cm^2) up to the eighteenth day of pregnancy.
There were stillbirths, a significant number of weak newborn, and a general
retardation of body weight gain and growth. Other researchers found similar effects in litters from females which had been exposed twice daily for
one hour to a 10 cm wavelength at an intensity of 10 mW/cm^2 for five months
prior to mating.

13

DST-1810S-074-76
March 1976

(U) Genetic effects of electromagnetic radiation were observed in other studies. Male rats, irradiated with microwaves at 50-55 mW/cm^2, were mated with nonirradiated females. Litters displayed reduced viability and abnormal development, reduced rate of development and nervous disorders.

(U) Although researchers noted a certain degree of specificity in the pathological changes induced by microwave irradiation of mice, they concluded that the pathological processes occurring in male or female animals resulted from different mechanisms of action.

(U) Both sexes of the fruit fly, Drosophila melanogaster, were exposed to microwaves to study the effects of radiation-induced mutation. Group A, exposed for five seconds to 38 MHz, showed an increased frequency of mutation when bred five to nine days after irradiation. The results were not statistically conclusive, however. Group B, exposed for ten minutes to 2375 MHz, showed no effect on frequency of mutations.

(U) A strain of Staphylococcus aureus, known to be resistant to penicillin, was exposed to an electromagnetic field. A mutant was found to be sensitive to penicillin, probably due to a change in lipid content.

(U) In summary, a large amount of research has been done on the reproductive effects of EMR. However, effects on human reproduction, especially on male fertility, have not been demonstrated.

PART 9 - VISUAL SYSTEMS

(U) The role of microwaves in cataract formation and visual damage has been studied extensively in the past and is reasonably well understood. Primary attention in many studies has been directed at the biological effects of superhigh frequency electromagnetic radiation on the crystalline lens of the eye. Biomicroscopic techniques have been used to study cataract development in persons regularly exposed to microwave fields. A four-year study involving 600 workers and 300 controls revealed no significant difference between the two groups. Cataracts were discovered in only one percent of those persons exposed to such radiation; most of these cases resulted from safety violations. Cataracts which occurred were characterized in their early stages by turbidity of the lens and changes in form and color.

(U) In another study, thirty-five workers regularly exposed to microwave fields and having pronounced congenital lenticular cataracts were examined over a one to three year period; the results of their examinations were compared to those of twelve persons with similar cataracts who had no history of exposure to radiation. No progression was noted in any of the exposed individuals; changes were slow and probably attributable solely to natural aging of the lens.

14

)

DST-1810S-074-76
March 1976

(U) Combined wavelengths over the range of the millimetric spectrum were
used in an animal study involving nine rabbits exposed for 35-70 minutes.
Although the radiation used was of considerable intensity (120-495 mW/cm^2),
no damage occurred in the deeper media of the eye, in particular the lens,
during the 2 to 2½ months observation period. However, erosion of the
epithelium of the cornea did occur along with damage to the conjunctiva
and its vessels. Multiple tiny hemorrhages in the mucosa and submucous
tissue were also evident.

(U) The Soviets have reported the occurence of "acute attacks" (sic) of
glaucoma (1304 cases) which were correlated with geomagnetic disturbances.
Moreover, recurring "acute attacks" came primarily on days when the mean
value of the horizontal component of the geomagnetic field varied significantly. The significance of this report is questionable, but it indicates that the Soviets are examining all aspects of magnetic and
electromagnetic radiation which might cause changes in vision.

(U) Although a growing body of evidence suggests that the microwave
power density required to produce cataracts is incompatible with life,
the Soviets will continue to investigate the visual effects of EMR but
their effort will be reduced from its previous level.

PART 10 - INTERNAL SOUND PERCEPTION

(U) Perception of modulated microwave signals which seem to be originating
intracranially as characteristic sounds is a phenomenon which was first
reported in the US open literature more than thirteen years ago. To produce sounds, peak power densities of up to 80 mW/cm^2 may be required, but
the average power density usually is 5 uW/cm^2. The Soviets have studied
this phenomenon in order to determine the underlying physiological mechan-
ism(s) and to define the optimum irradiation parameters needed to evoke the
response. They found that when the fundamental frequency of the electromagnetic stimulus was raised from 2050 to 2500 MHz, the reaction threshold
rose significantly, but at a frequency of 3000 MHz there was no reaction
in the auditory centers. The average intensity of electromagnetic radiation required to evoke the response was less than 10 mW/cm^2; it was
concluded that the fundamental signal frequency rather than the amount
of energy constituted the primary stimulus and that the observed phenomenon was sensory in nature.

(U) The Soviets will continue to investigate the nature of internal sound
perception. Their research will include studies on perceptual distortion
and other psychophysiological effects. The results of these investigations could have military applications if the Soviets develop methods for
disrupting or disturbing human behavior.

15
(Reverse Blank)

DST-1810S-074-76
March 1976

SECTION III

MISCELLANEOUS OBSERVATIONS

(U) Most of the reported biological effects from radiowaves and micro-waves result from exposure to the higher frequency ranges. Many of the observed physiological changes probably occur as a result of thermal effects arising from the vibration of ions and dipoles of water molecules in tissues; the vibrations are set into motion more efficiently by the shorter wavelength (high frequency) waves. For example, a radiowave of ten centimeters wavelength converts about fifty percent of its energy into heat in this manner, whereas a three-centimeter wave converts nearly ninety-eight percent of its energy into heat. A study of the biological activity of low frequency (seven KHz) impulse electromagnetic radiation of different intensities and durations was done on rats. It was found that the pathological changes were a function of dose; susceptibility to radi-ation was governed by metabolic processes and morphology and the organs and systems could be classified as to sensitivity in the following order: tes-ticles, liver, kidneys, heart, and central nervous system. Another study indicated that relatively low frequency electromagnetic fields generated sonic and ultrasonic oscillations in living organisms which in turn produced elastic deformations. If the frequency of the source field corresponded to the oscillation frequency of the cells (the resonance frequency most likely), the cells deteriorated as a result of the mechanical resonance.

(U) Clinical studies were done on thirty subjects, aged 25 to 40 years, ex-posed to industrial ultrahigh frequency centimeter waves at power densities of 10 to 500 mW/cm^2 for periods of time ranging from 4 to 13 years. Subjec-tive complaints included generalized weakness, afternoon and evening apathy, fatigue, headache, sleep disorders, and nonradiating precordial pain sugges-tive of asthenia or neurasthenia with autonomic dystonia. Electroencepha-lography revealed periods of absence of alpha wave activity alternating with low R waves, increased frequency of potentials, dysrhythmia, periodic low peak potentials, and reactions to afferent stimuli. Peripheral blood studies revealed lymphocytosis or monocytosis in eight subjects; increased alpha and gamma globulins were found in 18 subjects. Erythrocyte potassium was within the lower limits of normal, while urine potassium was within the upper limits of normal. Adrenal cortex function was evaluated by urine levels of 17-ketosteroids, which were elevated to 22 to 40 mg in 11 subjects; average levels were 20.5 mg. Urine levels of epinephrine and norepineph-rine were elevated in some subjects. Thyroid function was evaluated by rate of radioiodine uptake. Average uptake within two hours was 11.3 percent, and in four hours 16.9 percent. The 24 hour uptake did not differ from normal values. Electrocardiography revealed changes in the heart con-duction system in six subjects; the $T_{v1} > v6$ syndrome was found in ten

17

426

TIM RIFAT

DST-1810S-074-76
March 1976

subjects and a U wave was registered in lead V_3 in eight subjects. Hemodynamic and myocardial function parameters were studied by tachooscillo-
graphy and polysphygmography. Arterial pressure was usually within normal
limits, although it was of a labile nature. Bradycardia was present in
14 subjects and decreased minute volume was observed in eight; increased
peripheral resistance was found "in a significant number" of subjects.
Autonomic-vascular changes and emotional lability and reactivity were
attributed to CNS changes and increased pituitary-adrenal gland function.
It was also noted that such shifts in neuroendocrine function could lead
to circulatory disorders manifested by changes in the hemodynamic indices
and electrical activity of the heart.

(U) A second study was done on two groups of workers occupationally exposed
in the radio industry. The first group consisted of 100 subjects who had
worked for several years under conditions of periodic exposure to microwaves
of considerable intensity (up to several mW/cm^2). The second group consisted
of 115 subjects who had begun work after the introduction of protective
measures and had been exposed to microwave intensity levels approximately
the same as those to which the first group was exposed. A control group
of 100 subjects not exposed to the action of microwaves was also continu-
ously examined. The study showed adverse effects, primarily on the nervous
and cardiovascular systems, in both exposed groups. These effects were
more pronounced in the first group. They were manifested by more frequent
complaints of asthenic syndrome and vegetative vascular dysfunction.

(U) A lack of standards for measuring power levels represents a problem
which probably accounts for conflicting reports regarding the effects of
a given frequency and intensity. Other problems with dosimetry and experimental technique also exist. Such differences make comparison of results
from one investigator to another, as well as from one country to another,
extremely difficult.

(U) Only a few studies involving electromagnetic interaction with the
immunological system have been reported. In one, rabbits were employed
to study the body immunological reactivity under long-term irradiation.
The rabbits were immunized with typhoid antigen and divided into two groups.
One group was exposed to waves of 50 and 10 mW/cm^2 intensity for four hours
a day over a four-month period. Analysis of the data obtained indicated
that chronic exposure to the effects of low intensity high frequency radiowaves can influence the immunoreactive state of the body as evidenced by
differences in phagocytic activity of neutrophils, blood serum complement
level, and specific antibody titers.

18

427

DST-1810S-074-76
March 1976

(U) Soviet investigators have conducted studies on the effects of microwave frequencies in combination with ionizing radiation, magnetic fields,
drugs, and nonionizing electromagnetic radiation of other wavelengths.
Generally, synergistic effects have been observed. Continued work in
this area is expected, and possibly new safety standards for these combined effects will be developed.

(U) In summary, this section shows the rather broad front on which
Soviet researchers are investigating the biological effects of EMR. It
is apparent that their interest covers all body systems which could reasonably be expected to display responses to such radiation. As with Western
researchers, they have concentrated their efforts on the higher frequency
spectrum which would be expected to produce more thermal responses. However, they also continue to be interested in nonthermal effects, which,
by Western standards, they have yet to conclusively demonstrate.

Section IV (pp. 21–2) has not been made
available to the author

)

DST-1810S-074-76
March 1976

SECTION V

SAFETY PRECAUTIONS AND STANDARDS

(U) Safety precautions and standards have been established in both the
US and USSR to protect not only persons who are occupationally exposed
but also to protect the health of persons living or working near powerful
generating or transmitting facilities. Significant differences in these
standards exist and appear to be primarily due to different viewpoints
on nonthermal effects in the two countries. Both nations' standards take
into account the potentially lethal thermal effects resulting from high-
intensity exposure, but the biological effects of nonthermal irradiation
are not well defined or documented. In addition, some research has indicated the possibility of a cumulative effect on humans, but this is also
very poorly defined.

)

   Soviet research has produced guidelines which were used to establish
a value of 10 μW/cm^2 per working day as the maximum admissible value for
microwave irradiation. Higher exposures, at values of 0.01 to 0.1 mW/cm^2,
are permissible for up to two hours per day or 1 mW/cm^2 for 15 to 20 minutes
per day. Protective glasses are required in the latter case. The Czechoslovakian standards for frequencies above 300 MHz allow a maximum of
0.025 mW/cm^2 in the continuous wave mode for eight hour exposures. The
standard for pulsed operation for the same exposure period is 0.01 mW/cm^2.
In June 1973, Poland revised its exposure safety standards for nonionizing
radiation in the frequency range of 0.3 to 300 GHz. The new standard permits unlimited exposure of humans to field intensities of 0.01 mW/cm^2.
Eight hours per day exposure is permitted for intensities up to 0.2 mW/cm^2
for fixed fields and 1.0 mW/cm^2 for rotating fields. Exposures of up to
10 mW/cm^2 are permitted for limited periods of time without safety equipment. Exposures greater than 10 mW/cm^2 are prohibited without approved
safety equipment. Prior to June 1973, the maximum radiation exposure
level for all nonionizing radiation was 0.01 mW/cm^2 for up to eight hours
per day, which is the same as the safety standard for the USSR. The
0.1 mW/cm^2 limit remains in effect for 0.1 MHz to 300 MHz, but revised
standards for this frequency range are under consideration. The East
German maximum permissible exposure to microwaves is 10 mW/cm^2, but neither
the exact frequency range or duration for this exposure is specified.
By comparison, the United States Standards Institute recommends 10 mW/cm^2
as averaged over any 1/10 hour period. The US Army and Air Force use the
following equation to determine permissible exposure time (T_p).

$$T_p = \frac{6000}{W2}$$

where T_p = permissible exposure time in minutes
              during any one hour period and
      W = the power density in the area in mW/cm^2.

23

429

DST-1810S-074-76
March 1976

Potential problem areas for exposure to excessive electromagnetic radiation which were found in the Communist literature included a wood processing plant, coastal radiotransmitting centers, radio equipment on ships, and flight communications equipment in the crew cabins of aircraft. Open feeder lines were identified as major sources of exposure.

(U) Protective devices described for use in working near unacceptable intensity fields include protective (metal-coated) eye glasses and clothing and shielding of the source with special absorbers or sheet metal or wire mask shields. A small semiconductor indicator instrument used to warn workers of dangerous conditions from electromagnetic fields has been developed. It rings an alarm when the field intensity exceeds the allowable level. An indicator paper for visual determination of the intensity of an electromagnetic field has also been developed. The indicator is prepared by impregnating a filter paper with a thermosensitive chemical compound.

(U) In an animal study, it was reported that oral administration of caffeine in doses of 20 mg per kg lowered the duration of resistance against hyperthermia caused by microwave irradiation. Caffeine did not influence the temperature at which the animals died, but it shortened the time to death. The reason for the lowered resistance of rats to microwaves was attributed to caffeine's exciting effect on the CNS which caused increased metabolic activity and consumption of oxygen. Although caffeine might exert similar effects on the human CNS, any lowering of resistance to hyperthermia would be insignificant; trained personnel working with properly operating, adequately serviced microwave equipment would probably almost never be exposed, even accidentally, to the tremendous radiation intensity required to induce heating of the human body. Nevertheless, monitoring of Soviet research on the action of drugs in combination with microwave radiation should continue, since such studies may eventually result in the detection of nonthermal safety hazards resulting from the mutually potentiating effects of radiation fields and pharmacological compounds.

Should subsequent research result in adoption of the Soviet standard by other countries, industries whose practices are based on less stringent safety regulations could be required to make costly modifications in order to protect workers. Recognition of the .01 mW/cm^2 standard could also limit the applications of new electronic technology by making the commercial exploitation of some products unattractive because of increased costs imposed by the need for additional safeguards.

24

430

TIM RIFAT

)

DST-1810S-074-76
March 1976

SECTION VI

TRENDS, CONCLUSIONS, AND FORECAST

(U) A significant amount of research continues to be performed in the
Eurasian Communist countries to establish the effects of radiowaves and
microwaves on biological systems. It is often difficult to evaluate the
reported results, however, because details of the exposure in terms of
frequency, duration, and intensity are quite variable, and sometimes poorly
reported. This, coupled with problems of measurement encountered in such
studies, creates a rather confusing body of data from which to draw objective and absolute conclusions regarding the significance of the research.
The Eurasian Communist investigators tend to place greater importance
on the potential nonthermal effects than do their counterparts in the West,
but information regarding the precise nature of the exposure under consideration is often difficult to establish. A move toward improved statistical
analysis of data and standardization of dosimetry can be expected as Eastern
Bloc researchers react to criticism of their work by Western scientists.

)

(U) The types of responses reportedly exhibited by the various biological
organs, processes, or functions are in line with what has been reported by
Western investigators. Again, most of the responses which are reported can
be linked with the thermal action of the radiation. Studies which report
on nonthermal effects deal largely with subjective responses, relying on
reports of headache, sleepiness, loss of appetite, etc. The presence of
nonthermal effects, in addition to thermal effects at higher intensities,
has also been postulated by Eurasian Communist investigators, but no
detailed investigative support for this possibility was noted. Accordingly,
it is difficult to establish whether or not a trend toward this type of
research will begin. It is safe to say that research on nonthermal effects
at thermal intensities will be exceedingly difficult since another dimen-
sion to an already formidable problem will have been added.

No Eurasian Communist research activity has been identified which can
be clearly or directly related to any military offensive weapons program.
However, Soviet scientists are fully aware of the biological effects of
low-level microwave radiation which might have offensive weapons application.
Their internal sound perception research has great potential for development
into a system for disorienting or disrupting the behavior patterns of
military or diplomatic personnel; it could be used equally well as an
interrogation tool. The Soviets have also studied the psychophysiological
and metabolic changes and the alterations of brain function resulting from
exposure to mixed frequencies of electromagnetic radiation. One physiological effect which has been demonstrated is heart seizure. This has been
accomplished experimentally in frogs by synchronizing a pulsed ultrahigh

25

431

DST-1810S-074-76
March 1976

frequency microwave signal of low average-power density with the depolarization of the myocardium and beaming the signal at the thoracic area. A
frequency probably·could be found which would provide sufficient penetration of the chest wall of humans to accomplish the same effect. Another
possibility is alteration of the permeability of the blood-brain barrier.
This could allow neurotoxins in the blood to cross. As a result, an
individual could develop severe neuropathological symptoms and either
die or become seriously impaired neurologically.

A study published in 1972 by the US Army Mobility Equipment Research
and Development Center, titled "Analysis of Microwaves for Barrier Warfare"
examines the plausibility of using radio frequency energy in barrier-
counterbarrier warfare. It discusses both anti-personnel and anti-materiᴬl
effects for lethal and nonlethal applications for meeting the barrier
requirements of delay, immobilization, and increased target exposure.
The report concludes that:

a. It is possible to field a truck-portable microwave barrier system
that will completely immobilize personnel in the open with present-day
technology and equipment.

b. There is a strong potential for a microwave system that would be
capable of delaying or immobilizing personnel in vehicles.

c. With present technology no method could be identified for a microwave system to destroy the type of armored materiᴬl common to tanks.

The above study is recommended reading material for those consumers
who have an interest in the application of microwave energy to weapons.
A discussion of weapons is not within the scope of this study.

The immediate danger from microwave barrier weapons is burns. The
US Army Medical Research Laboratory at Fort Knox, Kentucky, has conducted
tests on burns with microwaves. They have produced third-degree burns on
human skin with $20W/cm^2$ in two seconds with frequencies of approximately
3 GHz. The study also points out that a microwave barrier can be set up
with existing state-of-the-art technology and off-the-shelf hardware.
Considering the Soviet expertise in the area of electromagnetic energy,
which is probably very close to, if not on a par with that of the US,
the possibility must be accepted that they too have investigated microwave
energy for barrier warfare and that they are also concerned with the
biological effects of this type of radiation. Close monitoring of their
research efforts on burns and burn therapy may possibly reveal Soviet
efforts to develop countermeasures against microwave barrier warfare.

Even though radiowaves and microwaves can exert their influence over
great distances, high intensities over large distances are not practical.

26

432

DST-1810S-074-76
March 1976

Accordingly, the potential for an offensive military capability employing such waves is small and any resulting thermal biological effects have not been sufficiently documented. Nonthermal effects, however, could be initiated over relatively large distances and areas, but the effects are not well enough defined to support possible offensive military appli-cation of this energy. The possibility of regulation of body function through nonthermal interactions with the neurological system has been postulated by some USSR investigators. If this is proven possible, it might prove militarily important, but no solid experimental evidence to support such a hypothesis has been presented.

Soviet research on the biological effects of microwave radiation is committed to clarification of the correlation between biological effects and power densities. The majority of their efforts will be concentrated on this objective. They will maintain their historical position that there are subtle effects that cannot be put in thermal terms but can be explained in terms of specific couplings to the central nervous system. Therefore, they will very likely continue to investigate the thermal effects, but will prob-ably place greater emphasis on investigations of nonthermal effects in the light of criticism of some of their previous reports by Western investigators.

A move to adopt stringent occupational and public health standards for microwave radiation is being led by Polish researchers. The impact of the enforcement of standards similar to the Soviet standards would be significant for both the military and civilian sectors of industrially developed countries. These limitations would probably be more closely monitored and tightly enforced in the free world than in the Communist nations where the needs of the state come first. It is possible that the Eastern European Communist countries hope to gain advantage in electronic warfare by giving lip service to "concern for the environmental effects" of nonionizing electromagnetic radiation and the need for its reduction while continuing the development of military electronic equipment.

The hazards of nonionizing electromagnetic radiation will be studied with greater attention to combined radiation effects, e.g., microwaves and soft X-rays, noise, changes in ambient temperatures, humidity, psycho-genic stimuli, and other factors. Reports of clinical applications should be forthcoming during the next five to ten years. There will be an in-creased number of medical-industrial investigations in which researchers will locate a facility where electromagnetic radiation is known to occur and study the workers at this location over a period of time. It is not clear what path they will follow regarding functional control of body processes through direct exposure of peripheral receptors, but any signif-icant results in this area would not be expected within the next five years.

27

433

DST-1810S-074-76
March 1976

Soviet electromagnetic radiation research will continue on a cautious level without straying very far from present approaches. No striking or surprisingly new developments are likely to occur in the next ten years. Within this time frame, however, Bloc researchers, particularly the Czechs and the Poles, will probably distinguish themselves by conducting better work in terms of quality than their Soviet counterparts. In the past, their investigations appeared to be generally independent of Soviet work and seemed to merit more credibility. While by no means unique, the methodologies employed by Czech researchers are distinctly different from those of the Soviets. Polish investigators will probably show more aggressive and dynamic approaches in their studies of the biological effects of nonionizing radiation.

28

Bibliography

By the same author

Alien Mind War – Psychic Warfare, *Alien Encounters* Issue 13, Summer 1997.

A Remote View of Delenn – From Babylon 5, *Sightings* Vol. 2 Issue 3, September 1997.

Changing Your Mind – Mind Control, *Alien Encounters* Issue 11, May 1997.

Exploring the Megaverse, *Enigma* Issue 4, June 1997.

It's All In The Mind, *Enigma* February/March 1997.

Losing Your Mind! – Mind Control Technology, *Sightings* Issue 12, April 1997.

Mind Control – Big Brother Is All In The Mind, *UFO Reality* Issue 8, June/July 1997.

Mind Wars – Big Brother is Out to Get You, *Enigma* Issue 6, October 1997.

Quantum Leap – Remote Viewing, *Sightings* Issue 9, January 1997.

Psychic spying UFOs, *Alien Encounters* Issue 23, April 1998.

Remote Controller – Psychic Spying with Tim Rifat, Europe's leading remote viewer, *X Factor* No. 24, November 1997.

Remote Viewing: A DIY Guide, A Complete Guide to Paranormal Phenomena, Paragon Publishing, 1996.

Remote Viewing – The ESP of ESPionage, *Nexus* October/November, December/January, February/March 1996-97.

Remote Viewing – Why The X-Files Is Good For Business, *Enigma* Issue 1 December 1996.

Room with a Remote View – Interview by Richard Forsyth, *Encounters* Issue 10, August 1996.

See The World – Remote Viewing Courses, interview by Nina Pendred, *Alien Encounters* Issue 16, September 1997.

Watching The Watchers – Remote Viewing, *Alien Encounters*, December 1997.

Web site: http://www.fastnet.uk.co/pms

An information package on remote viewing is available, price £3 plus an SAE, £5 sterling outside the UK, from Paranormal Management Systems, PO Box 2749, Brighton, BN2 2DR, UK.

Also available are correspondence courses:
REMOTE VIEWING CORRESPONDENCE COURSE: The RV course consists of ten modules. One module is posted to you every month. The course lasts about one year. It covers how to remotely view in beta, theta; How to remotely view using baroque music as an aid; Group remote viewing; Past and future remote viewing; RV of different dimensions, time-lines, stealth technology and boosted RV using biophysical augmented intelligences.

REMOTE SENSING CORRESPONDENCE COURSE: The RS course consists of ten modules on: how to enter the theta state so one can telepathically scan others minds. Protective technology to stop remote influences and alien entities, empathic awareness, as well as ESP and telepathy of interest to healers and business people.

Cost of each course is £160, and cheques for Paranormal Management Systems should be sent to PO Box 2749, Brighton, BN2 2DR, UK.

Adams, James, 'Day of the Pentagon Mindbenders', *Sunday Times*, 3 December 1995.

Anderson, Jack, and Binstein, Michael, 'Psychic Spies have a Home at the CIA', *United Features Syndicate*, 1 November 1995.

Chomsky, Noam, *Three Models for the Description of Language*, 1956.

Chomsky, Noam, *Syntactic Structures*, 1957.

Chomsky, Noam, *Cartesian Linguistics*, 1966.

Chomsky, Noam, *Language and Mind*, 1972.

Chomsky, Noam, *Reflections on Language*, 1975.

Chomsky, Noam, *Rules and Representations*, *Behavioural and Brain Sciences*, Vol. 3; Language and Problems of Knowledge, The Managua Lectures, 1988.

Constantine, Alex, *Psychic Dictatorship in the USA*, Feral House, Portland, Oregon USA, 1996.

Dennett, Daniel, *Darwin's Dangerous Idea*, Simon and Schuster, 1995.

Dowbenko, Uri, 'True Adventures Of A Psychic Spy', interview with David Morehouse, *Nexus* August/September, October/November 1997.

Edelman, Gerald, *Neural Darwinism*, 1987.

Fleming, Michael, 'Psychic Soldier sells his Bizarre Tale to Hollywood', *Variety* November 1995.

Goodwin, Brian, How The Leopard Changed Its Spots, Weidenfeld and Nicholson, London 1994.

Hameroff, Stuart, Kaszniak, Alfred, and Scott, Alwyn, 'Toward a Science of Consciousness', *The First Tucson Discussions and Debates*, MIT Press, 1996.

Keith, Jim, *Secret and Suppressed*, Feral House, Portland, Oregon USA, 1993.

Mathews, Robert, 'CIA Signed up Psychics as Spooks', *Sunday Telegraph*, 4 August 1996.

Marrs, Jim, *Alien Agenda*, HarperCollins, 1997.

Morehouse, David, *Psychic Warrior – Inside the CIA's Stargate Program*, St Martin's Press, 1996.

Ostrander, Sheila, and Schroeder, Lynn, *Psychic Discoveries – The Iron Curtain Lifted*, Souvenir Press, 1997.

Penrose, Roger, *The Emperor's New Mind*, Oxford University Press, 1989.

Rickard, Bob, 'From Russia with Anxiety', *Fortean Times*, June 1996.

Schnabel, Jim, *Remote Viewers: The Secret History of America's Psychic Spies*, Dell, 1997

Utts, Jessica, 'Scientific verification of RV', *The Journal of Scientific Exploration*, Stanford Vol. 10 No. 1 pages 1-111.

Vistica, Gregory, 'Psychics and Spooks', *Newsweek*, 11 December 1995.

Wittgenstein, Ludwig, *Tractuse Logico-philosphicus*, Routledge and Kegan Paul, London 1992.

Wolf, Jim, 'Psychic Power Real, but not good for Spying', says CIA, Reuter, 28 November 1995; ISCNI Flash, 1 December 1995.

Glossary

Adaptive energy   The bodies biophysical energy used to empower the immune system, fight internal and external stressors and uphold the structural integrity of the body and mind.

Algorithms   The step by step series of mathematical operations which computers use to process data.

Bilocation   The highly developed form of remote viewing in which the psychic viewer sees the target location as if actually there. A form of lucid dreaming while awake.

Biophysical field   The energy body around the physical form which can be detached from the human body and used for remote viewing. Composed of fields unknown in the West.

CIA: The Central Intelligence Agency   A branch of the U.S. Intelligence service.

Cinema method   The use of a mental cinema screen to receive information broadcast from the biophysical fields when remote viewing. Fixes attention on a TV image which we are conditioned to watch.

CRV: Co-ordinate Remote Viewing   A technique of psychic viewing invented by Ingo Swann, in which map co-ordinates are used, in a state of normal consciousness, to enable a trained remote viewer to give precise information on that location using a set of specialised protocols.

Directed attention   A focused, relaxed state of mind, centred on one specific function, this being RV. A tool to switch off internal chatter by use of the Cinema Method. A mental laser of attention emanating from the thalamus and used to command and control Psi-operations.

DIA: The Defence Intelligence Agency   A branch of the military which is involved with intelligence gathering.

EEG   Electroencephalograph, a device which is used to monitor brain waves.

ELF   Extremely low frequency waves – This form of wave penetrates the skull and is the set of frequencies that the brain uses for behaviour. Therefore ELF signals are used on microwave carrier waves to influence

438

the behaviour, make ill, or kill, high-profile people, routinely used by British intelligence services.

Entropy   A function of chaos, the more entropy the more chaos.

Epicentre of attention   The place the I part of your mind inhabits, place recreated to conform to reality so the I part of you can perceive itself and perform optimally inside or outside of your body.

ERV: extended remote viewing   An advanced form of psychic spying in which the clairvoyant descends into the theta state of consciousness, from which accurate psychic viewing can be established by following a special set of protocols.

ESP   Extra sensory perception, the ability to use psychic sensory means to read minds, see into the future, or to remotely view distant locations.

Genome   The full set of chromosomes with their complement of genes carried by the cell nucleus.

Group perception or the **Common consensus**   The perception of reality agreed upon by the group, not necessarily correct and very limiting.

Group reality   The picture of reality the group takes to be the absolute truth but in fact is only a construct, a list of what is thought possible and what is not.

High-order consciousness   A heightened state of self-awareness, e.g. when the biophysical field is aware of itself.

Hypnotic remote viewing   An advanced technique in which the remote viewer is placed in a deep trance and sees the target as if he or she was actually there; currently being developed in the USA.

Linear processing   One step at a time data processing, following a chain instructions to process data.

Lucid dreaming   Dreams observed while the dreamer is conscious that they are dreaming.

MASER   A microwave laser, used for burning holes in the blood brain barrier to give brain damage and tumours, also for synthetic telepathy.

Meme   A contagious idea that spreads through the population; term first coined by Dr Richard Dawkins. A biophysical field that is contagious.

Mental biofeedback   Using the mind to initiate changes in the body.

Mental feedback loop   Conscious thought is redirected back on to itself to fixate thoughts on one idea group. In this case fixating attention on the mental activity, or perception of reality.

Mind control   The use of microwave radiation, which carries specific signals to remotely influence people by electronic means. Developed by the Soviets and now endemic in the UK.

Morphogenetic field The biophysical field used by the developing embryo to tell genes in cells to differentiate into different cell types such as eye cells or hair cells. Cell development is controlled by these morphogenetic fields.

Negative entropy Order and structure.

Non-ionising Causing no ionisation of molecules and atoms, not radioactive.

OOBE Out of body experience, in which the person inhabits the biophysical field and sees the world from a vantage point outside the physical body. Commonly called astral projection.

OOBRV Out of body remote viewing is a state of consciousness where the viewer is aware of themselves floating in the biophysical field over the target site which is being remotely viewed.

Parallel processing Carrying out interconnected non linear data streams that have similar idea content, but may be of a different nature.

PDE: the Paranormal Damping Field A creation of the entire human populations Psi-fields which is used to suppress all paranormal abilities, to make agreed upon things and events real, while strongly exorcising events and phenomena that do not agree with the common consensus.

Primary consciousness Being aware of one's environment.

Precognition Foreknowledge of the future through extrasensory means.

PRV Precognitive remote viewing is the ability to use psychic viewing to see what may occur in the future.

PSI The use of psychic energy. Overall term encompassing remote viewing, remote influencing, psychotronics and all psychic ability.

Psychotronics The Russian research on the use of Psi-energy to effect people and influence reality. Also included are Soviet research on mind control using Psi and electromagnetic carrier waves for ELF signals.

RI: Remote influencing The use of telepathic hypnotism to plant thoughts in another person's mind, to control that person's thoughts, or to cause bodily changes.

RK: Remote killing The advanced application of Psi that enables high-level operators to telepathically influence the brain of the victim to give them a heart attack, or to use telekinesis to rupture capillaries in the victim's brain to cause a stroke. Advanced remote influencing to switch on suicide genes in the victim . . .

RS: Remote sensing The ability to psychically scan other people to telepathically sense what condition their body is in, or to begin to read thoughts and emotions running through their brain.

RV: Remote viewing The facility to use clairvoyance to psychically view distant locations.

Scanning The military use of remote sensing to psychically interrogate the brain of the victim to gain information by ESP and telepathy.

Schuman resonance The natural frequency which the planet resonates at, this being 7.82 Hz.

Situational awareness Having the clue, instinctively taking in a wealth of information, evaluating it, and reacting correctly.

Shaman A holy man of northern Asia in touch with spirits; also a medicine man.

Signal to noise ration A method of determining the accuracy of remote viewing information; reproducing exactly what you see (signal) without any attempt at interpretation (noise).

Suprameme The collection of memes which rule each person's life.

Synthetic telepathy Inducing telepathy by electronic means.

Telekinesis Psychokinesis.

Telepathic knockout Form of remote influencing which knocks people out.

Total order A state of affairs in which chaos is an absolute minimum and order is the rule.

Total reality The true nature of things stripped free of preconceptions and unfiltered by programming in the brain. Solid matter and influencing other people's brain functions by the power of the mind.

UHF Ultra high frequency waves.

Sources & Acknowledgements

The author and publisher wish to offer thanks and acknowledgement to the following individuals and institutions who have kindly permitted material to be reproduced in this book: Nick Redfern, the *Daily Express* (2.9.97), *Young Guard Magazine*, Michael Joseph Publishers for extracts from *Psychic Warfare: Threat or Illusion?* by Martin Ebon; *Lobster* magazine, Duncan Roads and Marcus Allen at *Nexus* magazine; and to Rodney Paull who produced the figures contained in this book.

The author has made all reasonable efforts to contact copyright holders for permission, and apologizes for any omissions or errors in the form of credit given. Corrections may be made in future printings.

The author would also like to thank his agent, Roger Houghton, at Lucas Alexander Whitley, and Mark Book and Liz Rowlinson at Century for all their work on the book.